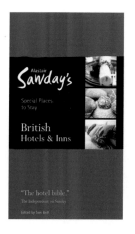

Alastair
Sawday's

Special Places to Stay

Thirteenth edition
Copyright © 2008 Alastair Sawday
Publishing Co. Ltd
Published in September 2008
ISBN-13: 978-1-906136-05-5

Alastair Sawday Publishing Co. Ltd,
The Old Farmyard, Yanley Lane,
Long Ashton, Bristol BS41 9LR, UK
Tel: +44 (0)1275 395430
Email: info@sawdays.co.uk
Web: www.sawdays.co.uk

The Globe Pequot Press,
P. O. Box 480, Guilford,
Connecticut 06437, USA
Tel: +1 203 458 4500
Email: info@globepequot.com
Web: www.globepequot.com

Series Editor Alastair Sawday
Editor Nicola Crosse
Assistant to Editor Wendy Ogden
Editorial Director Annie Shillito
Writing Nicola Crosse,
Jo Boissevain, Viv Cripps, Monica Guy
Inspections Jan Adam, David Ashby,
Neil Brown, Anne Coates,
Angie Collings, Trish Dugmore,
Jane Elliott, Becca Harris,
Vickie MacIver, Suzie Mickleburgh,
Robert & Glyn Newey, Scott Reeve,
Aideen Reid, Nicky Tennent,
Henrietta Thewes, Bridget Truman,
Mandy Wragg
And thanks to those people who did an
inspection or two!
Accounts Bridget Bishop,
Sally Ranahan
Production Julia Richardson,
Rachel Coe, Tom Germain,
Anny Mortada
Sales & Marketing & PR
Rob Richardson,
Sarah Bolton, Thomas Caldwell
Web & IT Joe Green,
Chris Banks, Mike Peake,
Russell Wilkinson

Alastair
Sawday's

Special Places
to Stay

British
Bed & Breakfast

4 Contents

The buildings

Beautiful as they were, our old offices leaked heat, used electricity to heat water and rooms, flooded spaces with light to illuminate one person, and were not ours to alter.

So in 2005 we created our own eco-offices by converting some old barns to create a low-emissions building. Heating and lighting the building, which houses over 30 employees, now produces only 0.28 tonnes of carbon dioxide per year. Not bad when you compare this with the 6 tonnes emitted by the average UK household. We achieved this through a variety of innovative and energy-saving building techniques, described below.

Insulation We went to great lengths to ensure that very little heat will escape, by:

- laying insulating board 90mm thick immediately under the roof tiles and on the floor
- lining the whole of the inside of the building with plastic sheeting to ensure air-tightness
- fixing further insulation underneath the roof and between the rafters
- fixing insulated plaster-board to add another layer of insulation.

All this means we are insulated for the Arctic, and almost totally air-tight.

Heating We installed a wood-pellet boiler from Austria, in order to be largely fossil-fuel free. The pellets are made from compressed sawdust, a waste product from timber mills that work only with sustainably managed forests. The heat is conveyed by water to all corners of the building via an under-floor system.

Water We installed a 6000-litre tank to collect rainwater from the roofs. This is pumped back, via an ultra-violet filter, to the lavatories, showers and basins. There are two solar thermal panels on the roof providing heat to the one (massively insulated) hot-water cylinder.

Lighting We have a carefully planned mix of low-energy lighting: task lighting and up-lighting. We also installed three sun-pipes – polished aluminium tubes that reflect the outside light down to chosen areas of the building.

Electricity All our electricity has long come from the Good Energy Company and is 100% renewable.

Materials Virtually all materials are non-toxic and natural. Our carpets, for example, are made from (80%) Herdwick sheep-wool from National Trust farms in the Lake District.

Doors and windows The doors are wooden, double-glazed, beautifully constructed in Norway. Old windows have been double-glazed.

We have a building we are proud of, and architects and designers are fascinated by. But best of all, we are now in a better position to encourage our 'owners' and readers to take sustainability more seriously.

Photo: Tom Germain

What we do

Besides moving the business to a low-carbon building, the company works in a number of ways to reduce its overall environmental footprint:

- all office travel is logged as part of a carbon sequestration programme, and money for compensatory tree-planting is dispatched to SCAD in India for a tree-planting and development project
- we avoid flying and take the train for business trips wherever possible; when we have to fly, we 'double offset'
- car-sharing and the use of a company pool car are part of company policy; recycled cooking oil is used in one car and LPG in the other
- organic and Fair Trade basic provisions are used in the staff kitchen and organic food is provided by the company at all in-house events
- green cleaning products are used throughout the office
- all kitchen waste is composted and used on the office organic allotment.

Our total 'operational' carbon footprint (including travel to and from work, plus all our trips to visit our Special Places to Stay) is just over 17 tonnes per year. We have come a long way, but we would like to get this figure as close to zero as possible.

For many years Alastair Sawday Publishing has been 'greening' the business in different ways. Our aim is to reduce our environmental footprint as far as possible – with almost everything we do we have the environmental implications in mind. (We once claimed to be the world's first carbon neutral publishing company, but are now wary of such claims). In recognition of our efforts we won a Business Commitment to the Environment Award in 2005, and in 2006 a Queen's Award for Enterprise in the Sustainable Development category. In that year Alastair was voted ITN's 'Eco Hero'.

We have created our own eco-offices by converting former barns to create a low-emissions building. Through a variety of innovative and energy-saving techniques this has reduced our carbon emissions by 35%.

Photo: Tom Germain

But becoming 'green' is a journey and, although we began long before most companies, we still have a long way to go.

In 2008 we won the Independent Publishers Guild Environmental Award. The judging panel were effusive in their praise, stating: "With green issues currently at the forefront of publishers' minds, Alastair Sawday Publishing was singled out in this category as a model for all independents to follow. Its efforts to reduce waste in its office and supply chain have reduced the company's environmental impact, and it works closely with staff to identify more areas of improvement. Here is a publisher who lives and breathes green. Alastair Sawday has all the right principles and is clearly committed to improving its practice further."

Our Fragile Earth series is a growing collection of campaigning books about the environment. Highlighting the perilous state of the world yet offering imaginative and radical solutions and some intriguing facts, these books will make you weep and smile. They will keep you up to date and well armed for the battle with apathy.

THE QUEEN'S AWARDS
FOR ENTERPRISE:
SUSTAINABLE DEVELOPMENT
2006

There is a whiff of nervousness in the air. Will the UK gently subside into recession? Will house prices bring us all down with them? Will the British stay put this year, rather than flock to where the sun promises to be?

I am determinedly optimistic about the role of B&Bs, for they are just what we need in times of uncertainty. They remind us that humanity matters more than mere profit, that one can arrive at the house of strangers and be welcomed, that one can avoid the vacuous uniformity of chain hotels. Going to a B&B is a 'risk', and risk-taking at this level is fun – you never know how delightful it is going to be.

They are, too, a refuge from bureaucratic interference, though their grim day may come. EU Fire Regulations intended largely for hotels are being rigorously enforced upon many B&Bs by zealous Fire Officers, with disastrous results. The same is true for food regulations. We must take up the cudgels for common sense, lest B&Bs are deemed too dangerous for us all!

The modern world, exciting though it is, does make business life more complex. B&B owners create websites and spend valuable time and money on them. So do we: how to retain our humanity and our sense of fun when glued to the screen all day, and also stay 'competitive'? There are the further challenges of rising oil prices and chaos threatened by climate change.

These will be severe, and our rural B&Bs, particularly, may suffer. The good news, however, is that local food producers are flourishing.

We, and a growing number of our owners, have always brought environmental awareness into all we do and I hope that few of you now feel it is unnecessary. We won a publishing prize for our environmental stance this year, so we will continue to encourage our staff, our owners and our readers to do their bit. Many of our B&B owners are extraordinarily imaginative in adapting to change and we celebrate them. The result is a collection of places to stay that is more eclectic, rewarding, green and inspiring than any in Britain.

Alastair Sawday

Photo: Tom Germain

"I hate staying in B&Bs." My 29-year-old daughter said this over lunch, at which point I nearly choked. When recovered, I asked her to explain. She replied that she hated talking to people in B&Bs. The owners or the other guests, I asked. Both, she said. But, I remonstrated, some of my happiest stays in Sawday places have been when I have talked to owners or other guests! There was that wonderful breakfast in Devon when we were all given champagne with our bacon and eggs because another guest was celebrating their birthday – we didn't move for two hours. And that gorgeous dinner in France with owners who joined us over boeuf en daube; we talked until after midnight. Sounds ghastly, she said.

Over pudding I silently simmered with anger. It is not that I mind people being a bit shy – loads of people are – I just absolutely hate it in my own child! But then I do remember her constantly

tugging at my arm every time we went anywhere when she was little; she was always trying to pry me away from talking to somebody so that we could actually get somewhere. Maybe I put her off?

After she had left – no doubt to phone a sibling and whinge about me being in a foul mood – I started thinking. She is representative of her generation in many ways, so maybe her friends have similar feelings about staying in B&Bs. And here was I fondly imagining that the reason younger people didn't stay in them often was that they were too expensive (although the amount my children spend on a night out staggers me).

So I thought I would try to find a place that would be perfect for somebody of Harriet's age. Of course, I got carried away looking at places that I would like. An old fog station on an RSPB reserve overlooking the Irish sea that you can't reach by car; a dear little buttery with a thatched roof and lovely owners; a colourful place in London with an owner who is guaranteed to entertain. It was hard to research from somebody else's point of view – but, as I'm always rattling on to anybody who will listen about how 'special' means different things to different people, I had to persevere.

Hmm, so I am pretending to be young like Harriet (odd) and that I don't like talking to other people (even odder) and

Photo right: 40 York Road, entry 262
Photo left: Beinn Bhracaigh, entry 629

I want to find somewhere to stay in this book. I have to start with what she does like. Food. She likes good food. And designed interiors. Her own house looks like something out of a magazine – I'm not even allowed to bring the dog round! Everything is stylish and modern and well thought-out. She also likes goose-down pillows, comfortable mattresses, lovely linen, walking in beautiful countryside. I key in the essential words and hey presto! Up pop at least thirty places in the south west that she would, I am sure, very much like. They are cool and funky, stylish and luxurious, serve the best of local and seasonal food and are surrounded by rolling hills or edged by coastal paths. But will she have to meet any other guests? Will she have to have an excruciatingly friendly chat with the owners?

In the end I narrow it down further and manage to find several places to stay where the above conditions are triumphantly met – with the added joy (depending on how you look at it) of total privacy and complete independence. I find a beautiful house in a garden overlooking a river estuary, with its own Rayburn and a canoe to use; a great restaurant that lets out rooms in a Georgian house down the road; a rocking little love nest with a plasma screen and a blasting sound system, hidden at the end of a long lane; and an annexe with a beach hut feel and a deck right on the sand.

All places where, once you've said hello and been shown where to go, you are on your own. She is spoiled for choice! I defy her not to have a wonderful time. And, as they are all Sawday places, I find myself forgiving Harriet (a bit) for being a curmudgeonly sort of socialite.

Next I should perhaps try to look for the ideal place for six middle-aged golfers, or a B&B for horse-lovers, with rosettes and brasses adorning the walls. I could hunt for somewhere to take Granny for a quiet weekend, where her favourite chintzes romp comfortingly across curtains and bedcovers. How about the perfect choice for families? Children do need the absolute freedom to charge about gardens and swoop through rooms without crushing or breaking anything. Sometimes parents need them to have a nursery tea and then the offer of a babysitter while they go to the pub for supper. What about bird watchers who don't care much what the bedroom looks like as long as the price is right and they can see their precious rare birds? Or people in love, who may care very much what the bedroom is like, and would prefer a late breakfast? How about somewhere for those devoted to hunting, shooting and fishing? And, for the body-weary, places to stay with massages and other treatments on offer?

Not a difficult task at all! They are all here – every one. Enjoy finding them.

Nicola Crosse

It's simple. There are no rules, no boxes to tick. We choose places that we like and are fiercely subjective in our choices. We also recognise that one person's idea of special is not necessarily someone else's so there is a huge variety of places, and prices, in the book. Those who are familiar with our Special Places series know that we look for comfort, originality, authenticity, and reject the insincere, the anonymous and the banal. The way guests are treated comes as high on our list as the setting, the architecture, the atmosphere and the food.

We choose places that we like and are fiercely subjective in our choices.

Inspections

We visit every place in the guide to get a feel for how both house and owner tick. We don't take a clipboard and we don't have a list of what is acceptable and what is not. Instead, we chat for an hour or so with the owner and look round. It's all very informal, but it gives us an excellent idea of who would enjoy staying there. If the visit happens to be the last of the day, we sometimes stay the night. Once in the book, properties are re-inspected every three to four years so that we can keep things fresh and accurate.

Photo: Brickfields Farm, entry 538

Feedback

In between inspections we rely on feedback from our army of readers, as well as from staff members who are encouraged to visit properties across the series. This feedback is invaluable to us and we always follow up on comments.

So do tell us whether your stay has been a joy or not, if the atmosphere was great or stuffy, the owners cheery or bored. The accuracy of the book depends on what you, and our inspectors, tell us. A lot of the new entries in each edition are recommended by our readers, so keep telling us about new places you've discovered too. Please use the forms on our website at www.sawdays.co.uk, or later in this book (p. 406).

However, please do not tell us if the bedside light was broken, or the shower head was scummy. Tell the owner, immediately, and get them to do something about it. Most owners are more than happy to correct problems and will bend over backwards to help. Far better than bottling it up and then writing to us a week later!

Subscriptions

Owners pay to appear in this guide. Their fee goes towards the high costs of inspecting, of producing an all-colour book and of maintaining our website. We only include places that we like and find special for one reason or another, so it is not possible for anyone to buy their way onto these pages. Nor is it possible for the owner to write their own description. We will say if the bedrooms are small, or if a main road is near. We do our best to avoid misleading people.

Disclaimer

We make no claims to pure objectivity in choosing these places. They are here simply because we like them. Our opinions and tastes are ours alone and this book is a statement of them; we hope you will share them. We have done our utmost to get our facts right but apologise unreservedly for any mistakes that may have crept in.

You should know that we don't check such things as fire regulations, swimming pool security or any other laws with which owners of properties receiving paying guests should comply. This is the responsibility of the owners.

Photo: The Old School, entry 183

Finding the right place for you

All these places are special in one way or another. All have been visited and then written about honestly so that you can take what you like and leave the rest. Those of you who swear by Sawday's books trust our write-ups precisely because we don't have a blanket standard; we include places simply because we like them. But we all have different priorities, so do read and choose carefully.

Our descriptions are carefully composed to help you steer clear of places that will not suit you, but instead lead you to personal paradise. If something is particularly important to you then do check when you book: a simple question or two can avoid misunderstandings.

We don't have a blanket standard; we include places simply because we like them

Maps

Each property is flagged with its entry number on the maps at the front. These maps are a great starting point for planning your trip, but please don't use them as anything other than a general guide — use a decent road map for real navigation. Most places will send you detailed instructions once you have booked your stay.

Photo: Clapton Manor, entry 189

Ethical Collection

We're always keen to draw attention to owners who are striving to have a positive impact on the world, so you'll notice that some entries are flagged as being part of our "Ethical Collection". These places are working hard to reduce their environmental footprint, making significant contributions to their local community, or are passionate about serving local or organic food. Owners have had to fill in a very detailed questionnaire before becoming part of this Collection – read more on page 400. This doesn't mean that other places in the guide are not taking similar initiatives – many are – but we may not yet know about them.

Sawday's Travel Club

We've recently launched a Travel Club, based around the Special Places to Stay series; you'll see a 💼 symbol on those places offering something extra to Club members, so to find out how to join see page 392.

Symbols

Below each entry you will see some symbols, which are explained at the very back of the book. They are based on the information given to us by the owners. However, things do change: bikes may be under repair or a new pool may have been put in. Please use the symbols as a guide rather than an absolute statement of fact and double-check anything that is important to you – owners occasionally bend their own rules, so it's worth asking if you may take your child or dog even if they don't have the symbol.

Do tell us whether your stay has been a joy or not, if the atmosphere was great or stuffy, the owners cheery or bored

Children – The 🕇 symbol shows places which are happy to accept children of all ages. This does not mean that they will necessarily have cots, high chairs, etc. If an owner welcomes children but only those above a certain age, we have put these details at the end of their write-up. These houses do not have the child

symbol, but even these folk may accept your younger child if you are the only guests. Many who say no to children do so not because they don't like them but because they may have a steep stair, an unfenced pond or they find balancing the needs of mixed age groups too challenging.

Pets – Our 🐕 symbol shows places which are happy to accept pets. It means they can sleep in the bedroom with you, but not on the bed. Be realistic about your pet – if it is nervous or excitable or doesn't like the company of other dogs, people, chickens, children, then say so.

Owners' pets – The 🐈 symbol is given when the owners have their own pet on the premises. It may not be a cat! But it is there to warn you that you may be greeted by a dog, serenaded by a parrot, or indeed sat upon by a cat.

Quick reference indices

At the back of the book you'll find a number of quick-reference indices showing those places that offer a particular service, perhaps a room for under £70 a night, or owners who are happy for you to stay all day. They are worth flicking through if you are looking for something specific.

A further listing refers to houses within two miles of a Sustrans National Cycle Network route. Take your own bike or check if you can hire or borrow one from the owners before you travel, and enjoy a cycle ride on your break.

Types of places

Some houses have rooms in annexes or stables, barns or garden 'wings', some of which feel part of the house, some of which don't. If you have a strong preference for being in the throng or for being apart, check those details. Consider your surroundings when you are packing: large, ancient country houses may be cooler than you are used to; city places and working farms may be noisy at times; and that peacock or cockerel we mention may disturb you. Light sleepers should pack ear plugs, and take a dressing gown if there's a separate bathroom (though these are sometimes provided).

Some owners give you a front door key so you may come and go as you please; others like to have the house empty between, say, 10am and 4pm.

Photo: Broad Bay House, entry 644

If you would prefer not to wander far during the day then look for the places that have the 'Stay all day' quick reference at the back of the book.

Rooms

Bedrooms – We tell you if a room is a double, twin/double (ie with zip and link beds), suite (with a sitting area), family or single. Most owners are flexible and can juggle beds or bedrooms; talk to them about what you need before you book. It is rare to be given your own room key in a B&B.

Often you will feast on local sausage and bacon, eggs from resident hens, homemade breads and jams

Bathrooms – Most bedrooms in this book have an en suite bath or shower room; we only mention bathroom details when they do not. So, you may get a 'separate' bathroom (yours alone but not in your room) or a shared bathroom. Under certain entries we mention that two rooms share a bathroom and are 'let to same party only'. Please do not assume this means you must be a group of friends to apply; it simply means that if you book one of these rooms you will not be sharing a bathroom with strangers.

If these things are important to you, please check when booking. Bath/shower means a bath with shower over; bath and shower means there is a separate shower unit.

Sitting rooms – Most B&B owners offer guests the family sitting room to share, or they provide a sitting room specially for guests. If neither option is available we generally say so, but do check. And do not assume that every bedroom or sitting room has a TV.

Meals

Unless we say otherwise, a full cooked breakfast is included. Some owners – particularly in London – will give you a good continental breakfast instead. Often you will feast on local sausage and bacon, eggs from resident hens, homemade breads and jams. In some you may have organic yogurts and beautifully presented fruit compotes. Some owners are fairly unbending about breakfast times, others are happy to just wait until you want it, or even bring it to you in bed.

Apart from breakfast, no meals should be expected unless you have arranged them in advance. Although we don't say so on each entry – the repetition a few hundred times would be tedious – all owners who provide packed lunch, lunch or dinner need ADVANCE NOTICE. And they want to get things right for you so, when booking, please discuss your diet and meal times. Meal prices are quoted per person, and dinner is often a social occasion shared with your hosts and other guests.

Do eat in if you can – this book is teeming with good cooks. And how much more relaxing after a day out to have to move no further than the dining room for an excellent dinner, and to eat and drink knowing there's only a flight of stairs between you and your bed. Very few of our houses are licensed, but most are happy for you to bring your own drink.

Prices and minimum stays

Each entry gives a price PER ROOM for two people. We also include prices for single rooms, and let you know if there is a supplement to pay should you choose to loll in a double bed on your own.

Photo: The Old Parsonage, entry 25

The price range for each B&B covers a one-night stay in the cheapest room in low season to the most expensive in high season. Some owners charge more at certain times (during regattas or festivals, for example) and some charge less for stays of more than one night. Some owners ask for a two-night minimum stay at weekends and we mention this where possible. Most of our houses could fill many times over on peak weekends and during the summer; book early, especially if you have specific needs.

Booking and cancellation

Do be clear about the room booked and the price for B&B and for meals. Requests for deposits vary; some are non-refundable, especially in our London homes, and some owners may charge you for the whole of the booked stay in advance.

Some cancellation policies are more stringent than others. It is also worth noting that some owners will take this deposit directly from your credit/debit card without contacting you to discuss it. So ask them to explain their cancellation policy clearly before booking so you understand exactly where you stand; it may well avoid a nasty surprise.

Payment

All our owners take cash and UK cheques with a cheque card. Few take credit cards but if they do, we have given them the appropriate symbol. Check that your particular credit card is acceptable.

Photo: Skirling House, entry 636

Tipping

Owners do not expect tips. If you have been treated with extraordinary kindness, write to them, or leave a small gift. Please tell us, too – we love to hear, and we do note, all feedback.

Arrivals and departures

Say roughly what time you will arrive (normally after 4pm), as most hosts like to welcome you personally. Be on time if you have booked dinner; if, despite best efforts, you are delayed, phone to give warning.

Closed

When given in months this means the whole of the month stated.

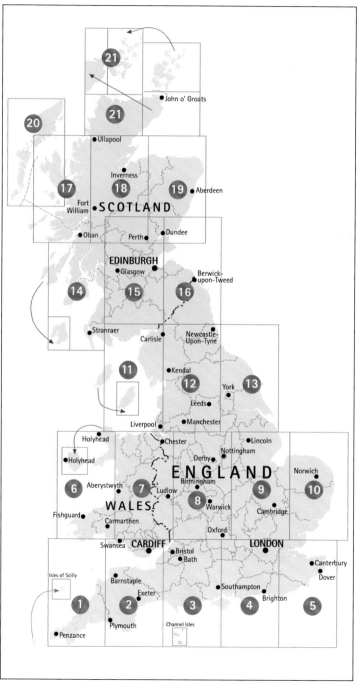

©Maidenhead Cartographic, 2008

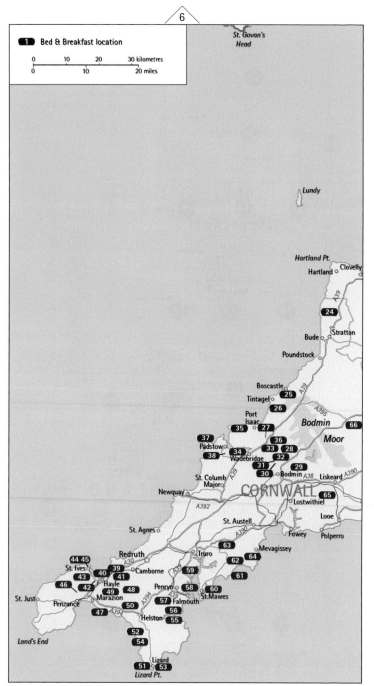

©Maidenhead Cartographic, 2008

Map 2   23

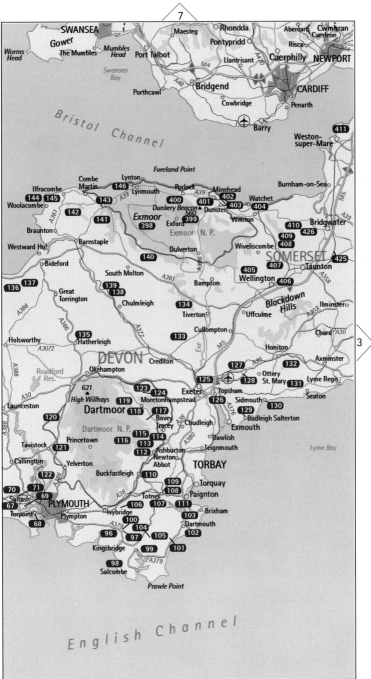

©Maidenhead Cartographic, 2008

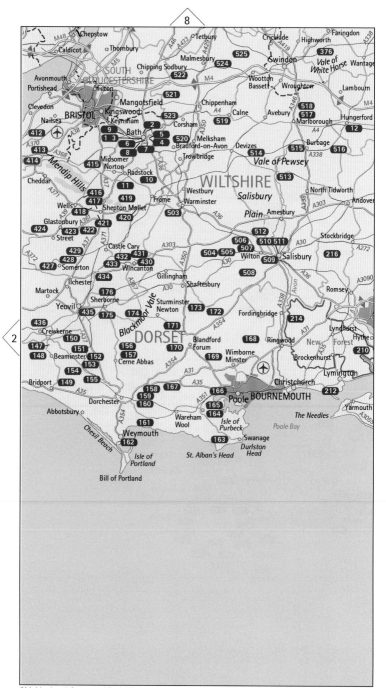

Map 4   25

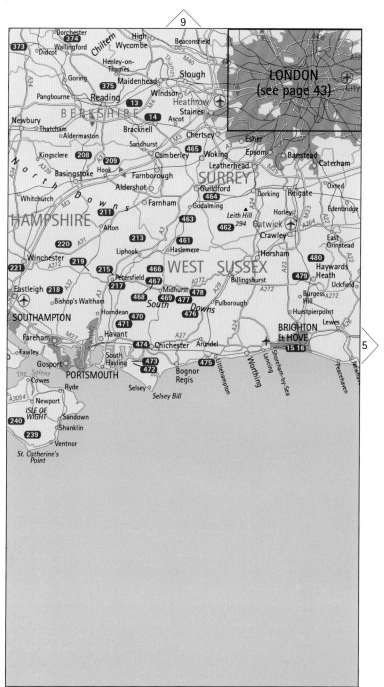

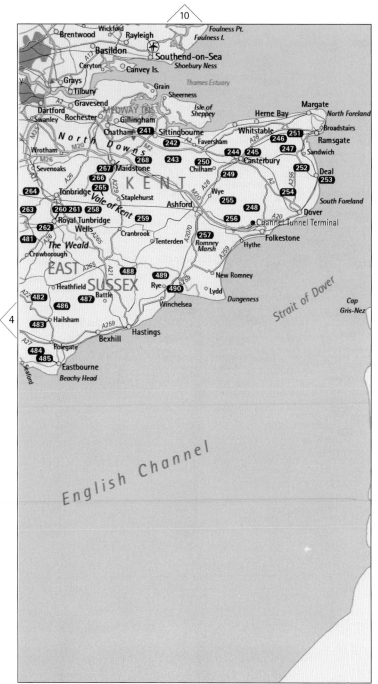

Map 6 27

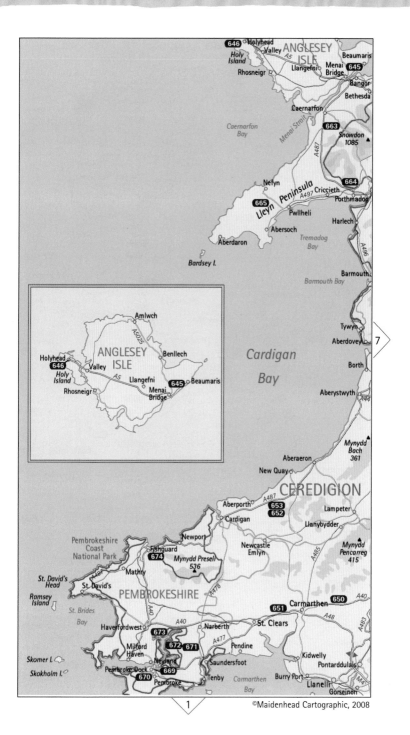

©Maidenhead Cartographic, 2008

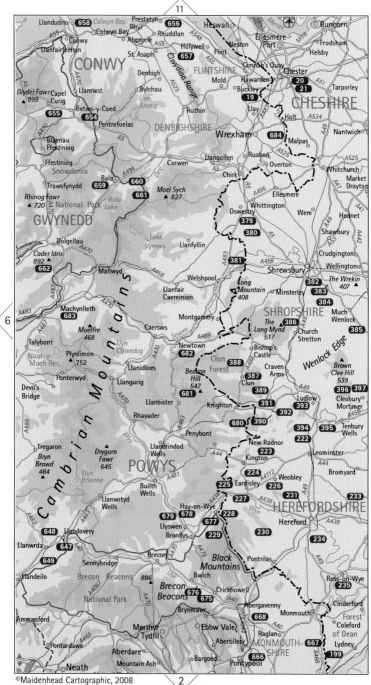

©Maidenhead Cartographic, 2008

Map 8   29

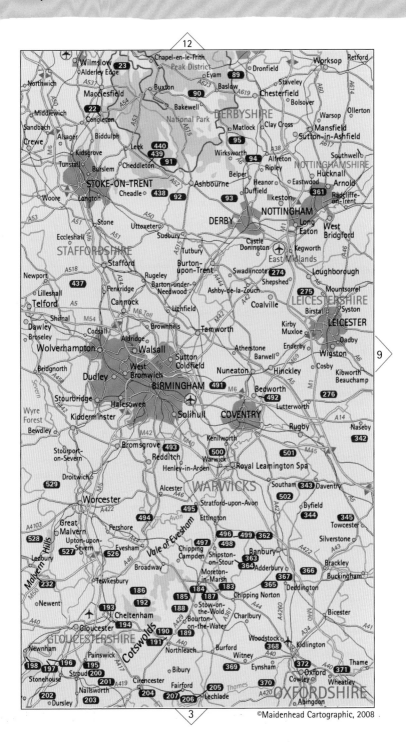

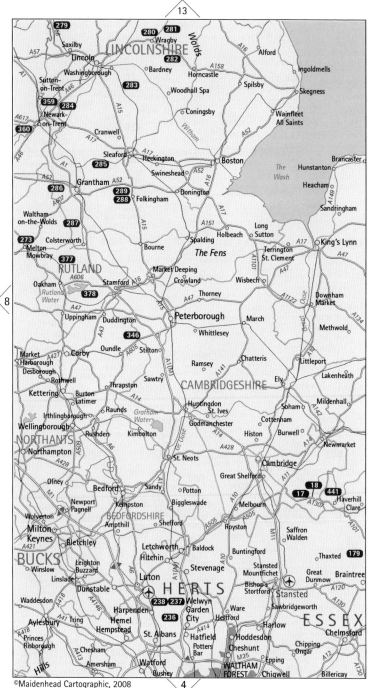

Map 10   31

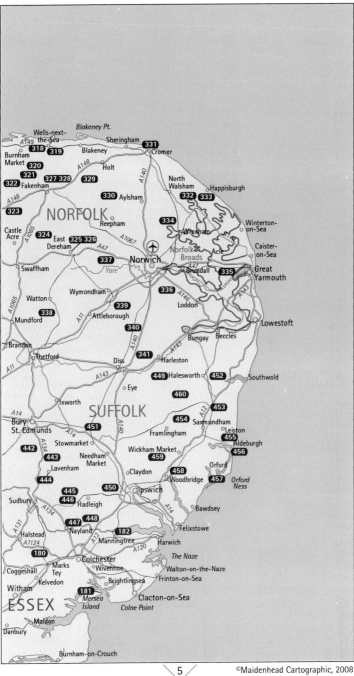

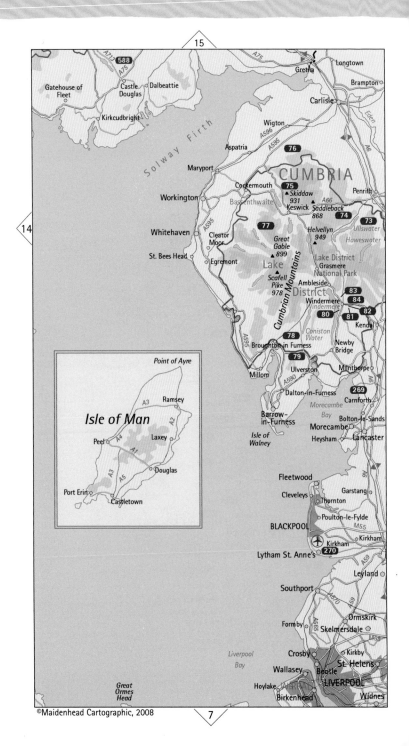

Map 12   33

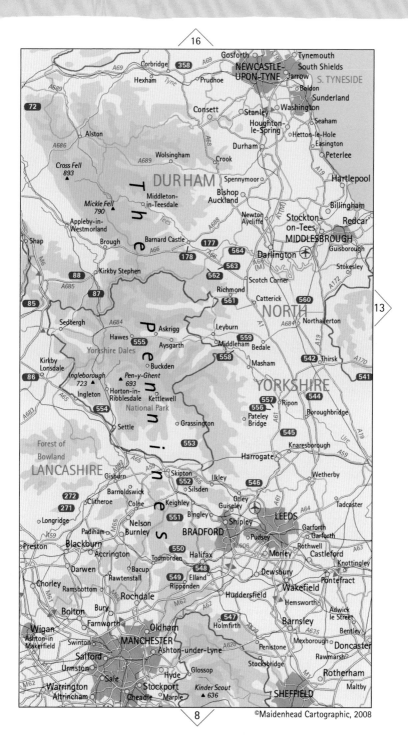

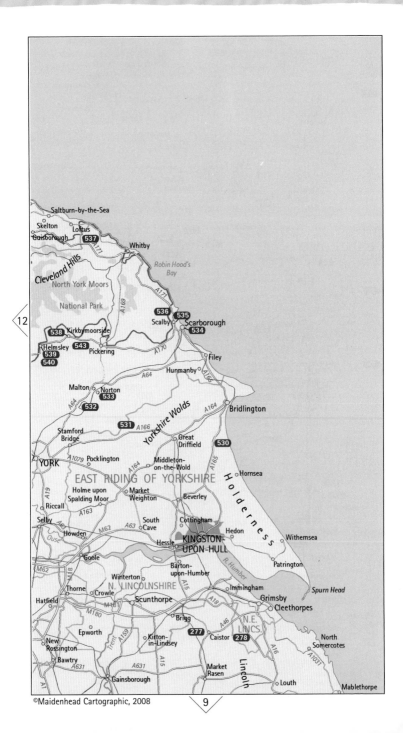

Map 14

35

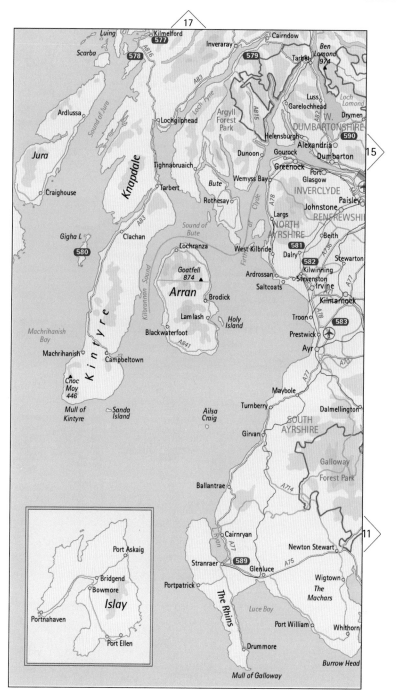

©Maidenhead Cartographic, 2008

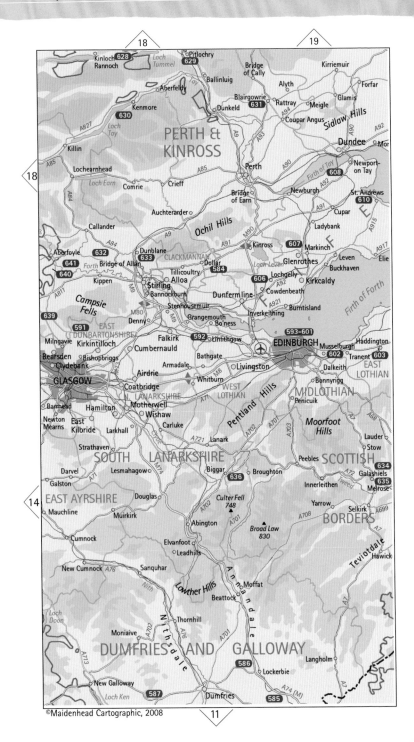

Map 16 37

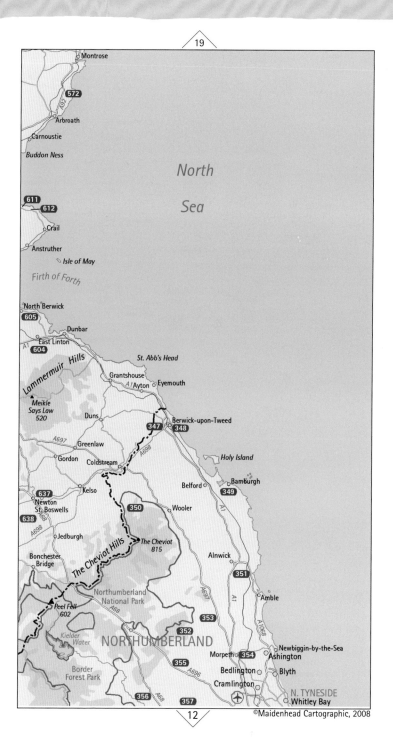

19

Montrose

572

Arbroath

Carnoustie

Buddon Ness

611
612

Crail

Anstruther

Isle of May

Firth of Forth

North

Sea

North Berwick

605

Dunbar

East Linton

604

Lammermuir Hills

St. Abb's Head

Grantshouse

Eyemouth

Ayton

▲ Meikle Says Law 520

Duns

Berwick-upon-Tweed

347
348

A697

Greenlaw

Gordon

Coldstream

Holy Island

Belford

Bamburgh

349

637

Kelso

Newton St. Boswells

638

350

Wooler

Jedburgh

The Cheviot Hills

The Cheviot 815

Alnwick

Bonchester Bridge

Northumberland National Park

351

Peel Fell 602

Kielder Water

NORTHUMBERLAND

Amble

353

352

Morpeth

354

Newbiggin-by-the-Sea

Ashington

Border Forest Park

355

Bedlington

Blyth

Cramlington

356

357

N. TYNESIDE

Whitley Bay

12

©Maidenhead Cartographic, 2008

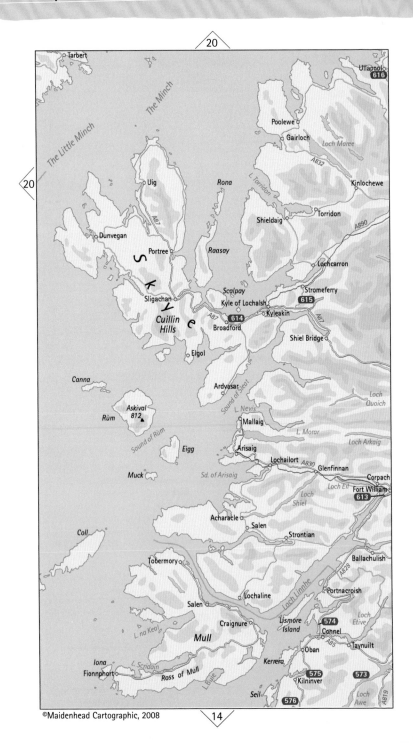

©Maidenhead Cartographic, 2008

Map 18   39

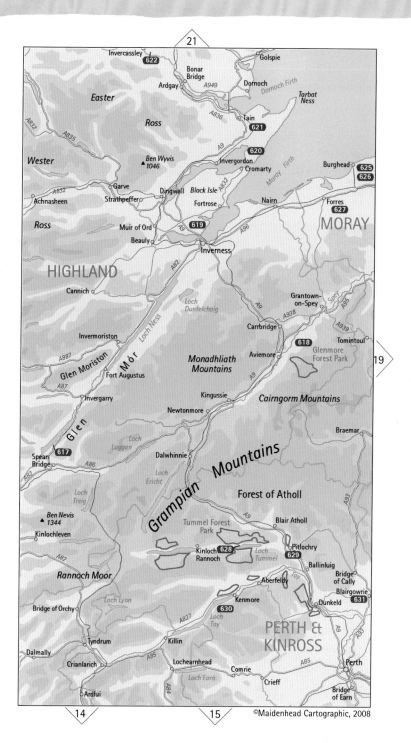

©Maidenhead Cartographic, 2008

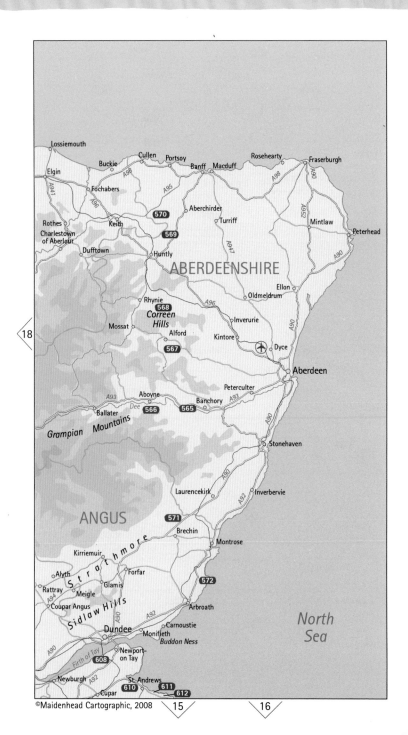

Map 20   41

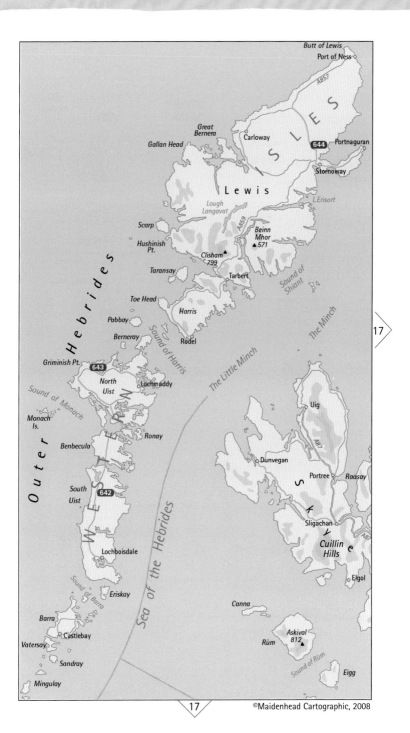

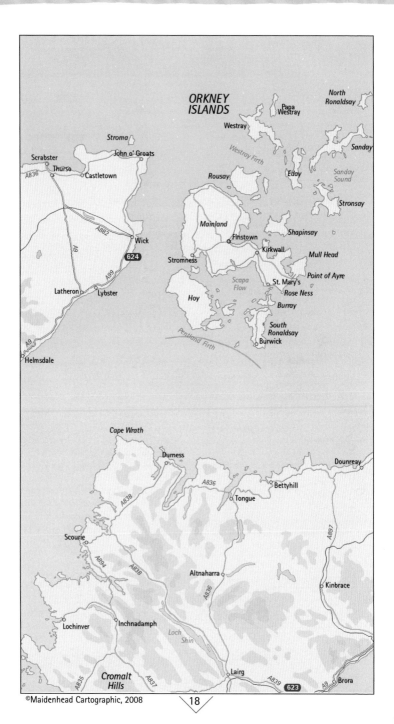

ORKNEY
ISLANDS

North
Ronaldsay

Papa
Westray

Westray

Sanday

Stroma

John o' Groats

Scrabster
Thurso
Castletown

Westray Firth

Eday

Sanday
Sound

Rousay

Stronsay

A836

Mainland

Finstown

Shapinsay

A882

Wick

Kirkwall

Mull Head

624

Stromness

Point of Ayre

A9

St. Mary's

Rose Ness

A99

Latheron
Lybster

Scapa
Flow

Hoy

Burray

South
Ronaldsay
Burwick

A9

Helmsdale

Pentland Firth

Cape Wrath

Durness

Dounreay

A838

A836

Bettyhill

Tongue

A897

Scourie

A894

A838

Altnaharra

Kinbrace

A836

Lochinver

Inchnadamph

Loch
Shin

Lairg

A839

623

A9

Brora

Cromalt
Hills

A835

A837

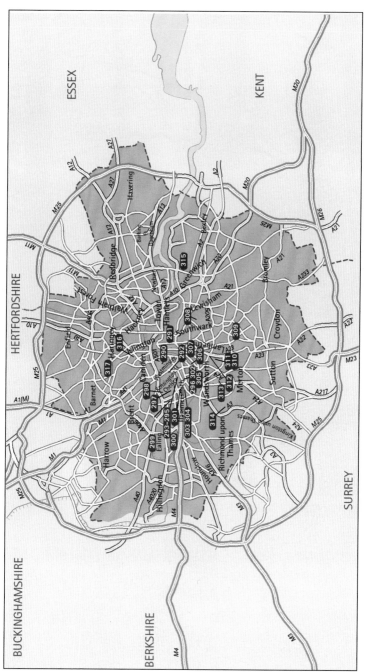

©Maidenhead Cartographic, 2008

England

Bath & N.E. Somerset

4 Brock Street

You'll be tickled pink here. Clever Minnie has performed a miracle at this natty Georgian townhouse tucked quietly behind The Circus and Royal Crescent. On either side of a sleek black door are box hedges with smart haircuts; walk in to a vast, elegant hallway, and up curved stairs to two softly coloured bedrooms. Find plump beds covered in soft woollen rug or baby blue quilt, painted furniture and a view from each. Loll in a roll top or blast yourself in the swish wet room, enjoy breakfast at the long dining table (or the garden on warm days), then go and have fun in town. A fabulous place to stay.

Bath & N.E. Somerset

77 Great Pulteney Street

Tea and cakes await down the elegant stone steps to a garden flat in this broad street of immaculate Georgian houses. Inside all is pale wood, modern art, bergère chairs and palms; the sitting room is light and airy; walls sport modern art and there's a view over the rugby pitch. Downstairs is a comfortable bedroom with loads of books and its own door to a small but delightfully well-designed garden. Breakfast here in summer at your own pace; Ian is a fanatic foodie and dinner will also be special. Henry may play the Northumbrian pipes for you if you ask nicely; the shops are a hop away.

Travel Club Offer: see page 392 for details.

Price	£95.
Rooms	2: 1 double, 1 twin sharing bath & wet room (let to same party only).
Meals	Pubs/restaurants within walking distance.
Closed	Christmas.
Directions	In centre of Bath.

Price	£75–£90. Singles from £55.
Rooms	1 double.
Meals	Dinner from £20. Packed lunch from £5.
Closed	Rarely.
Directions	A4 into centre of Bath. Last house before Laura Place on south side of Great Pulteney St. Parking by arrangement; 7-minute walk from station.

	Minnie Tatham
	4 Brock Street,
	Bath, Bath & N.E. Somerset BA1 2LN
Tel	01225 460536
Mobile	07812 042206
Email	enquiries@no4brockstreet.co.uk
Web	www.no4brockstreet.co.uk

	Ian Critchley & Henry Ford
	77 Great Pulteney Street,
	Bath,
	Bath & N.E. Somerset BA2 4DL
Tel	01225 466659
Email	critchford@77pulteneyst.co.uk.
Web	www.77pulteneyst.co.uk

Entry 1   Map 3

Entry 2   Map 3

Bath & N.E. Somerset

14 Raby Place

A listed Regency house within walking distance of one of Europe's most beautiful cities. Muriel likes modern art and has filled the elegant rooms with stunning pictures and objects, antique chairs and lovely fabrics. Beautifully proportioned double bedrooms are graceful and spotless with laundered linen; one on the top (third) floor has fabulous views over the city to the Abbey, the small single has a piano in case you get the urge. Breakfast is organic, delicious, and eaten at a communal table in the kitchen; chat to Muriel or bury your head in a paper. *Free parking permit for road outside.*

Price	£65–£70. Singles £35.
Rooms	5: 2 doubles, 1 family room; 1 twin with separate shower; 1 single with separate bath. (Cot available.)
Meals	Restaurants 8-minute walk.
Closed	Rarely.
Directions	Bathwick Hill is turning off the A36 towards Bristol; look for signs to university. No. 14 on left-hand side as you go uphill, before left turn into Raby Mews.

Muriel Guy
14 Raby Place,
Bathwick Hill,
Bath,
Bath & N.E. Somerset BA2 4EH
Tel 01225 465120

Entry 3   Map 3

Bath & N.E. Somerset

47 Sydney Buildings

Dazzling Simone has a natural sense of fun and a great deal of Franco-Caribbean colour: breakfasts of fruit, yogurt and cereals, or full English (much organic), are served on Limoges china overlooking the garden's box parterre and rambling roses. Immaculate bedrooms have a touch of 18th-century boudoir with their embroidered sheets, antique brass beds, frou-frou chairs and sumptuous drapes; views sail over the charming garden to the floodlit Abbey. Simone is wonderfully attentive and the delights of Bath, with its Thermae Spa, are a short walk along the canal.

Price	From £85. Singles £65.
Rooms	2: 1 double with separate bath; 1 twin/double with separate shower & wc.
Meals	Pubs/restaurants 10-minute walk.
Closed	Christmas.
Directions	From Bath centre, signs to American Museum. At A36 r'bout 1st exit onto Bathwick Hill. Sydney Buildings 1st road on right, house 300 yds on right. All-day parking.

Mrs Simone Johnson
47 Sydney Buildings,
Bathwick Hill, Bath,
Bath & N.E. Somerset BA2 6DB
Tel   01225 463033
Fax   01225 461054
Email sydneybuildings@mac.com
Web   www.sydneybuildings.com

Entry 4   Map 3

Bath & N.E. Somerset

Tolley Cottage

Breakfast on the patio and watch the barges pass the bottom of the gorgeous garden; raise your eyes to Bath Abbey on the skyline. This Victorian house is a ten-minute walk from the city centre, the spa and the fine old theatre. Sunny and bright, rooms are a comfortable mix of contemporary and classical; books, art and interesting glass pieces catch the eye. Bedrooms are small, calming and charming with toile de Jouy and elegant furniture; white bathrooms sparkle. Judy cooks special breakfasts; James, Master of Wine, can arrange tastings. Both are warm and relaxed, and love sharing their home.

Bath & N.E. Somerset

The Grove

Amble up the steep hill, past elegant railings and leafy gardens around bulky villas. At the top is the large house, split in two by jealous brothers in 1805, now elegant with creams and cushions, art and artefacts, books and bucolic views. Ample bedrooms are light and comfortable with fresh flowers, thick curtains or wooden shutters and modern bathrooms. Robert, a sculptor, will chat as he rustles up your delicious, lazy breakfast in the large, bright kitchen. An oversized town garden bordering woods is yours to explore – you may even meet deer – and Bath is a short stroll away. *Minimum stay two nights at weekends.*

Travel Club Offer: see page 392 for details.

Price	From £90. Singles from £80.
Rooms	2: 1 double, 1 twin.
Meals	Pubs/restaurants 10-minute walk.
Closed	Christmas.
Directions	Follow signs for American Museum & University up Bathwick Hill. Take 1st turn right to Sydney Buildings. House 200 yds on right.

Price	From £100. Singles from £80.
Rooms	3: 1 family room; 1 double with separate bathroom.
Meals	Pubs/restaurants within a mile.
Closed	Rarely.
Directions	Approx. 1 mile south of city centre. Lyncombe Hill opposite the railway & bus stations, 0.5 miles up Lyncombe Hill into Lyncombe Vale Rd. House 300 yds down the road, end of cul-de-sac.

Judy & James John
Tolley Cottage,
23 Sydney Buildings, Bath,
Bath & N.E. Somerset BA2 6BZ

Tel	01225 463365
Mobile	07703 534331
Email	jj@judyj.plus.com
Web	www.tolleycottage.co.uk

Robert & Dee Hornyold-Strickland
The Grove,
Lyncombe Vale Road, Bath,
Bath & N.E. Somerset BA2 4LR

Tel	01225 484282
Mobile	07899 757655
Email	robertstrickland44@yahoo.co.uk
Web	www.bathbandb.com

Entry 5   Map 3

Entry 6   Map 3

Bath & N.E. Somerset

Bath & N.E. Somerset

Grey Lodge

In a conservation area, yet only a short drive from the centre of Bath, the views are breathtaking from wherever you stand. The steep valley rolls out ahead of you from most of the rooms, and from the garden comes a confusion and a profusion of scents and colours – a glory in its own right. The friendly and likeable Sticklands are conservationists as well as gardeners and have a Green Certificate to prove it. Breakfasts are a feast: bacon and eggs, cereals, home-grown jam, smoked fish and much more. Jane will tell you all about wonderful local gardens to visit.

Manor Farm Barn

Duchy of Cornwall farmland stretches as far as the eye can see; the views from this converted barn – with light open-plan spaces – are splendid by any standards, but remarkable considering you are so close to Bath. There's much wildlife, too: sparrowhawks nest in the gable end, buzzards circle above the valley, and deer may gaze at you eating your breakfast. Giles, who pots, and Sue, who paints, are gentle and easygoing hosts; spruce guest rooms have built-in wardrobes, houseplants and excellent beds. For those in search of birdsong and country peace after a day on the hoof in Bath.

Price	£80–£90. Singles £50–£55.
Rooms	3: 2 twins/doubles, 1 family room.
Meals	Pub/restaurant 2 miles.
Closed	Rarely.
Directions	From A36, 3 miles out of Bath on Warminster road, take uphill road by lights & viaduct. 1st left, 100 yds, signed Monkton Combe. After village, house 1st on left; 0.5 miles on.

Price	£60–£70. Singles £40–£42.50.
Rooms	2: 1 twin/double; 1 double with separate shower.
Meals	Pubs/restaurants 2.5 miles.
Closed	Christmas & New Year.
Directions	From Bath, A367 (Wells Rd). At Red Lion r'bout right (Bristol A4). Straight on, pass Culverhay School on left. After 100 yds left to Englishcombe. There, right after postbox to church, fork right, follow road; last on right.

Jane & Anthony Stickland
Grey Lodge,
Summer Lane, Combe Down, Bath,
Bath & N.E. Somerset BA2 7EU

Tel	01225 832069
Fax	01225 830161
Email	greylodge@surfree.co.uk
Web	www.greylodge.co.uk

Sue & Giles Barber
Manor Farm Barn,
Englishcombe, Bath,
Bath & N.E. Somerset BA2 9DU

Tel	01225 424195
Mobile	07966 501016
Email	info@manorfarmbarn.com
Web	www.manorfarmbarn.com

Entry 7   Map 3

Entry 8   Map 3

Bath & N.E. Somerset

Corston Fields Farm

In rolling agricultural land, a short hop from Bath and its new spa, the Addicotts have given over swathes of their farm to natural habitat for indigenous wildlife – and have a Gold Award under the Duke of Cornwall's Habitat Award scheme to boot. Gerald, a keen rugby supporter, and Rosaline are utterly committed to the environment, and flax from the vibrant blue linseed crops is used to heat their sturdy, stone-mullioned and listed house. The large rooms – the best in the house – have all the mod cons. Come for the setting, the far-reaching views and the wonderful hosts.
Minimum stay two nights at weekends.

Price	From £94. Singles £60.
Rooms	4: 1 double; 1 double, 1 twin sharing bath (2nd room let to same party only). Annexe: 1 double.
Meals	Pub 300 yds.
Closed	Christmas & New Year.
Directions	From A4 west of Bath, A39 through Corston. 1 mile on, just before Wheatsheaf Pub (on right), right. Signed 200 yds along lane on right.

Gerald & Rosaline Addicott
Corston Fields Farm,
Corston, Bath,
Bath & N.E. Somerset BA2 9EZ
Tel   01225 873305
Mobile   07900 056568
Email   corston.fields@btinternet.com
Web   www.corstonfields.com

Entry 9   Map 3

Bath & N.E. Somerset

Hollytree Cottage

Meandering lanes lead to this 16th-century cottage, with roses round the door, a grandfather clock in the hall and an air of genteel tranquillity. The cottage charm has been updated with Regency mahogany and sumptuous sofas. There's even a four-poster bed and the bedrooms have long views over farmland and undulating countryside. Behind is a sloping, south-facing garden with a pond and some rare trees and shrubs. A place to come for absolute peace and quiet, birdsong and walks and the joys of elegant Bath 20 minutes away. Julia knows the city well so can help you plan trips.

Price	£80–£90. Singles £45.
Rooms	3: 1 double, 1 twin, 1 four-poster.
Meals	Pub/restaurant 0.5 miles.
Closed	Rarely.
Directions	From Bath, A36 to Wolverton. Just past Red Lion, turn for Laverton. 1 mile to x-roads; towards Faukland; downhill for 80 yds. On left, just above farm entrance on right.

Mrs Julia Naismith
Hollytree Cottage,
Laverton, Bath,
Bath & N.E. Somerset BA2 7QZ
Tel   01373 830786
Mobile   07854 783018
Email   julia@naismith.fsbusiness.co.uk
Web   www.hollytreecottagebath.co.uk

Entry 10   Map 3

Bath & N.E. Somerset

Melon Cottage Vineyard

Interesting, child-friendly hosts who are entirely natural and unbusinesslike make this place special; it's excellent value, too. The large Mendip-style 'long cottage' with mullioned windows and beams made of ships' timbers, fronted by a small vineyard, is temptingly close to dinner at Babington House, the treasures of Bath and Wells, the gardens and concerts at Stourhead, and Gregorian chant in Downside Abbey. Rooms are very simple, the jams are homemade and the hosts the kindest you may meet. No sitting room, but tea in the walled garden is rich compensation. *Children over five welcome. Minimum stay two nights.*

Price	£45–£55. Singles £25.
Rooms	1 double/family.
Meals	Pubs 2 miles.
Closed	Rarely.
Directions	From Bath A367, Wells road, through Radstock. After 3 miles, at large r'bout, B3139 for Trowbridge. After 1.1 miles, and Charlton sign, right up 2nd driveway on right. Pink house at top, visible from road.

Virginia & Hugh Pountney
Melon Cottage Vineyard,
Charlton, Radstock, Bath,
Bath & N.E. Somerset BA3 5TN

Tel	01761 435090
Email	a_pountney@sky.com
Web	www.meloncottage.co.uk

Entry 11   Map 3

Berkshire

Wilton House

With its handsome Queen Anne frontage, "the most ambitious house in Hungerford" (Pevsner) conceals medieval origins. A classic townhouse in a charming market town, its interior is a panelled, soft-painted delight. Light floods through sash windows onto paintings and prints, books, antiques and wide, inviting sofas; bedrooms are understatedly elegant and relaxing; bathrooms are grand. So is breakfast in the 18th-century dining room: the Welfares look after you perfectly. All this, antique shops to the front and a walled garden with cordon-trained fruit trees behind. *Children over eight welcome.*

Price	From £74. Singles from £62.
Rooms	2: 1 double, 1 twin/double.
Meals	Packed lunch £5. Pub 100 yds.
Closed	Christmas.
Directions	M4 exit 14; A338 to A4; right for Marlborough, turning at Bear Hotel onto Salisbury road (A338). Over canal bridge into High St. House 200 yds past Town Hall on right.

Deborah & Jonathan Welfare
Wilton House,
33 High Street, Hungerford,
Berkshire RG17 0NF

Tel	01488 684228
Fax	01488 685037
Email	welfares@hotmail.com
Web	www.wiltonhouse-hungerford.co.uk

Entry 12   Map 3

Berkshire

Eastmere

Opposite the duck pond in a pretty, tucked-away village, this Victorian redbrick house is near to Windsor, Ascot and Henley: Heathrow is an easy drive. Get a bouncy welcome from Whirly the curly poodle and homemade biscuits from Catherine, a successful artist who loves to cook: rare breed bacon from the village, eggs from the chickens who roam the garden. Your simple ground floor bedroom has its own entrance, lovely linen sheets, white painted Edwardian furniture, a sofa and a log burning stove. Settle in the conservatory with a good book from the library, stroll the commons or along the Thames. *French & Italian spoken*

Berkshire

Whitehouse Farm Cottage

Once you get past the housing estates of Bracknell, this is a fabulous find. A 17th-century farmhouse with a delightful garden, and two charmingly converted barns with their own entrances. Garden Cottage has a beamed drawing room downstairs and a gallery bedroom with creamy walls and a cast-iron bed. The Old Forge has the blacksmith's fireplace and lovely views onto the courtyard garden and its pebble mosaics. The single is in the house with its own comfortable sitting room. Locally sourced breakfasts with fresh bread are served in the house by friendly Keir and Louise, who are film prop makers.

Price	£75. Singles £45.
Rooms	1 double.
Meals	Dinner, 3-4 courses, £15-£18. Pubs 50 yds.
Closed	Christmas & New Year.
Directions	Leave M4 at Junction 8/9. A404 for High Wycombe, then left onto A4 towards Reading. After 3 miles, left signed to Waltham St Lawrence, then over staggered x-road. On right opposite pond.

Catherine & Peter Turner
Eastmere,
Shurlock Row,
Berkshire RG10 0PS
Tel   01189 340946
Mobile   07919 020704
Email   mrspturner@hotmail.co.uk

Entry 13   Map 4

Price	£75-£90. Singles £65.
Rooms	3: 1 single & sitting room. Old Forge: 1 double. Cottage: 1 double & sitting room.
Meals	Picnics by arrangement. Pubs/restaurants within 1 mile.
Closed	Christmas & occasionally.
Directions	From A329, take B3408 to Binfield. Left at r'bout, left at traffic lights, into St Marks Road. Then 2nd left Foxley Lane, 1st left Murrell Hill Lane. House is 1st on right.

Keir Lusby
Whitehouse Farm Cottage,
Murrell Hill Lane, Binfield,
Berkshire RG42 4BY
Tel   01344 423688
Mobile   07711 948889
Email   garden.cottages@ntlworld.com

Entry 14   Map 4

Brighton & Hove

Lansdowne Guest House

Fun, refreshing and bang in the middle of Pimlico-by-Sea. This is Hove: grand white Regency villas and the promenade a hop away. In this 1920s mansion built for a lord's mistress, the Bundys occupy the first floor. Enter a big friendly living room with a fire for winter nights, a sprinkling of modern art and a superb spread for the morning: Asian or English. Your hosts are attentive, interesting, well-travelled and love meeting their guests. Up under the roof are stylish creamy bedrooms separated by a curtain on a big sofa'd landing; bathrooms, cleverly compact, have lotions and bubbles. Brighton lies at your feet.

Price	£75–£85. Singles from £55.
Rooms	2: 1 double, 1 twin/double.
Meals	Dinner from £20. Packed lunch from £7.50. Picnic hampers from £10.
Closed	Christmas & occasionally.
Directions	A23 to seafront, then right towards Hove. 2nd right after Brunswick Square into Holland Rd; right at 2nd lights. House 2nd left behind red brick wall. Street parking with visitor's voucher.

	Diana & Michael Bundy
	Lansdowne Guest House,
	21 Lansdowne Road, Hove,
	Brighton & Hove BN3 1FE
Tel	01273 773700
Fax	01273 773718
Email	lansdowneguesthouse@hotmail.co.uk

Brighton & Hove

5 Palmeira Square

Drift along Brighton seafront, and emerge into the Regency splendour of Palmeira Square. Susie with the twinkling eyes welcomes you into a fun, bohemian, ground-floor flat in Hove. Rooms are flooded with light, ceilings are high, furnishings have pizzazz (kilims on bamboo floors, funky chandeliers). Your bedroom is deep lilac and lovely, your bathroom (big shower, stylish toiletries) is Susie's. She has lived in Portugal, Brazil, Bordeaux, works from home and delivers a delicious breakfast to your door. Or, at a pretty seat in the window bay; turn your head and you'll catch the sea. *Minimum stay two nights summer weekends.*

Price	£75–£85.
Rooms	1 double with shared bath.
Meals	Continental breakfast. Pub/restaurant 500 yds.
Closed	Rarely.
Directions	Seafront towards Hove. Right onto Adelaide Crescent (white Regency buildings) then immediate right, following road up into Palmeira Square. No 5 is just after Crescent becomes Square.

	Susie de Castilho
	5 Palmeira Square,
	Flat 1, Hove,
	Brighton & Hove BN3 2JA
Tel	01273 719087
Mobile	07917 562771
Email	stay@2staybrighton.co.uk
Web	www.2staybrighton.co.uk

Cambridgeshire

Springfield House

A fine mix of town and country: you are in a rural village yet wonderfully close to Cambridge. The former school house hugs the bend of a river, its French windows opening to rambling, delightful gardens. The conservatory, draped with a huge mimosa, is an exceptional spot for summer breakfasts. Beds and bedrooms are large and comfortable, with thick curtains, books, flowers and garden views. This is an old-fashionedly elegant home; there's Charlie the flat-coated retriever, a family bustle in the holidays, and Judith, a quietly nurturing hostess. Good value.

Price	£60-£65. Singles £45.
Rooms	2 doubles.
Meals	Pubs 150 yds.
Closed	Rarely.
Directions	A1307 from Cambridge, left into High St. 1st right after The Crown (on left) into Horn Lane. House on right next to chapel, before ford.

Judith Rossiter
Springfield House,
14-16 Horn Lane, Linton,
Cambridgeshire CB21 4HT
Tel   01223 891383
Fax   01223 890335
Email   fredrossiter@tiscali.co.uk
Web   www.springfieldhouse.org

🏃 🗡 📶 🐈

Entry 17   Map 9

Cambridgeshire

The Old Chapel

Tardis-like, this 1823 converted chapel opens out to a series of lovely light rooms and a gorgeous garden with cows peeping over the fence. You have a large drawing room with a wood-burner, a dining room with a grand piano, a verdant conservatory, a fabulous library, even a sauna. Bedrooms are beautifully dressed with cream bedspreads, pale carpets, fine antiques and heaps of cushions; bathrooms have gleaming tiles and fresh flowers. Alex and Ian are both keen cooks and love entertaining; the vast kitchen, with arched chapel windows, has a huge table and food is sourced as locally as possible. Good fun.

Ethical Collection: Environment; Food.
See page 400 for details.

Travel Club Offer: see page 392 for details.

Price	£65-£70. Singles £45.
Rooms	2: 1 double; 1 single with separate bath.
Meals	Dinner £25. Pubs easy walking distance. Restaurants 7 miles.
Closed	Rarely.
Directions	A1307 for Haverhill. Thro' Linton; after dual carriageway, left slip road into village. Left at sign of horse on green towards West Wickham. House 200 yds on left opposite thatched cottage.

Alexandra & Ian Rose
The Old Chapel,
West Wickham Road,
Horseheath,
Cambridgeshire CB21 4QA
Tel   01223 894027
Email   alexchapel@btinternet.com
Web   www.theoldchapelbandb.co.uk

🏃 🗡 🚂 🧴 📶 🐈

Entry 18   Map 9

Cheshire

The Mount

Britain at its best: rare trees planted in 1860, bountiful flowers, a pond, a vegetable garden and Rachel – delightful, warm and friendly. The Victorian house, built for a Chester corn merchant and furnished in a traditional style, has garden views from every light-filled window. You get an airy drawing room, a high-ceilinged dining room and comfortable, spacious, country-house bedrooms with attractive paintings and soft furnishings. A haven for garden buffs and walkers – and there's a tennis court too. Chester, North Wales and two airports are conveniently close. *Arrivals after 5pm.*

Cheshire

Cotton Farm

Only a four-mile hop from Roman Chester and its 900-year-old cathedral is this sprawling, red-brick farmhouse. Elegant chickens peck in hedges, ponies graze, lambs frisk and cats doze. The farm, run by conservationists Nigel and Clare, is under the Countryside Stewardship Scheme – there are wildflower meadows, summer swallows and 250 acres to roam. Bedrooms are large, stylish farmhouse with lovely fabrics and touches of luxury (bath towels are huge), but best of all is the relaxed family atmosphere. Breakfasts are delicious and beautifully presented. *Stabling available. Children over ten welcome.*

Price	£70. Singles from £40.
Rooms	3: 2 doubles, 1 twin.
Meals	Pub/restaurant 0.5 miles.
Closed	Christmas & New Year.
Directions	From A55 signed North Wales. Take A5104 Broughton; at 2nd r'bout left to Pennyfordd. Through village, cross over A55 then left Lesters Lane, signed Higher Kinnerton 1.25 miles. House 0.75 miles on right, sharp bend.

Price	£70. Singles £50.
Rooms	3: 2 doubles, 1 twin.
Meals	Pub 1.5 miles.
Closed	Rarely.
Directions	A51 Chester-Nantwich. 1.5 miles from outskirts, after golf course on left, right, down Cotton Lane, signed Cotton Edmunds; 1.5 miles, left on sharp right-hand bend; 2nd drive on right.

Jonathan & Rachel Major
The Mount,
Higher Kinnerton,
Chester,
Cheshire CH4 9BQ

Tel 01244 660275
Email themount@higherkinnerton.com
Web www.bandbchester.com

Clare & Nigel Hill
Cotton Farm,
Cotton Edmunds, Chester,
Cheshire CH3 7PG

Tel 01244 336616
Mobile 07840 682042
Email echill@btinternet.com
Web www.cottonfarm.co.uk

Entry 19   Map 7

Entry 20   Map 7

Cheshire

Greenlooms Cottage

This pretty cottage was where the estate's chief hedger and ditcher lived. The smallholding has gone but the walnuts, quinces and garden pump remain – and the views still reach to the Peckforton Hills. Now it is a stylishly simple and fun place to stay, thanks to Deborah – traveller, ex-potter, fabulous cook – and Peter, furniture-maker and restorer. Follow your nose to the Aga-cosy kitchen where the best black pudding and bacon are waiting to fuel you for a day on the Cheshire cycle route. Return to two sweet bedrooms, one up one down: crisp white duvets, Floris soaps in simple walk-in showers, ethnic touches.

Cheshire

Lower Key Green Farm

Aga-cooked breakfasts with home-baked bread, home-laid eggs and Staffordshire oatcakes: just the thing to set you up for a day's walking round this organic farm or in the Peak District. This is an unusual, quirky farmhouse filled with reclaimed things, good art (both David and Janet's own work too), flagged floors, leather bucket chairs round a wood-burning stove and grand views. The bedroom has a cottagey simplicity; a Victorian washstand and a slipper bath add delight, as do homemade biscuits and sherry. The garden is filled with interest; take a book and a cuppa and sit peacefully here, or find a good pub nearby.

Price	£70. Singles from £45.
Rooms	2: 1 double, 1 twin.
Meals	Dinner, £25 with wine. Pub 3 miles.
Closed	Never.
Directions	A41 Whitchurch; south from Chester. After petrol station, 2nd left at antiques shop. On for 1.5 miles thro' village, right into Martins Lane; 1 mile on right.

Price	£70. Singles £50.
Rooms	1 twin/double.
Meals	Pub 10-minute drive.
Closed	Rarely.
Directions	From A54, A523 towards Leek. Thro' Bosley village, turn right; after 40mph and Queen's Arms sign, onto Tunstall Rd; 2nd farm on left after 0.5 miles.

Deborah Newman
Greenlooms Cottage,
Martins Lane, Hargrave, Chester,
Cheshire CH3 7RX

Tel	01829 781475
Mobile	07791 014231
Email	dnewman@greenlooms.com
Web	www.greenlooms.com

Janet Heath
Lower Key Green Farm,
Bosley, Macclesfield,
Cheshire SK11 0PB

Tel	01260 223278
Email	lowerkeygreen@hotmail.com
Web	www.lowerkeygreen.co.uk

Entry 21   Map 7

Entry 22   Map 8

Cheshire

Harrop Fold Farm

Artists, foodies and walkers adore this antique-filled farmhouse with soul-lifting views. On the edge of the Peak District, the oldest building on the farm dates from 1694 (Bonnie Prince Charlie visited here!). The B&B part has a warm, peaceful breakfast room, a stone-flagged sitting room, a spectacular studio. Fresh flowers, antique beds, fine fabrics, hot water bottles with chic covers, bathrooms with fluffy robes: you get the best. Gregarious Sue and daughter Leah hold art and cookery courses so the food too is special. Bedrooms have stupendous views – and flat-screen TV and DVD just in case they pall.

Cornwall

The Old Vicarage

The first sight of quirky chimneys – the spires of former owner Reverend Hawker's parish churches – sets the scene for a huge house packed with interest and steeped in Victoriana. Jill and Richard, both delightful, know the local history – and the clifftop walks, which are glorious. Rooms are casually grand, dotted with *objets* – brass gramophone, magic lantern, eccentric Hawker memorabilia. Browse books in the study, play the grand piano, sip brandy over billiards. Bedrooms are country-house pretty, with most bathrooms refurbished, lawns well tended and views to the sea. Blissfully, mobiles don't work.

Travel Club Offer: see page 392 for details.

Price	£80. Singles £50.
Rooms	2 doubles.
Meals	Dinner, 5 courses, £30. Supper £15. Packed lunch available. Pub 0.25 miles.
Closed	Never.
Directions	B470 Macclesfield to Whaley Bridge. Continue for 4 miles to Highwayman pub; 0.25 miles further down track (rutted at top); on left, immed. before sharp right hand bend.

Price	£80. Singles £40.
Rooms	3: 1 double, 1 twin, 1 single.
Meals	Pub/tea rooms 5-10-minute walk.
Closed	December–January.
Directions	From A39 at Morwenstow, follow signs towards church. Small turning on right, just before church, marked 'public footpath'. Drive down to house.

	Sue Stevenson
	Harrop Fold Farm,
	Rainow, Macclesfield,
	Cheshire SK10 5UU
Tel	01625 560085
Email	stay@harropfoldfarm.co.uk
Web	www.harropfoldfarm.co.uk

	Jill & Richard Wellby
	The Old Vicarage,
	Morwenstow,
	Cornwall EX23 9SR
Tel	01288 331369
Fax	01288 356077
Web	www.rshawker.co.uk

Entry 23 Map 8

Entry 24 Map 1

Cornwall

The Old Parsonage

A spellbinding coastline, secret coves, spectacular walks. All this and a supremely comfortable Georgian rectory – with a drying room for wet togs! – to return to. Morag and Margaret have transformed the interior. Superb pitch pine floors and original woodwork add warmth and a fresh glow, the big engaging bedrooms (including one on the ground floor) have a quirky, upbeat mix of furniture and furnishings, and the bathrooms are pampering. In front of the house the land slopes away to the Atlantic, just a five-minute walk across a SSSI. There are plans afoot for the garden, which already has some pleasant corners.

Price	From £80. Singles from £55.
Rooms	3 twins/doubles.
Meals	Packed lunch £5.95. Pub/restaurant 600 yds.
Closed	Never.
Directions	In Boscastle head towards Tintagel on B3263. 500 yds after garage on left turn right into Green Lane. After bend, house 3rd on right.

Morag Reeve & Margaret Pickering
The Old Parsonage,
Forrabury, Boscastle,
Cornwall PL35 0DJ
Tel 01840 250339
Mobile 07890 531677
Email morag@old-parsonage.com
Web www.old-parsonage.com

Entry 25 Map 1

Cornwall

Upton Farm

A restored farmhouse set back from the rugged coastline with unrivalled views, from Tintagel to Port Isaac and beyond... sunsets are sublime. Bedrooms are traditional and smart, there's a games room and safe storage for surfers. Slate slabs in the hall, gentle colours throughout; from the depths of the sea-green sofa in your drawing room, breathe in those AONB views. Such seclusion! Yet ten minutes across fields is the coastal path and, nearby, serious surfing, great pub, restaurant and more. Kick-start your day with Ricardo's signature muesli. *Minimum stay two nights . Children over eight welcome.*

Price	From £90.
Rooms	4: 2 doubles, 1 twin, 1 family.
Meals	Pub/restaurant 1 mile.
Closed	Rarely.
Directions	South through Delabole, near end of village right into Treligga Downs Rd; 0.5 miles to T-junc; turn right. 1 mile on, pass Trecarne Farm on left; 100 yds, house on right.

Elizabeth & Ricardo Dorich
Upton Farm,
Trebarwith,
Cornwall PL33 9DG
Tel 01840 770225
Mobile 07975 710833
Email ricardo@dorich.co.uk
Web www.upton-farm.co.uk

Entry 26 Map 1

Cornwall

Tremoren

Views stretch sleepily over the Cornish countryside. You might feel inclined to do nothing more than snooze over your book on the terrace, but the surfing beaches, the Camel Trail and the Eden Project are all close by. The stone and slate former farmhouse has been smartly updated with a light and airy ground-floor bedroom – all soft colours, pretty china and crisp bed linen – and a swish, power-shower bathroom. Your red-walled sitting room, full of books and interesting maps, leads out onto the flower-filled terrace: perfect for that evening drink. Lanie is bubbly and engaging, and food is her passion.

Price	£80.
Rooms	1 double & sitting room.
Meals	Dinner, 4 courses, £25. Inn 0.5 miles.
Closed	Rarely.
Directions	A39 to St Kew Highway through village; left at Red Lion. Down lane, 1st left round sharp right-hand bend. 2nd drive on right; signed.

Philip & Lanie Calvert
Tremoren,
St Kew, Bodmin,
Cornwall PL30 3HA

Tel	01208 841790
Fax	01208 841031
Email	la.calvert@btopenworld.com
Web	www.sunsell.com/clients/tremoren

Entry 27   Map 1

Cornwall

Higher Lank Farm

Families rejoice: you can only come if you have a child under five! Celtic crosses in the garden and original panelling hint at the house's 500-year history; one bedroom is resplendent with oak, the other two more traditional. Nursery teas begin at 5pm, grown-up suppers are later and Lucy will cheerfully babysit while the rest of you slink off to the pub. Farm-themed playgrounds are covered in safety matting and grass, there are piglets and chicks, a pony to ride, eggs to collect, a nursery rhyme trail, a sand barn for little ones and cream teas in the garden. Oh, and real nappies are provided!

Price	From £95. Singles by arrangement.
Rooms	3 family rooms.
Meals	Supper £16.75. Nursery tea £4.75. Packed lunch £7.50. Pub 1.5 miles.
Closed	November–Easter.
Directions	From Launceston, A395, then A39 thro' Camelford. Left onto B3266 to Bodmin. After 4 miles, left signed Wenfordbridge Pottery; over bridge, past pottery & on brow of hill, left into lane; house at top.

Lucy Finnemore
Higher Lank Farm,
St Breward,
Bodmin,
Cornwall PL30 4NB

Tel	01208 850716
Email	higherlankfarm@waitrose.com
Web	www.higherlankfarm.co.uk

Entry 28   Map 1

Cornwall

Cabilla Manor

There's a treasure round every corner and an opera house in one of the barns. Instant seduction as you enter the old manor house out on the moor, brimful of interest and colour. Rich exotic rugs and cushions, artefacts from around the world, Louella's sumptuous hand-stencilled quilts, huge beds, coir carpets, garden flowers. There's a dining room crammed floor to ceiling with books, many of them Robin's (a writer and explorer) and a lofty conservatory for meals overlooking a semi-wild garden – with tennis and elegant lawns. The views are heavenly, the hosts wonderful and the final mile thrillingly wild.

Price	£80. Singles £40.
Rooms	4: 1 double; 1 double with separate bath; 1 double, 1 twin, sharing bath.
Meals	Dinner, 3 courses, £30. Pub 4 miles. Restaurant 8-10 miles.
Closed	Christmas & New Year.
Directions	6 miles after Jamaica Inn on A30, left for Cardinham. Through Millpool & straight on, ignoring further signs to Cardinham. After 2.5 miles, left to Manor 0.75 miles; on right down drive.

	Robin & Louella Hanbury-Tenison
	Cabilla Manor,
	Mount, Bodmin,
	Cornwall PL30 4DW
Tel	01208 821224
Mobile	07770 664218
Email	louella@cabilla.co.uk
Web	www.cabilla.co.uk

Entry 29   Map 1

Cornwall

Park Farmhouse

You are near to all the north Cornish coast delights – surfing, coastal path, Camel trail – but it feels quiet and peaceful in this Georgian slate-roofed farmhouse with generous windows; any road noise is muffled by mature trees. Flop in the guests' sitting room with a wood-burner and comfortable brocade sofa; bedrooms (one on the ground floor) are sumptuous with antique beds, fresh striped curtains and crisp linen. Justin and Sarah are both interested in food, especially local fish, and you dine surrounded by antlers at a gleaming table. Afterwards take a turn round the well-planned garden.

Price	£75. Singles £50.
Rooms	4: 2 doubles; 1 double, 1 single sharing bath.
Meals	Dinner, 3 courses, £25. Children's teas £10.
Closed	Never.
Directions	From Bodmin, A389 towards Wadebridge. Cross river, pass signs for Camelford & Pencarrow; through Washaway; for 1 mile, down long hill. At bottom, blue sign on right for Park Farmhouse.

	Justin & Sarah Mason
	Park Farmhouse,
	Washaway, Bodmin,
	Cornwall PL30 3AG
Tel	01208 841277
Email	masons@park-farmhouse.com
Web	www.park-farmhouse.com

Entry 30   Map 1

Cornwall

Menkee

From this handsome Georgian farmhouse there are long views towards the sea; you're 20 minutes away from the coastal path and wild surf but you may not want to budge. Gage and Liz are deliciously unstuffy and look after you well: newspapers and a weather forecast appear with a scrumptious breakfast, your gorgeously comfortable bed is turned down in the evening and walkers can be dropped off and collected. The elegant house is filled with beautiful things, gleaming furniture, fresh flowers, roaring fires and pretty fabrics – all you have to do is slacken your pace and wind down. *Minimum stay two nights in high season.*

Ethical Collection: Environment; Food. See page 400 for details.

Travel Club Offer: see page 392 for details.

Price	£80-£90. Singles from £40.
Rooms	2 doubles.
Meals	Pub/restaurant 1.3 miles.
Closed	Rarely.
Directions	A389 Bodmin-Wadebridge; 2.5 miles, then fork right on B3266; on for 2 miles for Camelford; 600 yds after St Mabyn turn-off, left down drive.

	Gage & Liz Williams
	Menkee,
	St Maybn, Bodmin,
	Cornwall PL30 3DD
Tel	01208 841378
Mobile	07999 549935, 07968 011653
Email	gagewillms@aol.com
Web	www.cornwall-online.co.uk/menkee

Entry 31   Map 1

Cornwall

Lavethan

A glorious house in the most glorious of settings: views sail down to the valley. It rambles on many levels and is part 15th-century: walls are stone, floors are flagged, stairs are oak. The bedrooms in the house are lovely; one, part of the old chapel, has stone lintels that cross it, all are sunny, with proper bathrooms and lovely old baths for wallowing in. Catherine, a warm hostess, has decorated lavishly in country style; the guest sitting room is hugely welcoming with books, flowers and piano. All this and acres of ancient woods, Celtic crosses and a heated pool in the old walled garden. *Children over ten welcome.*

Price	£70-£90. Singles £40-£50.
Rooms	4: 2 twins/doubles; 2 doubles, each with separate bath.
Meals	Occasional dinner £25. Pub 0.25 miles.
Closed	Rarely.
Directions	From A30, turn for Blisland. There, past church on left & pub on right. Take lane at bottom left of village green. 0.25 miles on, drive on left (granite pillars & cattle grid).

	Christopher & Catherine Hartley
	Lavethan,
	Blisland, Bodmin,
	Cornwall PL30 4QG
Tel	01208 850487
Fax	01208 851387
Email	chrishartley@btconnect.com
Web	www.lavethan.com

Entry 32   Map 1

Cornwall

Trewint

Sally, Charlie and Harry live in a fine old granite farmhouse on the edge of the moor. Anchored to the hillside, Bodmin's tors looming behind, Trewint is tidy (for a farm!) and friendly. Dinner is cooked in the Aga, breakfast includes compotes and farm eggs, water is from the spring. Your bedroom comes in simple, old-fashioned farmhouse style, with pretty sash windows; your sitting room has a wood-burner and chess for stormy nights; the plunge pool tempts on hot days. Mossy granite walls, sweet country lanes, stone circles and streams... this is fabulous walking country and you'll happily unwind.

Price	From £70.
Rooms	1 double & sitting room.
Meals	Dinner £15-£20. Packed lunch £5. Pub/restaurant 3 miles.
Closed	Never.
Directions	Thro' Camelford south on A39, then B3266 to Bodmin. Past sign on left for Advent Church; next left. House approx. 1 mile on.

Sally & Charlie Alford
Trewint,
Advent,
Camelford,
Cornwall PL32 9QR
Tel   01840 211438

🗙 🔊 🐱 🚜 🏊

Entry 33   Map 1

Cornwall

Roskear

Drive down the fields to this 17th-century working farmhouse, a blissfully peaceful escape. A large sitting room with log fire, a warm and smiling hostess, happy dogs, a comfortable bedroom, a cheerful Aga, fabulous estuary views – country life at its most charming. Delicious breakfasts are served on blue china, doors open to the garden on sunny days and there are acres of woodland and grassland to explore. Good restaurants include Rick Stein's, the ferry takes you to Rock, surfing is a short drive and the Camel cycle trail is nearby (hire bikes locally). Uncomplicated, good value B&B.

Price	From £70. Singles £35.
Rooms	2: 1 double with separate bath; 1 twin/double sharing bath (let to same party only).
Meals	Pubs/restaurants 0.5-6 miles.
Closed	Rarely.
Directions	Bypass Wadebridge on A39 for Redruth. Over bridge, pass garage on left; then 1st right to Edmonton. By modern houses turn immed. right to Roskear over cattle grid.

Rosina Messer-Bennetts
Roskear,
St Breock, Wadebridge,
Cornwall PL27 7HU
Tel   01208 812805
Mobile   07748 432013
Email   rosina@roskear.com
Web   www.roskear.com

👤 🐕 🐱 🚜

Entry 34   Map 1

Cornwall

Porteath Barn

What a spot! This upside-down house is elegantly uncluttered and cool with seagrass flooring and a wood-burner in the sitting room. Bedrooms – not vast – have fresh flowers, quilted bedspreads and there's an Italian marble shower room; the feel is private with your own doors to the lovely, large garden. Walks from here down a path with ponds will take you to Epphaven Cove and the beach at the bottom of the valley or to a good pub for supper if you're feeling hearty. The Bloors have perfected the art of B&B-ing, being kind and helpful without being intrusive. *Children over 12 or by arrangement.*

Price	From £80. Singles by arrangement.
Rooms	3: 2 twins/doubles, each with separate bath or shower; 1 double let to same party only.
Meals	Pub 1.5 miles.
Closed	Rarely.
Directions	A39 to Wadebridge. At r'bout follow signs to Polzeath, then to Porteath Bee Centre. Through Bee Centre shop car park, down farm track; house signed on right after 150 yds.

Jo & Michael Bloor
Porteath Barn,
St Minver,
Wadebridge,
Cornwall PL27 6RA
Tel   01208 863605
Email   m.bloor17@btinternet.com

Entry 35   Map 1

Cornwall

Polrode Mill Cottage

A lovely, beamy, 17th-century cottage in a birdsung valley. Inside, flagged floors, Chesterfields, a wood-burner and a light, open feel. Your friendly young hosts live next door; they are working hard on the informal flower and vegetable garden, much of the produce is used in David's delicious homemade dinners, there's pumpkin marmalade and eggs from the hens. Bedrooms are cottage-cosy with stripped floors, comfy wrought-iron beds and silver cast-iron radiators; fresh bathrooms have double-ended roll tops. A slight hum of traffic can be heard outside, but inside is blissfully peaceful. *Minimum stay two nights in high season.*

Travel Club Offer: see page 392 for details.

Price	£79–£90. Singles £60.
Rooms	3: 2 doubles; 1 double with separate bath.
Meals	Dinner, 3 courses, £28.
Closed	Rarely.
Directions	From A395 take A39 towards Camelford. Through Camelford; continue on A39 to Knightsmill. From there, 1.8 miles on left-hand side.

Deborah Hilborne & David Edwards
Polrode Mill Cottage,
Allen Valley,
St Tudy, Padstow,
Cornwall PL30 3NS
Tel   01208 850203
Email   polrode@tesco.net
Web   www.polrodeguesthouse.co.uk

Entry 36   Map 1

Cornwall

Mother Ivey Cottage

So close to the sea that there are salt splashes on the windows! Exceptionally lovely hosts here and a simple refuge (once a fish cellar for processing catches) from crashing surf and Atlantic winds. Look out of the window to the big blue below, swim to the lifeboat launch, barbecue on the beach. The coastal path is stunning and you can walk to surfing beaches or just drop down to the quiet bay beneath your window. Cultured, kind hosts and a relaxed atmosphere; bedrooms and bathrooms are not frilly or smart but come for the views. Families love it.

Price	From £60. Singles by arrangement.
Rooms	2 twins. Extra single bed.
Meals	Dinner from £20. Packed lunch from £5. Pub/restaurant 5 miles.
Closed	Rarely.
Directions	From St Merryn, right for Trevose Head. Over sleeping policemen. After tollgate ticket machine, right thro' 2nd farm gate. On towards sea; cottage gate at end of track, on right.

	Phyllida & Antony Woosnam-Mills
	Mother Ivey Cottage,
	Trevose Head,
	Padstow,
	Cornwall PL28 8SL
Tel	01841 520329
Email	antony@trevosehead.co.uk

Entry 37   Map 1

Cornwall

Molesworth Manor

It's a splendid old place, big enough to swallow hoards of people, peppered with art and interesting antiques. There are palms and a play area in the garden, a drawing room with an honesty bar and an open fire for cosy nights, a carved staircase leading to bedrooms that vary in style and size — His Lordship's at the front, the Maid's in the eaves — and bathrooms that are lovely and pampering. The whiff of homemade muffins lures you downstairs in the morning, the Cornish Riviera and its food scene will ravish you later — you're in the heart of it all. A superb bolthole run by Geoff and Jessica, youthful and fun.

Price	£60–£105. Singles from £45.
Rooms	9: 7 doubles, 1 twin/double; 1 twin with separate shower.
Meals	Pubs/restaurants 2 miles.
Closed	November-January. Open off-season by arrangement for larger parties.
Directions	Off A389 between Wadebridge & Padstow. Entrance clearly signed; 300 yds from bridge in Little Petherick.

	Geoff French & Jessica Clarke
	Molesworth Manor,
	Little Petherick, Padstow,
	Cornwall PL27 7QT
Tel	01841 540292
Email	molesworthmanor@aol.com
Web	www.molesworthmanor.co.uk

Entry 38   Map 1

Cornwall

Calize Country House

Beneath wheeling gulls and close to blond beaches, the big square 1870 house has amazing views of skies and sea. Virginia Woolf's lighthouse is in the bay and winter seals cavort at the colony nearby. A fresh, uncomplicated décor brings the tang of the sea to every room. Artworks recall a world of surf; deckchair stripes clothe the dining table and dress the window; traditional sofas call for quiet times with a book. Upstairs, patterned or pale walls, practical bath or shower rooms, perhaps a sea view. Jilly and Nigel are testament to the benefits of sea air and look after you beautifully.

Ethical Collection: Environment; Food.
See page 400 for details.

Travel Club Offer: see page 392 for details.

Price	£80-£90. Singles £55.
Rooms	4: 2 doubles, 1 twin, 1 single.
Meals	Packed lunch £5. Pub 350 yds.
Closed	Rarely.
Directions	Exit A30 at Camborne (west) A3047. Left, then right at r'bout. Right on entering Connor Downs, then on for 2 miles. House on right after sign for Gwithian.

Jilly Whitaker
Calize Country House,
Gwithian, Hayle,
Cornwall TR27 5BW
Tel   01736 753268
Fax   01736 753268
Email   jilly@calize.co.uk
Web   www.calize.co.uk

Entry 39   Map 1

Cornwall

Treglisson

A short drive from St Ives, the glorious bay and some nifty surfing beaches. Inside the old farmhouse, all is calm and peaceful. Stephen and Heather are thoughtful, fun, easy-going and filled with enthusiasm for looking after you: large light bedrooms in soft colours, generous beds with lovely linen, modern white bathrooms, good art on the walls, a beautiful antique-marble hall floor. Cornish Aga-cooked breakfasts can be relished late if you prefer; in the evening, take a sundowner to the garden in summer or relax by the log fire in winter. There's a heated indoor pool too.

Travel Club Offer: see page 392 for details.

Price	£55-£75. Singles from £35.
Rooms	4: 1 double, 1 twin, 2 family rooms.
Meals	Pubs/restaurants 2-5 miles.
Closed	Christmas & New Year.
Directions	A30 to Hayle; 4th exit on r'bout into Hayle. Left at mini r'bout into Guildford Rd; up hill for 1 mile. Turn left at green sign into lane.

Stephen & Heather Reeves
Treglisson,
Wheal Alfred Road,
Hayle,
Cornwall TR27 5JT
Tel   01736 753141
Email   steve@treglisson.co.uk
Web   www.treglisson.co.uk

Entry 40   Map 1

Cornwall

House at Gwinear

An island of calm – it sits, as it has for 500 years, in its own bird-trilled acres a short drive from St Ives. The Halls are devoted to the encouragement of the arts and crafts – Charles is a silversmith – which is reflected in their lifestyle. There's no stuffiness – just fresh flowers on the breakfast table, a piano in the corner, rugs on polished floors and masses of books. In a separate wing you have a cosy bedroom and sitting room and a fine view of the church from the bath. The big lawn-filled gardens are there for bare-footed solace, and you can have breakfast in the Italianate courtyard on sunny days.

Cornwall

The Old Vicarage

Artists will be inspired, not just with the proximity to St Ives but with Jackie's dazzling collection of her own and other artists' work. This is a light, airy, welcoming house whose big sash windows overlook a subtropical garden; wander at will after a grand breakfast of fresh fruit and local bacon and sausages. Bedrooms have soft coloured walls, deeply comfortable beds, period furniture and more lovely artwork adding spots of colour; bathrooms are gleaming and fresh. There's a sandy beach 20-minutes' walk away and you can join the coastal path just up the road. Wonderful house, lovely owners.

Travel Club Offer: see page 392 for details.

Price	From £70.
Rooms	1 twin/double & sitting room with separate bath.
Meals	Occasional dinner, 3 courses £25. Pub 1.5 miles.
Closed	Rarely.
Directions	From A30 exit Hayle (Loggans Moor r'bout); 100 yds left at mini-r'bout; 400 yds left for Gwinear; 1.5 miles, top of hill, driveway on right, just before 30mph Gwinear sign.

	Charles & Diana Hall
	House at Gwinear,
	Gwinear,
	St Ives,
	Cornwall TR27 5JZ
Tel	01736 850444
Fax	01736 850444
Email	charleshall@btinternet.com

Entry 41   Map 1

Price	£70-£75. Singles £40.
Rooms	3: 1 twin; 1 double with separate bath, 1 single sharing bath (same party only).
Meals	Pubs 5-8 minute walk. Restaurants in St Ives 2.5 miles.
Closed	1 November-30 March.
Directions	A30 for Penzance. At 2nd Hayle r'bout, A3074 St Ives. After Wyvale Garden Centre, over mini r'bout; right at next one & into Lelant. Brush End on left after sign for Elm Farm. House at end.

	Jackie & Howard Hollingsbee
	The Old Vicarage,
	Brush End, Lelant, St Ives,
	Cornwall TR26 3EF
Tel	01736 753324
Mobile	07841 522021
Email	bookings@oldvicaragelelant.co.uk
Web	www.oldvicaragelelant.co.uk

Entry 42   Map 1

Cornwall

Jamies

Breathe in the ocean views from this stylish 1920s villa. Airy bedrooms are hotel-smart with white bed linen, striped and checked curtains, fresh new bathrooms, a feeling of space and sea views; two have proper sitting areas. Crisp linen and silver at the breakfast table create an elegant mood – relish an exotic fruit salad in a perfect white room overlooking the bay, or admire some of artist Felicity's inspiring work. Generous, easy-going Felicity and Jamie are ex-hoteliers with a great sense of fun, the white sands of Carbis Bay are a five-minute walk, and St Ives lies just beyond. *Children over 12 welcome.*

Price	From £100. Singles £80.
Rooms	4: 3 twins/doubles, 1 suite.
Meals	Pub 3-minute walk. Restaurants 1.5 miles.
Closed	Rarely.
Directions	A30, then A3074 for St Ives. At Carbis Bay, Marshalls estate agents & Methodist church on left. Next right down Pannier Lane; 2nd right is Wheal Whidden; 1st house on left.

Felicity & Jamie Robertson
Jamies,
Wheal Whidden, Carbis Bay, St Ives,
Cornwall TR26 2QX

Tel	01736 794718
Mobile	07914 759454
Email	info@jamiesstives.co.uk
Web	www.jamiesstives.co.uk

Entry 43   Map 1

Cornwall

Organic Panda B&B & Gallery

A five-minute walk from busy St Ives, with a panoramic view of the bay, boutique B&B in perfect harmony with this artistic spot; come for a bold scattering of modern art and a ten-seater rustic table. Spacious contemporary bedrooms have a laid-back style with organic linen, bamboo towels, chunky beds, white walls and raw-silk cushions. Shower rooms are small but perfectly formed. Andrea is an artist and theatre designer, Peter a photographer and organic chef; the food is delicious and bread home baked. The most beautiful coastal road in all England leads to St Just. *Min. three nights: July/August, Easter & Christmas.*

Ethical Collection: Environment; Food. See page 400 for details.

Travel Club Offer: see page 392 for details.

Price	£75-£120.
Rooms	3: 2 doubles, 1 twin.
Meals	Packed lunch £10. Restaurants 10-minute walk.
Closed	Rarely.
Directions	A3074 to St Ives. Signs to leisure centre; house behind 3rd sign, on left-hand bend.

Peter Williams & Andrea Carr
Organic Panda B&B & Gallery,
1 Pednolver Terrace, St Ives,
Cornwall TR26 2EL

Tel	01736 793890
Mobile	07787 854380
Email	info@organicpanda.co.uk
Web	www.organicpanda.co.uk

Entry 44   Map 1

Cornwall

11 Sea View Terrace

In a smart row of Edwardian villas, with views over harbour, island and sea, is a delectable retreat. Sleek, softy coloured interiors are light and gentle on the eye – an Italian circular glass table here, a painted seascape there – deeply civilised. Bedrooms are perfect with crisp linen, vistas of whirling gulls, your own terrace; bathrooms are state-of-the-art. Rejoice in softly boiled eggs with anchovy and chive-butter soldiers for breakfast – or continental in bed if you prefer. Grahame looks after you impeccably and design aficionados will be happy. *Free admission to Tate Gallery & Barbara Hepworth Museum.*

Price	£95-£125. Singles from £70.
Rooms	3 suites.
Meals	Dinner, with wine, from £25 (groups only). Packed lunch £10. Pubs/restaurants 5-minute walk.
Closed	Rarely.
Directions	At Porthminster Hotel, signs for Tate; down Albert Rd, right just before Longships Hotel. Limited parking.

Grahame Wheelband
11 Sea View Terrace,
St Ives,
Cornwall TR26 2DH
Tel 01736 798440
Mobile 07973 953616
Email elevenseaviewterrace@btinternet.com
Web www.11stives.co.uk

Entry 45   Map 1

Cornwall

Trezelah Farmhouse

You'll feel high here, on the moor between Penzance and St Ives. The humble manor farmhouse with solid stone walls and huge chimney breast at one end has a light and fresh interior of waxed floors, limed walls, Indian scatter rugs, books, a wood-burner and soft white sofas. Small bedrooms with fine antiques and gentle lighting will calm you, as will the unusually pretty bathrooms – and the lovely Caro who painted many of the pictures here. Stride out round the north coastal path, then take a breather at the Tinners Arms in Zennor and go all Lawrencian; this is a wonderful part of Cornwall.

Travel Club Offer: see page 392 for details.

Price	£80.
Rooms	3: 2 doubles; 1 twin with separate bath.
Meals	Pub 3 miles.
Closed	October-March.
Directions	After Tesco r'bout heading into Penzance on A30, B3311 towards St Ives. Through Gulval, left at Badgers Cross towards Chysauster; left to Trezelah.

Caro Woods
Trezelah Farmhouse,
Trezelah, Badgers Cross,
Penzance, Cornwall TR20 8XD
Tel 01736 874388
Mobile 07717 008906
Email info@trezelah.co.uk
Web www.trezelah.co.uk

Entry 46   Map 1

Cornwall

Ednovean Farm

There's a terrace for each immaculate bedroom (one truly private) with views to the wild blue yonder and St Michael's Mount Bay – an enchanting outlook that changes with the passage of the day. Come for peace, space and the best of eclectic fabrics and colours, pretty lamps, gleaming copper, fluffy bathrobes and handmade soaps. The beamed, open-plan sitting/dining area is an absorbing mix of exotic, rustic and elegant; have full breakfast here, strictly on time, or continental in your room. A footpath through the field leads to the village; walk to glorious Prussia Cove and Cudden Point, or head west to Marazion.

Price	£80–£100. Singles £70–£80.
Rooms	3: 2 doubles, 1 four-poster.
Meals	Pub 5-minute walk.
Closed	Christmas & rarely.
Directions	From A30 after Crowlas r'bout, A394 to Helston. 0.25 miles after next r'bout, 1st right for Perranuthnoe. Drive on left, signed.

Christine & Charles Taylor
Ednovean Farm,
Perranuthnoe,
Penzance,
Cornwall TR20 9LZ
Tel 01736 711883
Email info@ednoveanfarm.co.uk
Web www.ednoveanfarm.co.uk

Entry 47   Map 1

Cornwall

Drym Farm

Rural, but not too deeply: the Tate at St Ives is a 15-minute drive. The 1705 farmhouse, beautifully revived, is surrounded by ancient barns, a dairy and a forge, fascinating to Cornish historians. Jan arrived in 2002, with an enthusiasm for authenticity and simple, stylish good taste. French limestone floors in the hall, striking art on the walls, a roll top bath, a *bateau lit*, an antique brass bed. Paintwork is fresh cream and taupe. There are old fruit trees and young camellias, a TV-free sitting room with two plump sofas and organic treats at breakfast. Charming and utterly peaceful.

Travel Club Offer: see page 392 for details.

Price	£70–£90. Singles from £55.
Rooms	2 doubles.
Meals	Pubs/restaurants within 1-4 miles.
Closed	Rarely.
Directions	From A30 to Hayle; through Hayle to r'bout, left to Helston. At Leedstown, left towards Drym. Follow road until right turn to Drym. Farm fourth on lane, on right after Drym House.

Jan Bright
Drym Farm,
Drym, Praze-an-Beeble,
Camborne,
Cornwall TR14 0NU
Tel 01209 831039
Email drymfarm@hotmail.co.uk
Web www.drymfarm.co.uk

Entry 48   Map 1

Cornwall

Ennys

Prepare to be spoiled. A fire smoulders in the sumptuous sitting room, tea is laid out in the Aga-warm kitchen, and bedrooms are luxurious: a king-size bed or an elegant modern four-poster, powerful showers and crisp white linen. The stylishness continues into the suites and everywhere there are fascinating artefacts from Gill's travels, designer fabrics and original art. The road ends at Ennys, so it is utterly peaceful; walk down to the river and along the old towpath to St Ives Bay. Or stay put: play tennis (on grass!) and swim in the heated pool sunk deep into the tropical gardens.

Price	£85-£125. Singles from £65.
Rooms	5: 3 doubles. Barn: 2 family suites.
Meals	Pub 3 miles.
Closed	1 November-25 March.
Directions	2 miles east of Marazion on B3280, look for sign & turn left leading down Trewhella Lane between St Hilary & Relubbus. On to Ennys.

Gill Charlton
Ennys,
St Hilary, Penzance, Cornwall
TR20 9BZ

Tel	01736 740262
Fax	01736 740055
Email	ennys@ennys.co.uk
Web	www.ennys.co.uk

Entry 49   Map 1

Cornwall

The Gardens

Two old miners' cottages combine to create this small, modest, pretty home. Irish Moira, a retired midwife, adores flowers and her posies brighten every corner; Goff, a potter and painter, tends the vegetables. Both are charming and kind. Sweet snug bedrooms have patchwork quilts, cotton sheets, antique linen runners and plenty of books. One is on the ground floor overlooking the pretty cottage garden, two are up a narrow stair. Aga-cooked breakfasts and homemade jams are brought to the sun-streamed conservatory and there's homemade cake in the sitting room by the wood-burner. Great value.

Price	From £65. Singles £32.50-£36.
Rooms	3: 2 doubles; 1 twin/double with separate bath.
Meals	Packed lunch from £7.50. Pubs & restaurants 10-min drive.
Closed	Christmas & New Year.
Directions	A394 Helston to Penzance, 2nd right after Ashton Post Office for Tresowes Green. After 0.25 miles, sign for house on right.

Moira & Goff Cattell
The Gardens,
Tresowes, Ashton,
Helston,
Cornwall TR13 9SY

Tel	01736 763299
Mobile	07881 758191
Email	moira.cattell@gmail.com

Entry 50   Map 1

Cornwall

Carmelin

The setting is sensational, looking straight out to sea from the Lizard, England's most southerly point. Breakfasts – a feast of breads and pastries, fruits, freshly made yogurt, homemade preserves – have to fight for your attention, so spectacular are the views. The bedroom has them too – and the sun room – making a private suite with its own entrance, sitting and dining area; a gorgeous spot to sit and watch sparkling waves and sunsets. John and Jane are gentle, relaxed people who enjoy their guests; walk the coastal path, return to a lovely home-cooked meal. *French & German spoken.*

Travel Club Offer: see page 392 for details.

Price	From £75. Singles by arrangement.
Rooms	1 suite for 2 with separate bath/shower.
Meals	Dinner from £20. BYO. Pub within walking distance.
Closed	Rarely.
Directions	From Helston to the Lizard; at Lizard Green, right, opp. Regent Café (head for Smugglers Fish & Chips); immed. right, pass wc on left. Road unmade; on for 500 yds; double bend; 2nd on right.

Jane & John Grierson
Carmelin,
Pentreath Lane,
The Lizard,
Cornwall TR12 7NY

Tel	01326 290677
Email	pjcarmelin@gmail.com
Web	www.bedandbreakfastcornwall.co.uk

Entry 51   Map 1

Cornwall

Chydane

All that separates you from the sand and sea is the coastal path. At the far end of the marvellous, three-mile beach is Porthleven; beyond, West Penwith stretches magically into the distance. All this, and lighthouses, basking sharks, dolphins. One elegant double room, with gorgeous linen, a superb bed and a chesterfield, opens onto a French balcony overlooking the waves. The bathrooms, too, are warm and you get thick white bathrobes, lovely candles, big showers. Upstairs is a second room with a porthole window and a new bathroom. Close to the spectacular Mullion links golf course. *Children over 12 welcome.*

Ethical Collection: Food. See page 400 for details.

Price	From £90.
Rooms	2 doubles.
Meals	Meals by arrangement. Pub 200 yds.
Closed	Christmas.
Directions	From Helston A3083 to the Lizard. After 2 miles right to Gunwalloe. Right before Halzephron Inn. Chydane on right immediately above beach.

Carla Caslin
Chydane,
Gunwalloe Fishing Cove,
Helston, Cornwall TR12 7QB

Tel	01326 241232
Mobile	07740 168805
Email	carla.caslin@btinternet.com
Web	www.chydane.co.uk

Entry 52   Map 1

Cornwall

Landewednack House

Susan and her pug dogs will greet you enthusiastically with tea and biscuits in the drawing room of this immaculate house. Antony the chef keeps the wheels oiled and the food coming – try his green crab soup or succulent lobster. Erik is a real gourmand and has a covetable cellar of over 2,000 bottles of wine. Bedrooms are not huge and not all have sea views, but everything you could possibly need is there, from robes to brandy. The pool area is stunning with a French feel, the garden is filled with interest and it's just a three-minute walk to the sea. *Minimum stay two nights July/August.*

Price	From £126. Singles £63-£75.
Rooms	3: 2 doubles, 1 twin.
Meals	Dinner, 4 courses, £33-£38.
Closed	Open all year.
Directions	From Helston, A3083 south. Just before Lizard, left to Church Cove. Follow signs for about 0.75 miles. House on left behind sage green gates.

Susan Thorbek
Landewednack House,
Church Cove, The Lizard,
Cornwall TR12 7PQ

Tel	01326 290877
Fax	01326 290192
Email	luxurybandb@landewednackhouse.com
Web	www.landewednackhouse.com

Entry 53   Map 1

Cornwall

Halftides

Hugely enjoyable and special, surrounded by three acres with a private path down to the beach. Funky bedrooms, not huge but filled with light, have gorgeous fabrics, pure white walls, crisp bedding, dreamy views; bathrooms (one a pod-shower in the room) are sleek in glass and chrome. Susie is an artist and chef and gives you a delicious organic breakfast and a dinner of seasonal food – perhaps a barbecue in the garden in summer. Take the coastal path north or south, visit the working harbour in the village – or snaffle a packed lunch from Susie and head for the beach. This is the perfect place to relax and unwind.

Price	£80-£110. Singles £60-£70.
Rooms	3: 1 double; 1 double, 1 single sharing separate bath.
Meals	Dinner £25-£30. Packed lunch £10.
Closed	February.
Directions	A3083 to Lizard, right to Cury, 5 miles; pass Poldhu beach & enter Mullion. Right into Laflouder Lane, follow bumpy track to very end, past sign 'Private Road'. House 1st on right.

Charles & Susie Holdsworth Hunt
Halftides,
Laflouder Lane, Mullion, Helston,
Cornwall TR12 7HU

Tel	01326 241935
Mobile	07970 821261
Email	halftides@btinternet.com
Web	www.halftides.co.uk

Entry 54   Map 1

Cornwall

The Hen House

Greenies will explode with delight: Sandy and Gary, truly welcoming, are passionately committed to sustainability and love guiding you to the best places to eat, to visit and to walk; there are even OS maps on loan for hikers. Enlightened souls will adore the spacious, colourful rooms, the bright fabrics, the wildflower meadow with inviting sun loungers, the pond, the tai chi, the fairy-lit courtyard at night, the scrumptious local food, the birdsong. There's even a sanctuary room for reiki and reflexology set deep into the earth. Join in or flounder. *Minimum stay two nights. Children over 12 welcome.*

Ethical Collection: Environment; Food. See page 400 for details.

Travel Club Offer: see page 392 for details.

Price	£70–£80. Singles £60.
Rooms	2 doubles.
Meals	Pub/restaurant 1 mile.
Closed	Rarely.
Directions	A3083 from Helston, then B3293 to St Keverne; left to Newtown-in-St Martin. After 2 miles right at T-junc. Follow road for 2-3 miles then left fork. Round 7 bends then right at triangulation stone for Tregarne.

Sandy & Gary Pulfrey
The Hen House,
Tregarne, Manaccan, Helston,
Cornwall TR12 6EW

Tel	01326 280236
Mobile	07809 229958
Email	henhouseuk@aol.com
Web	www.thehenhouse-cornwall.co.uk

Entry 55 Map 1

Cornwall

Trerose Manor

Follow winding lanes through glorious countryside to find the prettiest, listed manor house, a cheerful family atmosphere and a cup of tea from Tessa. Large, light bedrooms, one with floor-to-ceiling windows, sit peacefully in your own wing and have long views over the stunning garden. Both are dressed in pretty colours, have comfy seats for gazing and smartly tiled bathrooms. A sumptuous breakfast will set you up for anything; lovely walks over fields to river or beach, stacks of interesting places to visit, a warming gas wood-burner in the library for the lazy. Lovely. *French, German & Italian spoken.*

Price	£80–£100. Singles £70.
Rooms	2 doubles.
Meals	Pubs/restaurants within walking distance.
Closed	Christmas & New Year.
Directions	Left at Red Lion in Mawnan Smith. After 0.5 miles right down Old Church Road. 0.5 miles further on house is through white gate on right immediately after Trerose Farm.

Tessa Phipps
Trerose Manor,
Mawnan Smith,
Falmouth,
Cornwall TR11 5HX

Tel	01326 250784
Email	tmp@wisechoice.biz
Web	www.trerosemanor.co.uk

Entry 56 Map 1

Cornwall

Bosvathick

A huge old Cornish house that has been in Kate's family since 1760 along with all the pictures, books, heavy furniture, Indian rugs, ornate plasterwork, pianos and even a harp. Historians and garden lovers will be in their element: pass three Celtic crosses dating from the 7th century before the long drive finds the imposing house (all granite gate posts and lions) and a magnificent garden with grotto, lake, pasture and woodland. Bedrooms are traditional, full of books, antiques and lovely views; bathrooms are plain, functional and clean. Come then to experience a 'time warp' and Kate's good breakfasts.

Price	£80. Singles £40-£45.
Rooms	4: 1 twin with separate bath; 1 twin, 2 singles with 2 shared bathrooms.
Meals	Packed lunch £4. Pubs 2 miles.
Closed	Easter, Christmas & New Year.
Directions	From Constantine, signs to Falmouth. 2.5 miles, pass Bosvathick Riding Stables, next entrance on left. Drive thro' gate posts & green gate. A map can be sent to visitors.

	Kate & Stephen Tyrrell
	Bosvathick,
	Constantine,
	Falmouth,
	Cornwall TR11 5RD
Tel	01326 340103/340153
Email	kate@forgottenhouses.co.uk
Web	www.pasticcio.co.uk/bosvathick

Entry 57   Map 1

Cornwall

Tregew Vean

Once the home of a packet skipper, this pretty Georgian slate-hung house stands in a sunny spot above Flushing. From the garden with its palms, agapanthus, olive and fig trees, you glimpse the Fal estuary. The house is fresh and elegant, with tenderly cared-for antiques and an entertaining straw hat collection in the hall; Sandra and Rodney – both chatty and charming – give you comfortable bedrooms in your own part of the house. Flushing is a ten-minute walk and in the village there are two pubs that do food and a fish restaurant on the quay. There's plenty to do and you can catch the passenger ferry to Falmouth.

Travel Club Offer: see page 392 for details.

Price	From £80. Singles £45.
Rooms	2: 1 double, 1 double sharing bath (same party only).
Meals	Pubs/restaurants 0.25 miles.
Closed	Christmas.
Directions	From Penryn towards Mylor. After 1 mile right to Flushing. Entrance 1 mile down road on right, 40 yds before T-junction, opposite 'give way 40 yds' sign.

	Sandra & Rodney Myers
	Tregew Vean,
	Flushing, Falmouth,
	Cornwall TR11 5TF
Tel	01326 379462
Mobile	07770 663774
Email	tregewvean@aol.com
Web	www.tregewvean.co.uk

Entry 58   Map 1

Cornwall

Trevilla House

Come for the position: the sea and peninsula wrap around you, and the King Harry ferry gives you an easy reach into the glorious Roseland peninsula. Inside, find frog stencils in the bathroom, and old-fashioned, comfortable bedrooms – the twin with garden views and a sofa, the double with sea views. Jinty is warm and welcoming and rustles up delicious locally-sourced breakfasts in the sunny conservatory that looks south over the sea. Trelissick Gardens and the Copeland China Collection are just next door, and the Maritime Museum, Eden, Tate, cycling, watersports and coastal walks are close by.

Price	From £80. Singles £50.
Rooms	3: 1 twin; 1 double with separate bath/shower & sitting room. Extra single for same party, sharing bath.
Meals	Restaurants/pubs 1-2 miles.
Closed	Christmas & New Year.
Directions	A390 to Truro; A39 to Falmouth. At double r'bout with garage, left off 2nd r'bout (B3289); pass pub on left; at x-roads, left (B3289); 200 yds on, fork right to Feock. On to T-junc., then left; 1st on right.

Jinty & Peter Copeland
Trevilla House,
Feock, Truro,
Cornwall TR3 6QG

Tel	01872 862369
Mobile	07791 977621
Email	jinty@trevilla.com
Web	www.trevilla.com

Cornwall

Pelyn

Sheep on the hillside driveway remain curiously unmoved by the view that sweeps so lushly down to the creek. Set in its own green acres, minutes from golden beaches, this traditional house built around an 11th century dwelling, is a peaceful, yet accessible hideaway. Smugglers from a nearby cove once visited; nowadays a tap at the door brings a lobster instead. Fresh flowers are some of the personal touches in light, airy bedrooms (one cosy with sofa) and charming country bathrooms. Tuck into home eggs and local bacon in the conservatory in summer as you gaze out on rabbits and birds.

Price	From £80. Singles by arrangement.
Rooms	2: 1 twin/double; 1 double with separate bathroom.
Meals	Lobster & wine dinner from £40, by arrangement. Packed lunch £7.50. Pubs 5-minute drive.
Closed	Rarely.
Directions	To Gerrans & Portscatho. Thro' Gerrans, road to St Anthony Head. Just after Percuil turning, next drive right at 150 yds in dip in road & sharp bend (mirrored). Signed.

Graham & Bridget Reid
Pelyn,
Gerrans, Portscatho,
Truro,
Cornwall TR2 5ET

Tel	01872 580837
Email	pelyncreek@aol.com
Web	www.pelyncreek.com

Cornwall

Pine Cottage

The Cornish sea laps the steep quay of this narrow inlet's port, its blue horizon just visible from the window of the elegant bedroom high up on the coveside. A perfect spot to wake on a summer's morn. The house is as sunny as its owner, the guest bedroom charmingly informal with its hand-painted violet-strewn wallpaper, super big bed and shelves brimming with books. A handful of small open-top fishing boats slips out at dawn to bring back catches of crab and lobster. Clare will give you a splendid breakfast of warm fruit salad, local bacon and eggs and home-grown tomatoes.

Price	£85.
Rooms	1 double.
Meals	Pub 100 yds. Restaurants within 5 miles.
Closed	Rarely.
Directions	From Tregony, A3078 to St Mawes. After 2 miles, at garage, left to Portloe. Thro' village to Ship Inn. Right fork after pub car park. Cottage immed. on left between white gateposts up drive.

Clare Holdsworth
Pine Cottage,
Portloe,
Truro,
Cornwall TR2 5RB
Tel   01872 501385
Web   www.pine-cottage.net

✕ ⋑ ✕

Entry 61   Map 1

Cornwall

Hay Barton

Giant windows overlook many acres of farmland, well-stocked with South Devon cows and their calves. Jill and Blair give you locally sourced breakfast in the smart dining room with its giant flagstones and family antiques; later, retire to the guest sitting room with log fire. Bedrooms are fresh and pretty with garden flowers, soft white linen, floral green walls and stripped floors. Gloriously large panelled bathrooms have roll top baths and are painted in earthy colours. Guests are welcome to chuck a ball or two around the tennis court; you are near to good gardens and plenty of places to eat. *Min. two nights in summer.*

Price	£80. Singles £50.
Rooms	2 twins/doubles.
Meals	Pubs 1-2 miles.
Closed	Rarely.
Directions	A3078 from Tregony village towards St Mawes. After 1 mile, house on left, 100 yds down lane.

Jill & Blair Jobson
Hay Barton,
Tregony, Truro,
Cornwall TR2 5TF
Tel   01872 530288
Mobile   07813 643028
Email   jill@haybarton.com
Web   www.haybarton.com

✕ ⋑ ✕ 🚜 🐝

Entry 62   Map 1

Cornwall

Creed House

A light-filled Georgian former rectory surrounded by one of Cornwall's loveliest gardens. Complete independence is yours in a guest wing: two elegant bedrooms have antique furniture and gleaming bathrooms. Your fridge is filled with scrumptious local produce ready for a continental breakfast, taken in a beautifully decorated sitting room overlooking a courtyard. You are close to Heligan, the Eden Project and the beaches of the Roseland peninsular – wonderful. Nicely private: ideal for one couple, or two sets of friends together.

Price	£90.
Rooms	2 twins.
Meals	Pub/restaurant 1 mile.
Closed	Christmas & New Year.
Directions	From St Austell, A390 to Grampound. Just beyond clock tower, left into Creed Lane. After 1 mile, left at grass triangle opp. church. House behind 2nd white gates on left.

Jonathon & Annabel Croggon
Creed House,
Creed,
Grampound,
Truro,
Cornwall TR2 4SL
Tel   01872 530372

✕ 🐈

Entry 63   Map 1

Cornwall

Bodrugan Barton

Everything's lovely – the setting, the windy lanes, the gentle activity of the farm, the charming family who look after you with such enthusiasm. You get simple farmhouse bedrooms, good bathrooms, a super big living room (red walls, wood-burner, piano), family antiques and the promise of a fine breakfast. An ancient lane leads to Colona Bay: small, secluded and full of rock pools. There are an indoor pool and sauna here (shared by self-catering guests) and Heligan and the Eden Project nearby. A delightfully relaxing home. *Children over 12 welcome. Guided walks by arrangement. Painting courses.*

Price	£85. Singles £50.
Rooms	3: 1 twin/double; 1 twin/double with separate bath/shower, 1 single (let to same party only).
Meals	Pubs within 2 miles.
Closed	Christmas & New Year.
Directions	St Austell B3273 for Mevagissey. At x-roads on hill, right to Heligan, avoiding bottleneck in Mevagissey. Through Gorran, bend left to Portmellon. After 1.5 miles, right at grass triangle into farm, before hill.

Sally & Tim Kendall
Bodrugan Barton,
Mevagissey,
Cornwall PL26 6PT
Tel   01726 842094
Email   stay@bodrugan.co.uk
Web   www.bodrugan.co.uk

✕ 🐈 🚜 🏊

Entry 64   Map 1

Cornwall

Trussel Barn

Jo and Mike aim to look after you as beautifully as they can: large, light bedrooms with super views, squashy pillows, state-of-the-art bathrooms, fancy dressing gowns, your own hidden-away fridge. But they're dead keen on reducing their carbon footprint, too. View Mike's experimental straw walls in the garden, drink water from their borehole, enjoy a locally sourced breakfast cooked in an eco-Aga, ask about their plans for a windmill – it's all fascinating stuff. Explore acres of garden running down to a lake, or hike the four miles to the coast; come home to a roaring fire in the guest sitting room.

Price	£75-£80. Singles £50.
Rooms	2: 1 double; 1 double with separate bath.
Meals	Dinner £20. Cream tea £5. Pubs/restaurants within 2.5 miles.
Closed	Rarely.
Directions	A38 Plymouth-Liskeard, then B3254 to St Keyne for 1.5 miles. Climb steep hill; at bend, 1st left into Trussel Barn. Or train to Liskeard, 2 miles.

Jo Lawrence
Trussel Barn,
St Keyne,
Liskeard,
Cornwall PL14 4QL
Tel 01579 340450
Email jo@trusselbarn.co.uk
Web www.trusselbarn.co.uk

Entry 65   Map 1

Cornwall

Hornacott

The garden, in its lovely valley setting, has seats in little corners poised to catch the evening sun – perfect for a pre-dinner drink. The peaceful house is named after the hill and you have a private entrance to your wonderfully fresh and airy suite: a room with twin beds plus a large, square, high sitting room with windows that look down onto the wooded valley. With CD player, music, chocolates and magazines you'll feel beautifully self-contained. Jos, a kitchen designer, and Mary-Anne clearly enjoy having guests, and give you fresh local produce and free-range eggs for breakfast.

Travel Club Offer: see page 392 for details.

Price	From £80. Singles £50.
Rooms	1 suite; 1 single with separate shower.
Meals	Dinner, 3 courses, £20. BYO.
Closed	Christmas.
Directions	B3254 Launceston-Liskeard. Through South Petherwin, down steep hill, last left before little bridge. House 1st on left.

Jos & Mary-Anne Otway-Ruthven
Hornacott,
South Petherwin, Launceston,
Cornwall PL15 7LH
Tel 01566 782461
Fax 01566 782461
Email stay@hornacott.co.uk
Web www.hornacott.co.uk

Entry 66   Map 1

Cornwall

Buttervilla Farm

Gill and Robert are so good at growing vegetables (organically) they supply the local restaurants. They're pretty good at looking after you too, in a totally relaxed fashion, delivering breakfasts of superb rare-breed bacon and modern Cornish suppers; fish and Red Ruby steak are specialities. No sitting room but bedrooms are big, colourful, comfortable and cared for; bathrooms are smart with solar-powered showers. Explore these 15 beautiful eco acres, stride the coastal path or head for the surf. Young and fun – with soul. *Soil Association certified. Minimum stay three nights July/August.*

Ethical Collection: Environment; Food. See page 400 for details.

Travel Club Offer: see page 392 for details.

Price	£75-£85. Singles from £65.
Rooms	3 doubles.
Meals	Dinner, 3 courses, £30. Restaurants 2-7 miles.
Closed	Rarely.
Directions	Turn by Halfway House at Polbathic for Downderry. House 400 yds up hill from inn, on left; signed before lane.

	Gill & Robert Hocking Buttervilla Farm, Polbathic, St Germans, Torpoint, Cornwall PL11 3EY
Tel	01503 230315
Mobile	07887 124878
Email	info@buttervilla.com
Web	www.buttervilla.com

Entry 67   Map 2

Cornwall

Bulland House

Whether you come to this sleepy part of Cornwall by ferry or road you will find peaceful, gentle hosts and a 300-year-old chocolate-box farmhouse. Elke and Clive give you fresh and uncluttered bedrooms with plenty of sunshine, deliciious biscuits, pretty pink quilts, gleaming bathrooms and views to daffodil-strewn fields in spring. There's a guest sitting room with roaring wood-burner, maps and books; plan your day over a lazy breakfast of local bacon, farm eggs, homemade bread and honey from up the road. Snooze on a bench in the pretty garden or strike out for the coastal path and the most stunning walks.

Price	From £70. Singles £40.
Rooms	2: 1 double; 1 twin/double with separate bath.
Meals	Packed lunch £5. Pub/restaurant 1.5 miles.
Closed	Christmas & Boxing Day.
Directions	2.3 miles from Torpoint ferry on main road A374, sign on right.

	Elke & Clive Owen Bulland House, Antony, Torpoint, Cornwall PL11 2PE
Tel	01752 813823
Email	info@averywarmwelcome.co.uk
Web	www.averywarmwelcome.co.uk

Entry 68   Map 2

Cornwall

Erth Barton

Everyone is bowled over by this house; open to three tidal estuaries, it makes your heart leap. The manor house was once owned by the National Trust and is casually grand, with its own derelict chapel; a 14th-century fresco still clings to the walls. Relaxed Jenny and Nicholas, its privileged trustees, keep hens and an elderly retriever, and, in spite of the rabbits, grow their own salads and veg. You mostly get the run of the house – up the brown stair carpet lie no-nonsense bedrooms with floral fabrics and peaceful views. You can pick quiet spots in the large garden, and enjoy stunning walks.

Cornwall

Lantallack Farm

Life and art exist in happy communion: Nicky loves playing the piano and runs courses in landscape painting and sculpture. This is a heart-warming place – hens in the orchard, fine breakfasts in the walled garden, a super outdoor pool, a straw-yellow sitting room with a log fire… and bedrooms with delicious beds and books galore. The gorgeous old Georgian farmhouse has breathtaking views over countryside, streams and wooded valleys. Set off to discover the Walkers' leat-side trail, and make a fuss of Polly, the Gloucester Old Spot pig, on the way. You will be inspired. *Minimum stay two nights at weekends.*

Price	£60–£90. Singles £60.
Rooms	5: 3 doubles; 1 double, 1 twin with shared bath.
Meals	Packed lunch from £5. Dinner from £20. Pubs/restaurants 2 miles.
Closed	Rarely.
Directions	Plymouth, Tamar Bridge (A38); at 1st roundabout take exit Liskeard. Turn left Trematon, left Elmgate then right Elmgate. Right at White Cottage signed Erth Barton, keep straight on until the end.

Price	From £95. Singles by arrangement.
Rooms	2 doubles.
Meals	Pubs/restaurants 1 mile.
Closed	Rarely.
Directions	A38 through Saltash & on for 3 miles. At Landrake 2nd right at West Lane. After 1 mile, left at white cottage for Tideford. House 150 yds on, on right.

	Nicholas & Jenny Foster Erth Barton, Elmgate, Saltash, Cornwall PL12 4QY
Tel	01752 841560
Email	nicholasfoster@btopenworld.com
Web	www.erthbarton.co.uk

	Nicky Walker Lantallack Farm, Landrake, Saltash, Cornwall PL12 5AE
Tel	01752 851281
Fax	01752 851281
Email	nickywalker44@tiscali.co.uk
Web	www.lantallack.co.uk

Entry 69   Map 2

Entry 70   Map 2

Cornwall

Lower Treluggan

Surrounded by farmland, gardens and orchard, a typical old Cornish farmhouse, and a converted barn. Here you have complete independence in a swish, modern space with everything you need to hand. Kind Jane gives you farmhouse tea on arrival and a fridge full of breakfast; she will, if you wish, bring a delicious home-cooked dinner too. A contemporary sitting room has a wooden floor and blue and yellow checked curtains: on the same floor are a comfortable bedroom and a sparkling bathroom with power shower and fluffy towels. Minutes from the Saltash Bridge yet wonderfully quiet; good walking straight from the door.

Price	£75. Sofabed £20 p.p.
Rooms	1 double (with sofabed & cot).
Meals	Dinner from £15. Pub/restaurant 3 miles.
Closed	Rarely.
Directions	A38, over Tamar Bridge & on for 3 miles to Landrake. Left into Landrake following signs to St Erney (1 mile). Left before St Erney church between granite gate posts. Treluggan Manor & Lower Treluggan 100 yds on left.

Jane & Julian Trahair
Lower Treluggan,
Landrake,
Cornwall PL12 5ES

Tel 01752 851291
Mobile 07767 416478
Fax 01752 851291
Email juliantrahair@btinternet.com

Entry 71 Map 2

Cumbria

Sirelands

Sirelands, once a gardener's cottage, stands among rhododendrons and spreading trees on a sunny slope, a stream trickling gently by. The Carrs have lived here for many years and the house has a reassuringly lived-in feel. Enjoy home-grown produce over dinner at a polished country table, then retire to the sitting room, delightful with log basket and honesty bar. Sash windows overlook the lightly wooded garden, visited by roe deer and a variety of birds. Bedrooms and bathrooms are pleasant, carpeted and peaceful. Angela loves cooking and treats you to tea and homemade cake on arrival.

Price	£80.
Rooms	2: 1 twin; 1 double with separate bath/shower.
Meals	Dinner, 2–3 courses, £22–£27.50. Pubs 1.5 miles.
Closed	Christmas & New Year.
Directions	M6 north to junc. 43; A69 Newcastle; 3 miles to traffic lights. Right, on to Heads Nook; house 2 miles after village.

Angela Carr
Sirelands,
Heads Nook,
Brampton, Carlisle,
Cumbria CA8 9BT

Tel 01228 670389
Mobile 07748 101513
Email carr_sirelands@btconnect.com

Entry 72 Map 12

Cumbria

Whitbysteads

Swing into the yard of a gentleman's farmhouse at the end of a drive lined with gorse, stone walls and sheep. It's a working farm, so lots going on with four-wheel drives, dogs and bustle. Victoria does styles and periods well: warm rugs, flowery sofas with plain linen armchairs, modern family paintings. The main bedroom is sumptuous and stylish with grand views over fells, the smaller room simpler; bathrooms are old-fashioned and big. A touch of London in the country with native sheep and busy hens outside the front door – and great hosts! Dress up in the evening for dinner at Sharrow Bay. *Garden open for NGS.*

Price	£90–£110.
Rooms	2: 1 double; 1 double with separate bath.
Meals	Children's tea available £5. Pub 0.5 miles.
Closed	Rarely.
Directions	Exit 39 M6. A6 north, thro' Askham village past shop on right, thro' open gate, over 3 cattle grids. House on right after long drive.

Mrs Victoria Lowther
Whitbysteads,
Askham, Penrith,
Cumbria CA10 2PG

Tel	01931 712284
Mobile	07976 276961
Email	info@gnap.fsnet.co.uk
Web	www.whitbysteads.org

Entry 73   Map 11

Cumbria

Greenah

Tucked into the hillside off a narrow lane, this 1750s smallholding is surrounded by fells, so is perfect for walkers. Absolute privacy for four friends or family with your own entrance to a beamed and stone-flagged sitting room with wood-burning stove, creamy walls and cheery floral curtains. Warm bedrooms have original paintings, good beds, hot water bottles, bathrobes and a sparkling bathroom – which has a loo with a remarkable view. Malcolm is a climber; Marjorie is totally committed to organic food so you get a fabulous breakfast and good advice about the local area. Fell walking is not compulsory!

Ethical Collection: Food. See page 400 for details.

Price	£72–£80. Singles £45.
Rooms	2: 1 double, 1 twin sharing shower (let to same party only).
Meals	Pubs/restaurants 3 miles.
Closed	Rarely.
Directions	M6 junc. 40 follow A66 west. Left for Matterdale; after 1.5 miles, left for Dacre. Up hill, right fork to Lowthwaite, house 100 yds on right.

Marjorie & Malcolm Emery
Greenah,
Mattterdale, Penrith,
Cumbria CA11 0SA

Tel	01768 483387
Mobile	07767 213667
Email	info@greenah.co.uk
Web	www.greenah.co.uk

Entry 74   Map 11

Cumbria

Cumbria

Willow Cottage

Gaze across rooftops through tiny windows towards the towering mass of Skiddaw, the Lakes' third highest mountain. Here is a miniature cottage garden with sweet peas, herbs, vegetables and flowers... all suitably rambling. Roy and Chris have kept most of the old barn's features: wooden floorboards, wonderful beams. Dried flowers, pretty china, antique linen, glowing lamps and patchwork quilts, a collection of christening gowns... dear little bedrooms have panelled bathrooms and old pine furniture. TV is delightfully absent, classical music plays and you are in the heart of a farming village.

The Old Rectory

The setting of this lovely old house could hardly be more pastoral. Many of its rooms face south and have superb views, with mountains and fells beyond. History has created an intriguing house full of unexpected corners; the old rectory dates from around 1360 but bedrooms are freshly contemporary and have super big beds. Gill cooks in imaginative 'bistro' style, David knows his wines and you eat by candlelight in a 16th-century room. They're relaxed and charming and, when the place is full, create a fabulous house-party feel. Outside, red squirrels and well-fed rabbits, a croquet lawn and stunning Skiddaw.

Price	£60-£65. Singles £40-£45.
Rooms	2: 1 double, 1 twin.
Meals	Packed lunch £3.50. Pub 300 yds.
Closed	December-January.
Directions	From Keswick A591 for Carlisle (6.5 miles) right for Bassenthwaite village (0.5 miles). Straight on at village green, house on right.

Price	From £98. Singles from £65.
Rooms	3: 1 double, 1 twin/double; 1 double with separate bath.
Meals	Dinner, 3 courses, £30. Pub 10-minute drive.
Closed	Christmas & New Year.
Directions	B5305 to Wigton; at A595, left. After 5 miles, left to Boltongate. Left at T-junc.; in village, signs for Ireby; down hill, last driveway on left.

Roy & Chris Beaty
Willow Cottage,
Bassenthwaite,
Keswick,
Cumbria CA12 4QP
Tel   01768 776440
Email chriswillowbarn@googlemail.com
Web   www.willowbarncottage.co.uk

Gill & David Taylor
The Old Rectory,
Boltongate, Ireby,
Cumbria CA7 1DA
Tel   01697 371647
Mobile 07763 242969
Email boltongate@talk21.com
Web   www.boltongateoldrectory.com

Entry 75 Map 11

Entry 76 Map 11

Cumbria

New House Farm

The large, comfortable beds, the linen, the fabrics, the pillows – comfort par excellence. You'll be impressed by the renovation, too – the plasterwork stops here and there to reveal old beam, slate or stone. A trio of the bedrooms are named after the mountain each faces; Swinside brings the 1650s house its own spring water. The breakfast room has a woodburner, hunting prints and polished tables for Hazel's breakfasts which will fuel your adventures, the sitting room sports fireplaces and brocade sofas, and walkers will fall gratefully into the hot spring spa. *Children over six welcome.*

Cumbria

Cockenskell Farm

Sara loves her hill farm garden, with its wild rhododendrons and fruitful orchards. Inside are beamed bathrooms and faded lemon quilts, old pine and patterned walls, idiosyncratic touches of colour and dashes of eccentricity. Relax with a book in the conservatory, stroll through the magical garden or tackle a bit of the Cumbrian Way which meanders through the fields to the back. Sara, a delightful, energetic presence, gives you home-grown fruits in season, sometimes walnuts. History seeps from every pore, the place glows with loving care and to stay here is a treat. *Children over 12 welcome.*

Travel Club Offer: see page 392 for details.

Price	£140-£160. Singles £70-£120.
Rooms	5: 2 doubles, 1 twin/double. Stables: 2 four-posters.
Meals	Lunch from £6 (April-November), Dinner, 3-5 courses, £26-£36. Pubs 2.5 miles.
Closed	Never.
Directions	A66 to Cockermouth, then B5289 for Buttermere. Signed left 2.5 miles south of Lorton.

Price	£80. Singles from £40.
Rooms	3: 1 twin; 1 twin with separate bath; 1 single sharing bath.
Meals	Packed lunch £5. Pubs 2-4 miles.
Closed	November-February.
Directions	In Blawith, opp. church up narrow lane, through farmyard. Right after cattle grid, over fell, right at fork through gates & up drive.

	Hazel Thompson
	New House Farm,
	Lorton, Cockermouth,
	Cumbria CA13 9UU
Tel	01900 85404
Mobile	07841 159818
Email	enquiries@newhouse-farm.co.uk
Web	www.newhouse-farm.com

	Sara Keegan
	Cockenskell Farm,
	Blawith, Ulverston,
	Cumbria LA12 8EL
Tel	01229 885217
Mobile	07909 885086
Email	keegan@cockenskell.co.uk
Web	www.cockenskell.co.uk

Entry 77   Map 11

Entry 78   Map 11

Cumbria

Howe Foot

A cluster of buildings in a dell, tall hill above and trees along the trout beck. In a former centre for swill basket making, a miracle of restoration has taken place – and this dear little cottage for two. A patterned rug and a sofa on a new slate floor, a flowery duvet on a pine bed, fern-green towels in a spic and span shower. An immaculate wood pile fuels your wood-burner and the garden slips seamlessly into the nature that surrounds it. Roses and honeysuckle scent the air, pied wagtails nest in the wall and Sue and Martin, talented and full of life, are the warmest hosts; tasty breakfast is in their house.

Price	£80–£90. Singles £50.
Rooms	Cottage with 1 double & sitting room.
Meals	Pub 0.7 miles.
Closed	Christmas–end of January.
Directions	Through Greenodd on A5092, 2 miles to Farmer's Arms Pub. After 0.5 miles, left at crossroads up narrow fell road; 0.2 miles, 1st used track on left to house.

Sue & Martin Hawkard
Howe Foot,
Low Beck Bottom, Lowick, Ulverston,
Cumbria LA12 8EA

Tel	01229 885007
Fax	01229 885007
Email	info@howe-foot.co.uk
Web	www.howe-foot.co.uk

Entry 79 Map 11

Cumbria

Low Fell

The family is great fun, their warmth is infectious and their well-orchestrated house is packed with maps, lists, books and guides. Bedrooms are bright, sunny, pretty, with elegant patterned or checked fabrics, heavenly big beds, plump pillows, warm towels; the suite up in the loft is a super hideaway and you overlook trees animated with birds. Tuck into warm homemade bread and Aga pancakes at breakfast, warm your toes by the fire in winter, relax in the lovely secluded garden with a glass of wine in summer. The house is a five-minute stroll from the lake and busy Bowness. *Children over ten welcome.*

Price	£70–£90. Half-price for children.
Rooms	2: 1 double, 1 family suite (1 double, 1 twin).
Meals	Pubs/restaurants 200 yds.
Closed	Christmas.
Directions	From Kendal, A591 to Windermere; signs to Bowness. Bear left at bottom of hill & 1st left opp. church. Follow road past Burneside Hotel on right; 50 yds, on right.

Louise & Stephen Broughton
Low Fell, Ferney Green,
Bowness-on-Windermere, Windermere,
Cumbria LA23 3ES

Tel	01539 445612
Mobile	07921 057552
Email	louisebroughton@btinternet.com
Web	www.low-fell.co.uk

Entry 80 Map 11

Cumbria

Low House

A mile from Windermere bustle, 17th-century Low House is a hidden gem. Generosity is key here: immense fires, capacious dressers, grand beds piled with duvets, coverlets and pillows. The bathrooms, too – hugely thick towels and opulent mirrors. Breakfast? Wonderful, in bed or downstairs. Curl up by the fire in the snug or the drawing room, dip into a book, take tea, pour yourself a sherry. Set off on sunny days on walks from the door. Best of all, you may 'hire' Johnnie to take you on the lake in his 1930s sailing boat with picnics, swimming or fishing. What a treat!

Price	£80–£130. Singles £50–£80.
Rooms	3: 2 doubles, 1 twin/double.
Meals	Dinner £30 (min. 6). Pubs/restaurants 1 mile.
Closed	Christmas.
Directions	M6 exit 36; A590/591, past Kendal; 1st left at r'bout onto B5284 to Crook; 5 miles (past Windermere golf course); right signed Heathwaite; 100 yds on right.

Johnnie & Heather Curwen
Low House,
Windermere,
Cumbria LA23 3NA
Tel   01539 443156
Mobile 07711 840842
Email   info@lowhouse.co.uk
Web   www.lowhouse.co.uk

Entry 81   Map 11

Cumbria

Gillthwaite Rigg

All is calm and ordered in this light, airy and tranquil Arts and Crafts house. Come for nature and to be surrounded by countryside – you may spot a badger or deer. Find panelled window seats, gleaming oak floors, leaded windows, wooden latched doors and motifs moulded into white plaster. Bedrooms, reached via a spiral staircase, have an uncluttered simplicity and mountain and lake views. Banks of books, a wood-burner for cold nights and kind, affable hosts add cheer. Rhoda and Tony are passionate about conservation and wildlife in their 14 acres. *Babies & children over six welcome.*

Travel Club Offer: see page 392 for details

Price	£70–£80. Singles £55.
Rooms	2: 1 double, 1 twin/double.
Meals	Pubs/restaurants 1 mile.
Closed	Christmas & New Year.
Directions	M6 junc. 36; A590 & A591 to r'bout; B5284 (for 'Hawkshead via ferry') for 6 miles. After golf club, right for Heathwaite. Bear right up hill past nursery. Next drive on right; central part of manor.

Rhoda M & Tony Graham
Gillthwaite Rigg,
Heathwaite Manor,
Lickbarrow Road, Windermere,
Cumbria LA23 2NQ
Tel   01539 446212
Fax   01539 446212
Email tony_rhodagraham@hotmail.com

Entry 82   Map 11

Cumbria

Fellside Studios

Off the beaten tourist track, a piece of paradise in the Troutbeck valley: seclusion, stylishness and breathtaking views. Prepare your own candlelit dinners, rise when the mood takes you, come and go as you please. The flowerbeds spill with heathers, hens cluck, and there's a decked terrace for continental breakfast in the sun – delivered the night before for early risers; your gently hospitable hosts live in the attached house. You get oak floors, slate shower rooms, immaculate kitchenettes with designer touches, DVD players, comfy chairs, luxurious towels. Wonderful. *Minimum stay two nights.*

Price	£70-£90. Singles from £45.
Rooms	2 studios: each with 1 double, 1 twin/double & kitchen.
Meals	Pub/restaurant 0.5 miles.
Closed	Rarely.
Directions	From Windermere, A592 north for 3 miles; after bridge, immed. before church, left signed Troutbeck; 300 yds, 1st house on right.

Monica & Brian Liddell
Fellside Studios,
Troutbeck,
Cumbria LA23 1PE
Tel   01539 434000
Email   enquiry@fellsidestudios.co.uk
Web   www.fellsidestudios.co.uk

Entry 83   Map 11

Cumbria

Middle Reston

A proper Edwardian summer house in the heart of the Lakes (Windermere is the nearest) set high and with mature rhododendrons. Inside is crammed with beautiful dark furniture, Turkish rugs, gorgeous paintings, oak overmantles and fires in every room. Two traditional bedrooms have claret walls and dark carpets; the yellow attic room is more modern; all are a good size and entirely quiet. Make yourselves at home in two huge drawing rooms. Ginny and Simon are great fun and give you a stylish breakfast; then explore the magic outside – especially in spring, with curtseying daffodils and bobbing lambs.

Price	£90-£100.
Rooms	3: 1 double with shower; 2 twins sharing bath.
Meals	Pub 2 miles.
Closed	Christmas & occasionally.
Directions	A591 Kendal-Windermere; 500 yds past 2nd Staveley turning, turn right by small blue bicycle sign, then immediately hard left up drive.

Simon & Ginny Johnson
Middle Reston,
Staveley, Kendal,
Cumbria LA8 9PT
Tel   01539 821246
Mobile   07721 432530
Email   simonhj@btinternet.com
Web   www.lake-district-accomodation.com

Entry 84   Map 11

Cumbria

Howestone Barn

In the back of most-beautiful-beyond and reached down narrow lanes, this converted barn is a gorgeous retreat for two or four. Rick and Gillian give you privacy and an upstairs sitting room with log stove, comfy sofa, exposed beams and a balcony to take in the views. Bedrooms are plain and elegantly rustic with sweeping beams and modern, stone-tiled bathrooms. Breakfast is delivered: sausages and bacon from their Saddlebacks, eggs from their hens, homemade organic bread. Stroll along lowland tracks, watch curlews and lapwings, puff to the top of Whinfell. Windermere, Ambleside and Beatrix Potter's house are near.

Ethical Collection: Food. See page 400 for details.

Travel Club Offer: see page 392 for details.

Price	£50–£90. Singles from £35.
Rooms	Barn with 2 twins/doubles & sitting room.
Meals	Packed lunch £5. Pub/restaurant 3.5 miles.
Closed	Rarely.
Directions	A685 Kendal-Appleby. 500 yds after Morrison's petrol, left signed Mealbank; over long hill after Mealbank, after 2nd bridge at Patton, take middle road of 3. After Borrans Farm, left fork; 0.25 miles on left.

Rick & Gillian Rodriguez
Howestone Barn,
Whinfell, Kendal,
Cumbria LA8 9EQ

Tel	01539 824373
Mobile	07901 732379
Email	stay@lapwingsbarn.co.uk
Web	www.lapwingsbarn.co.uk

Entry 85   Map 12

Cumbria

Lavender House

An 1850s house – the local vet's for many years – a comfortable stroll away from the centre of the bustling little market town with its interesting shops and pubs; John can collect you if you come by train. Tea and homemade cake are served in the yellow sitting room – admire Diana's lovely paintings on the walls – with comfy chairs and a fire on chilly days. Bedrooms are bright, with vibrant cushions and antique furniture; bathrooms have big mirrors, thick towels and plenty of soaps and bubbles. On sunny mornings try a Manx kipper on the roof terrace with its 'Mary Poppins' views and smart potted plants.

Travel Club Offer: see page 392 for details.

Price	£65–£80. Singles from £35.
Rooms	2: 1 double; 1 twin/double with separate bath.
Meals	Packed lunch £6. Pub/restaurant 150 yds.
Closed	Rarely.
Directions	M6 junc. 36; A65 Kirkby Lonsdale. After 6.5 miles, left at roundabout. Pass Booth's supermarket. Right at junction. House 50 yds on left; park in drive.

John & Diana Craven
Lavender House,
17 New Road, Kirkby Lonsdale,
Cumbria LA6 2AB

Tel	01524 272086
Mobile	07775 564157
Email	info@lavenderhousebnb.co.uk
Web	www.lavenderhousebnb.co.uk

Entry 86   Map 12

Cumbria

A Corner of Eden

In the listed farmhouse surrounded by Cumbrian hills and infinite sky, tradition and comfort luxuriously combine. The sitting room has a cosy log fire; the dining room is red and gold; bedrooms glow with designer fireplaces and wooden floors; in one is a contemporary four-poster. Ochres, golds and rich fabrics embellish all, along with robes and slippers for shared bathrooms. Engaging Richard and Debbie live in the barn and show a passion for detail: sloe gin in the rooms, barbours by the door, an honesty bar and home-bakes in the dairy. Offset any indulgence by a walk to the pub – across three glorious fields.

Travel Club Offer: see page 392 for details.

Price	£120.
Rooms	4: 3 doubles, 1 twin, all sharing 2 bathrooms.
Meals	Supper, 2 courses, £19. Dinner, 3 courses, £24. Pub 3 miles.
Closed	Christmas.
Directions	M6 junc. 38, signs for Brough on A685. Right into Ravenstonedale; through village until The Fat Lamb, then right. After 0.5 miles left to Stennerskeugh, keep bearing left.

Debbie Temple & Richard Greaves
A Corner of Eden,
Ravenstonedale, Kirkby Stephen,
Cumbria CA17 4LL

Tel	01539 623370
Mobile	07759 469059
Email	enquiries@acornerofeden.co.uk
Web	www.acornerofeden.co.uk

Entry 87   Map 12

Cumbria

Coldbeck House

An old mill leat runs through the garden – elegant with trees, populated by woodpeckers and red squirrels; at breakfast they feed by the window. Belle's forte is her cooking and Richard assists with walks; both are natural hosts. The dignified 1820s house with Victorian additions has sanded and polished floors, antiques and splendid stained glass, a guest sitting room with a log-burning stove and a country-house feel. Bedrooms are delightful: fresh flowers, homemade biscuits, towels to match colourful walls. It's peaceful here, on the edge of a village with a green, and you are in unsurpassed walking country.

Price	£80–£90. Singles £50–£55.
Rooms	3: 2 doubles, 1 twin.
Meals	Dinner, 2–4 courses, £18.50–£30. Pubs within 5-minute walk.
Closed	Christmas.
Directions	M6 exit 38; A685 to Kirkby Stephen; 6 miles, then right to Ravenstonedale. 1st left opp. Kings Head pub; drive immed. on left.

Belle Hepworth
Coldbeck House,
Ravenstonedale, Kirkby Stephen,
Cumbria CA17 4LW

Tel	01539 623407
Mobile	07966 799171
Email	belle@coldbeckhouse.co.uk
Web	www.coldbeckhouse.co.uk

Entry 88   Map 12

Derbyshire

Horsleygate Hall

Hens and guinea fowl animate the charming old stable yard, and the gardens are vibrant and fascinating, with stone terraces and streams, hidden patios, modern sculptures and seats in every corner... the Fords, attentive and kind, encourage you to explore. Inside the 1783 house, Margaret has created yet more charm. There is a warm, timeless, harmonious feel, with worn kilims on pine boards, striped and floral wallpapers, deep sofas and pools of light. Breakfast is served round a big table in the old schoolroom — homemade jams and oatcakes, garden fruit, eggs from the hens. Special. *Children over five welcome.*

Price	£65-£75. Singles from £40.
Rooms	3: 1 double; 1 family room, 1 twin sharing bath.
Meals	Pub 1 mile.
Closed	23 December-4 January.
Directions	M1 exit 29; A617 to Chesterfield; B6051 to Millthorpe; Horsleygate Lane 1 mile on, on right. House 25 yds on left.

Robert & Margaret Ford
Horsleygate Hall,
Horsleygate Lane,
Holmesfield,
Derbyshire S18 7WD
Tel   01142 890333
Fax   01142 890333

Entry 89   Map 8

Derbyshire

River Cottage

Generous Gilly and well-travelled John have restored their large house — built in the 1740s almost entirely of marble — and given it a fresh modern twist. Interiors are light and airy; modern wallpapers, soft immaculate furnishings, mirrors and glowing antiques give each room a charm of its own. There's the beautiful little village to explore, and the Chatsworth estate ten minutes away. Fishing can be arranged through Gilly and John, and there's a lovely, tiered garden: watch the ducks and trout idle by on the Wye. Many guests come by bus: it stops outside the house. *Minimum stay two nights at weekends Easter-Oct.*

Price	£88-£120. Singles from £59.
Rooms	2 doubles.
Meals	Pubs 600 yds.
Closed	Rarely.
Directions	On northern edge of Ashford village, 1.5 miles N of Bakewell on A6. Buses from Nottingham, Matlock, Manchester & Buxton stop outside the door.

Gilly & John Deacon
River Cottage, The Duke's Drive,
Ashford-in-the-Water, Bakewell,
Derbyshire DE45 1QP
Tel   01629 813327
Email   info@rivercottageashford.co.uk
Web   www.rivercottageashford.co.uk

Entry 90   Map 8

Alstonefield Manor

Country manor house definitely, but delightfully understated and cleverly designed to look natural. Local girl Jo spoils you with warm, homemade scones and tea when you arrive, on the lawns overlooking the rolling hills, or in the elegant drawing room with its soft pale tones and warming fire. The bedroom soothes the soul with a painted wooden floor, antique iron bed, vintage linen, huge fluffy towels and a cool, quirky bathroom. Wake to birdsong – and a candlelit breakfast with local bacon and Staffordshire oatcakes. After a game or two of badminton or croquet, take supper at The George in the village. A joy.

Rose Cottage

Peaceful Rose Cottage lies up a tiny country lane – brighter and airier than 'cottage' would suggest. The hall sets the tone: Indian rugs on a tiled floor, a grandfather clock and ancestral paintings (there's one of Lord Byron!). Bedrooms are traditional and you may gaze on dreamy views across the Dove valley and the Dales. Although elegant, the house is nevertheless a home and guests are treated as friends. No off-limits: a small book-lined sitting room for guests and a big informal garden. Cynthia (Australian) and Peter are the most delightful couple for whom nothing is too much trouble.

Price	£80. Singles £50.
Rooms	1 double with separate bath.
Meals	Pub 100 yds.
Closed	Christmas & occasionally.
Directions	A515 north out of Ashbourne; 6 miles, left into Alstonefield. Over the bridge (river Dove) and up hill. Take 1st left on entering village, go towards the church. House on right.

Price	£70–£76.
Rooms	2: 1 double; 1 twin with separate bath.
Meals	Pub 2 miles.
Closed	Christmas.
Directions	From Ashbourne, A515 Lichfield road. After 4 miles, right onto B5033. After 1 mile, 2nd lane on right; 0.5 miles on, on right.

Robert & Jo Wood
Alstonefield Manor,
Alstonefield, Ashbourne,
Derbyshire DE6 2FX
Tel   01335 310393
Mobile   07968 143964
Email   stay@alstonefieldmanor.com
Web   www.alstonefieldmanor.com

Peter & Cynthia Moore
Rose Cottage,
Snelston,
Ashbourne,
Derbyshire DE6 2DL
Tel   01335 324230
Fax   01335 324651
Email   peter.moore.1@btinternet.com

Entry 91   Map 8

Entry 92   Map 8

Derbyshire

Park View Farm

An amazing farm stay, run by hospitable hosts. Daringly decadent, every inch of this plush Victorian farmhouse brims with flowers, sparkling trinkets, polished brass, plump cushions and swathes of chintz. The rooms dance in swirls of colour, frills, gleaming wood, lustrous glass, buttons and bows – it is an extravagant refuge after a long journey. New-laid eggs from the hens for breakfast, fresh fruits and homemade breads accompany the grand performance. The solid brick farmhouse sits in 370 organic acres and Kedleston Hall Park provides a stunning backdrop. *Children over eight welcome.*

Ethical Collection: Food. See page 400 for details.

 Travel Club Offer: see page 392 for details.

Price	£80–£90. Singles £50–£60.
Rooms	3: 2 doubles; 1 double with separate bath.
Meals	Pub/restaurant 1 mile.
Closed	Christmas.
Directions	From A52 & A38 r'bout west of Derby, A38 north, 1st left for Kedleston Hall. House 1.5 miles past park on x-roads in Weston Underwood.

Linda & Michael Adams
Park View Farm,
Weston Underwood, Ashbourne,
Derbyshire DE6 4PA

Tel	01335 360352
Mobile	07771 573057
Email	enquiries@parkviewfarm.co.uk
Web	www.parkviewfarm.co.uk

Entry 93   Map 8

Derbyshire

Mount Tabor House

On a steep hillside between the Peaks and the Dales, a chapel with a peaceful aura and great views. Enter a hall where light streams through stained-glass windows – this is a relaxed, easy place to stay with a distinctive and original interior. Breakfast, served in a kitchen with open stone walls, can be as carnivorous or as herbivorous as you wish, and enjoyed on the balcony in summer. Eat in, deliciously – or at the pub – on local seasonal food, then retire to a luxurious bed. Rooms, thanks to charming Fay, are as inviting as can be, and bathrooms a treat. *Usually minimum stay two nights at weekends.*

Price	£80. Singles £60.
Rooms	2: 1 twin/double, 1 suite.
Meals	Occasional dinner, £25. Pub 2 miles.
Closed	Christmas.
Directions	M1 exit 26; A610 towards Ripley. At Sawmills, right under r'way bridge, signed Crich. Right at marketplace onto Bowns Hill. Chapel 200 yds on right. Can collect from local stations.

Fay Whitehead
Mount Tabor House,
Bowns Hill, Crich, Matlock,
Derbyshire DE4 5DG

Tel	01773 857008
Mobile	07813 007478
Email	mountabor@msn.com
Web	www.mountabor.co.uk

Entry 94   Map 8

Derbyshire

Manor Farm

Between two small dales, close to great houses (Chatsworth), lies this cluster of ancient farms and church. Once the home of Anthony Babington, friend of Mary Queen of Scots, Manor Farm seems rooted in time. Simon and Gilly, warm and delightful, are sorting out their romantic new home, and Gilly raises prize pigs. The stunning arched kitchen is where guests are served breakfast (scrumptious, organic); the sitting room has less antiquity. Bedrooms have a simple country comfort, the beamy double is charming, shower rooms modernised, a pretty garden swoops to fields and distant river. *Children over six welcome.*

Devon

Orchard Cottage

Tucked into a quiet village corner, this is the last cottage in a row of three. Walk through the pretty garden, past seats that (sometimes!) bask in the sun and down to your own entrance and terrace… you may come and go as you please. Your bedroom is L-shaped and large, with a comfortable brass bed and a super en suite shower; it is spotless yet rustic. The Ewens are friendly and fun, their two spaniels equally so and you are brilliantly sited for Dartmoor, Plymouth, the sand and the sea. Breakfasts in the beamed dining room are generous and delicious; this is excellent value B&B.

Price	£60-£70. Singles £40-£50.
Rooms	3: 1 double, 1 twin/double; 1 double with shared bath.
Meals	Pubs 5-10 minute drive.
Closed	Christmas & New Year.
Directions	From M1 exit 28. A38 then A615 following Matlock signs all the way. Left 3 miles before Matlock, signed Dethick Lane. Down lane 1 mile.

Price	From £55. Singles £40.
Rooms	1 double.
Meals	Pubs 300 yds.
Closed	Christmas.
Directions	A379 from Plymouth for Modbury. On reaching Church St at top of hill, before Modbury, fork left at Palm Cross, then 1st right by school into Back St. Cottage 3rd on left, past village hall.

Simon & Gilly Groom
Manor Farm,
Dethick, Matlock,
Derbyshire DE4 5GG
Tel   01629 534302
Fax   01629 534008
Email   gilly.groom@virgin.net
Web   www.manorfarmdethick.co.uk

Maureen Ewen
Orchard Cottage,
Back Street, Palm Cross Green,
Modbury, Devon PL21 0QZ
Tel   01548 830633
Mobile   07979 558568
Fax   01548 830633
Email   moewen@talktalk.net

Entry 95   Map 8

Entry 96   Map 2

Devon

Annapurna

Rural bliss: the garden of this pretty, cream-painted longhouse surrounded by munching cows and happy hens looks down the folded valley to the steeple of Modbury Church. Inside, Carol and Peter spoil you with blueberry pancakes, organic home-baked bread, home-laid eggs and charming bedrooms with a fresh, country feel. Choose independence in the annexe with your own sitting room, or sleep in the main house; each room is lovely with garden flowers, good beds and sparkling bath or shower rooms. Fabulous walking starts from the door and you are close to the watery delights of Salcombe and Dartmouth.

Price	£65-£75. Singles £30-£40.
Rooms	3: 1 twin/double; 1 single with separate bath. Annexe: 1 double & sitting room (extra bed available).
Meals	Pubs/restaurants 1 mile.
Closed	Rarely.
Directions	A38 Modbury/Ermington. After 1.5 miles approx. Kittaford Cross straight on, through California Cross. After 2.4 miles left down unmarked lane. House 300 yds on right.

Carol Farrand & Peter Foster
Annapurna,
Mary Cross, Modbury,
Devon PL21 0SA

Tel	01548 831299
Mobile	07977 200324
Email	carolfarrand@tiscali.co.uk
Web	www.annapurna-devon.co.uk

Entry 97   Map 2

Devon

Rafters Barn

A delightful and peaceful 300-year-old barn along the narrowest of lanes and with soaring views down a valley to the sea. This is big sailing country but mostly agricultural so you will avoid the madding crowds. You have a comfy guest sitting room with big sofas and a wood-burner that belts out the heat, neat bedrooms in bright colours with pretty touches, tiled bathrooms that gleam and a great big breakfast in the open hallway. Elizabeth is thoughtful and smiley and will point you to the best beaches and places to eat in Salcombe. Or let her cook for you – with produce fresh from farmers' markets.

Travel Club Offer: see page 392 for details

Price	From £72. Singles £50.
Rooms	3: 1 double, 1 twin; 1 single with separate bath.
Meals	Dinner £20 by arrangement. Pubs/restaurants 4 miles.
Closed	Christmas & New Year.
Directions	A381 dir. Salcombe. Just before Hope Cove sign, right to Bagton & S. Huish. Follow lane for 1 mile; 30 yds past saw mill, right up farm lane; at bottom on left.

Elizabeth Hanson
Rafters Barn,
Holwell Farm, South Huish,
Kingsbridge, Devon TQ7 3EQ

Tel	01548 560460
Mobile	07971 293288
Email	raftersdevon@yahoo.co.uk
Web	www.raftersdevon.co.uk

Entry 98   Map 2

Devon

Washbrook Barn

Hard not to feel happy here – even the blue-painted windows on rosy stone walls make you want to smile. Inside is equally sunny. The barn – decrepit until Penny bought it six years ago – rests at the bottom of a quiet valley. She has transformed it into a series of big light-filled rooms with polished wooden floors, pale beams and richly coloured walls lined with fabulous watercolours: the effect is one of gaiety and panache. No sitting room as such, but armchairs in impeccable bedrooms from which one can admire the rural outlook. The beds are divinely comfortable and the fresh bathrooms sparkle.

Devon

High Barn

A quiet spot among rolling hills with artist Nick, cook Jill, two pointers, an inquisitive cat and some roaming chickens. This is a warm, generous household with an easy-going atmosphere: three large sofas round a wood-burner, big art, a snooker table, comfy bedrooms, patchwork quilts and one extremely pink bathroom. At breakfast you get freshly squeezed juice, homemade yogurt and bacon from the farm next door; suppers can be simple or elaborate, or a barbecue in the garden. Explore Dartmoor, walk the coastal paths or head for the beaches; there's plenty of space for storing boats, boards and sandy wetsuits.

Travel Club Offer: see page 392 for details.

Price	From £75. Singles £50.
Rooms	3: 1 double; 1 double, 1 twin, each with separate bath/shower.
Meals	Dinner occasionally in winter. Pubs/restaurants 10-min. walk.
Closed	Christmas & New Year.
Directions	From Kingsbridge quay to top of Fore St; right into Duncombe St; on to T-junc; left to Church St. Right into Belle Cross Rd; 150 yds, right into Washbrook Lane; 250 yds left; at bottom on right.

Price	From £65.
Rooms	2: 1 twin/double, 1 family.
Meals	Dinner, 2 courses, £15. Pubs within 2 miles.
Closed	Rarely.
Directions	A379 west from Kingsbridge to Aveton Gifford. Thro' village, then right past church. Continue 2 miles to Chillaton Cross, then left (after Lixton turning). House 1st on left.

Penny Cadogan
Washbrook Barn,
Washbrook Lane, Kingsbridge,
Devon TQ7 1NN
Tel 01548 856901
Mobile 07989 502194
Email penny.cadogan@homecall.co.uk
Web www.washbrookbarn.co.uk

Nick & Jill Bremer
High Barn,
Chillaton,
Loddiswell, Kingsbridge,
Devon TQ7 4EG
Tel 01548 550838
Email art@nickbremer.com
Web www.nickbremer.com

Entry 99   Map 2

Entry 100   Map 2

Devon

Strete Barton House

Contemporary, friendly, passionately green. There's much to love, and the coastal path runs outside the door. Your caring hosts live their dream running immaculate B&B by the sea. The old Manor House at the top end of the village has had a racy makeover – French sleigh beds and Asian art, white basins and black chandeliers – and the garden has sofas for the views. Breakfasts are exuberantly local (village eggs, sausages from Dartmouth, honey from the bay), there's a wood-burner in the sitting room and Kevin and Stuart know just which beach, walk or pub is perfect for you. *Min. two nights summer. Pets in cottage only.*

Price	£75-£120. Singles £65.
Rooms	6: 3 doubles, 1 twin; 1 twin with separate shower. Cottage: 1 suite & sitting room.
Meals	Pub & restaurant 50 yds.
Closed	Rarely.
Directions	From Dartmouth, A379 to Kingsbridge. At mini roundabout, left onto A379 signed Stoke Fleming. Follow A379 to Strete, then right into Totnes Road. House is 20 yds up the hill on right.

Stuart Litster & Kevin Hooper
Strete Barton House,
Totnes Road, Strete, Dartmouth,
Devon TQ6 0RU

Tel	01803 770364
Fax	01803 771182
Email	info@stretebarton.co.uk
Web	www.stretebarton.co.uk

Entry 101 Map 2

Devon

Nonsuch House

The photo says it all! You are in your own crow's nest, perched above the flotillas of yachts zipping in and out of the estuary mouth: stunning. Kit and Penny are great fun and look after you well; Kit is an ex-hotelier, smokes his own fish fresh from the quay and knocks out brilliant dinners. Further pleasures lie across the water: a five-minute walk brings you to the ferry that transports you and your car to the other side. Breakfasts in the conservatory are a delight, bedrooms are big and comfortable and fresh bathrooms sparkle. *Children over ten welcome. Minimum stay two nights at weekends.*

Ethical Collection: Food. See page 400 for details.

Price	£100-£140. Singles £75-£105.
Rooms	4: 3 twins/doubles, 1 double.
Meals	Dinner, 3 courses, £35. (Not Tues/Wed/Sat.) Pub/restaurant 5-minute walk & short boat trip.
Closed	Rarely.
Directions	2 miles before Brixham on A3022, A379. After r'bout, fork left (B3205) downhill, through woods, left up Higher Contour Rd, down Ridley Hill. At hairpin bend.

Kit & Penny Noble
Nonsuch House,
Church Hill, Kingswear, Dartmouth,
Devon TQ6 0BX

Tel	01803 752829
Fax	01803 752357
Email	enquiries@nonsuch-house.co.uk
Web	www.nonsuch-house.co.uk

Entry 102 Map 2

Devon

The White House

Gaze on the sparkling estuary from the comfort of your bed in this very friendly, very relaxing house at the top of the hill – filled with books and art. There's classical music and Hugh's homemade bread at breakfast, and a real fire for your sitting room in winter. Fresh, pretty bedrooms have sherry, chocolates, bathrobes and opera glasses for views; more village and estuary views from the garden terrace. A ferryman transports you to Agatha Christie's house just across the river: shake the bell opposite the Inn! Another ferry takes you to Dartmouth – catch the river boat on to Totnes. *Children by arrangement.*

Price	£85. Singles £55.
Rooms	2 doubles.
Meals	Pubs a short walk.
Closed	Christmas.
Directions	Down hill into Dittisham, sharp right immed. before Red Lion. Along The Level, up narrow hill & house entrance opp. at junc. of Manor St & Rectory Lane.

Hugh & Jill Treseder
The White House,
Manor Street,
Dittisham,
Devon TQ6 0EX

Tel	01803 722355
Fax	01803 722355
Email	jilltreseder@btinternet.com

Entry 103   Map 2

Devon

Riverside House

The loveliest 17th-century cottage with wisteria and honeysuckle growing up its walls and the tidal river estuary bobbing past with boats and birds; in summer you can dip your toes in the water while sitting in the garden. Felicity, an artist, and Roger, a passionate sailor, give you beautiful bedrooms, fresh flowers, thick towels and pretty china. No need to stir from your fine linen-and-down nest to use the binoculars: bedrooms have long views over the water and wide windows. Wander up to the pub for dinner – in fine weather they have quayside barbecues and live music. *Minimum stay two nights at weekends.*

Price	From £75. Singles from £60.
Rooms	2: 1 double; 1 double with separate shower.
Meals	Packed lunch £6. Pubs 100 yds.
Closed	Rarely.
Directions	In Tuckenhay, pass Maltsters Arms on left to 2nd thatched house on left, at right angle to road. Drive past, turn at bridge and return to slip lane.

Felicity & Roger Jobson
Riverside House,
Tuckenhay, Totnes,
Devon TQ9 7EQ

Tel	01803 732837
Mobile	07710 510007
Email	felicity.jobson@riverside-house.co.uk
Web	www.riverside-house.co.uk

Entry 104   Map 2

Devon

Lower Norton Farmhouse

Hard to believe the downstairs bedroom was a calving pen and its smart bathroom the dairy. Now it has a seagrass floor and a French walnut bed. All Glynis's rooms are freshly decorated, and she and Peter are the most amenable hosts, genuinely happy for you to potter around all day should you wish to do so. For the more active, a yacht on the Dart and a cream Bentley are to hand, with Peter as navigator and chauffeur – rare treats. Return to gardens, paddocks, peaceful views, super dinners and a big log fire. Off the beaten track, a tremendous find. *Children over ten welcome.*

Travel Club Offer: see page 392 for details.

Price	From £75. Singles £60.
Rooms	3: 2 doubles, 1 twin.
Meals	Dinner, 2 courses, £25. Lunch £9. Packed lunch £7. Pub/restaurant 1.5 miles.
Closed	Rarely.
Directions	From A381 at Halwell, 3rd left signed Slapton; 4th right after 2.3 miles signed Sherford, Kingsbridge at Wallaton Cross. House down 3rd drive on left.

Peter & Glynis Bidwell
Lower Norton Farmhouse,
Coles Cross, East Allington, Totnes,
Devon TQ9 7RL

Tel	01548 521246
Mobile	07790 288772
Email	peter@lowernortonfarmhouse.co.uk
Web	www.lowernortonfarmhouse.co.uk

Entry 105   Map 2

Devon

The Old Rectory

Fresh flowers and 18th-century elegance... Jill and John's Regency rectory, on the edge of Diptford, was once the home of William Gregor, a vicar who discovered titanium! (There are still some titanium bowls in the large and lovely hall with its fine staircase.) You'll enjoy eating here, in the splendour of the dining room, for Jill is a superb, Leith-trained cook and a vivacious hostess. Bedrooms are all large and light; one is downstairs, another has three lovely windows with views over the garden to the moors – and a chesterfield so you can appreciate them in comfort. Pets are exceedingly welcome.

Travel Club Offer: see page 392 for details.

Price	£85-£115. Singles £60.
Rooms	5: 3 doubles, 1 twin, 1 family suite for 4.
Meals	Dinner £27.50. Supper £18. Packed lunch available. Pub 5-minute drive.
Closed	Rarely.
Directions	Avonwick to Diptford road. First house on right after village sign.

Jill Hitchins
The Old Rectory,
Diptford, Totnes,
Devon TQ9 7NY

Tel	01548 821575
Mobile	07767 427722
Email	hitchins@oldrectorydiptford.co.uk
Web	www.oldrectorydiptford.co.uk

Entry 106   Map 2

Devon

Avenue Cottage

The tree-lined approach is steep and spectacular; the cottage sits in 11 wondrous acres of rhododendron, magnolia and wild flowers with a lily-strewn pond and paths that dip down towards the lovely river. Find a quiet spot in which to read or simply sit and absorb the tranquillity. Richard is a gifted gardener, and the archetypal gardener's modesty and calm have penetrated the house itself – it is uncluttered, comfortable. The old-fashioned twin room has a big bathroom with a faux-marble basin and a balcony with sweeping valley views; the pretty village and pub are a short walk away.

Price	£54–£70. Singles £32–£40.
Rooms	2: 1 twin/double; 1 double sharing shower.
Meals	Pub 0.5 miles.
Closed	Rarely.
Directions	A381 Totnes-Kingsbridge for 1 mile; left for Ashprington; into village, then left by pub ('Dead End' sign). House 0.25 miles on right.

Richard Pitts
Avenue Cottage,
Ashprington,
Totnes,
Devon TQ9 7UT

Tel	01803 732769
Mobile	07719 147475
Email	richard.pitts@btinternet.com

✗

Entry 107   Map 2

Devon

Parliament House

The ancient rambling house (where William of Orange held his first Parliament) is on the road at the bottom of the valley, and has been beautifully restored by two designers. This is a fresh, stylish and charming cottage where wallpapers, napkins and toile de Jouy are to Carole's own design. White walls and serene colours form a lovely backdrop for pretty touches. Breakfasts are feasts – creamy mushrooms on a toasted muffin, three sorts of bread – and bedrooms are low-ceilinged and cosy with cast-iron fireplaces and hand-stencilled paper. There's a sitting room and a library with a piano – and the garden is a joy.

Price	From £75.
Rooms	2: 1 double; 1 twin/double with separate bath/shower.
Meals	Pubs/restaurants within 2 miles.
Closed	Rarely.
Directions	From Totnes, A385 Paignton road; 2 miles on, right at Riviera Sports Cars. House 1st on right. Just past house to parking area on right.

Carole & Harry Grimley
Parliament House,
Longcombe,
Totnes,
Devon TQ9 6PR

Tel	01803 840288
Email	parliamenthouse@btopenworld.com

✗ 🚂 🐕

Entry 108   Map 2

Devon

Manor Farm

Capable Sarah is a keen gardener, and produces vegetables that will find their way into your (excellent) dinner, and raspberries for your muesli. She keeps bees and hens too, so you can have honey and eggs for breakfast, served in a smart red dining room. The farmhouse twists and turns around unexpected corners thanks to ancient origins, and the good-sized bedrooms, one with its own bathroom, both painted light yellow, are reached via two separate stairs – nicely private. The lovely village is surrounded by apple orchards and has two good pubs for eating out.

Price	£70. Singles £40-£45.
Rooms	2: 1 double; 1 twin with separate bath/shower.
Meals	Dinner £15-£21. Packed lunch £4-£5. Pubs 500 yds.
Closed	Rarely.
Directions	From Newton Abbot, A381 for Totnes. After approx. 2.5 miles, right for Broadhempston. Past village sign, down hill & 2nd left. Pass pub on right & left 170 yds on into courtyard.

Sarah Clapp
Manor Farm,
Broadhempston, Totnes,
Devon TQ9 6BD
Tel 01803 813260
Fax 01803 813260
Email mandsclapp@btinternet.com

Entry 109   Map 2

Devon

Kilbury Manor

You can stroll down to the Dart from the garden and onto their little island, when the river's not in spate! Back at the Manor – a listed longhouse from the 1700s – are four super-comfortable bedrooms, the most private in the stone barn. Your genuinely welcoming hosts (with dogs Dillon and Buster) moved to Devon to renovate a big handsome house and open it to guests. Julia does everything beautifully so there's organic smoked salmon for breakfast, baskets of toiletries by the bath, the best linen on the best beds and a drying room for wet gear – most handy if you've come to walk the Moor. Spot-on B&B.

Price	£67-£80. Singles from £45.
Rooms	4: 2 doubles. Barn: 1 twin/double; 1 double with separate bath.
Meals	Pubs/restaurants 1.5-4 miles.
Closed	Rarely.
Directions	Leaving A38, left for Totnes. After 0.5 miles, right over river on narrow bridge; follow lane over railway bridge then immed. left into Colston Rd. House 0.25 miles on left.

Julia & Martin Blundell
Kilbury Manor,
Colston Road, Buckfastleigh,
Devon TQ11 0LN
Tel 01364 644079
Email info@kilburymanor.co.uk
Web www.kilburymanor.co.uk

Entry 110   Map 2

Devon

Old Mill Farm

Position, position, position. Dazzling sunsets, resident kingfisher, the occasional seal, total seclusion; painters and birdwatchers will think they have died and gone to heaven. The approach is stunning: from the top of the hill you descend to the estuary's edge, and find a hugely refitted house with Elizabethan origins and glamorous Robert and Kate. Bedrooms are spacious, plush, stylish; bathrooms have thick fluffy towels and one has a bath with the best-ever view. Breakfast is posh (eggs benedict, homemade croissants, kippers) and eaten in the river room with slate floor, French windows and… views. A treat.

Travel Club Offer: see page 392 for details.

Price	£105–£130.
Rooms	3 doubles.
Meals	Occasional dinner, 3 courses, £30. Pub 1 mile.
Closed	Rarely.
Directions	From Brixham road into Galmpton, straight through (Greenway Road), with primary school on right. Up hill out of village, right at no-through road sign, down lane. Entrance on left.

Robert & Kate Chaston
Old Mill Farm,
Greenway, Galmpton, Devon TQ5 0ER
Tel   01803 842344
Mobile   07831 847796
Email   enquiries@oldmillfarm-dart.co.uk
Web   www.oldmillfarm-dart.co.uk

Entry 111   Map 2

Devon

Tudor House

A merchant's townhouse now happily given over to rooms for the Agaric Restaurant. Sophie and Nick are young, fun and very clever: in these mostly large, individually styled rooms, fabrics are plush, colours innovative and bathrooms have roll tops or a wet room style shower. A breakfast room is cool with leather and palms; full English or anything else you want is delivered here. Don't come without booking into the restaurant for fabulous modern British cooking – then stagger two steps down the street to your well-earned bed. Ashburton bustles with good food shops, antiques and books.

Price	£70–£125. Singles £50.
Rooms	5: 2 doubles, 1 family, 1 single; 1 double with separate bath.
Meals	Owner's restaurant next door. Packed lunch from £10 for 2.
Closed	Rarely.
Directions	From A38 follow signs to Ashburton. North Street is the main street, house is on the right after the Town Hall.

Sophie & Nick Coiley
Tudor House,
36 North Street, Ashburton,
Devon TQ13 7QD
Tel   01364 654478
Email   eat@agaricrestaurant.co.uk
Web   www.agaricrestaurant.co.uk

Entry 112   Map 2

Devon

Penpark

Clough Williams-Ellis of Portmeirion fame did more than design an elegant house; he made sure it communed with nature. Light pours in from every window and the views are long, across rolling farmland to Dartmoor and Hay Tor. The big double has a comfy sofa and its own balcony; the private suite has arched French doors to the garden and an extra room for young children. Antiques and heirlooms, African carvings, silk and fresh flowers — it is deeply traditional and comforting. Your generous hosts have been doing B&B for years; they and their two springer spaniels look after you well.

![] Travel Club Offer: see page 392 for details.

Price	From £70–£76. Singles by arrangement.
Rooms	3: 1 family suite; 1 twin/double with separate bath; 1 double with separate shower.
Meals	Pub 1 mile.
Closed	Rarely.
Directions	A38 west to Plymouth; A382 turn off; 3rd turning off r'bout, signed Bickington. There, right at junc. (to Plymouth), right again (to Sigford & Widecombe). Over top of A38 & up hill; 1st entrance on right.

Madeleine & Michael Gregson
Penpark,
Bickington, Ashburton,
Devon TQ12 6LH

Tel	01626 821314
Email	maddy@penpark.co.uk
Web	www.penpark.co.uk

Devon

Hooks Cottage

The hideaway mine captain's house may have few original features but the setting is special. At the end of a long bumpy track is a lush oasis carved out of woodland. Mary, gently spoken, and Dick have a finely judged sense of humour, and labradors Archie and Cobble will charm you. It is simple, rural, close to the Moors, with river and birdsong to unwind stressed souls. Carpeted bedrooms have a faded floral charm and pretty stream views; bathrooms are plain. Enjoy local sausages and Mary's marmalade for breakfast, bluebells in spring and 12 acres to explore. Your horse is welcome too!

Price	£55–£60. Singles £35.
Rooms	2: 1 double, 1 twin with separate bath.
Meals	Occasional dinner, £20. Pub/restaurant 2 miles.
Closed	Rarely.
Directions	From A38, A382 at Drumbridges for Newton Abbot; 3rd left at r'bout for Bickington. Down hill, right for Haytor. Under bridge, 1st left & down long, bumpy track, past thatched cottage to house.

Mary & Dick Lloyd-Williams
Hooks Cottage,
Bickington,
Ashburton,
Devon TQ12 6JS

Tel	01626 821312
Email	hookscottage@yahoo.com

Devon

Bagtor Manor House

What a setting! A ten-minute walk and you're on the moor. Enfolded by garden, green fields and sheep, the 15th-century house with the Georgian façade is the last remaining manor in the parish. Find ancient beauty in granite flagstones, oak-panelled walls, great fireplaces glowing with logs and country dressers brimming with china. Sue looks after hens, geese, labradors, guests, grows everything and makes her own bread. She offers you a large and elegant double room with an antique brass bed and, steeply up the stairs, a big attic-cosy suite perfect for families. Warm, homely, spacious, civilised.

Price	From £70. Singles by arrangement.
Rooms	2: 1 double, 1 family room, each with separate bath/shower.
Meals	Restaurants/pubs 1 mile.
Closed	Never.
Directions	From A38 to Plymouth, A382 turn off at r'bout, 3rd exit to Ilsington; up through village, 2nd left after hotel (to Bickington),1st crossroads right to Bagtor, 0.5 miles on, right next to Farm.

Sue Cookson
Bagtor Manor House,
Ilsington, Bovey Tracey,
Devon TQ13 9RT

Tel	01364 661538
Fax	01364 661538
Email	sawreysue@hotmail.com
Web	www.bagtormanor.co.uk

Entry 115   Map 2

Devon

Corndonford Farm

An ancient Devon longhouse and an engagingly chaotic haven run by warm and friendly Ann and Will, along with their Shire horses and Dartmoor ponies. Steep, stone circular stairs lead to bedrooms; bright lemon walls, a four poster with lacy curtains, gorgeous views over the cottage garden and a bathroom with a beam to duck. A place for those who want to get into the spirit of it all – maybe help catch an escaped foal, chatter to the farm workers around the table; not for fussy types or Mr and Mrs Tickety Boo. Good for walkers too – the Two Moors Way footpath is on the doorstep. *Children over ten by arrangement.*

Price	£60. Singles £30.
Rooms	2: 1 twin, 1 four-poster sharing bath.
Meals	Pub 2 miles.
Closed	Christmas.
Directions	From A38 2nd Ashburton turn for Dartmeet & Princetown. In Poundsgate pass pub on left; 3rd right on bad bend signed Corndon. Straight over x-roads, 0.5 miles, farm on left.

Ann & Will Williams
Corndonford Farm,
Poundsgate,
Newton Abbot,
Devon TQ13 7PP

Tel	01364 631595
Email	corndonford@btinternet.com

Entry 116   Map 2

Devon

Hammerslake Cottage

Be seduced by narrow lanes and high hedges before you arrive at this smartly painted 16th-century farm worker's cottage on the edge of Dartmoor. You are surrounded by a tranquil garden with twittering birds, a trickling stream and dramatic views; breakfast out here in summer, on eggs from Caroline's hens, local bacon, kedgeree. Two bedrooms (one with a balcony) are smartly dressed with big beds, goosey pillows, fresh flowers and chocolate, the third is a frill-free space for kids with bunks, comics and games. Tents can be put up in the garden, trees can be climbed; this is an affable place with a lovely owner.

Price	£65–£75.
Rooms	3: 2 doubles, 1 bunk room.
Meals	Pub 1 mile.
Closed	Rarely.
Directions	From Lustleigh, with church on right & shop opposite, turn left down lane to steep T-junc; right for North Bovey, Pethybridge & Cleave. On for 1 mile, to blind bend with thatched cottage on right. Next house on right, set back from road, signed 'B&B'.

	Caroline Byng
	Hammerslake Cottage,
	Ellimore Road, Lustleigh,
	Newton Abbot, Devon TQ13 9SQ
Tel	01647 277547
Mobile	07866 386084
Email	caroline.byng@btinternet.com
Web	www.lustleighbedandbreakfast.co.uk

Entry 117   Map 2

Devon

The Gate House

An idyllic house in an idyllic village, lost on the edge of the moor. The medieval longhouse (1460) has all the low beams and wonky walls you could hope for, and is beautifully looked after. Rose-print curtains and spruce quilts in the bedrooms, a wood-burner and flowers in the sitting room, robes, good soaps and soft towels in pretty bathrooms – and John and Sheila, delightful, attentive, serving you delicious Aga-side meals on white linen with candles. You will feel well and truly spoiled. A small pool in the lush garden overlooks beautiful woodland and moors… what more could you ask?

Price	£76–£80. Singles £50.
Rooms	3: 2 twins/doubles; 1 double with separate bath/shower.
Meals	Supper trays £12.50. BYO. Packed lunch available. Pub/restaurant 50 yds.
Closed	Rarely.
Directions	From Moretonhampstead via Pound St to North Bovey (1.5 miles). House 25 yds off village green, down Lower Hill past inn on left.

	John & Sheila Williams
	The Gate House,
	North Bovey,
	Devon TQ13 8RB
Tel	01647 440479
Fax	01647 440479
Email	srw.gatehouse@btinternet.com
Web	www.gatehouseondartmoor.co.uk

Entry 118   Map 2

Devon

Cyprian's Cot

A charming terraced cottage of 16th-century nooks and crannies and beams worth ducking. The setting is exquisite: the garden leads into fields of sheep, the Dartmoor Way goes through the town and the Two Moors Way skirts it. Shelagh, a lovely lady, gives guests their own sitting room with a fire, lit on cool nights; breakfasts, served in the cosy dining room, are fresh, free-range and tasty. Up the narrow stairs and into simple bedrooms – a small double and a tiny twin. A perfect house and hostess, and a perfect little town to discover, with its pubs, fine restaurant and delicatessen, organic shop and tearoom.

Devon

Burnville House

Granite gateposts, Georgian house, rhododendrons, beechwoods and rolling fields of sheep: that's the setting. But there's more. Beautifully proportioned rooms reveal subtle colours, elegant antiques, squishy sofas and bucolic views, stylish bathrooms are sprinkled with candles, there are sumptuous dinners and pancakes at breakfast. Your hosts left busy jobs in London to settle here, and their place breathes life – space, smiles, energy. Swim, play tennis, walk to Dartmoor from the door, take a trip to Eden or the sea. Or… just gaze at the moors and the church on the Tor and listen to the silence, and the sheep.

Travel Club Offer: see page 392 for details.

Price	£60. Singles from £30.
Rooms	2: 1 twin; 1 double with separate bath.
Meals	Pubs/restaurants 4-minute walk.
Closed	Rarely.
Directions	In Chagford pass church on left; 1st right beyond Globe Inn opposite. House 150 yds on right.

Price	From £70. Singles £45.
Rooms	2 doubles.
Meals	Dinner from £17.50. Pub 2 miles.
Closed	Rarely.
Directions	A30 Exeter-Okehampton; A386 dir. Tavistock. Right for Lydford opp. Dartmoor Inn; after 4 miles (thro' Lydford), Burnville Farm on left (convex traffic mirror on right).

Shelagh Weeden
Cyprian's Cot,
47 New Street,
Chagford,
Devon TQ13 8BB

Tel 01647 432256
Email shelaghweeden@btinternet.com
Web www.cyprianscot.co.uk

Victoria Cunningham
Burnville House,
Brentor, Tavistock,
Devon PL19 0NE

Tel 01822 820443
Mobile 07881 583471
Email burnvillef@aol.com
Web www.burnville.co.uk

Entry 119   Map 2

Entry 120   Map 2

Devon

Mount Tavy Cottage

Rural bliss – but just a short walk to Tavistock (best market town 2005). One guest wrote: "There's no better place to recover from stress." Everything is geared to your comfort – pretty rooms, four-poster and half-tester beds, deep, free-standing baths. Joanna and Graham, a lovely Devon couple, have worked hard to restore this former gardener's bothy, Graham making much of the furniture himself. Two new bedrooms have been created in the potting shed across the courtyard: bed and breakfast in glorious seclusion. Outside are ponds – one with a breezy pagoda for summer suppers – and a walled Victorian garden. *Arrivals after 5pm, unless previously arranged.*

Price	From £70. Singles from £35.
Rooms	3: 2 twins/doubles, 1 four-poster, each with separate bath.
Meals	Dinner, 3 courses, £20. Pub 2 miles.
Closed	Rarely.
Directions	From Tavistock B3357 towards Princetown; 0.25 miles on, after Mount House School, left. Drive past lake to house.

	Mr & Mrs G H Moule Mount Tavy Cottage, Tavistock, Devon PL19 9JL
Tel	01822 614253
Mobile	07776 181576
Email	mounttavy@btinternet.com
Web	www.mounttavy.co.uk

Entry 121   Map 2

Devon

South Hooe Count House

It's lovely here, so peaceful in your own private cottage perched above the river; steep steps lead to canoes for the intrepid. Delightful Trish leaves you homemade bread and marmalade, deep-yellow yolked eggs from her chickens and local bacon for you to cook. Choose a spot on the cushioned window seat or write your novel on the sheltered terrace which catches the sun; Martha the aged donkey may drop in for tea. There's a soft sofa and a wood-burner in the sitting room, and a large double bed in the light-filled bedroom. Live by the tide and emerge refreshed. *Babes in arms & children over eight welcome.*

Price	£70–£85. Singles from £35.
Rooms	1 twin/double.
Meals	Supper rarely. Pub 3 miles.
Closed	Rarely.
Directions	Into Bere Alston on B3257, left for Weir Quay. Over x-roads. Follow Hole's Hole sign, right for Hooe. Fork left for South Hooe Farm; 300 yds on, turn sharply back to your left (signed South Hooe Mine) & down track.

	Trish Dugmore South Hooe Count House, South Hooe Mine, Hole's Hole, Bere Alston, Yelverton, Devon PL20 7BW
Tel	01822 840329
Email	southhooe@aol.com

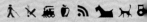

Entry 122   Map 2

Devon

Higher Eggbeer Farm

Over 900 years old and still humming with life: pigs, cows, ponies, rabbits, and chickens share the rambling gardens. Sally Anne and William are artistic, fun, slightly wacky and charming. It's an adventure to stay, so keep an open mind: the house is a historic gem and undeniably rustic. Huge inglenook fireplaces, interesting art, books, piano, wellies, muddle and charm. Your lovely hosts will take children to feed animals and collect eggs, and will babysit. Be wrapped in peace in your own half of the house (with beautiful drawing room), immersed in a magnificent panorama of forest, hills and fields of waving wheat.

Price	£65–£75. Singles £42.
Rooms	3: 2 twins/doubles sharing bath (2nd room let to same party); 1 double sharing owners' bath. Self-catering option.
Meals	Restaurants 5-minute walk.
Closed	Rarely.
Directions	A30 to Okehampton. After 10 miles left exit into Cheriton Bishop; 1st left after Old Thatch pub, signed Woodbrooke. Down & up hill; road turns sharp left but you don't. Turn right down private lane.

Sally Anne & William Selwyn
Higher Eggbeer Farm,
Cheriton Bishop,
Exeter,
Devon EX6 6JQ

Tel	01647 24427

Entry 123   Map 2

Devon

The Old Inn

Charlotte is fun and warm, and greatly enjoying her new project. The rambling building, on the village square, has 17th-century roots. But now the sitting and dining rooms – cream walls, big fireplaces, huge red chairs and sofa – are devoted to warmth and comfort. Breakfasts include local bacon and sausages, smoked haddock or delicious kedgeree. Bedrooms are dressed in pale colours, with stylish textiles and ultra comfy beds; bathrooms spoil you with locally made organic soaps and lotions. You are in fabulous walking country on the edge of Dartmoor, and Chagford is near with its music and arts festivals.

Price	£75–£85. Singles £50–£70.
Rooms	5: 3 doubles; 1 single with separate shower; 1 family room for 3 with separate bath.
Meals	Dinner, 2 courses, £20. Pub 100 yds.
Closed	22 December–mid-February.
Directions	A30 south from Exeter to Whiddon Down. Left off r'bout towards Mortonhampstead (A382); 400 yds, left to Drewsteignton. Enter village, house on right.

Charlotte Hammick
The Old Inn,
Drewsteignton,
Exeter, Devon EX6 6QR

Tel	01647 281276
Mobile	07973 757765
Email	charlotte.hammick@gmail.com
Web	www.old-inn.co.uk

Entry 124   Map 2

Devon

The Garden House

Refulgent! An extraordinary restoration of a 1930s house, carried out with passion. Bedrooms are sumptuous; beds plump with cushions, fabrics smooth, colours vibrant, scents divine. The exuberance reaches the garden; Jane's energy among the pots, quirky topiary and tulips is almost palpable. A huge collection of books are stacked hither and thither, the chandeliers sparkle, homemade cakes abound, candles flicker and there's a vast choice of locally-sourced breakfasts, beautifully served. It may not be minimalist but it is deeply comfortable, good-humoured and an easy walk into the city.

Price	£85-£90. Singles £50-£60.
Rooms	2: 1 double; 1 twin.
Meals	Pubs/restaurants nearby.
Closed	Rarely.
Directions	M5 junc. 30 for city centre & university. Behind Debenhams, Longbrook St into Pennsylvania Rd. Through lights, 2nd left into Hoopern Ave; house at end on left.

David & Jane Woolcock
The Garden House,
4 Hoopern Avenue, Pennsylvania,
Exeter, Devon EX4 6DN

Tel	01392 256255
Mobile	07968 374876
Email	david.woolcock1@virgin.net
Web	www.exeterbedandbreakfast.co.uk

Devon

Beach House

Lapping at the riverside garden is the Exe estuary, wide and serene. Birds and boats, the soft hills beyond, a gorgeous Georgian house on the river and kind hosts who have been here for years. The garden is pretty with quirky rooster-shaped hedges and old apple trees; you may have a locally sourced breakfast in the conservatory or in the dining room, with raspberries and blackberries in season. No guest sitting room but comfy chairs in the bedrooms, which are soft and chintzy, with antique white bedspreads, charmingly old-fashioned bathrooms and estuary views. Cycle into Exeter, for culture and Cathedral.

Price	From £80. Singles £50.
Rooms	2: 1 twin, 1 double.
Meals	Pubs/restaurants 8-minute walk.
Closed	Christmas & New Year; January-end March.
Directions	M5 exit 30; signs to Exmouth. Right at George & Dragon. After 1 mile, immed. left after level crossing. At mini r'bout, left down The Strand. House last on left by beach.

Trevor & Jane Coleman
Beach House,
The Strand, Topsham,
Exeter,
Devon EX3 0BB

Tel	01392 876456
Fax	01392 873159
Email	janecoleman45@hotmail.com

Devon

Larkbeare Grange

Expectations rise as you follow the tree-lined drive to the immaculate Georgian house... and are met, the second you enter this elegant, calm and characterful home. The upkeep is perfect, the feel is chic and the whole place exudes well-being. Sparkling sash windows fill big rooms with light, floors shine and the grandfather clock ticks away the hours. Expect the best: goose down duvets on king-size beds, contemporary luxury in fabric and fitting, flexible breakfasts and lovely views from the bedroom at the front. Charlie, Savoy-trained, and Julia are charming and fun: you are in perfect hands.

Travel Club Offer: see page 392 for details.

Price	£88–£110. Singles from £73.
Rooms	3: 2 doubles, 1 twin/double.
Meals	Pub 1.5 miles.
Closed	Rarely.
Directions	From A30 Exmouth & Ottery St Mary junc. At r'bouts follow Whimple signs. 0.25 miles, right; 0.5 miles, left signed Larkbeare. House 1 mile on left.

Charlie & Julia Hutchings
Larkbeare Grange,
Larkbeare, Talaton,
Exeter, Devon EX5 2RY

Tel	01404 822069
Fax	01404 823746
Email	stay@larkbeare.net
Web	www.larkbeare.net

Entry 127   Map 2

Devon

Lower Allercombe Farm

Horses in the paddock and no-frills bedrooms at this down-to-earth, very friendly B&B. Don't expect twinsets and pearls; Susie, ex-eventer, may greet you in two-tone jodphurs instead. She and Lizzie (her terrier) live at one end of the listed longhouse, guests at the other. There's a sitting room with horsey pictures and cosy wood-burner, and bedrooms upstairs that reflect the fair price. You'll feast on home eggs and tomatoes in the morning, and rashers from award-winning pigs. Very handy for the Devon County Show and Dartmoor; the airport is ten minutes away, the A30 is 300 yards. *Stabling available.*

Price	£55–£70. Singles £35–£45.
Rooms	3: 1 double, 1 twin; 1 double with separate bath.
Meals	Pub/restaurant 2 miles.
Closed	Rarely.
Directions	From Exeter junction 29, M5. A30 towards Honiton. At Daisymount exit to Ottery St Mary, take B3180 off roundabout. Go 200 yds, then right to Allercombe. 1 mile until crossroads, then right. House is 50 yds on right.

Susie Holroyd
Lower Allercombe Farm,
Rockbeare, Exeter,
Devon EX5 2HD

Tel	01404 822519
Mobile	07980 255107
Email	holroyd.s@gmail.com
Web	www.lowerallercombefarm.co.uk

Entry 128   Map 2

Devon

Simcoe House

A gem of a setting, this gracious 18th-century house was the summer home of General Simcoe in 1790 and is within strolling distance of the beach and town. There are stunning views from wide windows in the lovely guest sitting room, so find a book and settle in a comfy chair while the sun streams in. Jane gives you breakfast in the pretty conservatory or the dining room. Bedrooms are sunny and charming with fresh flowers and fabulous vistas. Laze on the terrace, look up the house history in the local museum or relish the Jurassic coast. A unique house with a beachy feel and delightful owners. *Children over ten welcome.*

Price	£70–£80. Singles £50.
Rooms	2: 1 double, 1 twin.
Meals	Pubs/restaurants 5 minute walk.
Closed	Christmas.
Directions	M5 junc. 30 onto A376. Then B3179 to Budleigh Salterton (approx. 8 miles). Into town centre then left opposite The Creamery, onto Fore Street Hill. 300 yds on right; steps lead to front door.

Jane Crosse
Simcoe House,
8 Fore Street Hill, Budleigh Salterton,
Devon EX9 6PE

Tel	01395 446013
Mobile	07747 633060
Email	simcoehouse@hotmail.co.uk
Web	www.simcoehouse.co.uk

Entry 129   Map 2

Devon

Rose Cottage

Step back in time to seaside fun and bracing walks. Tucked down a quiet street in sleepy Sidmouth, this is a quick hop to the beach – why not rent the family's beach hut? – or onto the coastal path. With stripped pine floorboards, stained-glass features and pretty cushions, Jackie has created a friendly, homely place. Bedrooms are small but jolly with quilted covers and sunny walls, two have tiny showers, another has a slipper bath. There's homemade muesli and organic bacon for breakfast in a room with a seaside teashop feel; no sitting room but a large garden with a slide and swing for children. *Children by arrangement.*

Price	From £70. Singles from £60.
Rooms	4: 2 doubles, 1 twin; 1 double with separate bath.
Meals	Packed lunch £5. Pubs/restaurants 300 yds.
Closed	Christmas, New Year & occasionally.
Directions	From Exeter A3052 to Sidmouth. Over r'bout at Woodlands Hotel. House is 100 yds on left just before zebra crossing.

Jacalyn & Neil Cole
Rose Cottage,
Coburg Road, Sidmouth,
Devon EX10 8NF

Tel	01395 577179
Mobile	07708 063820
Email	neilsurf@tesco.net
Web	www.rosecottage-sidmouth.co.uk

Entry 130   Map 2

Devon

Glebe House

Set on a hillside with fabulous views over the Coly valley, this late-Georgian vicarage has become a heart-warming B&B. The views will entice you, the hosts will delight you and the house is filled with interesting things. Chuck and Emma spent many years at sea – he a Master Mariner, she a chef – and have filled these big light rooms with cushions, kilims and treasured family pieces. There's a sitting room for guests, a lovely conservatory with a vintage vine, peaceful bedrooms with blissful views and bathrooms that sparkle. All this, two goats, wildlife beyond the ha-ha and the fabulous coast a hike away.

Travel Club Offer: see page 392 for details.

Price	From £70. Singles £40.
Rooms	3: 1 double, 1 twin/double, 1 family.
Meals	Pubs/restaurants 2.5 miles.
Closed	Christmas & New Year.
Directions	A375 from Honiton; left opposite Hare & Hounds on B3174 to Seaton. 2nd left to Southleigh, 1.5 miles. In village 1st left to Northleigh; 600 yds, drive on left.

Emma & Chuck Guest
Glebe House,
Southleigh, Colyton,
Devon EX24 6SD

Tel	01404 871276
Mobile	07867 568569
Email	emma_guest@talktalk.net
Web	www.guestsatglebe.com

Entry 131 Map 2

Devon

West Colwell Farm

Devon lanes, pheasants, bluebell walks *and* sparkling B&B. The Hayes clearly love what they do; ex-TV producers, they have converted this 18th-century farmhouse and barns into a cosy, warm and stylish place to stay. Be charmed by original beams and pine doors, heritage colours and clean lines. Bedrooms feel self-contained, two have terraces overlooking the wooded valley and the largest is tucked under the roof. Linen is luxurious, showers are huge and breakfasts (Frank's pancakes, lovely bacon, eggs from next door) are totally flexible. A pretty garden in front, beaches nearby, peace all around. Bliss.

Price	From £70. Singles £50.
Rooms	3 doubles.
Meals	Restaurants in Honiton.
Closed	Christmas.
Directions	3 miles from Honiton; Offwell signed off A35 Honiton–Axminster road. In centre of village, at church, down hill. Farm 0.5 miles on.

Frank & Carol Hayes
West Colwell Farm,
Offwell,
Honiton,
Devon EX14 9SL

Tel	01404 831130
Email	stay@westcolwell.co.uk
Web	www.westcolwell.co.uk

Entry 132 Map 2

Devon

The Devon Wine School

Alastair and Carol run their wine school from this delightfully rural spot – and look after you to perfection. Chill out in an open-plan sitting/dining room with wooden floors, smart chesterfields, Xian terracotta warriors, claret walls and rolling views. Bedrooms are light, unfussy and elegant, bathrooms are swish, food is taken seriously and sourced locally (an organic beef farmer lives next door). The atmosphere is relaxed and friendly; the wine, obviously, is a joy – and reasonably priced! There's a hard tennis court for working up an appetite and no light pollution; star-gazers will be happy.

Travel Club Offer: see page 392 for details.

Price	From £70. Singles £50.
Rooms	2: 1 twin/double, 1 double; 1 twin with shared bath (let to same party only).
Meals	Dinner, 3 courses, from £25. Occasional lunch. Pub 1 mile.
Closed	Rarely.
Directions	From Cadeleigh, 1.5 miles to Postbox Cross, turn left to Cheriton Fitzpaine. Follow road to Redyeates Cross x-roads, then right, house is 150 yds on left down track.

	Alastair & Carol Peebles
	The Devon Wine School, Redyeates Farm, Cheriton Fitzpaine, Crediton, Devon EX17 4HG
Tel	01363 866742
Email	alastair@devonwineschool.co.uk
Web	www.devonwineschool.co.uk

Entry 133 Map 2

Devon

West Bradley

Total immersion in beauty – doves in the farmyard, hens in the orchard, fields on either side of the long drive. Privacy, too, in your 18th-century upside-down barn on the side of the owners' Devon longhouse – and views. A handmade oak staircase, oak floors, two freshly furnished bedrooms (one up, one down), a gorgeous sitting room with plenty of comfy seats and a gas-fired wood-burner; even a little kitchen. Phillida can bring breakfast to you here, or you can tuck into full English in the farmhouse dining room. There will be homemade something on arrival and a good choice of local pubs.

Travel Club Offer: see page 392 for details.

Price	From £80. Singles £50.
Rooms	2: 1 twin/double; 1 twin with separate shower. Guest kitchen.
Meals	Pubs within 5 miles.
Closed	Rarely.
Directions	B3137 Tiverton-Witheridge; on towards Rackenford & Calverleigh. After pink thatched cottage (2 miles), fork left to Templeton; West Bradley 2 miles; on left before village hall.

	Martin & Phillida Strong
	West Bradley, Templeton, Tiverton, Devon EX16 8BJ
Tel	01884 253220
Mobile	07779 241048
Email	martinstrong@westbradley.eclipse.co.

Entry 134 Map 2

Devon

Raymont House

Delightful to be in the heart of a historic little town with a Tuesday market, good pubs and new bistro. No. 48 has been a shop, a pub, a tailor's, now it's a civilised B&B. Your charming hosts give you one bedroom (or, if you're a party, three), peaceful, pretty and serene, and a wow of a bathroom that mixes period features with beautiful modern fittings. No guest sitting room but TVs, homemade biscuits, delicious breakfasts, dressing gowns and fresh flowers... The breakfast room is warmed by a wood-burner, there's a drying room for wet gear, you're on the Tarka Trail and near to RHS Rosemoor. Great value.

Price	From £65. Singles £45.
Rooms	3: 2 doubles, 1 single all sharing bathroom (for one party only).
Meals	Pub/restaurant 50 yds.
Closed	Christmas to New Year.
Directions	From Okehampton, signs to Hatherleigh for 6 miles. At roundabout, right thro' Hatherleigh to top of Market St. House on left.

Jan & Alan Toogood
Raymont House,
49 Market Street, Hatherleigh,
Okehampton, Devon EX20 3JP
Tel   01837 810850
Email   alan.toogood@yahoo.co.uk
Web   www.raymonthouse.co.uk

Entry 135   Map 2

Devon

Leworthy Barton

Biscuits, scones, fresh flowers on arrival. Breakfasts are courtesy of their own Tamworth pigs with homemade bread, jams and marmalade; wellies and waxed jackets on tap. Rupert and Kim are busy farmers and artist/designers who choose to give guests what they would most like themselves. So... you have the whole of the stables, tranquil, beautifully restored and with field and sky views. Downstairs is open-plan plus kitchen; upstairs, sloping ceilings, warm wood floors, big bed, soft towels. It's cosy yet spacious, stylish yet homely, and the Atlantic coast is the shortest drive.

Ethical Collection: Food. See page 400 for details.

Price	£80. Singles £60.
Rooms	Barn for 2: 1 double, sitting room & kitchen.
Meals	Pub 3 miles.
Closed	Never.
Directions	A39 to Woolfardisworthy. At T-junc. in village, left. 0.5 miles left to Stibb X. Over bridge bear right, then left. Uphill, right towards Leworthy & Mill; 0.5 miles; on left.

Rupert & Kim Ashmore
Leworthy Barton,
Woolsery,
Bideford,
Devon EX39 5PY
Tel   01237 431140
Email   kim@westcountrylife.co.uk

Entry 136   Map 2

Devon

Beara Farmhouse

The moment you arrive at the whitewashed farmhouse you feel the affection your hosts have for the place. Richard is a lover of wood and a fine craftsman – every room echoes his talent; he also created the pond that's home to mallards and geese. Ann has laid brick paths, stencilled, stitched and painted, all with an eye for colour; bedrooms and guest sitting room are delectable and snug. Open farmland all around, sheep, pigs and hens in the yard, the Tarka Trail on your doorstep and hosts happy to give you 6.30am breakfast should you plan a day on Lundy Island. Readers love this place. *Minimum stay two nights June-Sept.*

Devon

Hillbrow House

You could be forgiven for thinking this 'house on the hill' is genuine Georgian – but it's mostly new, with a deep veranda and glorious views over the golf course (and, on a clear day, to distant Dartmoor). The light, uncluttered rooms are neat as a pin with coordinated colours, thick fabrics, antiques and your own upstairs studio sitting room; bedrooms have feather pillows, proper blankets and luxurious bathrooms. Golfers and walkers will be in paradise, surfers can reach Croyde easily and a plethora of gentler beaches lie in the other direction. Stoke up on delicious homemade granola for breakfast.

Travel Club Offer: see page 392 for details.

Price	£65. Singles by arrangement.
Rooms	2: 1 double, 1 twin.
Meals	Pub 1.5 miles.
Closed	20 December-5 January.
Directions	From A39, left into Bideford, round quay, past old bridge on left. Signs to Torrington; 1.5 miles, right for Buckland Brewer; 2.5 miles, left; 0.5 miles, right over cattle grid & down track.

Price	From £80. Singles £45.
Rooms	2: 1 double; 1 double with separate bath.
Meals	Dinner, 3 courses, £25. Pubs/restaurants within walking distance.
Closed	Christmas.
Directions	Take B3226 from South Molton for 5 miles. Right for Chittlehamholt, left at T-junc, then through village. House is last on right.

	Ann & Richard Dorsett
	Beara Farmhouse,
	Buckland Brewer,
	Bideford,
	Devon EX39 5EH
Tel	01237 451666
Web	www.bearafarmhouse.co.uk

	Clarissa Roe
	Hillbrow House,
	Chittlehamholt, Umberleigh,
	Devon EX37 9NS
Tel	01769 540214
Mobile	07774 784601
Email	clarissaroe@btinternet.com
Web	www.hillbrowhouse.com

Entry 137   Map 2

Entry 138   Map 2

Devon

Lower Hummacott

Bright clear colours, antique furniture, charming decorative touches. There are fresh fruit and flowers in the bedrooms (one with a king-size bed) and two guest sitting rooms. Delicious, organic and traditionally reared meat, veg and eggs, fresh fish, homemade cakes... As if that were not enough, the Georgian farmhouse has a stunning formal garden created from scratch – spring-fed pools, lime walk, pergola, arches, herbaceous beds and a new gazebo. Liz, a weaver, and Tony, an award-winning artist (he has a large gallery by the house) are charming and friendly and look after you beautifully.

Devon

Sannacott

On the southern fringes of Exmoor you're in huntin' and shootin' country. This is a stud farm – the Trickeys breed national hunt racehorses – and there's a riding stables close by. Downstairs is a happy mix of casual countryside living, antiques, open fires and family pictures. Bedrooms are traditional, clean and comfortable, all have lovely long views across rolling hills and trees, and you can come and go as you please. Clare bakes her own bread, most produce is organic or local and there's a pretty cottagey garden to wander through. Great for walkers, riders, birdwatchers and nature lovers.

Travel Club Offer: see page 392 for details.

Price	£68.
Rooms	2 doubles.
Meals	Dinner £27 (Sun & Mon only). Pub/restaurant 1.5 miles.
Closed	Rarely.
Directions	0.5 miles east of Kings Nympton village is Beara Cross; go straight over marked to Romansleigh for 0.75 miles; Hummacott is 1st entrance on left by iron wheel.

Price	£60-£70.
Rooms	3: 1 double; 1 twin/double sharing bath. Annexe: 1 twin with separate bath/shower.
Meals	Occasional dinner, 3 courses, £20. Pub 5 miles.
Closed	Rarely.
Directions	M5 J27; A361 for Barnstaple, past Tiverton, 15.5 miles; right at r'bout (small sign Whitechapel). 1.5 miles to junc., right for N. Molton; 1.5m to 3rd on left, black gates.

	Tony & Liz Williams
	Lower Hummacott,
	Kings Nympton,
	Umberleigh,
	Devon EX37 9TU
Tel	01769 581177
Fax	01769 581177

	Mrs Clare Trickey
	Sannacott,
	North Molton,
	Devon EX36 3JS
Tel	01598 740203
Fax	01598 740513
Email	mctrickey@hotmail.com
Web	www.sannacott.co.uk

Entry 139   Map 2

Entry 140   Map 2

Devon

Bratton Mill

Absolute privacy down the long track to a thickly wooded and beautifully secluded valley: watch for dragonflies, red deer, buzzards and the flash of the kingfisher. To the backdrop of a rushing stream is the house, painted traditional white and filled with treasure – including Marilyn who spoils you with elegant china, fresh flowers, warm bathrooms, crisp linen and a comforting decanter of port. Breakfast is locally sourced and superb; in summer, eat by the stream to almost deafening birdsong. There are simple strolls or robust hikes straight from the door. Wonderful. *Self-catering cottage & folly available.*

Devon

Hewish Barton

The second you arrive you're 'away from it all'. In the majestic Georgian house framed by green hills and a garden bouncing with birds, Maggi gives you delicious homemade cake for tea. You get a kitchen, too, and a lovely log-fired sitting room full of artefacts and books. Bedrooms have big sash windows, generous wardrobes and amazing views; baths encourage long soaks. Come for home comforts, home cooking, breakfasts by the Aga, woodland paths… and Woolacombe and Ilfracombe (the next Padstow?) down the road. Good value, great for couples *and* house parties, and the loveliest hosts.

Travel Club Offer: see page 392 for details.

Price	£75–£95. Singles from £45.
Rooms	2: 1 twin/double, 1 four-poster. Children's rooms available.
Meals	Dinner/supper available. Pub close walking distance.
Closed	Rarely.
Directions	From Bratton Fleming High Street turn into Mill Lane. Down road for 0.5 miles thro' railway cutting; turn right.

Price	From £70. Singles from £40.
Rooms	3 doubles. Guest kitchen.
Meals	Pub 2 miles.
Closed	Rarely.
Directions	A361 to Barnstaple. Follow A39 past hospital, left onto B3230 to Ilfracombe. Thro' Muddiford; 1 mile, quarry on left, right into drive.

	Marilyn Holloway
	Bratton Mill,
	Bratton Fleming,
	Barnstaple,
	Devon EX31 4RU
Tel	01598 710026
Email	contact@brattonmill.co.uk
Web	www.brattonmill.co.uk

	Maggi & Keith Wase
	Hewish Barton,
	Muddiford,
	Barnstaple,
	Devon EX31 4HH
Tel	01271 850245
Email	hewish_barton@mwase.freeserve.co.uk
Web	www.hewish-barton.co.uk

Entry 141   Map 2

Entry 142   Map 2

Devon

Beachborough Country House

A gracious 18th-century rectory with stone-flagged floors, lofty windows, wooden shutters, charming gardens. Viviane is vivacious and she spoils you with seemingly effortless food straight from the Aga, either in the kitchen or in the elegant dining room with twinkling fire. Chickens cluck, horses whinny but otherwise the peace is deep; this is perfect walking or cycling country. Ease any aches and pains in a steaming roll top; bathrooms are awash with fluffy towels, large bedrooms are fresh as a daisy with great views – admire them from the window seats. Combe Martin is a short hop for a grand beach day. *Dogs £5.*

Ethical Collection: Community; Food.
See page 400 for details.

Travel Club Offer: see page 392 for details.

Price	From £70. Singles £45.
Rooms	3: 1 twin/double, 2 doubles.
Meals	Dinner, 2-3 courses, from £16.
Closed	Rarely.
Directions	From A361 take A399 for 12 miles. At Blackmoor Gate, left onto A39. House 1.5 miles on right.

Viviane Clout
Beachborough Country House,
Kentisbury, Barnstaple,
Devon EX31 4NH
Tel   01271 882487
Mobile   07732 947755
Email   viviane@beachborough.freeserve.co.uk
Web   www.beachboroughcountryhouse.co.uk

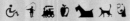

Entry 143   Map 2

Devon

Victoria House

Beachcombers, surfers and walkers will be in their element in this Edwardian seaside villa where all of the bedrooms have magnificent views. Choose between two in the main house with state-of-the-art bathrooms and one in the annexe with a beach-hut feel and a private deck. Heather is lively and fun, she and David are ex-RAF and clearly enjoy looking after you; breakfast is a main meal of nuts, fresh fruits, yogurts, eggs benedict, smoked salmon or The Full Monty. You are on the coastal road to Woolacombe for International Surf and Kite Surfing competitions; Lundy is always in view. Bucket and spade bliss.

Travel Club Offer: see page 392 for details.

Price	£90–£140.
Rooms	3 doubles.
Meals	Occasional dinner. Packed lunch £8. Pubs/restaurants 200 yds.
Closed	Rarely.
Directions	From B3343, right for Mortehoe. Through village & past the old chapel. Down steep hill, with the bay ahead; house 3rd on left.

Heather & David Burke
Victoria House,
Chapel Hill, Mortehoe, Woolacombe,
Devon EX34 7DZ
Tel   01271 871302
Fax   01271 871302
Email   heatherburke59@fsmail.net
Web   www.victoriahousebandb.co.uk

Entry 144   Map 2

Devon

Southcliffe Hall

An Argentinian chandelier, antique French radiators, a rediscovered Victorian garden; we love this gorgeous, grandly idiosyncratic house overlooking the sea. Eccentric owners have left their mark on what was originally the Manor House. Kate and Barry are young and enthusiastic. Vast bedrooms have rich carpets, big beds, antique flourishes. Bathrooms are fabulous one-offs – roll top baths to porcelain loos. Tea in the drawing room or the terraces, dinner in the panelled dining room; at breakfast, local produce. Spot deer in the woodland, walk to the beach, hike along the coast. Great fun.

Ethical Collection: Food. See page 400 for details.

Price	£100. Singles by arrangement.
Rooms	2 twins/doubles.
Meals	Dinner, 3 courses, £25. Pub 5-minute walk.
Closed	Rarely.
Directions	From A361, B3343 towards Woolacombe. Turn right, thro' Lincombe, into Lee. Long drive to house is on left, between village hall and Fuschia Tearoom.

Kate Seekings & Barry Jenkinson
Southcliffe Hall,
Lee,
Devon EX34 8LW
Tel	01271 867068
Mobile	07910 473725
Email	stay@southcliffehall.co.uk
Web	www.southcliffehall.co.uk

Entry 145   Map 2

Devon

Sea View Villa

The sea-captain's house gazes down from its wooded perch on beautiful Lynmouth below. There's a short, steep path up... then the pampering begins. Chris cooks, Steve does (sparkling) front of house. Bedrooms are warm and vibrant in black and silver, ochre and cream, and dinner is a full blown performance with theatrical touches: perfumed candles, soft music, maybe local lamb then "flambé Jamaican bananas". Rise early for a glorious Exmoor safari (spot the red deer) then ease away your aches and pains with an in-house holistic massage. The attention to detail here is fabulous.

Price	£90–£110. Singles £40.
Rooms	4: 2 doubles; 2 twins sharing bath.
Meals	Dinner, 5 courses, £30.
Closed	January–mid-February.
Directions	From M5 exit 23; A39 for Minehead; on to Porlock along coast to Lynmouth. Sea View Villa off Watersmeet Road, up path, directly opp. church.

Steve Williams & Chris Bissex
Sea View Villa,
6 Summerhouse Path, Lynmouth,
Devon EX35 6ES
Tel	01598 753460
Fax	01598 753496
Email	reservations@seaviewvilla.co.uk
Web	www.seaviewvilla.co.uk

Entry 146   Map 2

Dorset

Bowes House

A great place to blow the cobwebs away. The light, airy and spacious 1980s house with wide country views is at the end of a track, just where it peters out into a bridleway. With a gorgeous big garden and an orchard It's a great place for families... Lisa and Jeremy have two young sons, a dog, cats and a clutch of hens. No traffic – just the occasional passing horse – and walking from the door. Lisa is seriously eco-minded, so a wood has been planted to fuel the fires and the Rayburn; breakfast is local, homemade and organic. Super comfy bedrooms, too; the twin has Spanish bedheads.

Dorset

Crosskeys House

In previous lives a pub, a cobbler's shop and a smithy, this listed stone house, right on the village crossroads, is well settled into its B&B role. Robin and Liz offer you a fabulous breakfast menu and happily advise you on the glories of west Dorset (walks, pubs, stately homes): nothing is too much trouble. Their sitting room is softly traditional – plump sofas, family portraits and antiques, garden flowers, glossy magazines – while lovely cosy bedrooms have king-size beds and interesting books. The house is near the road but there's a courtyard garden for breakfast and water fresh from the well.

Travel Club Offer: see page 392 for details.

Price	From £60.
Rooms	3: 1 double; 1 twin/double, 1 single sharing bathroom (let to same party only).
Meals	Dinner, 2 courses, £15. Pub 2.5 miles.
Closed	Rarely.
Directions	A3066 from Beaminster to Mosterton. Having entered village from south, turn right immediately before Eeles Pottery into Bowes Lane. House is last on left.

Price	From £85. Singles from £60.
Rooms	2: 1 double, 1 twin/double.
Meals	Packed lunch from £6.50. Pub 200 yds.
Closed	Rarely.
Directions	A35 to Bridport then A3066 to Beaminster. B3163 to Broadwindsor. House is at end of one-way system, the last on the right (just before crossroads).

	Lisa & Jeremy Purkiss
	Bowes House,
	Bowes Lane, Mosterton,
	Beaminster, Dorset DT8 3HN
Tel	01308 868862
Mobile	07870 950666
Email	info@boweshousebandb.com
Web	www.boweshousebandb.com

	Robin & Liz Adeney
	Crosskeys House,
	High Street, Broadwindsor,
	Beaminster, Dorset DT8 3QP
Tel	01308 868063
Fax	01308 868063
Email	robin.adeney@care4free.net
Web	www.crosskeyshouse.com

Entry 147   Map 3

Entry 148   Map 3

Dorset

Orchard Barn

Immerse yourself in huge chalk cliffs, fabulous sea scapes and secret villages hiding in green folds. This is 'River Cottage' country and you will eat like kings – from the dazzling breakfast menu (try Jersey cream on your porridge) to delicious light suppers, all as local and organic as possible. Inside your own barn-like sitting room a fire burns brightly all day, bedrooms are nurturing and fresh, bathrooms awash with perfumed oils and fluffy towels. Nigel and Margaret are old hands at making everything very relaxing indeed. Sit on the terrace in summer and admire the lovely garden.

 Travel Club Offer: see page 392 for details.

Price	£115–£125. Singles from £75.
Rooms	2 twins/doubles.
Meals	Light supper £4.75–£15.50. Pubs/restaurants within 1 mile.
Closed	Rarely.
Directions	From A35 east of Bridport within 30mph limit, left into Lee Lane (with 6' 6" width restriction) & follow to bottom. Over bridge, round bend & into Dead End Lane. On right.

Nigel & Margaret Corbett
Orchard Barn,
Bradpole, Bridport,
Dorset DT6 4AR

Tel	01308 455655
Fax	01308 455655
Email	corbett@lodgeatorchardbarn.co.uk
Web	www.lodgeatorchardbarn.co.uk

Entry 149   Map 3

Dorset

Wooden Cabbage

Down a private driveway with stunning views across the unspoilt valley is a hamstone house with a misleading name ('stunted oak' in local parlance!). This is a spacious, stylish home: chintz and gorgeous bedspreads upstairs and a verdant garden room down, with a long oak table for breakfasts and a sofa for magical views. Or, in winter, breakfast by the Aga (the finest of local, Susie's own preserves). Pictures celebrate the country life, dogs Cracker and Rayburn work the shoots, Martyn and Susie look after guests – brilliantly; they used to run The Fox at Corscombe. *Children over 10 welcome.*

Travel Club Offer: see page 392 for details.

Price	From £85. Singles £50–£60.
Rooms	3: 1 double; 1 double, 1 twin sharing bath.
Meals	Dinner by arrangement. Pub/restaurant 3 miles.
Closed	Rarely.
Directions	3 miles S of Yeovil on A37, turn west to Closworth. Continue on this road, past turn to Halstock; 200 yds on right, over cattle grid. House 1st on left.

Martyn & Susie Lee
Wooden Cabbage,
East Chelborough,
Dorchester,
Dorset DT2 0QA

Tel	01935 83362
Email	relax@woodencabbage.co.uk
Web	www.woodencabbage.co.uk

Entry 150   Map 3

Dorset

Woodwalls House

Quiet seclusion among birds, badgers and wildflowers. The 1806 keeper's cottage sits in its own 12 acres where lovely walks lead in all directions. It is all thoroughly comforting and welcoming: heated towel rails and padded hangers, wonderful antiques and bits of china, lacy bedspreads, countryside views and a charming terrace for tea – nothing is too much trouble for Sally. Your kind, wildlife-loving hosts rustle up fine breakfasts of 'Beaminster bangers' and honey from their bees. There's great walking and you can try your hand at croquet or tennis. Perfect. *Minimum stay two nights.*

Price	£80. Singles from £50.
Rooms	2: 1 double; 1 twin with separate bath/shower.
Meals	Pub 500 yds.
Closed	December-February.
Directions	Leave Yeovil on A37 to Dorchester. After 1 mile, right for Corscombe; 6 miles to Corscombe; left after village sign down Norwood Lane; 300 yds, 1st white gate on right.

Sally & Tony Valdes-Scott
Woodwalls House,
Corscombe,
Dorchester,
Dorset DT2 0NT
Tel 01935 891477
Fax 01935 891477
Web www.woodwallshouse.co.uk

Entry 151   Map 3

Dorset

Higher Holway Farm

Heaven to walk here rather than drive. Hop over the cattle grid and amble down the quilted valley to find a listed, deliciously renovated farmhouse with a distinct 'designer-style' interior. Downstairs has chunky beams, soft colours, fresh flowers and a light, airy sitting room; ample bedrooms are deeply smart with the best linen, floaty goose down and restful views. Food is taken seriously; try a Beaminster banger for breakfast (on the elegant terrace in summer) or one of Sarah's Cordon Bleu dinners. The MacMillan Way is on the doorstep; for walkers who demand solace, this is perfect.

Travel Club Offer: see page 392 for details.

Price	£85. Singles £50.
Rooms	2: 1 twin, 1 twin/double.
Meals	Dinner with wine, £25. Pubs/restaurants 5-10 minute drive.
Closed	Christmas.
Directions	A37 Yeovil-Dorchester. Turn right to Evershot, left towards Cattistock. Left at x-roads to Cattistock. 1.5 miles; where telegraph poles finish on right, farm is on left.

Nigel & Sarah Hadden-Paton
Higher Holway Farm,
Cattistock,
Dorchester, Dorset DT2 0HH
Tel 01935 83822
Mobile 07767 494974
Email bumble@hadden-paton.com
Web www.higherholwayfarm.co.uk

Entry 152   Map 3

Dorset

Fullers Earth

Such an English feel: the village with pub, post office and stores, the walled garden with fruit trees beyond (source of perfect compotes and breakfast jams), the gentle church view. This listed house – its late-Georgian face added in 1820 – was where the Cattistock huntsmen lived; the unusual thatched stables alongside housed their steeds. Guests share a large and lovely sitting room in sand, cream and dove-blue; carpeted bedrooms have a lofty feel; the resplendent coastline – at times dramatic, at other times softly serene – is yours to discover, and Wendy and Ian will always plan your walks with you.

Price	£75-£85. Singles from £60.
Rooms	2 doubles.
Meals	Pub 500 yds.
Closed	Christmas.
Directions	From A37 take Cattistock turning downhill to T-junc. Left through village. Pub on left. After 90 degree right-hand bend, 5th house on right.

	Wendy Gregory
	Fullers Earth,
	Cattistock, Dorchester,
	Dorset DT2 0JL
Tel	01300 320190
Mobile	07968 325698
Email	stay@fullersearth.co.uk
Web	www.fullersearth.co.uk

✗ ⟡ ⌘

Entry 153   Map 3

Dorset

Gray's Farmhouse

Rosie greets you with tea and cake on arrival – in the lovely garden on warm days. Inside the former shooting lodge are huge flagstones, chunky pine doors and vibrant art on aqua walls; Rosie paints, Roger writes poetry. Light, bright bedrooms are peaceful and comfortable, dotted with pretty touches and fresh flowers. Breakfasts are worth getting up for – homemade breads, fruit compotes – as you plan a day exploring the valleys of Hardy country and the spectacular World Heritage coast. You are surrounded by bird-rich woods and flower-bedecked lanes; let Bertie the golden retriever be your guide. *Minimum stay two nights.*

📖 Travel Club Offer: see page 392 for details.

Price	£70-£95. Singles from £60.
Rooms	3: 1 double, 1 double/family; 1 twin/double across courtyard.
Meals	Pub 3 miles.
Closed	Rarely.
Directions	A356 from Dorchester, left at 1st sign for T. Porcorum. Through, & up hill 1 mile. Ignore right turn, cont. thro' village; on one mile, right signed Powerstock & Hooke. Under bridge, 0.3 miles, left at unmarked crossroads.

	Rosie & Roger Britton
	Gray's Farmhouse,
	Toller Porcorum,
	Dorchester,
	Dorset DT2 0EJ
Tel	01308 485574
Email	rosieroger@farmhousebnb.co.uk
Web	www.farmhousebnb.co.uk

♿ ✗ ⌘

Entry 154   Map 3

Dorset

Frampton House

A grand Grade II*-listed house in parkland landscaped by Capability Brown... and two labradors, Potter and Dumble, to greet you as you scrunch up the gravel. Beyond the Georgian façade lies a delicious mix of English and Gallic styles. Bedrooms combine comfort with outstanding views, a magnificent four-poster in one, everywhere fine linen and plump pillows. Georgina is a portrait painter and a food and arts writer. Breakfasts, served in the conservatory, are true-blue English, with spectacular bangers. Log fires in the drawing room in winter, tea on the terrace in summer, dinners accompanied by French wines.

Price	£90.
Rooms	3: 2 twins/doubles, 1 four-poster.
Meals	Dinner, 3 courses with wine, £25. Pub 2 miles.
Closed	Rarely.
Directions	A37 Dorchester-Yeovil; A356 for Crewkerne & Maiden Newton. In Frampton, left at green; over white bridge; left, opp. Frampton Roses. 'Private' track to house, signed 3rd on left.

Georgina & Nicholas Maynard
Frampton House,
Frampton, Dorchester,
Dorset DT2 9NH

Tel	01300 320308
Mobile	07785 391710
Email	maynardryder@btconnect.com
Web	www.frampton-house.co.uk

Entry 155   Map 3

Dorset

Holyleas House

Breakfast by a log fire in the elegant dining room in winter – a feast of free-range eggs, homemade jams and marmalades. All the rooms are stylish and well decorated, with lovely prints, many lamps and stunning views; bedrooms are full of light. After a day out or a good walk, hunker down by the fire in the drawing room with a good book. This is a fabulous house, comfortable and easy. Its walled half-acre garden with herbaceous borders is Tia's passion. She is genuinely welcoming – as are her two friendly dogs – and is happy to babysit. *Minimum stay two nights in high season & at weekends.*

Price	£75-£80. Singles £40.
Rooms	3: 1 double, 1 twin/double; 1 single with separate bath.
Meals	Supper tray £8 on first night. Pub a short walk.
Closed	Christmas & New Year.
Directions	From Dorchester, B3143 into Buckland Newton over x-roads; Holyleas on right opp. village cricket pitch.

Tia Bunkall
Holyleas House,
Buckland Newton, Dorchester,
Dorset DT2 7DP

Tel	01300 345214
Mobile	07968 341887
Email	tiabunkall@holyleas.fsnet.co.uk
Web	www.holyleashouse.co.uk

Entry 156   Map 3

Dorset

Chapel House

There's a mildly eccentric, Scottish hunting-lodge feel here, with battered leather sofas, bulging book shelves, a huge log fire, stuffed birds, outdoor dogs, polo sticks, ancient sabres and riding boots. Walls are covered with good art and sketches – some made by Malcolm as he roamed the countryside on horseback. Bedrooms are mostly large and old-fashioned, bathrooms small but modern and sleek with Porcelenosa tiles on the walls. No TV anywhere, shoes off before you go upstairs, and a generous, mostly organic breakfast served in the warm kitchen. An escape from blandness! *Children over five welcome.*

Price	£70. Singles £35.
Rooms	3 doubles.
Meals	Pub/restaurant 3.5 miles.
Closed	Christmas-New Year.
Directions	B3143 thro' Piddlehinton, Piddletrenthide & Alton Pancras. After 1.5 miles, red phone box & sign to Henley on left; 150 yds up this road, left at crossroads. House 50 yds on right.

Malcolm Scholes
Chapel House,
Henley, Dorchester,
Dorset DT2 7BN

Tel	01300 345822
Mobile	07814 705225
Email	enquiries@malcolmscholes.com
Web	wwwchapelhousebandb.com

Entry 157   Map 3

Dorset

The White Cottage

Strolling distance from magnificent Athelhampton House and its stunning gardens is this thatched cottage which Lindsay and Mark, escapees from London, have been renovating madly. It's a bright and sunny house with gorgeous bedrooms, super linen, fresh flowers, plump pillows, chocolates; generous bathrooms have thick white towels and lovely bottles of lotions. The suite has its own entrance, large sitting room, comfortable sofas and soft pink and cream bedroom. The river Piddle runs through the garden – fish for brown trout but put them back! You will be well fed – Lindsay's passion is cooking.

Travel Club Offer: see page 392 for details.

Price	£70-£120.
Rooms	3: 1 double, 1 suite for 2-4 (with sofabed); 1 twin with separate bath.
Meals	Dinner £16-£18. Pub 1 mile.
Closed	Open all year.
Directions	A35 exit Puddletown & Athelhampton; signs for Athelhampton House. Left at lights in Puddletown; house 200 yds on right, after Athelhampton House.

Lindsay & Mark Piper
The White Cottage,
Athelhampton, Dorchester,
Dorset DT2 7LG

Tel	01305 848622
Mobile	07778 987906
Email	markjamespiper@aol.com
Web	www.white-cottage-bandb.co.uk

Entry 158   Map 3

Dorset

The Old Manor

Few B&Bs are as stately as this – Pevsner described the magnificent manor as being "refined to a point of perfection". Gaze over the lake through mullioned windows, sleep in a hand-carved four-poster, warm yourself in front of a Jacobean fireplace. There are beautiful rugs on stone and wooden floors, lavish period fabrics and a spiral staircase made from just one oak tree. This is the perfect place to return to after a hearty walk straight from the door in rolling Hardy countryside and Andrew and Mulu pamper you; Mulu can even give you a beauty treatment in the salon. *Children by arrangement.*

Price	£104-£124. Singles £67-£77.
Rooms	3: 1 double, 1 twin, 1 four-poster.
Meals	Restaurant within walking distance.
Closed	Mid-December to mid-January.
Directions	At r'bout on A35, 1 mile NE of Dorchester, follow sign to Kingston Maurward gardens & animal park. In grounds, follow estate road, keep straight ahead past Kingston Maurward House, following signs to The Old Manor.

Andrew & Mulu Thomson
The Old Manor,
Kingston Maurward, Dorchester,
Dorset DT2 8PX

Tel	01305 261110
Mobile	07799 097219
Email	thomson@kingston-maurward.co.uk
Web	www.kingston-maurward.co.uk

Entry 159   Map 3

Dorset

Higher Came Farmhouse

A listed, handsome farmhouse dating from 1640, with honeysuckle and clematis clambering over the local stone front. Inside, winding corridors, sloping floors, the odd wonky wall and a large, comfortable sitting room with French windows to the informal garden. Bedrooms are a good size, particularly the cream triple, which has its own dressing room and good views. All are comfortable with good mattresses, thick bathrobes and a melée of patterns on walls and bed covers. Lisa and Tim, B&B pros, are terrific with guests and deliver great breakfasts. It's secluded and quiet here but Weymouth Bay is a short drive.

Price	£70-£80. Singles £40-£45.
Rooms	3: 1 triple; 1 twin/double, 1 triple, each with separate bath.
Meals	Packed lunch £4.50. Pub/restaurant 2.5 miles.
Closed	Rarely.
Directions	From Dorchester bypass A354 to Weymouth. 1st left to Winterbourne Herringston; at T-junc. right, on for 1 mile; look out for golf course, next left to house.

Lisa Bowden
Higher Came Farmhouse,
Higher Came, Dorchester,
Dorset DT2 8NR

Tel	01305 268908
Mobile	07970 498773
Email	enquiries@highercame.co.uk
Web	www.highercame.co.uk

Entry 160   Map 3

Dorset

Marren

On the Dorset coastal path, with spectacular views of Portland, a blissfully tranquil and bird-rich spot. Designers Peter and Wendy have transformed their 1920s house and the interiors sing with good taste; antique pine floors softened with kilims, colours contemporary. From six acres of terraced and wooded garden, step into your airy room, perfect with its own entrance, deep-mattressed bed, crisp sheets and luxurious bathroom. Breakfasts of farm produce and homemade bread will set you up for clifftop hikes – leave the low-slung Morgan at home: the track here is adventurously steep!

Price	£90.
Rooms	2 doubles.
Meals	Pub 1 mile.
Closed	Rarely.
Directions	On A353 after Poxwell, left at Ringstead sign; up hill (not to Ringstead), over cattle grid into NT car park; cross & drive through gate 'No Cars'; 2 more gates; 100 yds after 3rd gate, sharp right down steep track.

	Peter Cartwright
	Marren,
	Holworth, Dorchester,
	Dorset DT2 8NJ
Tel	01305 851503
Mobile	07957 886399
Email	marren@lineone.net
Web	www.marren.info

🛉 ⚒ 📶 🐾

Entry 161   Map 3

Dorset

Glenthorne

There are wide boat-spotted sea views all the way to Portland and Chesil, a secret informal garden where you may trip over a fossil or two, a heated pool, and a path to a secret sandy beach. A Victorian former rectory with turn-of-the-century tiles and staircase, vibrant colours, stuffed foxes, elephant tusks and ornate mahogany; character, too, in the drawing room with log fire and the roomy bedrooms Bring your boat or use your hosts' – they both paint and their work hangs on the walls here. Weymouth is bustling with restaurants, shops, kite and jazz festivals and has the best sunshine record on the south coast.

💼 Travel Club Offer: see page 392 for details.

Price	£70-£120. Singles from £40.
Rooms	3: 1 twin, 1 family; 1 family with separate bath/shower.
Meals	Pub 500 yds. Restaurants 10-min walk.
Closed	Rarely.
Directions	A354 Weymouth to Portland, 0.5 miles to top of hill. As road bears right, turn left into Old Castle Road. Follow signs to house.

	Mrs Olivia Nurrish
	Glenthorne,
	15 Old Castle Road, Weymouth,
	Dorset DT4 8QB
Tel	01305 777281
Mobile	07831 751526
Email	info@glenthorne-holidays.co.uk
Web	www.glenthorne-holidays.co.uk

🛉 ⚒ 📖 🚂 📶 🐕 🐾

Entry 162   Map 3

Dorset

Lower Lynch House

On the glorious Isle of Purbeck, between the old stone village of Corfe Castle and Kingston atop a hill, this wisteria-strewn house sits at the end of a long woodland track. Aga-cooked breakfast is served at tables overlooking courtyard and garden; cosy, old-fashioned bedrooms with pale colours and florals are as peaceful as can be. No sitting room, but a small sofa in the double. You are a five-minute drive from the coastal path: a great spot for walkers and peace-seekers. Warm, clean, comfortable B&B – and if you spot wild deer munching on the roses, tell Bron. *Minimum stay two nights.*

Price	From £70. Singles by arrangement.
Rooms	2: 1 twin;
	1 double with separate bath.
Meals	Inn 0.75 miles.
Closed	Christmas & New Year.
Directions	A351 from Wareham to Corfe Castle. At end of village fork right on B3069 for Kingston. Left 0.5 miles down track (sign on roadside).

Bron & Nick Burt
Lower Lynch House,
Kingston Hill,
Corfe Castle,
Dorset BH20 5LG
Tel   01929 480089
Email   bronburt@tiscali.co.uk

✕ ⛷

Entry 163   Map 3

Dorset

Gold Court House

Anthea and Michael have created a mood of restrained luxury and uncluttered, often beautiful, good taste in their Georgian townhouse. Bedrooms are restful in cream with mahogany furniture, sloping ceilings, beams, armchairs and radios. There's a large drawing room and good paintings. Your hosts are delightful – "they do everything to perfection," says a reader; both house and garden are a refuge. Views are soft and lush yet you are in the small square of this attractive town; the house was rebuilt in 1762 after a great fire, and the Hipwells added their creative spin seven years ago. *Children over ten welcome.*

Price	£70–£75. Singles £45.
Rooms	3: 1 twin/double; 2 twins/doubles, each with separate bath.
Meals	Dinner £17.50, available in winter. Restaurants 50 yds.
Closed	Rarely.
Directions	From A35, A351 to Wareham. Follow signs to town centre. In North St, over lights into South St. 1st left into St John's Hill; house on far right-hand corner of square.

Anthea & Michael Hipwell
Gold Court House,
St John's Hill, Wareham,
Dorset BH20 4LZ
Tel   01929 553320
Fax   01929 553320
Email   info@goldcourthouse.co.uk
Web   www.goldcourthouse.co.uk

✕ 🚂 ⛷

Entry 164   Map 3

Dorset

North Mill

It's the setting that does it. The river Piddle rushes past this pretty 16th-century listed mill house on the edge of the Saxon town of Wareham. The guest bedrooms (large double, smaller twin) overlook garden, river and water meadows, the guests' sitting/dining room has a wood-burner for chilly evenings and the house is furnished with lovely paintings and antiques. Breakfast includes fresh eggs from Sally's hens and homemade bread, marmalade and jams. Dorchester is close by and the World Heritage coastline and the beaches and hills of Purbeck beckon.

Ethical Collection: Environment.
See page 400 for details.

Price	From £80. Singles £45.
Rooms	2: 1 double; 1 twin with separate bath/shower.
Meals	Dinner, 3 courses with wine, £20. Pubs/restaurants 5-minute walk.
Closed	Rarely.
Directions	On entering Wareham, right up Shatters Hill just after garage. Right down footpath opp. Mill Lane.

	Sally Dubuis
	North Mill,
	Wareham,
	Dorset BH20 4QW
Tel	01929 555142
Mobile	07976 273385
Email	sally.dubuis@googlemail.com
Web	www.northmill.org.uk

Entry 165   Map 3

Dorset

Bering House

Fabulous in every way. Renate's attention to detail reveals a love of running B&B: the fluffy dressing gowns and bathroom treats, the biscuits, fruit and sherry. She and John are welcoming, enthusiastic, delightful — perfectly happy for you to potter around all day. Expect pretty little sofas, golden bath taps, a gleaming breakfast table, a big sumptuous suite that overlooks the sparkling harbour. Breakfasts are served on blue and white Spode china, among the birds and the breezes on summery days. Fresh fruit, Parma ham, smoked salmon, kedgeree: the choice is superb. An immaculate harbourside retreat.

Price	£70-£85. Singles by arrangement.
Rooms	2: 1 twin/double; 1 suite (twin/double) & kitchenette.
Meals	Pub 400 yds.
Closed	Rarely.
Directions	From A35 & A350 at Upton, take Blandford road B3068 south for Hamworthy & Rockley Park. 1.5 miles on at Red Lion pub on left, turn right into Lake Rd; under bridge past Yachtsman pub; 2nd left down Branksea Ave. House last on left.

	Renate & John Wadham
	Bering House,
	53 Branksea Avenue,
	Poole,
	Dorset BH15 4DP
Tel	01202 673419
Fax	01202 673419
Email	johnandrenate1@tiscali.co.uk

Entry 166   Map 3

Dorset

Honeycombe Cottage

As dreamy as its name, the 16th-century cottage in the village, with deep walls, open fireplaces and flagged floors houses two dogs, one cat and gentle, generous Heather. Now her children have flown the nest, she gives you a garden that blooms as wonderfully as the house and, up under the eaves, soft curtains, soothing colours, aromatic oils and a delicious bed. Have breakfast (pancakes with maple syrup, bacon from up the road) in the homely kitchen, or outside on fine days, where lawns and borders drift effortlessly into orchard, fields and hills. An all-year-round delight. *Children over five welcome.*

Price	From £70.
Rooms	2 twins/doubles.
Meals	Pubs/restaurant 5-minute walk.
Closed	Rarely.
Directions	From A31 to Bere Regis on West Street. At end of village, left down 'No Through Road', over bridge. Thatched wall on left, cottage at end.

Heather Loxton
Honeycombe Cottage,
Shitterton, Bere Regis,
Dorset BH20 7HU
Tel   01929 471660
Mobile   07746 497171
Email   heather.loxton@virgin.net
Web   www.honeycombecottage.com

Entry 167   Map 3

Dorset

Thornhill

Here is a pretty Thirties' thatched house, with peaceful views from every window... of fields, woods and two landscaped acres. Sara and John encourage the wildlife on their patch; you may spot a deer on the lawn. Inside are patterned fabrics and old-fashioned candlewick covers, pastel walls and polished antiques. All is neat, tidy, spacious and spotless, and Sara pays attention to detail: a toothbrush for the forgetful, fruit and chocolates in the rooms, a choice of teas. Walkers can stride out straight from the door, gardeners will be happy here – and bridge players, if they come on a Thursday!

Price	From £60. Singles from £30.
Rooms	3: 1 double, 1 twin, 1 single, all sharing 2 baths. Possible use of separate bath.
Meals	Pub/restaurant 400 yds.
Closed	Rarely.
Directions	From Wimborne B3078 towards Cranborne. Right to Holt. After 2 miles Thornhill on right, 200 yds beyond Old Inn.

John & Sara Turnbull
Thornhill,
Holt,
Wimborne,
Dorset BH21 7DJ
Tel   01202 889434
Email scturnbull@lineone.net

Entry 168   Map 3

Dorset

Crawford House

Below, the river Stour winds through the valley and under the medieval, nine-arched bridge. Above, an Iron Age hill fort; between is Crawford House. It's an elegant Georgian house in an acre of walled garden, soft and pretty inside with an easy, relaxed atmosphere. Carpeted bedrooms are homely and warm, with long curtains; one room has four-poster twin beds with chintz drapes. The sun streams through the floor-to-ceiling windows of the downstairs rooms, and charming 18th- and 19th-century oil paintings hang in the dining room. Visit the Isle of Purbeck coastline – a World Heritage Site.

Dorset

Stickland Farmhouse

Charming Dorset... and a soft, delightful thatched cottage in an enviably rural setting. Sandy and Paul have poured love into this listed farmhouse and garden, the latter bursting with lupins, poppies, foxgloves, clematis, delphiniums. Sandy gives you delicious breakfasts with homemade soda bread from the Aga. Cottagey bedrooms have crisp white dressing gowns and lots of books and pictures – one room opens onto your own seating area in the garden. You are in a village with a good pub, and Cranbourne Chase, rich in barrows and hill forts, is close by. *Children over ten welcome. Min. stay two nights summer weekends.*

Travel Club Offer: see page 392 for details.

Price	From £60. Singles £30.
Rooms	3: 1 twin/double;
	1 twin with separate bath;
	1 twin with separate shower.
Meals	Pub in village 0.5 miles.
Closed	Mid-October-mid-April.
Directions	A350 north; after entering Spetisbury, 1st gateway immed. on left after crossroads (B3075).

Price	£65-£70. Singles £45.
Rooms	3: 2 doubles, 1 twin.
Meals	Pub 3-minute walk.
Closed	Never.
Directions	Leave Blandford for SW, cross river Stour. Hard right after Bryanston school for W. Stickland (4.5 miles). Down North St, right signed W. Houghton. House 150 yds on left with 5-bar gate.

Andrea Lea
Crawford House,
Spetisbury,
Blandford Forum,
Dorset DT11 9DP

Tel	01258 857338
Fax	01258 858152
Email	andrea@lea8.wanadoo.co.uk

Sandy & Paul Crofton-Atkins
Stickland Farmhouse,
Winterborne Stickland,
Blandford Forum,
Dorset DT11 0NT

Tel	01258 880119
Mobile	07932 897774
Email	sandysticklandfarm@tiscali.co.uk

Dorset

Dorset

Manor Barn

What was once an L-shaped cow shed is now a rather smart self-contained barn – attached to the main house and with views to an Iron Age hill. Relax in a roomy and beamed sitting room with squashy sofas, white walls, a wood-burning stove; down a corridor are two restful bedrooms with delightful linen and huge fluffy pillows. It is all very rustic-contemporary. A huge breakfast is brought to you, and kind Carolyn will cook a delicious, locally sourced supper if you want a night in with a DVD. Perfect for friends or families and you have complete independence. *Children over eight welcome.*

The Old Rectory

Walk all day on Cranborne Chase, return for tea at The Old Rectory, then stroll off for a meal at the much-fêted pub down the road... What could be nicer? Vicky's brick-and-flint Victorian house is in the middle of the village, yet feels wonderfully peaceful in its ten-acre grounds. Bedrooms are simple, comfortable and restful; bathrooms clean and functional. The drawing and dining rooms have the warm, gracious air of a much-loved and lived-in home, family portraits hang on the walls, the furniture is polished, the spaniel is friendly and big windows overlook sweeping lawns and summer terrace.

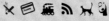 Travel Club Offer: see page 392 for details.

Price	£90. Singles £60.
Rooms	2 twins/doubles.
Meals	Dinner £20-£30.
	Light supper £10-£15.
	Pub in village & more within 3 miles.
Closed	Rarely.
Directions	South on A350 from Shaftesbury; right at sign 'Child Okeford 3 miles'. Just before village, drive is on left, opposite 30 ft high hedge.

Price	£80.
Rooms	2: 1 double, 1 twin.
Meals	Pub within walking distance.
Closed	Christmas.
Directions	16 miles south west of Salisbury on A354 Blandford Forum road. Farnham is signed off main road; house is in Farnham opposite Museum pub.

	Carolyn Sorby
	Manor Barn,
	Upper Street, Child Okeford,
	Blandford Forum, Dorset DT11 8EF
Tel	01258 860638
Mobile	07973 595344
Email	carisorby@btinternet.com
Web	www.manorbarnbedandbreakfast.co.uk

	Vicky Forbes
	The Old Rectory,
	Farnham,
	Blandford Forum,
	Dorset DT11 8DE
Tel	01725 516474
Email	forbescopper@compuserve.com

Entry 171   Map 3

Entry 172   Map 3

Dorset

The Old Forge, Fanners Yard

Tim and Lucy are tangibly happy in this beautifully restored forge. It was built in the 1700s; the wheelwright and carriage-builder from the local estate used to work here. Tim has beautifully restored the cosy gypsy caravan which has super views and a picnic table outside. The attic bedrooms are snug, with Lucy's quilts, country antiques and sparkling bathrooms. Delicious Aga-cooked breakfasts include eggs from their own free-strutting hens, organic sausages and bacon, home-grown jams, apple juice straight from the orchard. The Downs beckon walkers; warm corners invite readers. Utterly genuine.

Price	From £70.
Rooms	3: 1 double, 1 family; 1 double in gypsy caravan with separate shower & wc (20 yds).
Meals	Pub/restaurant 1 mile.
Closed	Rarely.
Directions	From Shaftesbury, A350 to Compton Abbas. House 1st on left before Compton Abbas sign. Left; entrance on left.

Tim & Lucy Kerridge
The Old Forge, Fanners Yard,
Compton Abbas, Shaftesbury,
Dorset SP7 0NQ
Tel 01747 811881
Fax 01747 811881
Email theoldforge@hotmail.com
Web www.theoldforgedorset.co.uk

Entry 173   Map 3

Dorset

Golden Hill Cottage

Deep in the countryside lies Stourton Caundle and this charming thatched cottage. The sitting room, traditionally furnished with antiques, paintings and coal fire, is all yours if you stay, along with a carpeted twin room and small shower up a private stair. Anna, courteous and kind, brings you splendid platefuls of local bacon and sausage, homemade jams and Dorset honey for breakfast; nothing is too much trouble for these owners. There are glorious walks from the village, a good pub that serves real ales, and Sherborne, Montacute and Stourhead for landscape, culture and history. *Babes in arms welcome.*

Price	£60-£70. Singles from £30.
Rooms	1 twin & sitting room.
Meals	Pubs/restaurants within 3 miles.
Closed	Rarely.
Directions	From Sherborne, A352 to Dorchester; after 1 mile, left onto A3030; on to far end of Bishops Caundle, left to Stourton Caundle; after sharp left into village street, house 200 yds on right.

Anna & Andrew Oliver
Golden Hill Cottage,
Stourton Caundle,
Sturminster Newton,
Dorset DT10 2JW
Tel 01963 362109
Email anna@goldenhillcottage.co.uk
Web www.goldenhillcottage.co.uk

Entry 174   Map 3

Dorset

Holt Cottage

The house stands on high ground and the views are amazing – enough to seduce Richard and Annabel from the west country. She is a whizz in the kitchen, he loves classic cars, both give you a big welcome and two super bedrooms in the annexe a step away. One is upstairs, with a sitting space and views, the other, perfect for children, is down. Both are fresh, light and inviting, with elegant prints on the walls, white towels on the rails, fabulous mattresses. You may use the lovely main sitting room too, with books and wood-burner. In the garden: dogs romp, hens hatch, and orchard and pergola are on their way.

Price	From £70. Singles from £50.
Rooms	Annexe: 1 double & sitting room; 1 twin/double with separate bath.
Meals	Packed lunch from £5. Dinner, 3 courses, £22.50. Pub/restaurant 1 mile.
Closed	Christmas & occasionally.
Directions	From Sherborne, A352 south. After 1 mile, left onto A3030 Blandford road. In Bishops Caundle, left at Murco garage. House 1 mile on left.

Richard & Annabel Buxton
Holt Cottage,
Alweston,
Sherborne,
Dorset DT9 5JF
Tel   01963 23014
Mobile   07766 583344
Email   annabelbuxton@hotmail.com

Entry 175   Map 3

Dorset

Windrush Farm

Fun to breakfast in the farmhouse kitchen with its polished oak table and rag-rolled dresser full of colourful plates. Upstairs, too, is delightful – creaky carpeted floors, sloping ceilings, a maze of corridors and cubby holes. Well-furnished bedrooms are in soft yellows and blues, pinks and creams; paintings, prints and books catch your eye. On colder evenings, your charming hosts will light a fire for you in the sitting room, traditional and snug, while for summer there's a scented, rambler-strewn garden and a terrace with the loveliest views. Bustling Sherborne is a ten-minute drive.

Price	From £75. Singles from £45.
Rooms	2: 1 double with separate bath; 1 twin sharing bath (2nd room let to same party only).
Meals	Dinner £20. Pub/restaurant 2 miles.
Closed	Christmas.
Directions	A357 Wincanton-Templecombe; 2nd turn Stowell, on right opp. entrance to Horsington House. Down hill past church for 0.5 miles; house on left.

Richard & Jenny Gold
Windrush Farm,
Stowell,
Sherborne,
Dorset DT9 4PD
Tel   01963 370799
Email   jennygold@hotmail.co.uk

Entry 176   Map 3

Durham

The Coach House

There's so much to gladden your heart – the cobbled courtyard that evokes memories of its days as a coaching inn, the river running through the estate, the drawing room's log fire, the delicious breakfasts, the blackberry crumbles with cream… and Peter and Mary, your kind, unstuffy, dog-adoring hosts (they have three well-behaved ones). Every creature comfort has been attended to in this small, perfect, English country house: lined chintz, starched linen, cushioned window seats, cut flowers, heated towel rails. Friendly, delightful, and the perfect stepping stone to Scotland or the south.

Price	£80. Singles £50.
Rooms	2: 1 twin/double; 1 twin/double with separate bath.
Meals	Dinner, 3 courses, £25. Pub/restaurants within 3 miles.
Closed	Rarely.
Directions	A1(M) to Scotch Corner. A66 west for 8 miles until Greta Bridge turn-off. House on left just before bridge.

Peter & Mary Gilbertson
The Coach House,
Greta Bridge,
Barnard Castle,
Durham DL12 9SD
Tel   01833 627201
Email   info@coachhousegreta.co.uk
Web   www.coachhousegreta.co.uk

Entry 177   Map 12

Durham

34 The Bank

In this impressive Georgian townhouse live Eva, Ian, Otto the wire-haired Hungarian vizsla and Georgina. Georgina is the resident ghost whose manners are unfailingly polite; Eva and Ian merely run the place. Ian cooks the breakfasts and Eva arranges them artistically because that's her thing. They love their guests and provide beautiful rooms – white quilts, bold walls, easy chairs – and much comfort in the sitting room with open fire. Sally forth to see the rest of bonny Barney on the Tees: the castle, the antique shops and the restaurant next door where Cromwell really stayed. Marvellous.

Price	From £55. Singles from £40.
Rooms	3: 1 double, 1 twin, 1 four-poster.
Meals	Pubs/restaurants 50 yds.
Closed	Rarely.
Directions	At A1 Scotch Corner, A66 west for 14 miles. Then 1st dual carriageway; right for Barnard Castle. At lights right over bridge, left at T-junc. to Butter Market. Left down bank, house on left.

Ian & Eva Reid
34 The Bank,
Barnard Castle,
Durham DL12 8PN
Tel   01833 631304
Email   evasreid@aol.com
Web   www.number34.com

Entry 178   Map 12

Essex

Brook Farm

Large low Georgian windows fill the house with light, unpretentious family pieces warm the bedrooms and the stunning carved crossbeam in the largest is late-medieval. Anne, country lover and B&B-er, has farmed here for over 30 years; outbuildings dot the yard, sheep and horses roam the acres. In Anne's sitting room logs fill the copper and hunting prints line the walls – no TV, but magazines and books aplenty – and you breakfast (deliciously) at a long table with fine antique benches. The handsome bright farmhouse oozes history and a faded country charm – yet is 30 minutes from Stansted.

Price	£70–£80. Singles £35–£45.
Rooms	3: 1 twin; 1 double, 1 family room, both with separate bath.
Meals	Packed lunch £3–£5. Pubs within 2 miles.
Closed	Rarely.
Directions	House on B1053, 500 yds south of Wethersfield.

Mrs Anne Butler
Brook Farm,
Wethersfield, Braintree,
Essex CM7 4BX

Tel	01371 850284
Mobile	07770 881966
Fax	01371 850284
Email	abutlerbrookfarm@aol.com

Entry 179 Map 9

Essex

Caterpillar Cottage

Traditional brick and clapboard, dormer windows, tall chimneys – this looks like the real thing. But the 'converted farm building' in the grounds of Patricia's former grand house is brand new! Filled with fine furniture, family photographs and *objets* from far-flung travels, it invites relaxation. The double-height, vaulted sitting room brims with sofas and books, logs crackle on chilly nights and bedrooms are simple and comfortable with decent-sized bathrooms. Patricia, a lively grandmother, adores children while her big garden promises home-grown fruit and tranquillity.

Travel Club Offer: see page 392 for details.

Price	From £65. Singles from £35.
Rooms	2: 1 triple; 1 double with separate bath/shower.
Meals	Packed lunch available. Pubs 50 yds.
Closed	Rarely.
Directions	A12 to A1124. In Fordstreet, cottage through gateway shared with Old House, opposite Old Queens Head pub.

Patricia Mitchell
Caterpillar Cottage,
Fordstreet,
Aldham,
Colchester,
Essex CO6 3PH

Tel	01206 240456
Fax	01206 240456

Entry 180 Map 10

Essex

Bromans Farm

The island of Mersea is surprisingly secluded, and Bromans Farm is in the most tranquil corner; the sea murmurs across the Saltings where the Brent geese wheel and the great Constable skies stretch. The house began in 1343 – nearly as old as the exquisite church. The Georgians added their bit, but the venerable beams and uneven old construction shine through. It is a sunny, comfortable house, with good bedrooms and warm bathrooms, a snug book-filled sitting room, a beautiful Welsh oak dresser in the breakfast room, and a conservatory gazing over the large garden. Wild walks beckon.

Price	£70–£80. Singles £40.
Rooms	2: 1 double, 1 twin, each with separate bath.
Meals	Pub 0.5 miles.
Closed	Rarely.
Directions	From Colchester B1025, over causeway, bear left. After 3 miles, pass Dog & Pheasant pub; 3rd right into Bromans Lane. 1st on left.

Mrs Ruth Dence
Bromans Farm,
East Mersea,
Essex CO5 8UE
Tel   01206 383235
Fax   01206 383235
Email   ruth.dence@homecall.co.uk
Web   www.bromansfarm.co.uk

Entry 181   Map 10

Essex

Emsworth House

Unexpectedly tranquil, this 1937 vicarage – with wide views over the Stour and some wonderful light for painting – will both energise and calm you. Penny, an artist, is a generous host and looks after you well. This is Constable country so great for walking, you are near to Frinton beach and good golf, sailing and riding. Return to comfy sofas and chairs, open fires and good books, fairly basic bedrooms with a country feel and the odd African throw or splash of colour, lots of lovely paintings and a garden filled with birds. Perfect for families too – Penny has camp beds and a can-do attitude.

Price	From £55. Singles from £45.
Rooms	3: 1 double, 1 twin; 1 double with separate bath.
Meals	Pub/restaurant 0.5 miles.
Closed	Rarely.
Directions	A12-A120 (to Harwich) & left to B1035; right at TV mast to Bradfield, 2 miles; house on right.

Penny Linton
Emsworth House,
Ship Hill, Station Road, Bradfield,
Maningtree, Essex CO11 2UP
Tel   01255 870860
Mobile   07767 477771
Email   emsworthhouse@hotmail.com
Web   www.emsworthhouse.co.uk

Entry 182   Map 10

Gloucestershire

The Old School

Comfortable, warm and filled with understated style is this 1854 Cotswold stone house. Wendy and John are generous, beds are enormous, linen is laundered, towels and robes are thick and fluffy. Your own mini fridge is carefully hidden and lighting is well thought-out. Best of all is the upstairs sitting room: a chic, open-plan space with church style windows letting the light flood in and super sofas, good art, lovely fabrics. A wood-burner keeps you toasty, Wendy is a grand cook and all is flexible. A gorgeous, relaxing place to stay – on the A44 but peaceful at night – where absolutely nothing is too much trouble.

Price	£88. Singles £60.
Rooms	4: 3 doubles, 1 twin/double.
Meals	Dinner, 4 courses, £28. Supper, 2 courses, £18. Supper tray £12. Pub 0.5 miles.
Closed	Rarely.
Directions	From Moreton-in-Marsh, A44 towards Chipping Norton & Oxford. Little Compton 3.5 miles; stay on main road, then right signed Chastleton village. House on corner, immed. left into drive.

Wendy Veale & John Scott-Lee
The Old School,
Little Compton, Moreton-in-Marsh,
Gloucestershire GL56 0SL
Tel   01608 674588
Mobile   07831 098271
Email   wendy@theoldschoolbedandbreakfast.com
Web   www.theoldschoolbedandbreakfast.com

Entry 183   Map 8

Gloucestershire

Wren House

Barely two miles from Stow-on-the-Wold, peaceful Wren House sits charmingly in a tiny hamlet. The stylish stone house was built before the English Civil War and Kiloran spent two years renovating it; the results are a joy. Downstairs, light-filled, elegant rooms with glowing rugs on pale Cotswold stone; upstairs, delicious bedrooms, spotless bathrooms and a doorway to duck. Breakfast can include cream from the Jerseys in the fields over the wall, and the well-planted garden, in which you are encouraged to sit, has far-reaching views. Explore rolling valleys and glorious gardens. Perfect. *Children over six welcome.*

Travel Club Offer: see page 392 for details.

Price	£90–£100. Singles from £70.
Rooms	2: 1 twin/double; 1 twin/double with separate bath/shower.
Meals	Pubs/restaurants 2 miles.
Closed	Rarely.
Directions	A429 between Stow & Moreton; turn to Donnington; 400 yds, bear left uphill; 100 yds, sign on right in wall and entrance set back from lane beside The Granary Cottage.

Kiloran McGrigor
Wren House,
Donnington, Moreton-in-Marsh,
Gloucestershire GL56 0XZ
Tel   01451 831 787
Mobile   07802 676673
Email   enquiries@wrenhouse.net
Web   www.wrenhouse.net

Entry 184   Map 8

Gloucestershire

Windy Ridge House

Astonishing! Find mullioned windows, gables, roofs of stone slate and thatch, winding staircases and unexpected corners. The bonhomie starts on arrival: Nick and Jennifer are the second generation to own this family home and they are delighted to throw open house, arboretum and prize-winning gardens to guests. All is polished to perfection, there's a grand country-house feel; bedrooms are warm, carpeted and cosy. Take a book to the pine-panelled drawing room, help yourself from the honesty bar, or fling yourself into tennis, croquet and a swim in the summer heated pool. Sumptuous, generous, great fun.

Price	From £90. Singles from £70.
Rooms	4: 2 doubles; 1 double, 1 twin, each with separate bath.
Meals	Pub 100 yds.
Closed	Rarely.
Directions	From Stow, north for Broadway on A424 for 2 miles to Coach & Horses pub on left. Opposite, turn right by post box & 30mph signs down single-track lane. Entrance 100 yds down on left, bear left up drive.

Nick & Jennifer Williams
Windy Ridge House,
Longborough, Moreton-in-Marsh,
Gloucestershire GL56 0QY

Tel	01451 830465
Fax	01451 831489
Email	nick@windy-ridge.co.uk
Web	www.windy-ridge.co.uk

Entry 185   Map 8

Gloucestershire

Isbourne Manor House

The part-Tudor, part Georgian house is named after the river flowing through its garden. Sudeley Castle is next door – just nip through the kissing gate into the glorious grounds. David, an organic grain merchant, and Felicity are gentle-mannered and easy, and treat you to breakfasts of homemade and local produce. One bedroom has an ornately carved, comfortable four-poster; the twin, under the eaves, has its own sun terrace. In the drawing room: oils on walls, antiques, an honesty bar and open fire. Winchcombe is a satisfying little town, with useful shops, buzzing inns and a real sense of community.

Price	£75-£100. Singles from £60.
Rooms	3: 1 double, 1 four-poster; 1 twin with separate shower.
Meals	Pubs/restaurants 2-5 minute walk.
Closed	Christmas & possibly Easter.
Directions	On B4632 between Cheltenham & Broadway. Turn into Castle St by White Hart in village centre. On left at bottom of steep hill.

Felicity & David King
Isbourne Manor House,
Castle Street, Winchcombe,
Gloucestershire GL54 5JA

Tel	01242 602281
Mobile	07818 290109
Email	felicity@isbourne-manor.co.uk
Web	www.isbourne-manor.co.uk

Entry 186   Map 8

Gloucestershire

Lower Farm House

Nicholas and Zelie are charming and articulate hosts who love entertaining and nurturing their guests: nothing is too much trouble. In peaceful little Aldestrop, a perfect Georgian house – high ceilings, sash windows, elegant proportions, gracious furnishings. The bedrooms are generous in size (as are the sumptuous double beds) and have restful views over the garden – a joy to wander through or sit out in. Meals – everything as organic and locally sourced as possible – sound superb: cooking and gardening are Zelie's passions. Bustling little Stow-on-the-Wold is a hop and a skip away. Readers are full of praise.

Travel Club Offer: see page 392 for details.

Price	From £92. Singles £66.
Rooms	2: 1 double, 1 twin.
Meals	Dinner £30. Pubs/restaurants 1.5 miles.
Closed	Rarely.
Directions	A436 from Stow; after 3 miles, left to Adlestrop; right at T-junc; after double bend, drive 50 yds on right; sign at end of drive.

Nicholas & Zelie Mason
Lower Farm House,
Adlestrop, Stow-on-the-Wold,
Gloucestershire GL56 0YR
Tel 01608 658756
Mobile 07809 429365
Email info@adlestrop-lowerfarm.com
Web www.adlestrop-lowerfarm.com

Entry 187 Map 8

Gloucestershire

Rectory Farmhouse

Once a monastery, now a farmhouse with style. Passing a development of converted farm buildings to reach the Rectory's warm Cotswold stones makes the discovery doubly exciting. More glory within: Sybil, a talented designer, has created something immaculate, fresh and uplifting. A wood-burner glows in the sitting room, bed linen is white, walls cream; beds are superb, bathrooms sport cast-iron slipper baths and power showers and views are to the church. Sybil used to own a restaurant and her breakfasts – by the Aga or in the conservatory under a rampant vine – are a further treat.

Price	From £90. Singles £60.
Rooms	2 doubles.
Meals	Pubs/restaurants 1 mile.
Closed	Christmas & New Year.
Directions	B4068 from Stow to Lower Swell, left just before Golden Ball Inn. Far end of gravel drive on right.

Sybil Gisby
Rectory Farmhouse,
Lower Swell,
Stow-on-the-Wold,
Gloucestershire GL54 1LH
Tel 01451 832351
Email rectory.farmhouse@cw-warwick.co.uk

Entry 188 Map 8

Gloucestershire

Clapton Manor

Karin and James's 16th-century manor is as all homes should be: loved and lived-in. And, with three-foot-thick walls, flagstoned floors, sit-in fireplaces and stone-mullioned windows, it's gorgeous. The enclosed garden, full of birdsong and roses, wraps itself around the house. One bedroom has a secret door that leads to a fuchsia-pink bathroom; the other room, smaller, is wallpapered in a honeysuckle trellis and has wonderful garden views. Wellies, dogs, barbours, log fires… and breakfast by a vast Tudor fireplace on homemade bread and jams and eggs from the hens. A happy, charming family home.

Price	From £95. Singles £85.
Rooms	2: 1 double, 1 twin/double.
Meals	Pub/restaurants within 15-min drive.
Closed	Rarely.
Directions	A429 Cirencester-Stow. Right signed Sherborne & Clapton. In village, pass grassy area to left, postbox in one corner; house straight ahead on left on corner.

Karin & James Bolton
Clapton Manor,
Clapton-on-the-Hill,
Gloucestershire GL54 2LG

Tel	01451 810202
Mobile	07967 144416
Email	bandb@claptonmanor.co.uk
Web	www.claptonmanor.co.uk

Entry 189   Map 8

Gloucestershire

Grove Farm House

Masses of charm and style here – the 1789 Cotswold farmhouse is much loved and is a restful place to stay. Outbuildings, courtyards and granary are in the same warm stone as the house, and your hosts are friendly, fun and terrific cooks. Angela is Cordon Bleu trained. Breakfasts and occasional dinners are served in the dining room, where lovely oils complement the oak beams and flagged floors. Country bedrooms are stylish with curtains in Colefax florals and there are robes in the bathrooms. Walking and riding all around, a good village pub and a pool for summer swims.

Price	From £90. Singles £60.
Rooms	3: 1 double, 1 twin; 1 double with extra single bed.
Meals	Occasional dinner £25. Pub 50 yds.
Closed	Christmas.
Directions	In middle of village, pass Plough Inn on left; look for gates on right.

Angela Storey
Grove Farm House,
Cold Aston,
Gloucestershire GL54 3BJ

Tel	01451 821801
Fax	01451 821108
Email	angela@cotswoldbedandbreakfast.com
Web	www.cotswoldbedandbreakfast.com

Entry 190   Map 8

Gloucestershire

Blanche House

A fun and engaging home with walks from the door and masses to see. The Flemings are young, talented (he studying architecture, she interior design) and keen on the country life. The drawing room brims with family photos, well-worn sofas, interesting books, a warm fire and views to the superb garden; bedrooms have an upmarket rustic feel with smart new beds and bright fabrics and rugs. Breakfast on apple juice from the orchard, eggs from their chickens and (usually) homemade bread, all served in the glass barn at a hand-made oak table. Brilliant for stressed-out young Londoners and lovers of the outdoors.

Price	£65–£105. Singles £55.
Rooms	4: 2 doubles, 1 family, 1 single.
Meals	Packed lunch £10. Pub 1.5 miles.
Closed	23 December–2 January.
Directions	A429 from Northleach towards Bourton-on-the-Water. 1st left after roundabout to Turkdean. House 3rd on left at bottom of hill.

Jessica & Christian Fleming
Blanche House,
Turkdean,
Cheltenham,
Gloucestershire GL54 3NX
Tel   01451 861176
Email blanchehouse@gmail.com
Web   www.blanchehousebandb.co.uk

Entry 191   Map 8

Gloucestershire

Westward, Sudeley Lodge

Susie and Jim are highly organised and efficient, juggling farm, horses and B&B. She's also a great cook (Leith trained). The grand, but cosy, house sits above Sudeley Castle surrounded by its own 600 acres; all bedrooms look west to long views. Colours, fabrics and furniture are in perfect harmony, beds and linen are inviting, and the easy mix of elegant living and family bustle is delightful. There's tea on the terrace in summer and by a log fire in winter… your hosts delight in sharing this very English home. Wonderful walks on your doorstep and all those honey-hued Cotswold villages just beyond.

Price	From £80. Singles £55.
Rooms	3: 1 double, 2 twins/doubles.
Meals	Pubs/restaurants 1 mile.
Closed	December–January.
Directions	From Abbey Sq., Winchcombe, go north; after 50 yds, right into Castle St. Follow for 1 mile; after farm buildings, right for Sudeley Lodge; follow for 600 yds. House on right; first oak door.

Susie & Jim Wilson
Westward, Sudeley Lodge,
Winchcombe, Cheltenham,
Gloucestershire GL54 5JB
Tel   01242 604372
Mobile 07879 643197
Email   jimw@haldon.co.uk
Web   www.westward-sudeley.co.uk

Entry 192   Map 8

Gloucestershire

5 Ewlyn Road

In a bustling suburb of Cheltenham, Barbara's red-brick villa remains firmly unmodernised. The clock ticks sonorously, the whiff of beeswax fills the air and Barbara looks after you with old-fashioned ease; there's a proper front room with an open fire where you can read a book or chatter away. Your bedroom is peaceful, the bed firm and the white cotton sheets are robustly pressed; the clean and purposeful bathroom is shared but not noticeably. In the warm parlour Barbara cooks best Gloucester Old Spot bacon, sausage and free-range eggs – have it outside the sunny back door in summer. Authentic, great value B&B.

Gloucestershire

Hanover House

The former home of Elgar's wife, set in an early-Victorian terrace in Cheltenham's heart, is warm, elegant, inviting – and surprisingly peaceful. There are big trees all around and the river Chelt laps at the foot of the garden. Inside, a graceful period décor is enlivened by Bracken and Sophie (the dogs!) and exuberant splashes of colour; the delectable drawing room, with pale walls and trio of arched windows, is the perfect foil for paintings, books and rugs. Bedrooms have vivid Indian throws, bathrooms are simple and stylish. But best of all are Veronica and James: musical, well-travelled, irresistible.

Price	£50. Singles £25.
Rooms	1 twin sharing bath (& separate shower).
Meals	Pubs/restaurants 5-minute walk.
Closed	Rarely.
Directions	From A40, signs to Stroud then Cheltenham College. Up Bath Road past shops; at x-roads, veg shop on left. Left signed Emmanuel Church; 2nd on right; front door to side.

Barbara Jameson
5 Ewlyn Road,
Cheltenham,
Gloucestershire GL53 7PB
Tel 01242 261243

Entry 193 Map 8

Price	£80-£100. Singles £60-£70.
Rooms	3: 1 double; 1 double, 1 twin each with separate bath.
Meals	Pubs/restaurants 500 yds.
Closed	Rarely.
Directions	In Cheltenham town centre, 200 yds from bus/coach station; 600 yds from railway station. Parking available.

Veronica & James Ritchie
Hanover House,
65 St George's Road, Cheltenham,
Gloucestershire GL50 3DU
Tel 01242 541297
Email hanoverhouse@tiscali.co.uk
Web www.hanoverhouse.org

Entry 194 Map 8

Gloucestershire

St Annes

Step straight off the narrow pavement into a sunny hall – and a welcome to match. Iris worked in tourism for years and lives here with antique restorer Greg, two smiling children and Rollo the dog. They've also made this pretty 17th-century house in the centre of a captivating village (some road noise) as eco-friendly as possible. The biggest and most beautiful bedroom has a four-poster and a bathroom down the hall; the smallish double and the twin rooms will charm you. Farmer's market breakfasts are a warm, cosy, stylish feast. Brilliant all-round B&B. *Minimum stay two nights weekends April-Sept.*

Ethical Collection: Environment; Food. See page 400 for details.

Price	£65. Singles £40.
Rooms	3: 1 double, 1 twin; 1 four-poster with separate bathroom.
Meals	Packed lunch £5. Restaurants/pubs in village.
Closed	Rarely.
Directions	A46 Stroud-Painswick; in Painswick, left after lights; house 3rd door on right. Bus: from Cheltenham & Stroud.

	Iris McCormick St Annes, Gloucester Street, Painswick, Gloucestershire GL6 6QN
Tel	01452 812879
Email	greg.iris@btinternet.com
Web	www.st-annes-painswick.co.uk

Entry 195   Map 8

Gloucestershire

The Old School House

The perfect English scene: a late 18th-century house tucked down a lane off the country's longest village green; a garden alive with colourful posies; walks by the canal. Bedrooms are large with fluffy towels, crisp linen, muted yellows and rich velvety plums. It's a wonderful house that feels freshly decorated and Carol wants you to treat it as home. When we visited, there was a jigsaw puzzle that invited a challenge, dogs and cats happily co-existed and the visitors' book was inscribed: "We'll be back" (and return they do). At breakfast: fresh eggs, elegant china, pots of homemade jam. *Children over ten welcome.*

Price	£80. Singles £40.
Rooms	1 twin/double, 1 twin.
Meals	Pub 0.5 miles. Restaurant 5 miles.
Closed	Christmas & New Year.
Directions	A38 for Bristol, west onto B4071; 1st left & drive length of village green; 300 yds after end, right into Whittles Lane. House last on right. 3 miles from junc. 13 on M5.

	Carol & William Alexander The Old School House, Whittles Lane, Frampton-on-Severn, Gloucestershire GL2 7EB
Tel	01452 740457
Mobile	07769 578767
Email	theoldies@the-oldschoolhouse.wanadoo.co.uk
Web	www.the-oldschoolhouse.co.uk

Entry 196   Map 8

Gloucestershire

Frampton Court

Deep authenticity in this magnificent Grade I-listed house. The manor of Frampton-on-Severn has been in the family since the 11th century and although Rollo and Janie look after the estate, it is Gillian who greets you on behalf of the family and looks after you (very well). Exquisite examples of decorative woodwork and, in the hall, a cheerful log fire; perch on the mouseman fire seat. Bedrooms are traditional with antiques, panelling and long views. Beds have fine linen, bathrooms are delectably antiquated. Stroll around the ornamental canal, soak up the old-master views. An architectural masterpiece.

Price	£125.
Rooms	3: 1 twin/double, 1 double, 1 four-poster.
Meals	Dinner £27. Pub across the green. Restaurant 3 miles.
Closed	Rarely.
Directions	From M5 junc. 13 west, then B4071. Left down village green, 400 yds, then look to left! 2nd turning left, between two chestnut trees & thro' ornamental gates in wall.

	Rollo & Janie Clifford
	Frampton Court,
	Frampton-on-Severn,
	Gloucestershire GL2 7EQ
Tel	01452 740267
Mobile	07795 116086
Email	framptoncourt@framptoncourtestate.co.uk
Web	www.framptoncourtestate.co.uk

Entry 197 Map 8

Gloucestershire

Grove Farm

Boards creak and you duck, in a farmhouse of the best kind: simple, small-roomed, stone-flagged, beamed, delightful. The walls are white, the furniture is good and there are pictures everywhere. In spite of great age (16th-century), it's light, with lots of windows. You'll be fed well, too; the 400 acres are farmed organically and Penny makes a grand breakfast – continental at busy times. Stupendous views across the Severn estuary to the Cotswolds, the Forest of Dean on the doorstep and woodland walks, carpeted with spring flowers. And there is simply no noise – unless the guinea fowl are in voice.

Price	£60-£70. Singles £35.
Rooms	2: 1 double; 1 twin/double with separate bath.
Meals	Packed lunch £4. Pub 2 miles.
Closed	Rarely.
Directions	2 miles south of Newnham on A48, opp. turn for Bullo Pill, large 'pull-in' with phone box on right; turn here; follow farm track to end.

	Penny & David Hill
	Grove Farm,
	Bullo Pill, Newnham,
	Gloucestershire GL14 1DZ
Tel	01594 516304
Fax	01594 516304
Email	davidandpennyhill@btopenworld.com
Web	www.grovefarm-uk.com

Entry 198 Map 8

Gloucestershire

The Old Rectory

Behind the Georgian façade, a ravishing interior. Be seduced by flamboyant flowers on choice antique pieces, deep sofas sprinkled with cushions, and gilt-framed ancestors surveying cut glass and acres of mahogany. Up the wrought-iron stairs more sumptuousness awaits, and every bedroom has views of the Severn. Jane decorates houses for a living and has an impressive design workshop in the barn next door. Feel free to wander the 30 acres bordered by the ha-ha, where sheep, horses, dogs and cats roam. This is a big house with a big-hearted owner and you will be thoroughly spoiled. *Stabling available.*

Price	From £70. Singles £40.
Rooms	4: 2 twins/doubles, 1 four-poster; 1 four-poster with separate bath.
Meals	Occasional dinner. Pubs/restaurants 1-4 miles.
Closed	Rarely.
Directions	A48 from Chepstow for approx. 4 miles. At Woolaston, left after picnic area into Keynsham Lane. Road forks, take left at end, drive for house on left of church gates.

	Jane Bowyer
	The Old Rectory,
	Woolaston, Lydney,
	Gloucestershire GL15 6PR
Tel	01594 528179/529825
Mobile	07771 656521
Email	jane@rectorydesign.co.uk

Entry 199   Map 7

Gloucestershire

Nation House

Three cottages were knocked together to create this house, now listed and wisteria-clad. Beams are exposed, walls are pale and hung with prints, floors are close-carpeted in pinky beige, the sitting room is formally cosy and quiet. Bedrooms show off a cottage garden theme with fat quilts, low beams and lattice windows; the bathroom is spotless and the shower room compact. In summer, breakfast in the conservatory on still-warm homemade bread, local bacon and sausages, Brenda's preserves. The village is a Cotswold treasure, with two good eating places and with many walks from the door.

Travel Club Offer: see page 392 for details.

Price	£70-£80. Singles £50.
Rooms	3: 1 suite; 2 doubles sharing bath.
Meals	Pubs 50 yds.
Closed	Rarely.
Directions	From Cirencester A419 for Stroud. After 7 miles right to Bisley. Left at village shop. House 50 yds on right.

	Brenda & Mike Hammond
	Nation House,
	George Street,
	Bisley,
	Gloucestershire GL6 7BB
Tel	01452 770197
Email	nation.house@homecall.co.uk

Entry 200   Map 8

Gloucestershire

Well Farm

Perhaps it's the gentle, unstuffy attitude of Kate and Edward. Or the great position of the house with its glorious views across the valley. Whatever, you'll feel comforted and invigorated by your stay here. It's a real family home and guests have a fresh, pretty bedroom that feels very private, and the use of a comfortable, book-filled sitting room that opens to a courtyard – Kate is an inspired gardener. Sleep soundly on crisp linen with the softest of pillows, wake to the deep peace of the countryside and tuck in to eggs from their own hens, local sausages, good bacon. The area teems with great walks.

Travel Club Offer: see page 392 for details.

Price	From £80.
Rooms	1 twin/double & sitting room.
Meals	Dinner from £20. Pubs nearby.
Closed	Rarely.
Directions	Directions on booking.

Kate & Edward Gordon Lennox
Well Farm,
Frampton Mansell,
Stroud,
Gloucestershire GL6 8JB
Tel   01285 760651
Email   kategl@btinternet.com
Web   www.well-farm.co.uk

Entry 201   Map 8

Gloucestershire

Drakestone House

A treat by anyone's reckoning. Utterly delightful people with wide-ranging interests (ex British Council and college lecturing; arts, travel, gardening) in a manor-type house full of beautiful furniture. The house was born of the Arts and Crafts movement: wooden panels painted green, a log-fired drawing room for guests, handsome old furniture, comfortable proportions, good beds with proper blankets. The garden's massive clipped hedges, Monterey Pines and smooth, great lawn are impressive, as is the whole place – and the views stretch to the Severn Estuary and Wales.

Price	£78. Singles £49.
Rooms	3: 1 twin/double, 1 double, 1 twin, each with separate bath/shower.
Meals	Dinner £25. BYO. Pub/restaurant under 1 mile.
Closed	December-January.
Directions	B4060 from Stinchcombe to Wotton-under-Edge. 0.25 miles out of Stinchcombe village. Driveway on left marked, before long bend.

Hugh & Crystal Mildmay
Drakestone House,
Stinchcombe,
Dursley,
Gloucestershire GL11 6AS
Tel   01453 542140
Fax   01453 542140

Entry 202   Map 8

Gloucestershire

Lodge Farm

A plum Cotswolds position, a striking garden, stylish décor, exceptional linen — there are plenty of reasons to stay here. Then there are your flexible hosts, who can help wedding groups, give you supper en famille next to the Aga or something smarter round the dining-room table with crystal and silver: perfect for a house party. The sitting room has flowers, family photographs and lots of magazines; throughout are flagstones, Bath stone and wood. Sometimes home-produced lamb for dinner, always excellent coffee at breakfast and their own free range eggs. The Salmons breed thoroughbreds and can stable your horse.

Gloucestershire

107 Gloucester Street

Slip through gates into a narrow courtyard of potted shrubs and honey-coloured Cotswold stone. This modest Georgian merchant's house is three minutes from the charming town centre yet blissfully quiet. Inside: buttery colours, well-loved antiques, soft uncluttered spaces. Restful, understated bedrooms are small, chic and spotless. Kitchen breakfasts overlook the sheltered garden — a verdant spot for relaxing in summer. For evenings, a creamy first-floor sitting room with a small log fire. Ethne and her ex-army husband are full of fun and good humour — very special. *Children over ten welcome.*

Travel Club Offer: see page 392 for details.

Price	£60–£75. Singles from £55. Family room £80.
Rooms	4: 2 twins/doubles; 1 twin/double, 1 family room sharing bath.
Meals	Dinner, 2–3 courses, £15–£25. Pub/bistro 2.5 miles.
Closed	Rarely.
Directions	From Cirencester A433 to Tetbury, right B4014 to Avening. After 250 yds, left onto Chavenage Lane. Lodge Farm 1.3 miles on right; left of barn on drive.

Price	£70. Singles £50.
Rooms	2: 1 double, 1 twin.
Meals	Hotel 300 yds & restaurants 8-minute walk.
Closed	Easter & Christmas.
Directions	Directions on booking.

Mrs Nicola Salmon
Lodge Farm,
Chavenage, Tetbury,
Gloucestershire GL8 8XW

Tel	01666 505339
Mobile	07836 221457
Email	rsalmon@lodgefarm.vianw.co.uk
Web	www.lodgefarm.co.uk

Ethne McGuinness
107 Gloucester Street,
Cirencester,
Gloucestershire GL7 2DW

Tel	01285 657861
Mobile	07746 100789
Fax	01285 657861
Email	ethne@mcguinness78.freeserve.co.uk

Entry 203 Map 8

Entry 204 Map 8

Gloucestershire

Lady Lamb Farm

Light pours into perfectly proportioned rooms through windows hung with velvet and chintz; soft sofas entice; china sits in alcoves on both sides of the fireplace. Jeanie and James, farmers, inventors, built the honey-stone house years ago and have kept their Cotswold dream ship-shape. You can play tennis and swim in the pool, bedrooms are a good size and have dreamy views, Aga breakfasts are scrumptious; locally cured bacon and eggs from the chickens that strut on the manicured lawn. Fishing, cycling and golf can all be organised for you and Kelmscott Manor (the country home of William Morris) is close.

Price	From £65. Singles £45.
Rooms	2: 1 twin; 1 twin/double with separate bath.
Meals	Pubs/restaurants 1-4 miles.
Closed	Christmas & New Year.
Directions	From Fairford on A417. After 0.5 miles look for sign for Waitenhill and Cherry Tree House. Entrance directly opposite on left.

Jeanie Keyser
Lady Lamb Farm,
Meysey Hampton, Cirencester,
Gloucestershire GL7 5LH

Tel	01285 712206
Mobile	07876 418966
Fax	01285 712206
Email	jeanie@jameskeyser.co.uk

Entry 205   Map 8

Gloucestershire

The Old Rectory

English to the core – and to the bottom of its lovely garden, with a new woodland walk and plenty of quiet places to sit. You sweep into the circular driveway to a yellow labrador welcome. The house, despite its magnificent age, throbs with family energy and warmth – Caroline is calmly competent and amiable, with a talent for understated interior décor. The two large, airy bedrooms are furnished with antiques, very good beds, a chaise longue or an easy chair, even a bottle opener and wine glasses. Elsewhere, old furniture and creaky floorboards complete the sense of well-being in a very special place.

Price	£80-£95. Singles from £50.
Rooms	2: 1 double, 1 twin.
Meals	Pub 200 yds.
Closed	December-January.
Directions	South through village from A417. Right after Masons Arms. 200 yds on left, through stone pillars.

Roger & Caroline Carne
The Old Rectory,
Meysey Hampton, Cirencester,
Gloucestershire GL7 5JX

Tel	01285 851200
Fax	01285 850602
Email	carolinecarne@cotswoldwireless.co.uk
Web	www.meyseyoldrectory.co.uk

Entry 206   Map 8

Gloucestershire

Kempsford Manor

On the edge of the Cotswolds, this 17th-century village house is surrounded by large hedges and mature trees. Crunch up the gravelled drive to find floor-to-ceiling bay windows, dark pine floors with patterned rugs, wood panelling and built-in bookcases. Bedrooms vary hugely – one has a Chinese theme – but all are a good size and have super garden views; bathrooms are functional and old-fashioned. Two acres of beautifully tended gardens (snowdrops are special here) lead to an orchard and a canal walk; stoke up on Zehra's homemade muesli and come back for dinner – vegetables are homegrown.

Price	£60-£70. Singles £40.
Rooms	3: 1 double; 1 double, 1 single, each with separate bath.
Meals	Dinner available by arrangement. Pub 200 yds.
Closed	Open all year.
Directions	A419 Cirencester-Swindon; Kempsford is signed with Fairford. Right into village, past small village green; on right, through stone columns. Glass front door, by a fountain.

Mrs Zehra I Williamson
Kempsford Manor,
High Street, Kempsford, Fairford,
Gloucestershire GL7 4EQ

Tel	01285 810131
Mobile	07980 543882
Email	ipek@kempsfordmanor.co.uk
Web	www.kempsfordmanor.co.uk

Entry 207   Map 8

Hampshire

Manor House

Outside is a pretty courtyard for breakfasts on balmy mornings. This glorious house, built in 1546, is one of the finest hearth-passage manors in Hampshire. There are rosy bricks, dark timbers and diamond-leaded windows without; ancient witches' marks on the massive fireplace (to ward off evil) and Wren's impeccable upholstery within. But this is no museum – your kind, friendly hosts make you comfortably at home aided by their well-mannered spaniel. Up a private staircase are two bedrooms with a warm, peaceful elegance, and a spotless cream bathroom in between.

Price	£80. Singles from £45.
Rooms	2: 1 double, 1 single sharing bath.
Meals	Pubs/restaurants 2 miles.
Closed	Christmas & New Year.
Directions	M4 junc 11; A33 to Bramley, 14 miles. House at western end of village in Vyne Road, close to junc. with The Street.

Wren & Rhydian Vaughan
Manor House,
Bramley, Tadley, Basingstoke,
Hampshire RG26 5DW

Tel	01256 881141
Mobile	07771 514152
Email	info@manorhouse.biz
Web	www.manorhousebramley.co.uk

Entry 208   Map 4

Hampshire

Little Cottage

Just 45 minutes from Heathrow but the peace is deep, the views are long and the wildlife thrives – watch fox and deer, hear the rare nightjar. Chris and Therese grow many of their own vegetables and fruit, source meat locally and give you superb home cooking; guests have a lovely sitting room with an eclectic mix of modern and antique furniture, and a pretty terrace overlooks the garden. Bedrooms are all ground-floor, fresh and light, the double has distant views; perfect for walkers and those who seek solace from urban life but don't want to go too far. *Minimum stay two nights at weekends. Children over 12 welcome.*

Ethical Collection: Food. See page 400 for details.

Travel Club Offer: see page 392 for details.

Price	£70-£80. Singles £50.
Rooms	3: 1 twin/double, 1 double, 1 single.
Meals	Dinner from £15. Pub 1.5 miles.
Closed	Between Christmas & New Year & occasionally.
Directions	B3011 from A30 in Hartley Wintney for 1.5 miles. Cottage just before the continuous double white line down the middle of road becomes a single line.

	Chris & Therese Abbott
	Little Cottage,
	Hazeley Heath, Hook,
	Hampshire RG27 8LY
Tel	01252 845050
Mobile	07721 462214
Email	info@little-cottage.co.uk
Web	www.little-cottage.co.uk

Entry 209   Map 4

Hampshire

Home Close

The setting is gorgeous, surrounded by the New Forest – walks start from the gate. The house, once a farm belonging to the Beaulieu estate, is now home to friendly Sally and Bob. You sleep in a sunshine-yellow bedroom overlooking the lovely garden, there are Lloyd Loom chairs for reading or TV, bottled water, proper milk, homemade shortbread. A generous breakfast, sometimes with home-baked bread, is taken in the pretty blue dining room at a solid oak table, from where you can watch the comings and goings of the birds beneath the arbour. Perfect for exploring the New Forest or a day trip to the Isle of Wight.

Price	From £80.
Rooms	1 double.
Meals	Packed lunch £5. Pubs/restaurants within 7 miles.
Closed	Christmas, New Year & occasionally.
Directions	M27 junc. 2. A326, then B3054 signed Beaulieu 1.1 miles from New Forest cattle grid, down gravel track signed Home Close & Vanguard. Left past cottage to gate.

	Sally Brearley
	Home Close,
	Hill Top,
	Beaulieu,
	Hampshire SO42 7YR
Tel	01590 612287
Email	homeclose@talktalk.net
Web	www.homeclosebedandbreakfast.co.

Entry 210   Map 3

Hampshire

The Manor House

Gracious yet informal, a crisp Regency house in this little corner of Hampshire where Jane Austen wrote most of her books. Clare will spoil you, even collect you from the station if you come without a car. Bedrooms are airy and light with space for chairs, knick-knacks and family pictures; bathrooms are smart. Eat a delicious home-cooked breakfast in the elegant dining room whose French windows overlook glorious lawns, impressive herbaceous borders and mature trees. Clare has a good knowledge of places to visit locally – especially gardens; she even organises garden tours to Normandy.

Price	£80. Singles £55.
Rooms	2: 1 double;
	1 twin with separate bath.
Meals	Pub 0.25 miles.
Closed	Never.
Directions	Turn West at r'bout on A31 north of Alton, signed for Alton, Bordon & Holybourne. Over railway; 1st right into Holybourne. After 300 yds road dips, proceed up hill and at top turn left into Church Lane; 100 yds on left up 2nd gravel drive without gate.

Clare Whately
The Manor House,
Holybourne, Alton,
Hampshire GU34 4HD

Tel	01420 541321
Mobile	07711 655450
Fax	01420 83175
Email	clare@whately.net

Entry 211   Map 4

Hampshire

Bay Trees

Step in from the village street and you find yourself in a striking hall where the guest book perches on the music stand! Comfortable bedrooms have just been refurbished, the double with French windows opening to a lush suntrap of a garden – a wonderful surprise – full of arbours and weeping willow and a brook at the end with a seat for two. Breakfasts are gourmet here, served in the conservatory overlooking the magnolia. Robert, humorous and down-to-earth, makes you feel at ease the moment you arrive. The shingle beach with views to the Isle of Wight is a sprint away. *Minimum stay two nights at weekends.*

Travel Club Offer: see page 392 for details.

Price	£80–£130. Singles from £50.
Rooms	3: 1 double, 1 four-poster;
	1 triple, 1 single sharing bath
	(2nd room let to same party only).
Meals	Restaurants/pubs 100 yds.
Closed	Rarely.
Directions	From Lymington follow signs for Milford-on-Sea (B3058). On left, just past village green.

Robert Fry
Bay Trees,
8 High Street,
Milford-on-Sea, Lymington,
Hampshire SO41 0QD

Tel	01590 642186
Email	rp.fry@virgin.net
Web	www.baytreebedandbreakfast.co.uk

Entry 212   Map 3

Hampshire

Land of Nod

A 1939 house of character with hosts to match and one of the greatest gardens in the book… seven tended acres within 100 acres of woodland. There are azaleas and camellias, specimen trees, croquet, tennis, a white wisteria 40 years old – and orchids: Jeremy's passion. Breakfast in the chinoiserie dining room – the allegorical tableau is charming, the needlework on the walls dates from 1901. Bedrooms are spacious, with views over the garden; original baths have vast taps. Flexible breakfasts are locally sourced and seasonal fruit and preserves come from the garden. *Children over ten welcome.*

Price	From £80. Singles from £50.
Rooms	2: 1 twin; 1 twin with separate bath.
Meals	Restaurants 5-minute drive.
Closed	Rarely.
Directions	South on A3 to lights at Hindhead. Straight across & after 400 yds, right onto B3002. On for 3 miles. Entrance (signed) on right in a wood.

Jeremy & Philippa Whitaker
Land of Nod,
Headley, Bordon,
Hampshire GU35 8SJ
Tel   01428 713609
Fax   01428 717698

Entry 213   Map 4

Hampshire

Sandy Corner

Stride straight onto open moorland from this smallholding on the edge of the New Forest – a great place for anyone who loves walking, cycling, riding, wildlife and the great outdoors. And there's plenty of room for wet clothes and muddy boots. Cattle graze within ten feet of the window, you may hear the call of a nightjar in June, Dartford warblers nest nearby, happy hens cluck around the yard. Sue also keeps a horse, two cats, a few sheep. You have a little guest sitting room, lovely fresh bedrooms, your own spot in the garden and a marvellous, away-from-it-all feel. You can walk to one pub; others are nearby.

Price	From £70. Singles from £45.
Rooms	2 doubles.
Meals	Packed lunch £6. Pub within walking distance, restaurant 2.5 miles.
Closed	Rarely.
Directions	On A338, 1 mile S of Fordingbridge, at small x-roads, turn for Hyde & Hungerford. Up hill & right at school for Ogdens; left at next x-roads for Ogdens North; on right at bottom of hill.

Sue Browne
Sandy Corner,
Ogdens North,
Fordingbridge,
Hampshire SP6 2QD
Tel   01425 657295

Entry 214   Map 3

Hampshire

Little Shackles

Gaze upon the pretty Arts and Crafts house from the comfort of the hammock or solar-heated pool: this is a charming place to stay. Rosemary advises on local gardens to visit (her own two acres are also special) and is the loveliest of hosts. Your bedroom has an elegant country air – homemade quilts on firm beds, new armchairs and a new TV – and a spring-like bathroom with fluffy bathrobes and views to fresh green fields. Breakfast is plentiful; dinner, at the lovely old drover's pub down the sleepy lane, is a simple treat. Goodwood and Portsmouth are close, and the walks on the South Downs are marvellous.

Price	£68. Singles From £30.
Rooms	2: 1 twin/double, 1 single sharing bath (2nd room let to same party only).
Meals	Packed lunch £7. Pub 0.5 miles.
Closed	Rarely.
Directions	From London A3 take A272 junc. Petersfield, right at r'bout. 1st right into Kingsfernsden Lane, over level crossing into Reservoir Lane. Right into Harrow Lane. House 2nd driveway on right.

Rosemary & Martin Griffiths
Little Shackles,
Harrow Lane, Petersfield,
Hampshire GU32 2BZ

Tel 01730 263464
Fax 01730 263464
Email martgriff@freenet.co.uk

Entry 215   Map 4

Hampshire

Yew Tree House

A charming papier-mâché cat welcomes you at the front door, setting the tone for this artistic, tranquil house. The views, the house and the villagers are said to have inspired Dickens, who escaped London for the peace of the valley. The exquisite red brick was there 200 years before him; the rare dovecote, to which you may have the key, 300 years before that. Thoughtful hosts, interesting to talk to, have created a house of understated elegance: a yellow-ochre bedroom with Descamps bed linen, cashmere/silk curtains designed by their son, a view onto an enchanting garden, a profusion of flowers. Great value.

Price	£65. Singles by arrangement.
Rooms	2: 1 twin; 1 double with separate bath.
Meals	Pub in village.
Closed	Rarely.
Directions	From A30 west of Stockbridge for 1.5 miles, left at minor x-roads. After 2 miles left at T-junction House on left at next junction opp. Greyhound.

Philip & Janet Mutton
Yew Tree House,
Broughton, Stockbridge,
Hampshire SO20 8AA

Tel 01794 301227
Email pandjmutton@onetel.com

Entry 216   Map 3

Hampshire

Mizzards Farm

Wow! The central hall is three storeys high, its vaulted roof open to the rafters. This is the oldest part of this rambling, mostly 16th-century farmhouse: kilims and fine antiques look splendid with the ancient flagstones. There's a drawing room for musical evenings and an upstairs conservatory from which you can see the garden with its lake, swimming pool, outdoor chess and sculptures. The four-poster is extraordinarily kitsch with electric curtains, the other bedrooms traditional and fresh. Come in the summer for mini Glyndebourne on the lawn. *Children over eight welcome. Minimum stay two nights.*

Price	£80–£88. Singles by arrangement.
Rooms	3: 1 double, 1 twin, 1 four-poster.
Meals	Pubs 0.5 miles.
Closed	Christmas & New Year.
Directions	From A272 at Rogate, turn for Harting & Nyewood. Cross humpback bridge; drive signed to right after 300 yds.

Harriet & Julian Francis
Mizzards Farm,
Rogate,
Petersfield,
Hampshire GU31 5HS
Tel   01730 821656
Fax   01730 821655
Email   francis@mizzards.co.uk

Hampshire

Little Ashton Farm

Part 18th-century farm cottage, part extended Victorian extension; this is a laid-back, friendly house, full of joyful, arty clutter. Felicity is a keen cook with a burgeoning kitchen garden: plums, peaches, figs for bottling and jamming. You eat in the dining room or conservatory; delicious "everything's local" breakfasts and dinners that are hard to resist. Separate staircases lead to the large triple under the rafters and the small cottage double; both have garden views, good linen and furniture, books and paintings, cosy Guatamalan throws. Country walks from the doorstep, yet close to the M27, M3 and Winchester.

Price	£70. Singles £40.
Rooms	2: 1 double, 1 triple.
Meals	Lunch £10. Dinner, 3 courses, £20. Packed lunch £5. Pubs/restaurants nearby.
Closed	Mid-December–28 March.
Directions	B2177 Winchester to Portsmouth. Just after 40mph sign into Bishop's Waltham, left into Ashton Lane. 0.75 miles up on left, black wrought-iron gates into drive.

Felicity & David Webb-Carter
Little Ashton Farm,
Ashton Lane, Bishop's Waltham,
Hampshire SO32 1FR
Tel   01489 894055
Mobile   07760 221785
Email   flossywebb@hotmail.com
Web   www.littleashtonfarm.20m.com

Hampshire

The Threshing Barn

You are on the edge of the rolling Meon valley, the approach through hedge-lined lanes is bucolic and the beautifully restored barn sits on a conservation award-winning farm run by John. Choose between a colourful and homely double in the main house or independence in the glorious bothy – a beamed and light space with a double walk-in shower. Find fresh flowers, good mattresses and feather and down pillows. All guests are greeted with tea and scones, breakfast is a local or homegrown extravaganza (check out Emma's borage honey) and views are to one of the tallest village church spires in Hampshire.

Travel Club Offer: see page 392 for details.

Price	£75-£85. Singles £55.
Rooms	3: 1 double,
	1 single with shared bath
	(let to same party only).
	Bothy: 1 twin/double.
Meals	Packed lunch £7-£8. Pub 2 miles.
Closed	Rarely.
Directions	A272 Winchester to Petersfield. After A32/A272 crossing, on for 0.8 miles towards Petersfield. Then left up Stocks Lane, 0.5 miles to house.

Emma Bird
The Threshing Barn,
Stocks Lane, Privett,
Hampshire GU34 3NZ

Tel	01730 828382
Mobile	07980 841154
Email	emmacbird@stocksfarmprivett.co.uk
Web	www.thethreshingbarn.co.uk

Entry 219   Map 4

Hampshire

Mulberry House

Deep into Jane Austen country, among ancient apple trees and rosebushes in Hampshire parkland, is Mulberry House – the red-brick stable block of Old Alresford House. Peter and Sue's charm permeates their lovely home and B&B. Private, quietly elegant guest rooms share a sitting room and kitchenette; the one in the eaves overlooks a pretty courtyard where a fountain plays. When the weather is fine, breakfast beneath the wisteria and vine-hung pergola on home-laid eggs and homemade jams. Suppers promise lively conversation, delicious food, fresh flowers. Comfortably English.

Travel Club Offer: see page 392 for details.

Price	£70. Singles £50.
Rooms	2: 1 double, 1 twin/double.
Meals	Supper from £20. Packed lunch £8. Pubs/restaurants within 10-minute walk.
Closed	Rarely.
Directions	M3 exit 9, signs to Alresford. In town centre, left onto B3046 to church on right. Then right into Colden Lane. House is 3rd on right through field gate.

Sue & Peter Paice
Mulberry House,
Colden Lane, Old Alresford,
Hampshire SO24 9DY

Tel	01962 735518
Mobile	07801 931905
Email	suepaice@btinternet.com
Web	www.mulberryhousebnb.com

Entry 220   Map 4

Hampshire

Brymer House

Complete privacy in a B&B is rare. Here you have it, a 12-minute walk from town, cathedral and water meadows. Relax in your own half of a Victorian townhouse immaculately furnished and decorated and with a garden to match – all roses and lilac in the spring. Fizzy serves sumptuous breakfasts, there's a log fire in the guests' sitting room and fresh flowers abound – guests have been delighted. You are also left with an 'honesty box' so you may help yourselves to drinks. Bedrooms are small and elegant, with antique mirrors, furniture and bedspreads; bathrooms are first class. *Children over seven welcome.*

Price	£70-£80. Singles £50-£54.
Rooms	2: 1 double, 1 twin.
Meals	Pubs/restaurants nearby.
Closed	Christmas.
Directions	M3 junc. 9; A272 Winchester exit, then signs for Winchester Park & Ride. Under m'way, straight on at r'bout signed St Cross. Left at T-junc. St Faith's Rd veers off 100 yds ahead to the left on reaching bend.

Guy & Fizzy Warren
Brymer House,
29/30 St Faith's Road, St Cross,
Winchester, Hampshire SO23 9QD
Tel   01962 867428
Mobile 07762 201076
Web   www.brymerhouse.co.uk

Entry 221   Map 4

Herefordshire

Bunns Croft

The timbers of the medieval house are probably 1,000 years old. Little of the structure has ever been altered and it is an absolute delight: stone floors, rich colours, a piano, dogs, books and cosy chairs – all give a homely feel. Cruck-beamed bedrooms are snugly small, the stairs are steep – this was a yeoman's house – and the twin's bathroom has its own sweet fireplace. The countryside is 'pure', too, with 1,500 acres of National Trust land five miles away. Anita is charming, loves her garden and her guests, grows her own fruit and veg and makes fabulous dinners. Just mind your head.

Price	£70-£80. Singles £35.
Rooms	4: 1 double, 2 singles, sharing bath (let to same party only); 1 twin.
Meals	Dinner, 3 courses, £20. Pub 3 miles.
Closed	Rarely.
Directions	From Leominster, A49 towards Ludlow; 4 miles to village of Ashton, then left. House on right behind postbox after 1 mile.

Mrs Anita Syers-Gibson
Bunns Croft,
Moreton Eye,
Leominster,
Herefordshire HR6 0DP
Tel   01568 615836

Entry 222   Map 7

Herefordshire

Staunton House

The Georgian rectory's well-proportioned rooms, painstakingly restored, brim with beautiful furnishings and fine furniture. The original oak staircase leads to peaceful bedrooms with comfortable, well-dressed beds; the blue room looks onto garden and pond. It's a house that matches its owners – quiet, traditional and country-loving. Wander through the lovely garden, drive to Hay or Ludlow, stride some ravishing countryside, play golf near Offa's Dyke; return to Rosie and Richard's delicious dinner in the elegant dining room or in the large kitchen if you prefer. You will be well tended here.

Price	From £70. Singles from £40.
Rooms	2: 1 double, 1 twin/double.
Meals	Dinner, 2-3 courses, £18-£25. Pub/restaurant 2.5 miles.
Closed	Rarely.
Directions	A44 Leominster-Pembridge; right to Shobdon. After 0.5 miles, left to Staunton-on-Arrow; at x-roads, over to village. House opp. church, with black wrought-iron gates.

Rosie & Richard Bowen
Staunton House,
Staunton-on-Arrow, Pembridge,
Leominster, Herefordshire HR6 9HR
Tel   01544 388313
Mobile   07780 961994
Email   rosbown@aol.com
Web   www.stauntonhouse.co.uk

Entry 223   Map 7

Herefordshire

Bollingham House

The views alone might earn the house a place in this book. But there's more... a beautifully furnished interior and an interesting four-acre garden with a perfumed rose walk. Stephanie and John, working unobtrusively to make your stay enjoyable, are natural hosts. Bedrooms are large, bright and comfortable, and Stephanie has cleverly brought vibrant colours, fine furniture and paintings together with a dash of elegance. Gaze from your windows across the Wye Valley to the Malvern Hills, or west to the Black Mountains. Stephanie's cooking is worth a detour.

Price	From £75. Singles from £40.
Rooms	2: 1 twin; 1 double with separate bath.
Meals	Dinner from £23. Packed lunch £5. Pub 2 miles.
Closed	Occasionally.
Directions	A438 Hereford to Brecon road, towards Kington on A4111; through Eardisley; house 2 miles up hill on left, behind long line of conifers.

Stephanie & John Grant
Bollingham House,
Eardisley,
Herefordshire HR5 3LE
Tel   01544 327326
Email   grant@bollinghamhouse.com
Web   www.bollinghamhouse.com

Entry 224   Map 7

Herefordshire

Hall's Mill House

Remote lanes bring you, finally, to this most idyllic spot – a stone cottage tucked into a wooded valley. The sitting room is snug with wood-burner and sofas but the kitchen is the hub of the place – delicious breakfasts and dinners are cooked on the Aga. Grace, chatty and easy-going, obviously enjoys living in her modernised mill house. Rooms are small, fresh, with exposed beams and slate sills; only the old mill interrupts the far-reaching, all-green views. Drift off to sleep to the sound of the Arrow burbling by – a blissful tonic for city-dwellers. Great value, too. *Children over four welcome.*

Price	£45-£55. Singles £22.50-£27.50.
Rooms	3: 1 double; 1 double, 1 twin, sharing bath.
Meals	Dinner from £15. Pub/restaurant 3 miles.
Closed	Christmas.
Directions	A438 from Hereford. After Winforton, Whitney-on-Wye & toll bridge, sharp right for Brilley. Left fork to Huntington, over x-roads & next right to Huntington. Next right into 'No Through Road', then 1st right.

	Grace Watson Hall's Mill House, Huntington, Kington, Herefordshire HR5 3QA
Tel	01497 831409

Entry 225   Map 7

Herefordshire

Garnstone House

Come for peace and quiet in the Welsh Marches, good food and lovely, humorous, down-to-earth hosts. The atmosphere is easy, and the furniture a lifetime's accumulation of eclectic pieces and pictures and prints of horses, hounds and country scenes. After dinner and good conversation, climb the picture-lined stairs to a comfortingly carpeted bedroom – either a twin or a double – and a bathroom that is properly old-fashioned. Delicious breakfasts, good dinners and a stunning garden to explore – the variety and colour of the springtime flowers are astonishing and the clematis is a glory.

Travel Club Offer: see page 392 for details.

Price	From £70. Singles from £35.
Rooms	1 twin or double with separate bath.
Meals	Dinner from £20. Pub/restaurant 1 mile.
Closed	Rarely.
Directions	A480 from Hereford; after 10 miles, right onto B4230 for Weobley. After 1.75 miles, right onto level tarmac private road; 2nd on left over cattle grid.

	Dawn & Michael MacLeod Garnstone House, Weobley, Herefordshire HR4 8QP
Tel	01544 318943
Email	macleod@garnstonehouse.co.uk
Web	www.garnstonehouse.co.uk

Entry 226   Map 7

Herefordshire

Winforton Court

Dating from 1500, the Court is dignified in its old age – undulating floors, great oak beams, thick walls. It is a dramatic, colourful home with exceptional timber-framed bedrooms; one room has an Indian-style bathroom and huge roll top bath, the suite a sitting area with two sofas. You also have a roomy guest sitting room and a small library for restful evenings. Your hosts are delightful and spoil you with decanters of sherry and bedside chocolates; the long room gallery seats up to 35 – great for family get-togethers. Visit Hay, walk down to the Wye or relax in the splendid garden. *Fishing can be arranged.*

Herefordshire

Lower House

I was in the equatorial forest, surely. The view reached over a pattern of tree tops to a distant hill, whose mist hovered as it awaited the day's heat. The house, itself a forest of old timber, is almost lost within the beautiful garden. It is old, but restored with affection. Stairs twist and creak, the unexpected awaits you. Bedrooms are panelled or timber-clad, bathrooms are neat, there is a handsome room where you eat breakfast, read or play the piano. Nicky and Pete are unpretentious and easy, steeped in good taste and this exquisite project, next to Offa's Dyke path and on the Welsh border. *Minimum stay two nights.*

Travel Club Offer: see page 392 for details.

Price	From £80–£100. Singles from £65.
Rooms	3: 1 double, 1 four-poster, 1 four-poster suite.
Meals	Pub/restaurant 2-minute walk.
Closed	Christmas.
Directions	From Hereford, A438 into village. House on left with a green sign & iron gates.

Price	From £80.
Rooms	2: 1 double; 1 double with separate bath.
Meals	Pubs/restaurants 1 mile.
Closed	Rarely.
Directions	East through Hay on B4348 for Bredwardine. On edge of Hay, right into Cusop Dingle; 0.75 miles, old mill house on left; drive on right, across stone bridge over stream.

	Jackie Kingdon
	Winforton Court,
	Winforton,
	Herefordshire HR3 6EA
Tel	01544 328498
Fax	01544 328498
Web	www.winfortoncourt.co.uk

	Nicky & Peter Daw
	Lower House,
	Cusop Dingle, Hay-on-Wye,
	Herefordshire HR3 5RQ
Tel	01497 820773
Mobile	07779 480783
Email	nicky.daw@btinternet.com
Web	www.lowerhousegardenhay.co.uk

Entry 227   Map 7

Entry 228   Map 7

Herefordshire

Ty-Mynydd

Six miles over open heathland from Hay-on-Wye, it is a bumpy, precipitous approach up the mountainside to Ty-Mynydd, but this renovated, stone-flagged farmhouse is worth every jolt. Sheep graze the hillside, the views are simply the best and the garden is colourful, informal, delightful. Turn on the taps and taste water straight from your hosts' own mountain stream; awake to bacon and eggs produced in the fields around you (this is a working organic farm). The lovely young family give you two sweetly restful rooms on the ground floor, one with 'that view', and a simple country bathroom. The sunsets are magical.

Ethical Collection: Environment; Food.
See page 400 for details

Price	From £80. Singles £50.
Rooms	2 doubles sharing bath (2nd room let to same party only).
Meals	Pubs 6-8 miles.
Closed	Rarely except Christmas & New Year.
Directions	From Hay on A438, 1st left after Swan Hotel; 6 miles uphill to open heath under Hay Bluff; 1st right signed Capel Y Ffin; 1 mile, signed.

	Miss N Spenceley
	Ty-Mynydd,
	Llanigon,
	Hay-on-Wye,
	Herefordshire HR3 5RJ
Tel	01497 821593
Email	nikibarber@tiscali.co.uk
Web	www.tymynydd.co.uk

Entry 229   Map 7

Herefordshire

Ladywell House

Snuggling in the Golden Valley, wrapped by ancient oaks and a deep peacefulness, you will relax here. The whitewashed Edwardian dower house is welcoming and informal with understated good taste: soft colours, family paintings and antiques. The four-poster bedroom is regal, the twin is fresh in blues and creams, and bathrooms are stylish and spoiling – one has a corner spa bath. Breakfast in the light conservatory, take drinks to the new Breeze House in the garden, dine well by candlelight at a rustic oak table. Sarah and Charles are warm and generous – this is very much 'open house'.

Price	From £60. Singles from £50.
Rooms	2: 1 four-poster; 1 twin with separate bath.
Meals	Dinner, 3 courses, from £25. Bistro 10-minute drive. Pub 15-minute drive.
Closed	Rarely.
Directions	From A465 Hereford-Abergavenny, B4348 for Hay-on-Wye. In Vowchurch, left for Michaelchurch. Through hamlet of Turnastone, house 0.5 miles on right.

	Charles & Sarah Drury
	Ladywell House,
	Turnastone, Vowchurch,
	Herefordshire HR2 ORE
Tel	01981 550235
Mobile	07970 510110
Email	sarah@ladywellhouse.com
Web	www.ladywellhouse.com

Entry 230   Map 7

Herefordshire

Burghill Grange

A big, happy, friendly, family house. Harriet and John have sandblasted beams, waxed elm floors, uncovered some fine 18th-century ceilings and put in three smart bathrooms. Your sitting room is cosy – bright with fire, bold fabrics and interesting books; enjoy home-laid eggs, delicious coffee and sausages from Ludlow while looking over the peacefully twittering garden. A first-floor double is calm and uncluttered, the others beamed and large with great views to church tower and orchards; bathrooms have chunky roll tops, big towels and organic bubbles and creams. Handy for Hay, golf, antiques and the Brecons.

🛄 Travel Club Offer: see page 392 for details.

Price	£90. Singles £55.
Rooms	3: 1 double; 1 twin/double with separate shower; 1 twin with separate bath.
Meals	Occasional dinner £20. Pubs/restaurants 1-4 miles.
Closed	Christmas.
Directions	A4103 north of Hereford, then A4100 north to Cannon Pyon. After 2 miles, after Portway sign, left to Burghill. After Burghill sign, house 1st on left.

	Harriet Gordon
	Burghill Grange,
	Burghill,
	Herefordshire HR4 7SE
Tel	01432 761016
Mobile	07525 215414
Email	enquiries@burghillgrange.com
Web	www.burghillgrange.com

🕇 ✗ 🚃 🐾

Entry 231　Map 7

Herefordshire

The Grove House

Pimms and pomp in 13 acres of gardens and pastures, this house is cosseting, Beams gleam richly in winter firelight and the guests' drawing room is large, elegant and generous, with plump sofas. You sleep either in the house's heart, among 14th-century timbers, or in the garden house with its more modern style. Dinner is a smart affair or a buffet for a large party, cooked deliciously by Ellen. It is delightfully chic, a tad shabby in parts, and you can have fun poking your head round the French windows trilling "anyone for tennis?" The court is yours, and a swimming pool next door. *Minimum stay two nights at weekends.*

🛄 Travel Club Offer: see page 392 for details.

Price	£85-£90. Singles £60.
Rooms	3: 1 twin/double, 2 four-posters.
Meals	Dinner £32 (min. 4). Pubs/restaurants in Ledbury, 3 miles.
Closed	Christmas.
Directions	M50 exit 2, for Ledbury; 1st left to Bromsberrow Heath; right by post office, up hill, house on right.

	Michael & Ellen Ross
	The Grove House,
	Bromsberrow Heath, Ledbury,
	Herefordshire HR8 1PE
Tel	01531 650584
Mobile	07960 166903
Email	ross@the-grovehouse.co.uk
Web	www.the-grovehouse.com

🕇 ✗ 🚃 🐾 🐕 🚲

Entry 232　Map 8

Herefordshire

Moor Court Farm

The buildings, about 500 years old, ramble and enfold both gardens and guests. This is an honest, authentic farmhouse in a deeply rural position. Elizabeth, a busy farmer's wife, manages it all efficiently with husband Peter; they were lambing when we were there. They also dry their own hops and in September you can watch the lovely old oast house (with resident owls and bats) at work. Elizabeth is an excellent, traditional cook – make the most of the home-produced meat, preserves and vegetables. Cottagey bedrooms have plump pillows and goose down duvets; one has views to the Malvern hills.

Price	From £60. Singles £35.
Rooms	3: 1 double, 2 twins.
Meals	Dinner, 3 courses, from £19.
Closed	Rarely.
Directions	From Hereford, east on A438. A417 into Stretton Grandison; 1st right past village sign, through Holmend Park. Bear left past phone box. House on left.

Elizabeth & Peter Godsall
Moor Court Farm,
Stretton Grandison, Ledbury,
Herefordshire HR8 2TP

Tel	01531 670408
Fax	01531 670408
Email	elizabeth@moorcourtfarm.co.uk
Web	www.moorcourtfarm.co.uk

Entry 233   Map 7

Herefordshire

Pullastone

Find a quiet, secluded corner in the two acres of garden hugging this ancient black and white farmhouse: watch the Indian Runner Ducks on their pond, spot deer, buzzards and shy hedgehogs. Inside is lovely: soaring beams, sculptures, turned wood chairs, prints, pictures and photos, all interesting, all beautiful. Two bedrooms on the ground floor have good beds, quilted covers, fresh flowers; one upstairs has a high vaulted ceiling and abstract art. Breakfast comes with a weather forecast and duck eggs; in season you get asparagus soldiers. Alison just wants you to be comfortable, to relax and feel at home. You will.

 Travel Club Offer: see page 392 for details.

Price	£70–£80. Singles from £30.
Rooms	3: 2 doubles, 1 twin.
Meals	Pubs within 2 miles.
Closed	Christmas.
Directions	A49 from Hereford towards Ross. Past car show rooms, then up hill. Where road narrows turn left to Aconbury; 2nd drive on left.

Alison Davies
Pullastone,
Kingsthorn,
Herefordshire HR2 8AQ

Tel	01981 540450
Fax	01981 540450
Email	info@pullastone.com
Web	www.pullastone.com

Entry 234   Map 7

Herefordshire

Treetops

Retreat seekers will love it here – up in the treetops (it is well named) with fine views, at the end of a steep narrow track. The modernised farmworker's cottage has a calm serenity within, and kind hosts whose wish is that you truly unwind. You will: woods and wildlife surround you, the owls hoot you to sleep at night. The very private bedroom is feminine and pretty with a neat bathroom, all smells fresh and lovely, breakfast times are bendy, there's a summerhouse in the garden and you can stay all day. Walks start from the door, yet you are just three miles from Ross. *Minimum stay two nights at weekends.*

Hertfordshire

The Old Rectory

A happy spirit pervades the Grade II*-listed rectory, thanks to the likeable, relaxed and very spoiling Dunns. Warm, light, candy-striped rooms lie across a cobbled courtyard and bathrooms are equally inviting. Enjoy a very delicious breakfast on the sunny terrace overlooking gardens in summer; finish the day with a nightcap in the inglenook-cosy, deep-red walled dining room. The conservation village trumpets George Bernard Shaw's house and a gem of an inn, there are concerts at Knebworth, green walks aplenty and you're just 35 minutes from London. *Children by arrangement.*

Travel Club Offer: see page 392 for details.

Price	£60-£70.
Rooms	1 double.
Meals	Packed lunch £5. Pub/restaurant 1.5 miles.
Closed	Rarely.
Directions	B4234 Ross to Walford. Left at Coughton (Howle Hill). Ignore right turn Howle Hill, take right to Ruardean/Deepdean. Stop under vision mirror on left; take unmade track opposite. Left at fork.

Sandra & Steve Gibbens
Treetops,
Howle Hill,
Ross-on-Wye,
Herefordshire HR9 5SP
Tel   01989 567537
Email   info@treetopscottage.co.uk
Web   www.treetopscottage.co.uk

Entry 235   Map 7

Price	£95. Singles by arrangement.
Rooms	3 twins/doubles.
Meals	Meals by arrangement. Pub 2-minute walk.
Closed	Rarely.
Directions	Exit A1 junc. 4. Follow signs to B653, towards Wheathampstead. At r'bout on to B653; 1st right for Codicote & Ayot St Lawrence. Left up Bride Hall Lane, signed Shaws Corner. Right into drive before red phone box in village.

Helen & Dick Dunn
The Old Rectory,
Ayot St Lawrence,
Welwyn,
Hertfordshire AL6 9BT
Tel   01438 820429
Fax   01438 821844
Email   ayotbandb@aol.com

Entry 236   Map 9

Hertfordshire

Homewood

Lutyens built this wonderful 1901 house for his mother-in-law, Lady Lytton. It is set down a long drive in six acres of gardens and fields, and architectural peculiarities abound. Samantha has applied her considerable artistic skills to the interior; new is the double bedroom's pretty stencilled floor. The reception rooms are particularly elegant and formal: unusual colour schemes offset magnificent antiques, tapestries and chinoiserie. Your hosts give you an excellent breakfast, can converse in a clutch of languages, will book tables and taxis if required. And their pets are happy to welcome yours.

Price	£80. Singles £50. Suite £80–£120.
Rooms	3: 1 double, 1 family suite for 4. 1 double with separate shower also available.
Meals	Pub 15-minute drive. Occasional dinner, including wine, £30 (min. 4).
Closed	20 December–3 January.
Directions	Into Knebworth B197, into Station Rd (becomes Park Lane); 300 yds after m'way bridge, left into public footpath; 300 yds; bear left through gates; house at end.

Samantha Pollock-Hill
Homewood,
Old Knebworth,
Hertfordshire SG3 6PP

Tel	01438 812105
Email	sami@homewood-bb.co.uk
Web	www.homewood-bb.co.uk

Entry 237 Map 9

Hertfordshire

West Lodge

With Luton Airport a short drive, it is an unexpected treat to find somewhere so tranquil. At the end of country lanes, behind a sweep of gravel drive, the imposing red-brick edifice is new, well-designed and sits in an acre of garden; fields and woodland are visible beyond the lawns. Inside, an abundance of windows and light and a smart and luxurious décor. Rooms range from a voluptuous double to a more functional single; colourful bathrooms gleam. Downstairs, traditional sofas, chintz and some good antiques – all very swish. Best of all, Jean-Christophe Novelli's restaurant is a 15-minute drive!

Price	£75–£90. Singles from £50.
Rooms	3: 1 twin; 1 double with separate bath/shower; 1 single with separate shower.
Meals	Pub in village.
Closed	Rarely.
Directions	A1 exit 4 take B653. At Wheathampstead, B651 towards Kimpton. Just before village, left on single track road to Porters End & house. Airport parking £6 per day.

Pauline & Graeme Tarbox
West Lodge,
Porters End, Kimpton, Hitchin,
Hertfordshire SG4 8ER

Tel	01438 832633
Fax	01438 832633
Email	westlodgebb@yahoo.co.uk

Entry 238 Map 9

Isle of Wight

Gotten Manor

Such character, such style – miles from the beaten track, bordered by beautiful stone barns. There's a refreshing simplicity to this unique Saxon house where living space was above, downstairs was for storage. Romantic bedrooms, one hidden up a steep open stair, have limewashed walls, wooden floors, A-frame beams, sofas. You sleep on a French rosewood bed, you bathe in a roll top tub in the room! Wallow by candlelight with a glass of wine. The garden bursts with magnificent fruit trees; Caroline's breakfasts include smoked salmon and smoothies. Rustic perfection, ancient peace. *Minimum stay two nights at weekends.*

Ethical Collection: Environment.
See page 400 for details.

Price	£70-£95. Singles by arrangement.
Rooms	2 doubles.
Meals	Pub 1.5 miles.
Closed	Rarely.
Directions	0.5 miles south of Chale Green on B3399. After village, left at Gotten Lane. House at end of lane.

Caroline Gurney-Champion
Gotten Manor,
Gotten Lane, Chale,
Isle of Wight PO38 2HQ

Tel	01983 551368
Mobile	07746 453398
Email	as@gottenmanor.co.uk
Web	www.gottenmanor.co.uk

Entry 239   Map 4

Isle of Wight

North Court

The Harrisons bought this glorious Jacobean house for its matchless grounds: 15 acres of pathed terraced gardens, exotica and subtropical flowers. The house, too, is magnificent, with 80 rooms, its big, comfortable guest bedrooms in two wings. The library houses a full-size snooker table (yes, you may use it) and the vast music room a grand piano (yours to play). The dining room has separate tables and delightful Nina Campbell wallpaper. Step back in time – in a quiet, untouristy village in lovely downland, this large house is very much a family home, and the perfect base for walkers and garden lovers.

Price	£65-£100. Singles £40-£50.
Rooms	6 twins/doubles.
Meals	Occasional light meals. Pub 3-minute walk through gardens.
Closed	Rarely.
Directions	From Newport, drive into Shorwell; down a steep hill, under a rustic bridge & right opp. thatched cottage. Signed.

John & Christine Harrison
North Court,
Shorwell,
Isle of Wight PO30 3JG

Tel	01983 740415
Mobile	07955 174699
Email	christine@northcourt.info
Web	www.northcourt.info

Entry 240   Map 4

Kent

Hartlip Place

The house resonates with a faded, funky grandeur. Family portraits and mahogany pieces, a drawing room to die for, an antique table shimmering with hyacinths, sash windows with sweeping views, happy dogs, chirpy peacocks, a garden intricate and special. After a candlelit dinner, up the circular stair to a colonial-style bedroom (or delightful four-poster) with garden views, decanter for sherry, old-fashioned bathroom and – big treat – real winter fire. John is unflappable and a touch mischievous, Gillian cooks, daughter Sophie greets – you'll like the whole family. *Children over 12 welcome.*

Price	From £90. Singles £50.
Rooms	2: 1 four-poster; 1 twin/double with separate bath.
Meals	Dinner £25. Pub 1 mile.
Closed	Christmas & New Year.
Directions	From Dover, M2 to Medway Services. Into station, on past pumps. Ignore no exit signs. Left at T-junc., 1st left & on for 2 miles. Left at next T-junc. House 3rd on left.

Gillian & John Yerburgh & Sophie & Richard Ratcliffe
Hartlip Place, Place Lane,
Sittingbourne, Kent ME9 7TR
Tel   01795 842323
Mobile   07990 971614
Email   hartlipplace@btinternet.com
Web   www.hartlipplace.co.uk

Entry 241   Map 5

Kent

Dadmans

Ease into a more gracious way of life at this listed Tudor dower house. Amanda is cheery company and enthuses about art history and her rare-breed hens – the breakfast eggs are ambrosial. There's good local food for dinner, too, served in the dining room on gleaming mahogany or in the Aga-warmed kitchen. Bedrooms have patterned fabrics, indulgent beds, fresh flowers and good bathrooms, one heavily beamed with a claw-foot bath. Ancient trees in the garden, orchards and fields all around, and Doddington Place with its gardens (and opera in summer) a five-minute drive. *Children over four welcome.*

Price	£80. Singles by arrangement.
Rooms	2: 1 twin; 1 double with separate bath.
Meals	Dinner, 3 courses, £25. Supper from £12.50. Pubs/restaurants nearby.
Closed	Rarely.
Directions	M20 junc. 8, then east on A20; left in Lenham for Doddington. At The Chequers in Doddington, left; house 1.7 miles on left before Lynsted.

Amanda Strevens
Dadmans,
Lynsted, Sittingbourne,
Kent ME9 0JJ
Tel   01795 521293
Mobile   07931 153253
Email   amanda.strevens@btopenworld.com
Web   www.dadmans.co.uk

Entry 242   Map 5

Kent

Frith Farm House

Eight beautifully tended acres of garden with pond, obelisk and orchards – yours to explore. Magnificent views, too – and a very pretty indoor pool that is heated all year round. The house is large, traditional, luxurious. Bold Traviata-type fabrics abound and walls are vividly coloured. Feel grand in the four-poster, enjoy Chinese carpets, oriental pictures, exotic antiques. There's a music room with an organ, too. Markham will play – but only if you will sing! He and Susan enjoy meeting new people over breakfast – local and delicious – and are lovely hosts. Canterbury and Leeds Castle are easily reached.

Price	£75. Singles £60.
Rooms	3: 1 double, 1 twin, 1 four-poster.
Meals	Pubs/restaurant nearby.
Closed	Christmas.
Directions	From A2 at Faversham, Brogdale Road to Eastling. 1.5 miles past Carpenters Arms, right (by postbox). House 0.5 miles on right.

	Susan & Markham Chesterfield
	Frith Farm House,
	Otterden,
	Faversham,
	Kent ME13 0DD
Tel	01795 890701
Email	stay@frithfarmhouse.co.uk
Web	www.frithfarmhouse.co.uk

Entry 243   Map 5

Kent

7 Longport

A delightful, unexpected hideaway bang opposite the site of St Augustine's Abbey and a five-minute walk to the Cathedral. You pass through Ursula and Christopher's elegant Georgian house to emerge in a pretty courtyard, on the other side of which is the self-contained cottage. Downstairs is a cosy sitting room with pale walls, tiled floors and plenty of books, and a clever, compact wet room with mosaic tiles. Then up steep stairs to a swish bedroom with crisp cotton sheets on a handmade bed and views of magnolia and ancient wisteria. You breakfast in the main house or in the courtyard on sunny days. Perfect.

Ethical Collection: Food. See page 400 for details.

 Travel Club Offer: see page 392 for details.

Price	£80. Singles £60.
Rooms	Cottage with 1 double & sitting room.
Meals	Restaurant 30 yds (closed Mondays).
Closed	Rarely.
Directions	Follow ring road around Canterbury. Signs for Sandwich A257, at St George's r'bout turn for Dover. After 300 yds left for Sandwich. At mini r'bout, left; house on left just before corner.

	Ursula & Christopher Wacher
	7 Longport,
	Canterbury,
	Kent CT1 1PE
Tel	01227 455367
Email	ursula.wacher@btopenworld.com

Entry 244   Map 5

Kent

14 Westgate Grove

Slap bang in the city, overlooking the river Stour and within strolling distance of the cathedral... step through the understated door and you will be astonished. Pippa is an interior designer, her husband an architect, and bedrooms are cool, smooth and fresh with good lighting, smart fabrics and pretty flowers. Bathrooms dazzle with rain showers, Brazilian black slate and the fluffiest of towels; don't feel guilty – it's rainwater heated by solar panels. On warm days you breakfast in the rosy-walled garden with its ancient vines, olives, lemons, mimosa; for cooler evenings there is an outdoor fireplace. Lovely.

Price	£80-£100.
Rooms	2: 1 double; 1 double with separate bath.
Meals	Pub/restaurant 50 yds.
Closed	Rarely.
Directions	Centre of Canterbury, on river by the Westgate Towers.

Pippa Clague
14 Westgate Grove,
Canterbury,
Kent CT2 8AA

Tel	01227 769624
Mobile	07815 107032
Email	pippa@clague.plus.com

✕ 🚃 🔊

Entry 245   Map 5

Kent

Forstal House

Where to begin – the house or the garden? Both are a rare delight. The interiors are beautiful, lived-in, quietly traditional: muted colours in a sunlit drawing room; a riot of paintings; masses of books. Cosy, welcoming bedrooms (it feels like staying with friends), one up, one down, look onto the gardens – graceful, formal, tantalising; Duncan, a painter, sculptor and printmaker, redesigned much after the 1987 storm. Your hosts love their 17th- and 18th-century home and look after you well; fruit from the orchards ends up in crumbles, pies and delicious breakfast jams. *Children over seven welcome.*

Price	£70-£80. Singles from £50.
Rooms	2: 1 twin/double, 1 double.
Meals	Dinner, 3 courses, £22.50. Pub/restaurant 2 miles.
Closed	Christmas.
Directions	From A257, Canterbury to Sandwich; left at Wingham, north to Preston. In Preston, The Forstal is 2nd left; 500 yds to house.

Elizabeth Scott
Forstal House,
The Forstal, Preston,
Canterbury,
Kent CT3 1DT

Tel	01227 722282
Email	emscott@forstal.fsnet.co.uk

✕ 🐕 🏊

Entry 246   Map 5

Kent

Great Weddington

The listed house of perfect proportions was built by a Sandwich brewer of ginger beer. The décor is delicious, the bedrooms desirable and cosy, the bathrooms snug and spotless, and Katie fills the rooms with flowers; she also arranges the flowers for Canterbury Cathedral. Dinner is followed by coffee and chocolates in the drawing room – rich fabrics, shelves of books, fine watercolours, much-loved antiques. Outside, stunning hedges and lawns and a terrace for tea in the summer. An enchanting home in a farmland setting, and the area hums with history. *Min. stay two nights weekends April-Sept. Pets by arrangement.*

Price	£90–£110. Singles £72–£82.
Rooms	2 twins/doubles.
Meals	Dinner, 4 courses, £33 (not Sunday).
Closed	Christmas & New Year.
Directions	From Canterbury, A257 for Sandwich. On approach to Ash, stay on A257 (do not enter village), then 3rd left at sign to Weddington. House 200 yds down on left.

Katie & Neil Gunn
Great Weddington,
Ash, Canterbury, Kent CT3 2AR
Tel   01304 813407
Fax   01304 812531
Email   greatweddington@hotmail.com
Web   www.greatweddington.co.uk

🚶 🏃 ✕ 🗐 🐾 🔊 🍷 🐕

Kent

Park Gate

Peter and Mary are a generous team and their conversation is informed and easy. Behind the wisteria-clad façade are two sitting rooms (one with chesterfield, one with wood-burner), ancient beams and polished wood. Bedrooms are freshly comfortable with gorgeous views over the garden to the fields beyond; bathrooms gleam, meals are delicious. More magic outside: croquet, tennis and thatched pavilions, wildlife and roses and a sprinkling of sheep to mow the paddock. The house has a noble history: Sir Anthony Eden lived here and Churchill visited during the war. Great value, and convenient for the Channel Tunnel.

Price	£80. Singles £40.
Rooms	3: 2 twins/doubles; 1 single with separate shower.
Meals	Dinner, 3 courses, £25. Pubs/restaurants 1 mile.
Closed	Christmas & New Year.
Directions	A2 Canterbury to Dover road; Barham exit. Through Barham to Elham. After Elham sign 1st right signed Park Gate 0.75 miles. Over brow of hill; house on left.

Peter & Mary Morgan
Park Gate,
Elham,
Canterbury,
Kent CT4 6NE
Tel   01303 840304
Email   marylmorgan@hotmail.co.uk

✕ 🐾 🐕 🌿

Kent

Little Mystole

All is reassuringly traditional and peaceful in this corner of Kent. The small Georgian house and delightful garden is run with the lightest of touches by your well-travelled, charming hosts. Cosy, comfortable bedrooms have a touch of chintz, inviting beds and glorious views. Tuck into a delicious breakfast in the handsome dining room, relax in the beamed sitting room filled with antiques, plump sofas, gilt-framed portraits and pretty flower arrangements. Golf at Royal St George's can be arranged and there are walks through rolling downland, hop fields and orchards. *10 mins from Canterbury, 30 mins from ferry & tunnel.*

Price	£85. Singles £20–£50.
Rooms	2: 1 double with extra single bed, 1 twin.
Meals	Occasional dinner. Pubs/restaurants 1.5 miles.
Closed	Christmas & Easter.
Directions	A28 Canterbury–Ashford. Left to Shalmsford Street; right immed. after post office at Bobbin Lodge Hill. Road bends left, then right at T-junc.; 2nd drive on left at junc. with Pickelden Lane.

Hugh & Patricia Tennent
Little Mystole,
Mystole Park, Canterbury,
Kent CT4 7DB

Tel	01227 738210
Fax	01227 738210
Email	little_mystole@yahoo.co.uk
Web	www.littlemystole.co.uk

Entry 249 Map 5

Kent

Pond Cottage

Don't be fooled by the rural exterior and rolling countryside — inside is cool, funky and fabulously colourful. Off the garden: a designer bedroom with an Indian theme — hot pink rubber floor, electric blue shiny bedcover, sixties chair and eastern wall hanging. You have your own walk-in shower and the use of a gorgeous roll top upstairs. Try Jude's specialist juices at breakfast (celery, ginger, cucumber) or tuck into kippers, smoked salmon, eggs from the hens, enjoyed outside on your own terrace on fine days. Walk it off well, then stagger back for an aromatherapy massage — and a delicious healthy supper.

 Travel Club Offer: see page 392 for details.

Price	From £95.
Rooms	1 double.
Meals	Dinner from £15. Packed lunch £8. Pub 2 miles.
Closed	Rarely.
Directions	A28 Canterbury to Ashford. At junction with A252, turn up Cobbs Hill to Old Wives Lees. Past Star Inn, then continue on Selling Road. House 0.5 miles on left.

Jude Adams
Pond Cottage,
Selling Road, Old Wives Lees,
Canterbury, Kent CT4 8BD

Tel	01227 751828
Mobile	07795 424570
Email	jude@pondstays.com
Web	www.pondstays.com

Entry 250 Map 5

Kent

Hoo Farmhouse

Jane and Nicolas are keen shrimpers – let them take you to Minnis Bay and cook your catch for supper! Passionate about the coastline and the area, Jane is also a generous hostess, baking cakes for your arrival and giving you greengages and flowers from the garden. Bedrooms are big and sunny and have Georgian skirting boards and elegant sash windows; new bathrooms have soaps from Provence. The large Georgian-fronted house, surrounded on three sides by garden and rosy-brick outbuildings, has pale classic colours within, a breakfast conservatory, a drawing room with a fire – and a cathedral down the road.

Price	£80. Singles £60.
Rooms	2 twins/doubles.
Meals	Supper, 2 courses, £10.
	Dinner, 3 courses, £20. Pub 1 mile.
Closed	Rarely.
Directions	A28 from Canterbury to Sarre, then A253 to Ramsgate. 4th exit at Monkton r'bout onto Willets Hill. Left at mini r'bout. House 0.75 miles on left.

Jane Irwin
Hoo Farmhouse,
Monkton Road,
Minster,
Ramsgate, Kent CT12 4JB
Tel   01843 821322
Email   stay@hoofarmhouse.com
Web   www.hoofarmhouse.com

Entry 251   Map 5

Kent

Orchard Barn

Alison loves to spoil (big beds, fluffy towels, bread from the mill), David knows the wildlife. Now their twins have flown the nest, they are loving B&B. The big beautiful barn has been sympathetically restored and eclectically furnished, its middle section left open to create a stunning covered courtyard. You get two snug bedrooms up in the eaves – pale beams and pretty velux windows onto the garden, and a sweet bath (or shower) room. A delightful village here, the ancient port of Sandwich nearby and egrets, kingfishers, swallows and squirrels a walk away. *Children over seven welcome.*

Price	£65–£75. Singles from £40.
Rooms	2: 1 double, 1 twin/double.
Meals	Pubs/restaurants within 1.5 miles.
Closed	20 December–15 January.
Directions	A258 Sandwich to Deal. 1st right after Worth sign into Federland Lane; 0.5 miles concealed entrance on left, opp. black barn.

David & Alison Ross
Orchard Barn,
Felderland Lane,
Worth, Deal,
Kent CT14 0BT
Tel   01304 615045
Mobile   07950 599304
Web   www.orchardbarn-worth.co.uk

Entry 252   Map 5

Kent

Beaches

A proper seaside townhouse on The Strand, facing Walmer Green and the sea. But no fierce landlady inside – just cheery Rosie and two sleek, cool bedrooms, one on the ground floor, one on the first. Both are light, bright and fresh, dressed mainly in pale colours but with the odd striped headboard or bright cushion, and with comfy chairs for admiring views. Bathrooms are funky in a nautical way, there's a super little garden for breakfast on sunny days, and a fabulous fish and chip shop close by. Start your day with eggs Benedict, cinnamon brioche, fresh croissants, good coffee. The perfect English seaside treat.

Kent

West End House

The very smart red-bricked Georgian house, formerly the village surgery, is now a gorgeous retreat. Choose between complete independence in the spacious suite at the 'North End' of the house, or the Tulip room in the main house. Lovely easy-going Lynne gives you homemade cake when you arrive, and delicious breakfasts (including smoked salmon and scrambled eggs) in an elegant family dining room with garden views. Bedrooms are crisp and pretty in shades of blue and green, mattresses are excellent and bathrooms have scented goodies. There's a deeply peaceful and rural feel, yet you are near to Dover and Canterbury.

 Travel Club Offer: see page 392 for details.

Price	£75-£85. Singles £60-£70.
Rooms	2 doubles.
Meals	Breakfast brunch for the beach. Pubs/restaurants 0.5 miles.
Closed	Rarely.
Directions	From Deal station or town centre, south along Victoria Road passing Deal Castle. Then on to The Strand which opens onto Walmer Green. House opposite bandstand.

Price	£65-£95. Singles £40-£55.
Rooms	2: 1 suite & sitting room; 1 double with separate bath, sitting room & kitchen.
Meals	Dinner on request. Pub 800 yds.
Closed	Christmas & New Year.
Directions	A2 towards Dover. Follow signs for Coldred. With the green on left, take right fork for Eythorne. House is on left after village sign.

	Rosanna Lillycrop
	Beaches,
	34 The Strand, Walmer,
	Kent CT14 7DX
Tel	01304 369692
Mobile	07752 720022
Email	enquiries@beaches.uk.com
Web	www.beaches.uk.com

	Lynne Backhouse
	West End House,
	Coldred Road,
	Eythorne,
	Kent CT15 4BE
Tel	01304 830594
Email	lynne_backhouse@yahoo.co.uk
Web	www.westendhousekent.co.uk

Entry 253 Map 5

Entry 254 Map 5

Kent

Woodmans

No traffic noise, just blissful peace – and you're no more than a short hop to Canterbury. Your cosy ground-floor bedroom has its own entrance via the glorious garden where there are plenty of places to sit when its sunny. Tuck into local bacon and eggs (from Sarah's own rescued hens) in the breakfast room with its old pine table, dresser and flowers – or decide to be lazy and let Sarah bring it to your room. You can eat delicious dinner here too, perhaps after some hearty walking on the Wye Downs with its magnificent Chalk Crown and far-reaching views to Dungeness and the coast. *Babies welcome but cot not available.*

Price	£65. Singles £35.
Rooms	1 double.
Meals	Dinner, 3 courses, £22.50. Packed lunch £6.50. Pub/restaurant 1 mile.
Closed	Rarely.
Directions	From A2, 2nd exit to Canterbury. Follow ring road & B2068 for Hythe. Over A2, through Lower Hardres, past Granville pub. Right to Waltham; 1.5 miles after Waltham, right into Hassell St; 4th on left.

Sarah Rainbird
Woodmans,
Hassell Street,
Hastingleigh,
Ashford, Kent TN25 5JE

Tel	01233 750250
Mobile	07836 505575
Email	sarah.rainbird@googlemail.com

Entry 255 Map 5

Kent

Stowting Hill House

A classic manor house in an idyllic setting, close to Canterbury and the North Downs Way. This warm, civilised home mixes Tudor beams with Georgian proportions, there's a huge conservatory full of greenery, a guest sitting room with sofas and log fire, and breakfasts fresh from the Aga. Traditional bedrooms are carpeted and cosily furnished. Your charming, country-loving hosts welcome you with tea and flowers from the garden – a perfect summer spot with its lawns, tree-lined avenue and stone obelisk. You are ten minutes from the Chunnel but this is worth more than one night. *Children over ten welcome.*

Price	From £80. Singles £50.
Rooms	2: 1 twin/double, 1 twin.
Meals	Dinner from £25. Pub 1 mile.
Closed	Christmas & New Year.
Directions	From M20 junc. 11, B2068 north. After 4.6 miles, sharp left opp. Jet garage. House at bottom of hill on left, after 1.7 miles. Left into drive.

Richard & Virginia Latham
Stowting Hill House,
Stowting, Ashford,
Kent TN25 6BE

Tel	01303 862881
Mobile	07803 157987
Fax	01303 863433
Email	vjlatham@hotmail.com

Entry 256 Map 5

Kent

The Old Rectory

On a really good day (about once every five years) you can see France. But you'll be more than happy to settle for the superb views over Romney Marsh, the Channel in the distance. The big, friendly house, built in 1850, has impeccable, elegant bedrooms and good bathrooms; the large, many-windowed sitting room is full of books, pictures and flowers from the south-facing garden. Marion and David are both charming and can organise transport to Ashford International for you. It's remarkably peaceful – perfect for walking (right on the Saxon Shore path), cycling and birdwatching. *Children over ten welcome.*

Price	£65–£75. Singles £45.
Rooms	2: 1 twin; 1 twin with separate bath/shower.
Meals	Pubs within 4 miles.
Closed	Christmas & New Year.
Directions	M20, exit 10 for Brenzett & Hastings on A2070. After 6 miles, right for Hamstreet; immed. left; in Hamstreet, left B2067. After 1.5 miles, left (Ash Hill); 700 yds on right.

Marion & David Hanbury
The Old Rectory,
Ruckinge,
Ashford,
Kent TN26 2PE
Tel   01233 732328
Email   oldrectory@hotmail.com
Web   www.oldrectoryruckinge.co.uk

Entry 257   Map 5

Kent

West Winchet

Annie has got hospitality down to a fine art: homemade compotes and scrumptious rashers at breakfast, the run of the gardens, treats in your room. The house is spotless but infectiously informal, the Parkers are great company and Annie is a treasure. Light, bright, ground-floor bedrooms are in the post-Edwardian wing, one opening to the terraced lawns; all is polished, nothing looks out of place: floral fabrics, soft carpeting, fresh flowers. Breakfast in the splendid drawing room with huge windows – or in bed. Beautifully, traditionally English. *Children over five welcome. Min. stay two nights summer weekends.*

Price	From £70. Singles from £50.
Rooms	2: 1 double, 1 twin.
Meals	Pubs 2 miles.
Closed	Christmas & New Year.
Directions	A262 to Goudhurst. There, B2079 to Marden. House 2.5 miles from village, on left.

Annie Parker
West Winchet,
Winchet Hill, Goudhurst,
Cranbrook, Kent TN17 1JX
Tel   01580 212024
Fax   01580 212250
Email   annieparker@jpa-ltd.co.uk
Web   www.westwinchet.co.uk

Entry 258   Map 5

Kent

Barclay Farmhouse

Lynn's breakfasts are fabulous: fresh fruits, warm croissants, banana bread, eggs en cocotte. The weatherboarded guest barn may be in perfect trim but has a been-here-for-ever feel; you have a country-cosy dining room for breakfast or playing cards, a patio for summer, a big peaceful garden, a bird-happy pond. Gleaming bedrooms have brocade bedspreads, French oak furniture, chocolates, slippers, flat-screen TVs; shower rooms are in perfect order. Couples, honeymooners, garden lovers – many would love it here (but no children: the pond is deep). Warm-hearted B&B, and glorious Sissinghurst nearby. *Min. two nights weekends.*

Price	£75. Singles from £60.
Rooms	Barn: 3 doubles.
Meals	Pubs/restaurants 1 mile.
Closed	Rarely.
Directions	From Biddenden centre, south on A262: Tenterden road. 0.7 miles, bear right (for Par3 Golf, Vineyard & Benenden). Immed. on right.

	Lynn Ruse
	Barclay Farmhouse,
	Woolpack Corner, Biddenden,
	Kent TN27 8BQ
Tel	01580 292626
Fax	01580 292288
Email	info@barclayfarmhouse.co.uk
Web	www.barclayfarmhouse.co.uk

Entry 259   Map 5

Kent

22 Lansdowne Road

Built in 1861, the house in leafy Tunbridge Wells "has never been as Victorian as it is now". So says Harold, whose devotion to Victoriana knows no bounds. Deep colours, rich velvets, marble tables, authentic wallpapers, tasselled lamps, portraits of Queen Vic, tea and scones by the fire… be prepared to take a serious step back in time. Bedrooms are simple in comparison: ruched chintz in the ground-floor double, damask in the twin below – and a door to the conservatory. Bathrooms have large mirrors and brand new fittings, breakfast is a spread. Those in search of heritage will marvel.

Price	£80–£120. Singles £80.
Rooms	3: 1 double, 1 twin/double, 1 studio.
Meals	Dinner, 2 courses, £15. Pubs/restaurants within 5-min. walk.
Closed	January.
Directions	From A21 to Tonbridge A26 to T. Wells centre. Grosvenor Rd one way system turn left onto Victoria Rd. Onto Garden Rd turn right onto Lansdowne Rd.

	Harold Brown
	22 Lansdowne Road,
	Tunbridge Wells,
	Kent TN1 2NJ
Tel	01892 533633
Mobile	07714 264489

Entry 260   Map 5

Kent

Swan Cottage

A delightful Georgian townhouse in Tunbridge Wells, just near the Pantiles with its covered walkways between shops, coffee houses and spas. Your genial host is an artist, his studio can be seen through the glass wall in the open-plan dining room and his engaging pen and ink drawings dot every wall. Bedrooms have plenty of space, are comfortable and contemporary with big sash windows and fresh flowers; bathrooms are roomy, light and white, one with rooftop views. In summer there's a little patio for local sausages and eggs at a pink table under the magnolia tree. And the High Street is at the bottom of the road.

Travel Club Offer: see page 392 for details.

Price	£80. Singles £50.
Rooms	2: 1 twin/double; 1 single with separate bath.
Meals	Pubs/restaurants 200 yds.
Closed	Rarely.
Directions	From railway station follow High Street for 300 yds, left up Little Mt Sion. House faces you at top of hill. Parking to left of house.

	David Gurdon
	Swan Cottage,
	17 Warwick Road, Tunbridge Wells,
	Kent TN1 1YL
Tel	01892 525910
Email	swancot@btinternet.com
Web	www.swancottage.co.uk

Entry 261   Map 5

Kent

40 York Road

A smart Regency townhouse, slap bang in the centre of Royal Tunbridge Wells and a five-minute walk from the delightfully preserved Pantiles. Patricia will enjoy cooking for you – in another life she served up delights for hungry skiers coming off the French mountains. She is a gentle presence and leaves you to come and go as you please; guests have a comfortable sitting room and bright, spotless bedrooms that are quieter than you may think. In the summer you may breakfast outside in the pretty courtyard garden before wandering into town for the cluster of great little shops and restaurants. *Children over 12 welcome.*

Travel Club Offer: see page 392 for details.

Price	From £70. Singles from £40.
Rooms	2 twins/doubles.
Meals	Dinner, 4 courses with wine, £25. Picnic available. Pub/restaurant nearby.
Closed	23 December-2 January.
Directions	From M25 junc. 5 onto A21, then A26 through Southborough to T. Wells. Take sign for Lewes, incline left taking 4th road left. Halfway along, on left. Car parks nearby, from £3.50 per 24 hours.

	Patricia Lobo
	40 York Road,
	Tunbridge Wells,
	Kent TN1 1JY
Tel	01892 531342
Email	yorkroad@tiscali.co.uk
Web	www.yorkroad.co.uk

Entry 262   Map 5

Kent

Hoath House

Mervyn and Jane are fun. They live in a fascinating house which creaks under its own history, and takes you on a journey through medieval, Tudor and Edwardian times. Breakfast in what was a medieval hall, all heavy panelling, low ceilings and small, leaded windows; wander through 23 acres of formal and informal gardens. Ancestors, and a new charcoal drawing of Mervyn, gaze from the walls, dark staircases wind up to roomy, traditional bedrooms with super views, bathrooms are 1930s with chunky taps. Not for shallow style-seekers, but imaginative souls will adore it. *Minimum stay two nights at weekends.*

Price	£60-£70. Singles £35-£40.
Rooms	3: 1 double with separate bath; 2 twins sharing bath.
Meals	Supper/dinner £12.50-£20. Pubs 2.5 miles.
Closed	Christmas & New Year.
Directions	From A21, signs to Penshurst Place; go past vineyard up Grove Road; right at T-junc. for Edenbridge; through village, bearing left, for Edenbridge. House 0.5 miles on left.

Mr & Mrs Mervyn Streatfeild
Hoath House,
Chiddingstone Hoath,
Edenbridge, Kent TN8 7DB
Tel   01342 850362
Email   jstreatfeild@hoath-house.freeserve.co.uk
Web   www.hoathhouse.co.uk

Entry 263   Map 5

Kent

Charcott Farmhouse

The 1750 tile-hung brick farmhouse is very much a family home, so don't come expecting a sterile, immaculate environment and you should love it here. You share a pretty sitting room in the old bakehouse with the original beams and bread oven, and bedrooms are simple and fresh, with traditional fabrics and country views. Ginny is charming and Nicholas – a tad eccentric for some – is highly knowledgeable about the area and a brilliant chef. Breakfast is an unrushed, happy affair with heaps of homemade bread and marmalade and free-range eggs from the family flock. Best of all, you can come and go as you please.

Travel Club Offer: see page 392 for details.

Price	£60-£70. Singles £45-£55.
Rooms	3: 2 twins; 1 twin with separate bath.
Meals	Pub 5-minute walk.
Closed	Christmas Day & very occasionally.
Directions	B2027 0.5 miles north of Chiddingstone Causeway. Equidistant between Tonbridge, Sevenoaks & Edenbridge.

Nicholas & Ginny Morris
Charcott Farmhouse,
Charcott, Leigh,
Tonbridge, Kent TN11 8LG
Tel   01892 870024
Mobile   07714 023021
Email   charcottfarmhouse@btinternet.com

Entry 264   Map 5

Kent

Merzie Meadows

You get your own suite in this modern, ranch-style house with huge windows, pergolas groaning with climbers, and a mediterranean-style swimming pool in the twittering garden. Pamela is just as light and bright: she keeps horses and hens and gives you locally sourced breakfasts. Your bedroom has a contemporary, uncluttered feel and is beautifully dressed in pale colours with pretty fabrics and a super bed, your own sitting room looks out onto the garden and the bathroom is sleek with Italian marble and plump towels. All is quiet and calm; garden and nature lovers will adore it here. *Minimum stay two nights at weekends.*

Kent

Reason Hill

Brian and Antonia's 200-acre fruit farm is perched on the edge of the Weald of Kent, with stunning views over orchards and oast houses. The farmhouse has 17th-century origins (low ceilings, wonky floors, stone flags) and there's a new conservatory; colours are soft, antiques gleam and the mood is relaxed. The roomy double has a bay window and armchairs, the pretty twin looks over the garden. Come in spring for the blossom, summer for the fresh fruit and anytime for a break – the Greensand Way runs along the bottom of the farm, you are close to Sissinghurst Castle and 45 minutes from the Channel tunnel.

Travel Club Offer: see page 392 for details.

Price	£85–£95.
Rooms	1 suite.
Meals	Pub 2.5 miles.
Closed	Mid-December–mid-February.
Directions	A229 Maidstone to Hastings road, then B2079 for Marden. 1st right into Underlyn Lane, 2.5 miles, large Chainhurst sign, right onto drive.

Price	£70.
Rooms	3: 1 double; 1 twin with separate shower, 1 single sharing shower (let to same party only).
Meals	Pubs within 3 miles.
Closed	Christmas & New Year.
Directions	From Maidstone A229 for Hastings. After 4.5 miles, right at lights on B2163. In Coxheath, left up Westerhill Rd, 0.2 miles then right into private road. Leave large white house on left, follow road through fruit trees to Reason Hill.

	Pamela Mumford
	Merzie Meadows,
	Hunton Road, Marden,
	Maidstone, Kent TN12 9SL
Tel	01622 820500
Mobile	07762 713077
Email	pamela@merziemeadows.co.uk
Web	www.merziemeadows.co.uk

	Brian & Antonia Allfrey
	Reason Hill,
	Linton,
	Maidstone,
	Kent ME17 4BT
Tel	01622 743679
Mobile	07775 745580
Email	antonia@allfrey.net

Entry 265   Map 5

Entry 266   Map 5

Kent

The Limes

A three-minute motor from 'the loveliest castle in the world' (magnificent Leeds, on two islands) is a well-renovated, oak-beamed, inglenook'd and thoroughly refurbished Wealdon hall house overlooking the village green. Your hostess greets you with a lovely bright smile and ushers you in to an immaculate interior traditionally decorated with a crisp, modern slant – and bedrooms that delight in fine fabrics and bedding. (Sonia has her own bed linen business so you are assured of the best.) The breakfast buffet is equally splendid: fresh, organic, and served, on warm days, on the sun-trap terrace.

Price	From £90. Singles from £75.
Rooms	2 doubles.
Meals	Pubs/restaurant a short walk.
Closed	Christmas & New Year.
Directions	M20 exit 7 for Maidstone. At 2nd r'bout, signs for Bearsted. Past railway station on left, past shops. House 50 yds on left overlooking green.

Sonia Ashdown
The Limes,
The Green,
Bearsted, Maidstone,
Kent ME14 4DR
Tel   01622 730908
Email   info@limesonthegreen.co.uk
Web   www.limesonthegreen.co.uk

Entry 267 Map 5

Kent

Thurnham Keep

A grand house in every sense. Through wrought-iron gates and up a winding drive edged by immaculate lawns, find an Edwardian house with fabulous views to the Weald of Kent. Bubbly Amanda grew up here and gives you the run of the place: snooker room, sitting room with roaring fire and comfy sofas, conservatory, terraces, croquet on the lawn. Bedrooms are brobdingnagian! Gaze out of stone mullion windows, leap onto half-tester beds with clouds of goose down, pamper yourself in marble bathrooms. Breakfast is a treat: try omelettes, American pancakes, good bacon, proper coffee. The perfect country house retreat.

Price	£105-£130. Singles from £85.
Rooms	3 doubles.
Meals	Dinner on request. Packed lunch £10. Pub/restaurant 300 yds.
Closed	Christmas.
Directions	M20, junction 7 to Maidstone. Turn to Bearsted then to Bearsted Green. 1.5 Take sharp left at shops up Thurnham Lane. 1.2 miles, entrance next to Black Horse pub.

Mrs Amanda Lane
Thurnham Keep,
Castle Hill, Thurnham,
Maidstone, Kent ME14 3LE
Tel   01622 734149
Mobile   07906 399380
Email   info@thurnhamkeep.co.uk
Web   www.thurnhamkeep.co.uk

Entry 268 Map 5

Lancashire

Challan Hall

The wind in the trees, the boom of a bittern and birdsong. That's about as noisy as it gets. On the edge of the village, the Victorian former farmhouse overlooks fields, woods and Lake Haweswater. Deer, squirrels and Leighton Moss Nature Reserve are your neighbours. The Cassons are well-travelled and the house is filled with a colourful mishmash of mementos. Comfortably traditional, there's a sofa-strewn sitting room, a smart red and polished-wood dining room and two cosily floral bedrooms. Morecambe Bay and the Lakes are on the doorstep – come back for peaceful views and stunning sunsets.

Price	£70. Singles from £40.
Rooms	2: 1 twin/double; 1 twin with separate bath.
Meals	Packed lunch available. Pubs 2 miles.
Closed	Rarely.
Directions	M6 exit 35. Thro' Carnforth for Warton. Left for Silverdale. Past railway station, signed Silverdale. Over level crossing, right at T-junc, signs to Arnside. After 1 mile house on right.

Mrs Charlotte Casson
Challan Hall,
Silverdale,
Lancashire LA5 0UH
Tel   01524 701054
Mobile   07790 360776
Email   cassons@btopenworld.com
Web   www.challanhall.co.uk

Entry 269   Map 11

Lancashire

Northwood

A super stretch of golden beach with sand dunes is just across the road and delightful Lytham is a couple of miles away. The Victorian façade conceals light, lofty rooms mixing vintage and modern; bold wallpaper on odd walls, huge displays of flowers, original artwork. Your hosts happily find babysitters, advise on restaurants (then drive you there) and offer you maple syrup pancakes at breakfast, along with other treats. Bedrooms are generous: find coir carpets, baskets of plump blankets and towels, lovely colours and DVDs to watch on wet days. The whole place has an informal, warm and happy family vibe.

Travel Club Offer: see page 392 for details.

Price	£80. Family £90. Singles from £75.
Rooms	2: 1 double, 1 double/family room.
Meals	Restaurants 5-minute walk.
Closed	Christmas & New Year.
Directions	M6 exit 32 then M55 to Blackpool. Follow signs for Lytham St Annes then St Annes. Head for the promenade.

Shannon Kuspira
Northwood,
24 North Promenade,
St Annes on Sea,
Lancashire FY8 2NQ
Tel   01253 782356
Email   skuspira@hotmail.com
Web   www.24northwood.co.uk

Entry 270   Map 11

Lancashire

Sagar Fold House

Helen transformed this 17th century dairy and created two perfect studio apartments, self contained, all mod cons, very here and now. Your own entrance leads to large, beamed spaces that bring together comfort, immaculate efficiency and unusual beauty. There are books, DVDs, and comfortable sofas to curl up on; continental breakfast is supplied, using homemade, organic or local produce whenever possible. Now gaze over the Italian knot garden, which ties in lines of a lovely landscape. Take wonderful walks in deeply peaceful countryside, and it's not far to top-notch places to eat.

Price	£70.
Rooms	2:1 double, 1 studio both with kitchenette.
Meals	Continental breakfast in fridge. Pubs/restaurants 1-2 miles.
Closed	Rarely.
Directions	A59 through centre of Whalley. At 2nd mini r'bout left to Mitton; 3 miles, Three Fishes pub on left. Right to Whitewell Chaigely; 1 mile, left to Whitewell Chaigely; 0.5 miles, 3rd drive left to house.

Helen & John Cook
Sagar Fold House,
Higher Hodder,
Clitheroe,
Lancashire BB7 3LW
Tel   01254 826844
Mobile   07787 587437
Email   cookj@thomas-cook.co.uk

Entry 271   Map 12

Lancashire

Peter Barn Country House

Wild deer roam – this is the Ribble Valley, an AONB that feels like a time-locked land. In this former 18th-century tithe barn, where old church rafters support the big yet cosy guest sitting room, you settle in among plump sofas, log fire and flat-screen TV. Bedrooms, too, are on the top floor – nicely private. The Smiths couldn't be more helpful and breakfast is a feast: jams and muesli are homemade, stewed fruits are from the gardens. Step outside: Jean has transformed a field into a riot of colour and scent, there are pretty corners, a meandering stream and water lilies bask in still pools. *Minimum stay two nights.*

Price	£60–£64. Singles £36.
Rooms	3: 1 double, 1 twin/double; 1 double with separate bath.
Meals	Restaurants/pubs 1.5 miles.
Closed	Christmas & New Year.
Directions	M6 junc. 31, A59 to Clitheroe. Through Clitheroe to Waddington. Through village 0.5 miles, left on Cross Lane for 0.75 miles, past Colthurst Hall, house on left.

Jean & Gordon Smith
Peter Barn Country House,
Cross Lane/Rabbit Lane,
Waddington, Clitheroe,
Lancashire BB7 3JH
Tel   01200 428585
Mobile   07970 826370
Email   jean@peterbarn.co.uk

Entry 272   Map 12

Leicestershire

The Gorse House

Passing cars are less frequent than passing horses – this is a peaceful spot in a pretty village. The lasting impression of this 17th-century cottage is of lightness, brightness and space. There's a fine collection of paintings and furniture, everything gleams and oak doors lead from dining room to guest sitting room. Bedrooms are restful and fresh, the largest with three views. The garden was designed by Bunny Guinness, the stables accommodate up to six horses and it's strolling distance to dinner at the village pub. The house is filled with laughter and the Cowdells are terrific hosts.

Price	From £60. Singles £32.50.
Rooms	3: 1 double, 1 family for 3. Stable: 1 triple & kitchenette.
Meals	Packed lunch £5. Pub 100 yds.
Closed	Rarely.
Directions	From A46 Newark-Leicester; B676 for Melton. At x-roads, straight for 1 mile; right to Grimston. There, up hill, past church. House on left, just after right-hand bend at top.

	Mr & Mrs R L Cowdell
	The Gorse House, 33 Main Street, Grimston, Melton Mowbray, Leicestershire LE14 3BZ
Tel	01664 813537
Mobile	07780 600792
Email	cowdell@gorsehouse.co.uk
Web	www.gorsehouse.co.uk

Entry 273   Map 9

Leicestershire

White House Fields Farm

A house with a very pretty front – Georgian with a leaded porch and sash windows – but you arrive at the back, past rather modern farm buildings. You have your own entrance from the courtyard garden into a light, beamed bedroom – painted a cheerful yellow, brightened with fresh flowers and soothing with linen and goose down. This is a comfortable, lived-in farm with no pretensions – but Charlotte gives you very special food indeed, either a smart affair in the dining room or a kitchen supper with her young family. Very convenient for Donington race track and East Midlands Airport, yet peaceful.

 Travel Club Offer: see page 392 for details.

Price	£80–£85. Singles £55–£60.
Rooms	1 double.
Meals	Dinner, 3 courses with coffee & wine, £25. Pub/restaurant 0.5 miles.
Closed	Christmas & New Year.
Directions	M1 junc. 23a. Head for East Midlands Airport, follow signs to Breedon on the Hill. Left signed Worthington. 0.5 miles on right.

	Mrs Charlotte Meynell
	White House Fields Farm, Worthington, Ashby de la Zouch, Leicestershire LE65 1RA
Tel	01332 862312
Mobile	07973 105467
Email	charlottemeynell@aol.com
Web	www.whitehousefieldsfarm.co.uk

Entry 274   Map 8

Leicestershire

Curtain Cottage

A pretty village setting for this cottage on the main street, next door to Sarah's interior design shop. You have your own entrance by the side and through a large garden, which backs onto fields with horses and the National Forest beyond. A conservatory is your sitting room: wicker armchairs, wooden floors, a contemporary take on the country look. Bedrooms are light and fresh, linen from The White Company on sumptuous beds, a slate-tiled bathroom, stunning fabrics. Breakfast is anything, anytime, full English or fresh fruit and croissants from the local shop – all is delivered to you. Perfect privacy.

Leicestershire

The Grange

Behind the mellow brick exterior (Queen Anne in front, Georgian at the back) is a warm family home. Log fires brighten chilly days and you are greeted with kindness and generosity by Mary and Shaun, whose young family includes two sweet dogs. Big, beautifully quiet bedrooms, one in the attic, are hung with strikingly unusual wallpapers and furnished with excellent beds and pretty antiques, bathrooms are simple yet impeccable and there's a fireplace in the big, flagstoned hall decorated with sporting prints and deeds. The garden has a treehouse and is large enough to roam.

Travel Club Offer: see page 392 for details.

Price	£80. Singles £55.
Rooms	2: 1 double, 1 twin.
Meals	Pubs/restaurants 150 yds.
Closed	Rarely.
Directions	Gravel driveway to left of Barkers Interiors Design Showroom on Main Street. From car park, access to cottage via gate into garden at rear of showroom.

Price	£70. Singles £45.
Rooms	2: 1 twin, 1 double.
Meals	Pubs/restaurants 0.5-1.5 miles.
Closed	Christmas & New Year.
Directions	M1 exit 20; A4304 towards Market Harborough. First left after Walcote marked 'Gt Central Cycle Ride'; 2 miles, then right into Kimcote, pass church on left. On right after Poultney Lane.

Sarah Barker
Curtain Cottage,
92-94 Main Street, Woodhouse Eaves,
Leicestershire LE12 8RZ

Tel	01509 891361
Fax	01509 890100
Email	barkerID@aol.com
Web	www.barkersinteriors.com

Entry 275   Map 8

Shaun & Mary Mackaness
The Grange,
Kimcote,
Leicestershire LE17 5RU

Tel	01455 203155
Mobile	07808 242530
Email	shaunandmarymac@hotmail.com
Web	www.thegrangekimcote.co.uk

Entry 276   Map 8

Lincolnshire

1 Waterhills Court

Follow a lane from Caistor's marketplace to this contemporary townhouse, a haven of comfort for those trekking the Viking Way. Built into the eaves on the second floor, your suite is a seductively large and airy space with crisp white walls, wooden blinds and clever plays on lighting – with power jets in the bathroom to invigorate aching limbs. Vivacious Suzy, a therapist and yoga teacher, treats you to an organic English breakfast in the wood-floored kitchen, bright with the works of her art student daughter. Restorative B&B in the Lincolnshire Wolds – yet minutes from Humberside airport. Great value, too.

Price	£60. Singles £40-£50.
Rooms	1 suite for 2-4.
Meals	Pub/restaurant 170 yds.
Closed	Occasionally.
Directions	From A46, turn into Caistor sign. In Caistor through market place, left for Brigg. Then 1st right into North Street. House 150 yds on left.

	Suzy Gibson
	1 Waterhills Court,
	North Street,
	Caistor,
	Lincolnshire LN7 6QW
Mobile	07876 466989
Email	suzy@waterhills.org

✗ 🚂 🔊 🐾

Entry 277   Map 13

Lincolnshire

The Old Farm House

Hidden in the Lincolnshire Wolds, an 18th-century, ivy-covered house – and Nicola's father still farms the fields beyond the ha-ha. The stone-flagged, terracotta-washed hall gives a hint of warm colours to come; creamy walls show off tawny fabrics, prints and antiques; the beamed sitting/breakfast room has a big, rosy brick inglenook fireplace and tranquil views. Such a welcoming, tucked-away place, hopping with pheasant but just a 10-15-minute drive from shops, golf and racing in the nearby towns. Excellent value, and perfect if you fancy privacy and space. *Children over eight welcome.*

Price	£70. Singles £50.
Rooms	2: 1 double; 1 triple with separate bath.
Meals	Pub 2 miles.
Closed	Christmas, New Year & occasionally.
Directions	M180 exit 5; A18 signed Louth. Past airport; 2.5 miles after junction of A46 take right signed Hatcliffe. House is third on right, before village.

	Nicola Clarke
	The Old Farm House,
	Low Road, Hatcliffe,
	Lincolnshire DN37 0SH
Tel	01472 824455
Mobile	07818 272523
Email	clarky.hatcliffe@btinternet.com
Web	www.oldfarmhousebandbgrimsby.co.u

✗ 🐾 ♿

Entry 278   Map 13

Lincolnshire

Knaith Hall

This intriguing place, medieval church at its gate, dates from the 16th century. Lawns slope down to the river Trent, daffodils, lambs, a passing barge and waterfowl pattern the serenity. And the skyscapes are terrific! At night, a distant power station shines, actually enhancing that 'great rurality of taste' referred to in Pevsner. Indoors, diamond-paned windows, a domed dining room and fine furniture are softened by easy décor and a log fire. An appealing family house, with a relaxed atmosphere. Your own room is comfortable and restful with the very best of old-fashioned bedding.

Lincolnshire

The Manor House

One guest's summing up reads: "Absolutely perfect – hostess, house, garden and marmalade." Delightful Ann – interested in horses, food, photography, people – makes you feel immediately at home. You have the run of downstairs: all family antiques, fresh flowers and space. Chintzy, carpeted bedrooms have dreamy views of the lovely sweeping gardens and duck-dabbled lake; dinners are adventurous and delicious: game casserole, ginger meringue bombe… Perfect stillness at the base of the Wolds and a pretty one-mile walk along the route of the old railway that starts from the front door. Very special, great value.

Travel Club Offer: see page 392 for details.

Price	From £70. Singles £40.
Rooms	2: 1 double with separate shower, 1 twin with separate bath.
Meals	Dinner, 3 courses with wine, £20. Pub 4 miles.
Closed	Rarely.
Directions	Knaith 3 miles south of Gainsborough on A156 Lincoln-Gainsborough road. After Knaith signs, look for white gateposts on west side with sign for St Mary's Church.

Price	From £65. Singles £50.
Rooms	2: 1 double, 1 twin.
Meals	Dinner from £18. BYO. Pub/restaurant 2 miles.
Closed	Christmas.
Directions	From Wragby A157 for Louth. After approx. 2 miles, at triple road sign, right. Red postbox & bus shelter at drive entrance, before graveyard.

John & Rosie Burke
Knaith Hall,
Knaith, Gainsborough,
Lincolnshire DN21 5PE

Tel	01427 613005
Mobile	07796 881328
Fax	01427 613005
Email	jandrburke@aol.com

Ann Hobbins
The Manor House,
West Barkwith,
Lincolnshire LN8 5LF

Tel	01673 858253
Mobile	07751 891274
Fax	01673 858253

Entry 279   Map 9

Entry 280   Map 9

Lincolnshire

The Grange

Wide open Lincolnshire farmland on the edge of the Wolds. This immaculately kept farm has been in the family for five generations; their award-winning farm trail helps you explore. Listen to birdsong, catch the sun setting by the trout lake, have supper before the fire in a dining room whose elegant Georgian windows are generously draped. Sarah is a young and energetic host and offers you delicious homemade cake on arrival. Comfortable bedrooms have spick and span bath or shower rooms and fabulous views that stretch to Lincoln Cathedral. A delightful couple running good farmhouse B&B.

Travel Club Offer: see page 392 for details.

Price	From £60. Singles £40.
Rooms	2 doubles.
Meals	Supper from £13. Dinner, 3 courses, from £17. BYO. Packed lunch £6. (No meals at harvest time.) Pub/restaurant 1 mile.
Closed	Christmas & New Year.
Directions	Exit A157 in East Barkwith at War Memorial, into Torrington Lane. House 0.75 miles on right after sharp right-hand bend.

Sarah & Jonathan Stamp
The Grange,
Torrington Lane, East Barkwith,
Lincolnshire LN8 5RY

Tel	01673 858670
Mobile	07951 079474
Email	sarahstamp@farmersweekly.net
Web	www.thegrange-lincolnshire.co.uk

Entry 281 Map 9

Lincolnshire

Baumber Park

Lincoln red cows and Longwool sheep ruminate in the fields around this rosy-brick farmhouse – once a stud that bred a Derby winner. The old watering pond is now a haven for frogs, newts and toads; birds sing lustily. Maran hens conjure delicious eggs and Clare, a botanist, is hugely knowledgeable about the area. Bedrooms are light and traditional, not swish, with mahogany furniture. There's a heart-stopping view through an arched window on the landing, a grass tennis court, a sitting room with a log fire, a dining room with local books. This is good walking, riding and cycling country, with quiet lanes.

Travel Club Offer: see page 392 for details.

Price	£58-£62. Singles from £35.
Rooms	3: 2 doubles; 1 twin with separate bath.
Meals	Pubs/restaurants 4 miles.
Closed	Christmas & New Year.
Directions	From A158 in Baumber take road towards Wispington & Bardney. House 300 yds down on right.

Mike and Clare Harrison
Baumber Park,
Baumber, Horncastle, Lincolnshire
LN9 5NE

Tel	01507 578235
Mobile	07977 722776
Email	mail@baumberpark.com
Web	www.baumberpark.com

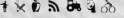

Entry 282 Map 9

Lincolnshire

Ryelands House

Farmer Mike and charming Caroline built this large red-brick and slate house on their land and are much committed to the Countryside Stewardship programme; hang out of your bedroom window to watch waders, even deer, round the nearby pond. Inside is warm with underfloor heating and spacious. Your bedroom has a boutique hotel feel in shades of cream and brown, while two beautifully lit sitting rooms are smoothly uncluttered and have comfortable armchairs. Pedal along those lovely flat lanes after breakfast, head to Lincoln and its cathedral or Horncastle for antiques; walk to the local pub for excellent bar food.

Price	From £65. Singles from £40.
Rooms	1 twin/double & sitting room.
Meals	Packed lunch from £2.50. Restaurant 0.5 miles.
Closed	Christmas, New Year & occasionally.
Directions	A15 Lincoln, Sleaford turn. Left at Mere onto B1178 for 3 miles; over staggered x-roads into Potterhanworth. At T-junc. right for 100 yds to War Memorial; left onto Barff Rd, 0.5 miles, drive on left.

Michael & Caroline Norcross
Ryelands House,
Barff Road, Potterhanworth, Lincoln,
Lincolnshire LN4 2DU
Tel   01522 793563
Mobile   07977 590375
Email   norcross@ukfarming.co.uk
Web   www.ryelands-house.co.uk

Entry 283   Map 9

Lincolnshire

Brills Farm

There aren't many hills in Lincolnshire, but Sophie and Charlie's early Georgian farmhouse is at the top of one of them. Built of warm brick, right next door to the site of a Roman settlement, it is restful and elegant inside, with subtle colours and charming furniture. The drawing and dining rooms, filled with fresh flowers, overlook the valley, the beautiful, airy bedrooms hold some lovely old pieces. The Whites are a delightful young couple, enthusiastic and hospitable (Sophie is a professional cook) and obviously enjoy what they do. Breakfast on home-produced eggs, bacon, and just-made bread. *Children over 12 welcome.*

Travel Club Offer: see page 392 for details.

Price	£82. Singles £51.
Rooms	3: 2 doubles, 1 twin/double.
Meals	Supper £15.50. Dinner £25. Packed lunches £8. Pubs 5-minute drive.
Closed	Christmas & New Year.
Directions	A46 Newark–Lincoln. Exit Brough, Norton Disney & Stapleford. Right at T-junc.; 0.5 miles; 1st left onto lane; 0.75 miles; wide gravel entrance, on right before hill.

Charles & Sophie White
Brills Farm,
Brills Hill, Norton Disney, Lincoln,
Lincolnshire LN6 9JN
Tel   01636 892311
Mobile   07947 136228
Email   admin@brillsfarm-bedandbreakfast.co.uk
Web   www.brillsfarm-bedandbreakfast.co.uk

Entry 284   Map 9

Lincolnshire

Churchfield House

The little house was built in the sixties; inside glows with character and charm. Bridget is an interior decorator whose eye for detail and sense of fun will delight you. A snug bedroom sports fresh checks in creams and greens, firm mattress, down pillows, interesting pictures, even a gilt-trimmed copy of a Louis XIV chair. The bathroom is small but spotless, and there's a conservatory mood to the warm red, stone-tiled dining room, where glass doors open to a large, lush garden in summer. You're close to a good golf course, Bridget cooks and chats with warmth and humour – this is a gem.

Price	£55. Singles £35.
Rooms	1 twin with bath.
Meals	Dinner from £15.
	Pubs/restaurants 3 miles.
Closed	Christmas & New Year.
Directions	A607 Grantham to Lincoln road. On reaching Carlton Scroop, 1st left for Hough Lane. Last house on left.

Mrs Bridget Hankinson
Churchfield House,
Carlton Scroop, Grantham,
Lincolnshire NG32 3BA
Tel   01400 250387
Fax   01400 250241
Email   info@churchfield-house.co.uk
Web   www.churchfield-house.co.uk

Entry 285   Map 9

Lincolnshire

Belvoir Vale Cottage

The Vale of Belvoir is gloriously quiet and you are just 200 yards from the Viking Way. Kindly Norman and Suzie have restored two old roadside cottages, charmingly; the emphasis is on warmth, lovely colours, beautifully arranged fresh flowers, good food and gorgeous views over the pretty garden to Belvoir Castle. Bedrooms and bathrooms are a good size and have thick carpets and new windows to keep out the blast; expect original brass beds, fluffy towels, crisp white linen. Start the day with a full English or undyed haddock with poached eggs; you'll be truly spoiled. *Children welcome if rooms let to one party.*

Travel Club Offer: see page 392 for details.

Price	£65–£75. Singles from £40.
Rooms	3: 1 double & sitting room; 1 double, 1 twin.
Meals	Dinner from £25.
	Packed lunch available.
	Pubs/restaurants 1.2 miles.
Closed	Rarely.
Directions	A52 Nottingham-Grantham. At Sedgebrook x-roads, turn for Stenwith & Woolsthorpe. After 1.5 miles cross double bridges - private car park 300 yds.

Suzie & Norman Davis
Belvoir Vale Cottage,
Stenwith, Woolsthorpe-by-Belvoir,
Grantham, Lincolnshire NG32 2HE
Tel   01949 842434
Mobile 07976 562845
Email   reservations@belvoirvale-cottage.co.uk
Web   www.belvoirvale-cottage.co.uk

Entry 286   Map 9

Lincolnshire

Tanyard House

The old tanner's house (it dates from 1643) is listed and the Knights Templar convened in the cellar. Sloping ceilings, twisting stairs and tiny doors – a house of immense history which has been completely refurbished inside. Claire, full of enthusiasm for guests, gives you a long sunny living room overlooking a young garden, replete with dining table, generous sofas and deep sills. Upstairs are soft carpets, gentle hues, seductive linen, aromatic oils. One bedroom is in the old part (mullion windows, copse views), one (big and beautiful) in the new. Expect to be stylishly spoiled.

Price	£70. Singles £45.
Rooms	2 twins, each with separate bath/shower.
Meals	Occasional dinner with wine, £25. Pubs 0.75 miles.
Closed	Rarely.
Directions	North on A1, exit after Ram Jam Inn to S. Witham. Or: going south on A1, exit after Fox Inn to S. Witham; enter village, 1st right into Church Lane; 2nd drive on right.

Alex & Claire van Straubenzee
Tanyard House,
South Witham, Grantham,
Lincolnshire NG33 5PL

Tel	01572 767976
Mobile	07765 241354
Email	tanyardhouse@btinternet.com
Web	www.tanyardhouse.co.uk

Entry 287   Map 9

Lincolnshire

The Barn

Simon and Jane, the nicest people, have farmed for 30 years and love having guests to stay. Breakfasts are entirely local or homemade, home-grown and delicious; there are endless extras and nothing is too much trouble. In this light-filled barn conversion find old beams, new walls and good antiques; a brick-flanked fireplace glows and heated floors keep toes warm. Above the high-raftered main living/dining room is a comfy, good-sized double; in the adjoining stables, two further rooms, a crisp feel, sparkling showers, restful privacy. Views are to sheep-dotted fields and the village is on a 25-mile cycle trail.

Travel Club Offer: see page 392 for details.

Price	£70. Singles £40.
Rooms	3: 1 double, 1 twin/double; 1 single with separate bath/shower.
Meals	Supper, 2 courses, £15. Dinner, 3 courses, £20. BYO. Pub in village & 2 miles.
Closed	Rarely.
Directions	Midway between Lincoln & Peterborough. From A15, in Folkingham, turn west into Spring Lane next to village hall; 200 yds on right.

Simon & Jane Wright
The Barn,
Spring Lane, Folkingham, Sleaford,
Lincolnshire NG34 0SJ

Tel	01529 497199
Mobile	07876 363292
Email	sjwright@farming.co.uk
Web	www.thebarnspringlane.co.uk

Entry 288   Map 9

Lincolnshire

The White House

The wisteria-clad, smart Georgian house is right by the village green in this conservation village. Victoria and David, understandably passionate about the place, have filled the rooms with gorgeous things. Feel free to discover interesting books in the library; admire the fine moulded fireplace and the etchings, the watercolours and the English and Chinese porcelain. The bedrooms, too, are striking, one with an antique four-poster canopied in green silk; bathrooms are fresh and appealing. Your friendly hosts give you afternoon tea in the pretty walled garden in summer, by a roaring fire in winter.

Price	£70. Singles £45.
Rooms	2: 1 twin/double; 1 four-poster (with adjoining room if required) with separate bath.
Meals	Occasional dinner, with wine, £25. Pub/restaurant in village.
Closed	Rarely.
Directions	A15 to Folkingham; on village green.

Victoria & David Strauss
The White House,
25 Market Place, Folkingham,
Sleaford, Lincolnshire NG34 0SE

Tel	01529 497298
Email	victoria.strauss@btinternet.com
Web	www.bedandbreakfastfolkinghamlincolnshire.co.uk

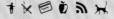

Entry 289   Map 9

London

Hyde Park Gate

Virginia Woolf was born in the sitting room (there's a library of her books here) which entitles this smart London house to a blue plaque – in fact it has three! Jasmyne is well-travelled, cultured, and gives you a full English breakfast (smoked salmon on Sundays) in a deep green and blue dining room. Your bedroom sits quietly at the back, sweetly decorated in corals and with fresh flowers, fruit, chocolates and a tea tray with proper china; the compact shower room sparkles. You are a step away from the Albert Hall, Kensington Gardens, Hyde Park and Knightsbridge – an excellent choice of restaurants too.

Price	From £75. Singles from £55.
Rooms	1 double.
Meals	Pubs/restaurants nearby.
Closed	Occasionally.
Directions	Tube: Gloucester Road; Kensington High Street. Bus: 9, 10, 52, 452, 70. Car park £25 per 24 hrs.

Jasmyne King-Leeder
Hyde Park Gate,
Flat 3, Kensington, London SW7 5DH

Tel	020 7584 9404
Mobile	07940 872807
Email	jkingleeder@yahoo.co.uk
Web	www.22hydeparkgate.com

Entry 290   Map 4

London

6 Oakfield Street

This district dates from the mid-1660s and Simon, who knows his Chelsea onions, has maps to prove it. Enter their 1860s house and you glimpse a collection of Egyptian prints – they once lived in Cairo. There's an open-plan feel to the kitchen, a marble-topped table and beautiful roof mural in the dining room, and a roof terrace where you can sit in summer under a smart green umbrella. Bedrooms are at the top of the house. The twin is tiny but, being at the back, is silent at night; the double has a big wooden bed and an antique armoire. Restaurants on Hollywood Road are a 30-second stroll.

London

37 Trevor Square

A fabulous find, luxury in the middle of Knightsbridge. The square is impossibly pretty, unexpectedly peaceful and a three-minute walk from Hyde Park or Harrods. Margaret runs an interior design company – rather successfully, by the look of things. You breakfast in the dining room (smoked salmon with scrambled eggs, if you wish) elegant with toile de Jouy walls, stone busts, warm rugs and fire in winter. Upstairs: electric blankets, duvets, a maple table, a gorgeous marbled bathroom, a minibar, DVDs and CDs. There's a snug conservatory/sitting room you're welcome to use, too.

Price	£80. Singles £60.
Rooms	2: 1 double, 1 twin.
Meals	Restaurants nearby.
Closed	Occasionally.
Directions	Tube: Earl's Court 15-minute walk. Nearest car park £25 for 24 hrs. South Kensington 20-minute walk.

Price	£160. Singles £100.
Rooms	2: 1 double, 1 twin sharing bath & shower (2nd room let to same party only).
Meals	Restaurants 200 yds.
Closed	Occasionally.
Directions	Tube: Knightsbridge. Nearest car park £25 for 24 hrs (closed overnight).

Margaret & Simon de Maré
6 Oakfield Street,
Little Chelsea, London SW10 9JB

Tel	020 7352 2970
Mobile	07990 844008
Email	demare@easynet.co.uk
Web	www.athomeinnchelsea.com

Margaret & Holly Palmer
37 Trevor Square,
Knightsbridge, London SW7 1DY

Tel	020 7823 8186
Fax	020 7823 9801
Email	margaret@37trevorsquare.co.uk
Web	www.37trevorsquare.co.uk

Entry 291 Map 4

Entry 292 Map 4

London

4 First Street

This is a smart London home in one of London's most desirable quarters. You get the top floor to yourself, and some floor it is. You're nicely private, it's surprisingly quiet, there's masses of space and the luxuries are unremitting... trim carpets, comfy armchairs, traditonal pictures, stencilled borders, a bathroom of marble and mirrors – and a wall of glass opening to a tiny muralled balcony. Shirley is the kindest hostess. Breakfast in the basement by an open fire or catch the sun on the potted terrace. This is shop-till-you-drop land and you can't get posher. Charming.

Price	£110.
Rooms	1 double.
Meals	Continental breakfast. Pub/restaurant 2 mins.
Closed	Occasionally.
Directions	Tubes: Sloane Square; Knightsbridge; South Kensington. Nearest car park £25 for 24 hrs.

Shirley Eaton
4 First Street,
Chelsea,
London SW3 2LD

Tel	020 7581 8429
Mobile	07831 292888
Email	shirley@eaton3176.fsnet.co.uk

✕ 🐈

Entry 293   Map 4

London

20 Bywater Street

In a quiet, pretty cul-de-sac off the fashionable King's Road, a delightful pastel-coloured house and a welcoming B&B. Caroline and Richard give you a pretty, bright bedroom downstairs, with a cherry blossom theme, a trim carpet and a wicker chair, fresh flowers, lots of magazines and a CD player. The private shower room is next door – fluffy towels, white tiles – while breakfast is taken across the hall in the kitchen/conservatory, a cheery room that swims in morning sun, with doors opening onto a smallish Yorkstone garden full of terracotta pots. The best of London laps at the door.

📖 Travel Club Offer: see page 392 for details.

Price	From £99. Singles from £80.
Rooms	1 double with separate shower.
Meals	Continental breakfast. Pubs/restaurants/cafes nearby.
Closed	Occasionally.
Directions	Tube: Sloane Square 5-min. walk (down King's Rd, 6th street on right). Parking available locally.

Caroline & Richard Heaton-Watson
20 Bywater Street,
Chelsea,
London SW3 4XD

Tel	020 7581 2222
Email	caheatonw@aol.com
Web	www.20bywaterstreet.com

✕

Entry 294   Map 4

London

90 Old Church Street

In a quiet street facing the Chelsea Arts Club, an enticing, contemporary haven. Softly spoken Nina is passionate about the arts, knows Chelsea inside out and takes real pleasure in looking after her guests. Antique shop spoils stand alongside more modern delights, the attention to detail is amazing and there are plentiful bunches of flowers. A lush carpet takes you up to the second floor and your super-private, surprisingly peaceful and deliciously designed bedroom. Breakfast – an array of fresh fruit, yogurts and croissants – is shared with Nina in the kitchen. We love this place.

Price	From £95. Singles from £80.
Rooms	1 double.
Meals	Continental breakfast. Restaurants/coffee shops/pubs nearby.
Closed	Occasionally.
Directions	Tube: South Kensington.

Nina Holland
90 Old Church Street,
Chelsea,
London SW3 6EP

Tel	020 7352 4758
Mobile	07831 689167
Email	ninastcharles@btinternet.com

Entry 295   Map 4

London

12A Evelyn Mansions

Your passport to Pimlico – one of the last 'villages' left in London with proper shops and a good choice of restaurants. Find comfort and elegance in this Edwardian mansion flat, its lovely drawing room sprinkled with interesting objects from Moranna's travels as the wife of a diplomat – she is a charming hostess. Your bedroom (double glazed) has a great view of the junction between Victoria Street and the station – a people-watcher's paradise – and is spoiling: goose down, easy chairs, good books, a shining white bathroom. It is the perfect city bolthole and good value too.

Price	£90. Singles £50.
Rooms	1 twin/double with separate bath.
Meals	After-theatre supper £15. Pubs/restaurants nearby.
Closed	Rarely.
Directions	3-minute walk to Victoria bus & tube; 5-minute walk to coach station. Carlisle Place is just off Victoria Street.

Moranna Colvin
12A Evelyn Mansions,
Carlisle Place,
London SW1P 1NH

Tel	020 7834 1889

Entry 296   Map 4

London

101 Abbotsbury Road

The area is one of London's most desirable and Sunny's family home is opposite the borough's loveliest park, with open-air opera in summer. The whole top floor is generally given over to visitors. Cosy, spotless bedrooms are in gentle yellows and greens, with pale carpets, white duvets, pelmeted windows and a dressing table in the double. The bathroom, marble-tiled and sky-lit, shines. You are well placed for Kensington High Street, Olympia, Notting Hill, Portobello Market, Kensington Gardens, the Albert Hall, Knightsbridge and Piccadilly. Feel free to come and go. *Children over ten welcome.*

Price	£100. Singles from £50.
Rooms	2: 1 double, 1 single, sharing bath.
Meals	Continental breakfast. Pubs/restaurants 5-minute walk.
Closed	Occasionally.
Directions	Tube: Holland Park 7-minute walk. Off-street parking sometimes available.

Sunny Murray
101 Abbotsbury Road,
Holland Park,
London W14 8EP
Tel 020 7602 0179
Mobile 07768 362562
Email sunny.murray@googlemail.com

Entry 297   Map 4

London

26 Hillgate Place

You are in luxurious, bohemian Notting Hill: a movie at the Coronet, a pint at the Windsor Castle, the best Thai at the Churchill and the chic-est shops. Whatever you do, roll back to Hilary and Maryo's easy-going home for a bit of eastern spice; Indian textiles, old teak dressers, the odd wooden elephant, wildly colourful art (Hilary paints). The bigger double has an Indo-Caribbean influence and shares a bathroom up a flight of stairs; the smaller is smarter – immaculate, actually – with a sofa and a claw-foot bath. Both rooms come with bathrobes and small fridge, and there are two gardens to look out on, one on a roof.

Travel Club Offer: see page 392 for details.

Price	£70-£97.50. Singles £60-£75.
Rooms	2: 1 double; 1 twin/double sharing family bath.
Meals	Pubs/restaurants nearby.
Closed	Occasionally.
Directions	Tube: Notting Hill Gate 5-min. walk.

Hilary Dunne & Maryo Josef
26 Hillgate Place,
Notting Hill Gate,
London W8 7ST
Tel 020 7727 7717
Email hilary.dunne@virgin.net
Web www.26hillgateplace.co.uk

Entry 298   Map 4

London

31 Rowan Road

Terrific value for money in Brook Green, and perfect privacy. Vicky's top-floor pied-à-terre is big and airy and delightfully decorated in white, pink and lime green. Under the eaves are a sofa, a window seat spilling cushions, a big comfy bed and a bathroom with a deep cast-iron bath from which you can gaze out at the birds; a continental breakfast is popped into the fridge the night before. The larger, lower-ground-floor studio is also private, furnished in contemporary style and equally inviting with its own wisteria-strewn entrance. There's a garden full of blossom and super restaurants close by.

Price	£60-£95. Extra person £10.
Rooms	2 studios for 2-3: with twin or twin/double & kitchen or kitchenette.
Meals	Continental breakfast. Pubs/restaurants 2 mins.
Closed	Occasionally.
Directions	Tube: Hammersmith. Off-street parking £12 a day.

Vicky & Edmund Sixsmith
31 Rowan Road,
Brook Green, London W6 7DT
Tel   020 8748 0930
Mobile   07966 829359
Email   vickysixsmith@btconnect.com
Web   www.abetterwaytostay.co.uk

Entry 299   Map 4

London

Roof Tops

This Edwardian terraced house, with a cool-lemon breakfast room and south-facing garden, makes a refreshing alternative to a central London stay – and is good value indeed. If you're after some respite before a trip abroad or a long day's shopping, leafy Northfields, with its peaceful park, is within easy reach of both Heathrow and Harvey Nics. A warm smile from Vanessa or Sheila greets you at the door, then it's up the thick poppy-red carpet to the new loft conversion high up, with trim twin beds and French windows admiring the roof tops. It's bright and south-facing and the sandstone bathroom is a treat.

Price	£68. Singles £47.
Rooms	2: 1 twin; 1 single sharing bath (let to same party only).
Meals	Continental breakfast only. Pub/restaurant 200 yds.
Closed	Never.
Directions	Tube: Northfields 5-minute walk. No parking restrictions.

Vanessa Scales
Roof Tops,
59 Altenburg Avenue,
London W13 9RN
Tel   020 8810 1502
Mobile   07958 234381
Email   info@wrightapartments.co.uk

Entry 300   Map 4

London

50a Penywern Road

In a grand central London street, a luxurious slice of peace. Past potted pansies and down limestone steps to warm, smiling, Irish Breege, who leads you into a light lower ground-floor space zinging with art and good taste. Off the kitchen is the guest bedroom. Find a huge bed, chrome chairs, subtle lights, white walls splashed with art and through to your own magnificent shower that designer Breege drove with Jack all the way to Paris to claim. More steps up to a lovely garden where statues peep out of bushes and seats beckon. Easy, fun and *so* spoiling – readers are full of praise. *Minimum stay two nights.*

Price	£85. Singles £60.
Rooms	1 double.
Meals	Continental breakfast.
Closed	Rarely.
Directions	Tube: Earl's Court 2-minute walk. Pay and display parking 8.30-6.30 Mon-Sat. Free at all other times in P&D bays and on yellow lines.

Breege Collins
50a Penywern Road,
Earl's Court,
London SW5 9SX
Tel 020 7244 7178
Email info@breegecollins.com

✕ ⌇ 🐾

Entry 301   Map 4

London

21 Barclay Road

The grand piano is a magnet for esteemed conductors and music professors from around the world. Charlotte, who does something unspeakably high-powered by day, happily advises on the best London sites. You pretty much get the run of the house: a large sitting room with an open fire, two tiny but beautifully laid out bedrooms with waffle bathrobes, a decanter of sherry and a book-filled bathroom. Breakfast is a feast of homemade cranberry muffins, French toast, fresh fruit salad, the best coffee – eat on the tree-top terrace in summer. Delightful people, a great city find. *Use of grand piano by arrangement.*

 Travel Club Offer: see page 392 for details.

Price	£88. Singles £68.
Rooms	2 doubles sharing bathroom.
Meals	Food & music evenings Thursdays. Restaurants 2-minute walk.
Closed	Occasionally.
Directions	Tube: Fulham Broadway 2-minute walk. Parking free 8pm-9am & all Sunday. 9am-8pm pay & display.

Charlotte Dexter
21 Barclay Road,
Fulham, London SW6 1EJ
Tel 020 7384 3390
Mobile 07767 420943
Email info@barclayhouselondon.com
Web www.barclayhouselondon.com

✕ ▭ ⌇ ⚲

Entry 302   Map 4

London

22 Marville Road

Smart railings help a pink rose climb, orange lilies add a touch of colour, and breakfast is in the pretty back garden in good weather. Tess, the spaniel, and Christine – music lover, traveller, rowing coach – make you feel at home. A generous single on the first floor shares the main bathroom (claw-foot bath, huge shower) with the owner. The spacious room in the eaves comes in elegant French grey and has a chaise longue; it was tested and vacated with regret. Treasures from Christine's travels, gentle music at breakfast, crisp linen, restaurants and shops a stroll away – and the Boat Race down the river.

Price	From £90. Singles from £50.
Rooms	2: 1 twin/double; 1 single with shared bath/shower. Extra single bed available.
Meals	Occasional dinner. Pubs nearby.
Closed	Rarely.
Directions	At Fulham Rd junc. with Parson's Green Lane, turn down Kelvedon Rd. Cross Bishop Rd into Homestead Rd; 1st left into Marville Rd.

Christine Drake
22 Marville Road,
Fulham, London SW6 7BD

Tel	020 7381 3205
Mobile	07973 113757
Email	christine.drake@btinternet.com
Web	www.londonguestsathome.com

Entry 303   Map 4

London

15 Delaford Street

A pretty Victorian terraced home, unassuming from the front but with space and charm inside. In a tiny, sun-trapping courtyard you can have continental breakfast in good weather – tropical fruits are a favourite; a second miniature garden bursts with life at the back. The bedroom, up a spiral staircase, looks down on it all. Expect perfectly ironed sheets, a quilted throw, books in the alcove, a sunny bathroom and fluffy white towels. The tennis at Queen's is in June and on your doorstep. Tim and Margot – she's from Melbourne – are fun, helpful and happy to pick you up from the nearest tube.

Price	£80. Singles £55.
Rooms	1 double.
Meals	Restaurants nearby.
Closed	Occasionally.
Directions	Tube: West Brompton. Parking free eves & weekends; otherwise pay & display. 74 bus to West End nearby.

Margot & Tim Woods
15 Delaford Street,
Fulham,
London SW6 7LT

Tel	020 7385 9671
Fax	020 7385 9671
Email	woodsmargot@hotmail.co.uk

Entry 304   Map 4

London

8 Parthenia Road

Caroline, an interior designer, mixes the sophistication of the city with the feel of the countryside and her handsome big kitchen is clearly the engine-room of the house. It leads through to a light breakfast room with doors onto a pretty brick garden with chairs and table – hope for fine days. The house is long and thin, Fulham style, and reaches up to a large, sloping-ceilinged bedroom in the eaves that is sunny and bright. A surprisingly quiet place to stay in an accessible part of town, near the King's Road with its antique and designer shops and Chelsea Football ground.

Price	£80–£100. Singles from £75.
Rooms	1 twin/double.
Meals	Continental breakfast. Restaurants nearby.
Closed	Rarely.
Directions	Tube: Parsons Green 4-minute walk. Parking £12.80 per day in street. Bus: no. 22, 2-minute walk.

Caroline & George Docker
8 Parthenia Road,
Fulham,
London SW6 4BD

Tel	020 7384 1165
Fax	020 7371 8819
Email	carolined@angelwings.co.uk

Entry 305   Map 4

London

20 St Philip Street

Come for peace and undemanding luxury: the 1890 Victorian cottage with delightful courtyard garden protects you from the frenzy of city life. You breakfast in the dining room on freshly squeezed juice, homemade bread and jams and marmalade, organic full English; across the hall is the sitting room, with gilt-framed mirrors, wooden blinds, plump-cushioned sofas and a piano you are welcome to play. Upstairs is a bright and restful bedroom with pretty linen and a cloud of goose down to snuggle into. Your bathroom next door is fabulous with its porthole windows and huge mirror. Nothing has been overlooked.

Price	£100. Singles £65.
Rooms	1 double with separate bath & shower.
Meals	Restaurants 200 yds.
Closed	Occasionally.
Directions	Nearby r'way stations (6-min ride Waterloo, 3-min ride Victoria). Or 137 & 452 bus (Sloane Sq) & 156 (Vauxhall) tubes 10 mins. Parking limited to 4 hrs (£1.80 per hr) or £10 day ticket, 9.30-5.30 Mon-Fri. Otherwise free.

Barbara Graham
20 St Philip Street,
Battersea,
London SW8 3SL

Tel	020 7498 9967
Email	stay@bed-breakfast-battersea.co.uk
Web	www.bed-breakfast-battersea.co.uk

Entry 306   Map 4

London

Bowling Hall

Walking distance from both Tates, a self-contained wonderland of cool lines and soothing colours. The mix of old and new is delicious: rugs on limestone tiles, a satinwood chest, hints of the orient – architect Peter has renovated with style. Stand at the front door and look down the expansive hall: the view floats seamlessly through each room. On the walls, dazzling art, much of it Katherine's. You stay in a lovely private apartment (with kitchen) at the front of the house – maple floors, linen curtains, light colours – opening onto a tropical treasure of a courtyard. *Parking free at weekends.*

Price	£90. Singles £50.
Rooms	Apartment with 1 double, 1 single, sitting room & kitchenette.
Meals	Continental breakfast. Pubs/restaurants 5-minute walk.
Closed	Occasionally.
Directions	Details on booking. Near underground & bus routes. Parking charge (no charge at weekend).

Peter Camp & Katherine Virgils
Bowling Hall,
346 Kennington Road,
London SE11 4LD

Tel	020 7840 0454
Fax	020 7840 0454
Email	bowlinghall@freenet.co.uk

Entry 307   Map 4

London

113 Pepys Road

Anne is Chinese, well-travelled, loves this house, loves her guests, and is a trained Cordon Bleu cook; convivial breakfast can be English or oriental. The house overlooks the first landscaped park of its kind in south-east London; at night you see a carpet of lights. There are hats on the hat stand, batiks on the walls, orchids (Anne's passion). The downstairs room has a huge bed, bamboo blinds, a kimono for the bathroom; our favourites are upstairs, airy, bright, overlooking the garden (the magnolias are majestic). It's a ten-minute walk downhill to buses, tubes and trains… and blissfully quiet for London.

Price	From £100. Singles from £70.
Rooms	3: 1 double, 1 twin/double; 1 twin with separate bath.
Meals	Dinner from £30. BYO. Restaurant 0.5 miles.
Closed	Rarely.
Directions	Directions on booking.

Anne Marten
113 Pepys Road,
New Cross, London SE14 5SE

Tel	020 7639 1060
Fax	020 7639 8780
Email	annemarten@pepysroad.com
Web	www.pepysroad.com

Entry 308   Map 4

London

24 Fox Hill

This part of London is full of sky, trees and wildlife; Pissarro captured on canvas the view up the hill in 1870 (the painting is in the National Gallery). There's good stuff everywhere – things hang off walls and peep over the tops of dressers; bedrooms are stunning, with antiques, textiles, paintings and big, firm beds. Sue, a graduate from Chelsea Art College, employs humour and intelligence to put guests at ease and has created a special garden, too. Tim often helps with breakfasts. Frogs sing at night, woodpeckers wake you in the morning, in this lofty, peaceful retreat. *Victoria is 20 minutes by train.*

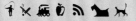 Travel Club Offer: see page 392 for details.

Price	£90–£100. Singles £50.
Rooms	3: 1 twin/double; 1 double, 1 twin sharing shower.
Meals	Dinner £30–£35. Pubs/restaurants 5-minute walk.
Closed	Rarely.
Directions	Train: Crystal Palace (7-min. walk). Collection possible. Good buses to West End & Westminster.

	Sue & Tim Haigh
	24 Fox Hill,
	Crystal Palace,
	London SE19 2XE
Tel	020 8768 0059
Email	suehaigh@hotmail.co.uk
Web	www.foxhill-bandb.co.uk

Entry 309   Map 4

London

108 Streathbourne Road

It's a handsome house in a conservation area that manages to be both elegant and cosy. The cream-coloured double bedroom has an armchair, a writing desk, pretty curtains and a big, comfy walnut bed; the twin is light and airy. The dining room overlooks a secluded terrace and garden and there are newspapers at breakfast. Dine in – David, who works in the wine trade, always puts a bottle on the table – or eat out at one of the trendy new restaurants in Balham. A friendly city base on a quiet, tree-lined street – maximum comfort and good value for London. Delightful. *Minimum stay two nights.*

Price	£85–£95. Singles £70–£80.
Rooms	2: 1 double with separate bath; 1 twin sharing bath (let to same party only).
Meals	Dinner £30. Restaurants 5-minute walk.
Closed	Occasionally.
Directions	Tube: Tooting Bec 7-minute walk. Free parking weekends, otherwise meters or £7.50 daily.

	Mary & David Hodges
	108 Streathbourne Road,
	Balham, London SW17 8QY
Tel	020 8767 6931
Fax	020 8672 8839
Email	mary.hodges@virgin.net
Web	www.streathbourneroad.com

Entry 310   Map 4

London

The Coach House

A rare privacy: you have your own coach house, separated from the Notts' home by a stylish terracotta-potted courtyard with Indian sandstone paving and various fruit trees (peach, pear, nectarine). Breakfast in your own sunny kitchen, or let Meena treat you to an all-organic full English in hers (she makes fine porridge, too). The big main attic bedroom has toile de Jouy bedcovers, cream curtains, rugs on dark polished floors; the brick-walled ground-floor twin is pleasant, light and airy, and both look over the peaceful garden. *Minimum stay three nights; two nights in Jan/Feb.*

Price	£75-£165.
Rooms	Coach House for 2-5 (1 family room; 1 twin with separate shower). Same-party bookings only.
Meals	Pub/restaurant 200 yds.
Closed	Occasionally.
Directions	From r'bout on south side of Wandsworth Bridge, south down Trinity Rd on A214. At 3rd set of lights, 1.7 miles on, left into Upper Tooting Park. 4th left into Marius Rd, then 3rd left.

Meena & Harley Nott
The Coach House,
2 Tunley Road, Balham,
London SW17 7QJ
Tel 020 8772 1939
Fax 08701 334957
Email coachhouse@chslondon.com
Web www.coachhouse.chslondon.com

Entry 311   Map 4

London

39 Telford Avenue

A very pretty Edwardian home, a family enclave, with logs piled high at the front door and a fire in the hall on cold afternoons. Warm interiors come with stripped floors, bright colours, fresh flowers and a piano in the dining room. There's a sofa in the homely double bedroom, a wall of good books and an electric pink bathroom two paces across the landing. Breakfast is a treat: homemade bread and yogurt, the full cooked works, a good selection of teas. Richard, an architect, loves his cricket; prints of Lords hang on the walls. You can be in Victoria in 15 minutes, and there's off-street parking, too.

Ethical Collection: Food. See page 400 for details.

Price	From £60. Singles from £30.
Rooms	2: 1 twin/double, 1 single each with separate bath.
Meals	Restaurants 2-minute walk.
Closed	Occasionally.
Directions	Train: Streatham Hill (to Victoria) 5-minute walk. Or ring on arrival at Clapham South tube (Northern line) & you will be collected.

Katharine & Richard Wolstenholme
39 Telford Avenue,
Streatham Hill,
London SW2 4XL
Tel 020 8674 4343
Mobile 07930 470619
Email rwolstenholme@aol.com

Entry 312   Map 4

London

33 Barmouth Road

Good value, family-friendly B&B in a smart 1880s terraced house of which only the exterior walls survive. Everything else is new, from the four flights of stairs to the Farrow & Ball paints. Expect neutral colours, a refined elegance, old pine dressers and a bit of helping yourself to things like breakfast. Uncluttered bedrooms at the top have good linen and all mod cons, the kitchen's floors are warm underfoot, there's a pretty Arts and Crafts feel and curtains made by Nessie. She, a stationery designer, and Duncan, a sports editor on a national paper, are most welcoming and full of enthusiasm for their B&B.

Price	From £65. Singles from £45.
Rooms	2: 1 twin/double, 1 double.
Meals	Continental breakfast. Pubs/restaurants nearby.
Closed	Occasionally.
Directions	From A217 at Wandsworth r'bout into Trinity Rd; under bypass & right at lights into Windmill Rd; right at lights into Heathfield Rd; 1st left into Westover Rd; Barmouth Rd 3rd right. Wandsworth station ten-min. walk.

	Nessie & Duncan Maclay
	33 Barmouth Road,
	Wandsworth Common,
	London SW18 2DT
Tel	020 8877 0331
Mobile	07885 379136
Email	beds@maclayworld.com
Web	www.maclayworld.com

London

P&P's B&B

Pinky and Perky Piggins, your porky hosts are not what you'd call trotters on – they're too busy making improvements to the garden – digging and more digging (to be honest they've made a bit of a pig's ear of it). They met on the way to market but managed to run wee wee wee all the way back to this B&B with its rolling wood chip hills and attractive fencing. "We really love having guests," squeals Pinky, as she dives headlong into a trough of filthy water, "they're as happy as pigs in ordure here." An absolute pigsty is how a reader described this place; we couldn't agree more (a patio is planned for spring).

Price	Sty high.
Rooms	Just the one (thankfully).
Meals	Snap, crackling and pop, truffles (order ahead and they'll dig them out).
Closed	Market days only.
Directions	Into village, left into orchard, across fields (no car porking).

	Pinky & Perky Piggins
	P&P's B&B,
	Banger Lane,
	Ringinnose,
	South Hams SN0 UTS
Web	www.pigsinblankets.oink

London

16 St Alfege Passage

The approach is along the passage between the Hawksmoor church and its graveyard, away from the village's hubbub. At the end of the lane is a 'cottage' set about with greenery, lamp posts and benches. Inside, a cup of tea and flapjack await you in the eccentrically furnished (stuffed cat on dentist chair, huge parasol) sitting room. Bedrooms are cosy and colourful, with double beds (not huge) that positively encourage intimacy. Breakfast is in the basement, another engagingly furnished room awash with character. Robert, an actor, is easy, funny, chatty – and has created an unusual and attractive place.

Price	From £90. Singles from £60.
Rooms	3: 1 four-poster, 1 double, 1 single.
Meals	Pubs/restaurants 2-minute walk.
Closed	Rarely.
Directions	3-minute walk from Greenwich train & Docklands Light Railway station or Cutty Sark DLR station. Parking free from 5pm (6pm Sundays) to 9am.

	Nicholas Mesure & Robert Gray
	16 St Alfege Passage,
	Greenwich, London SE10 9JS
Tel	020 8853 4337
Email	info@st-alfeges.co.uk
Web	www.st-alfeges.co.uk

Entry 315 Map 4

London

66 Camden Square

A modern, architect designed house made of African teak, brick and glass. Climb wooden stairs under a glazed pyramid to light-filled, Japanese-style bedrooms with low platform beds, modern chairs and adjacent sitting room/study. Sue and Rodger have travelled widely so there are pictures, photographs and ethnic pieces everywhere – and a parrot called Peckham. Share their lovely open-plan dining space at breakfast overlooking a bird-filled courtyard or eat outside on warmer days. Camden's bustling market and the zoo are near, and a huge choice of places to eat. *Children by arrangement.*

Price	£100–£110. Singles £50–£55.
Rooms	2: 1 double, 1 single sharing bath (2nd room let to same party only).
Meals	Pubs/restaurants nearby.
Closed	Occasionally.
Directions	Tube: Camden Town or Kentish Town. Parking free at weekends; meters during week. 10 minutes by taxi from St Pancras Eurostar Terminal.

	Sue & Rodger Davis
	66 Camden Square,
	Camden Town,
	London NW1 9XD
Tel	020 7485 4622
Email	rodgerdavis@btopenworld.com

Entry 316 Map 4

London

29 Woodberry Crescent

London life, but not as we know it. A leafy suburb, an Edwardian house, a huge birdsung garden with a terrace and a thriving pond, delicious food grown on an allotment or bought from the farmers' market... you could be in the countryside but you can cycle to Hampstead Heath in 30 minutes. Inside is an eclectic mix of old and new, a comfortable sitting room with a wood-burner overlooking the garden and a bright bedroom upstairs with white walls and a modern metal bed. There are flowers from Edwina and Nigel's lovely garden, plenty of books, and on sunny days you can eat outside – a huge treat.

Norfolk

The Merchants House

The oak four-poster – a beauty – came with the house. Part of the building (1400) is the oldest in Wells; in those days, the merchant could bring his boats up to the door. Liz and Dennis know the history, and happily share it. Inside is warm, friendly, inviting: the mahogany shines, the bathrooms sparkle, there are papers for breakfast, books to borrow and pretty sash windows overlooking salt marshes. As for Wells, it is on the famous Coastal Path, has a quay bustling with sailing boats and 16 miles of sands. Birdwatch by day, dine out at night – easy when you're in the centre. Breakfasts are a treat.

Travel Club Offer: see page 392 for details.

Price	£85. Singles £75.
Rooms	1 double.
Meals	Dinner, 3 courses with wine, £25. Packed lunch £6-£7. Pubs/restaurants 200 yds.
Closed	Rarely.
Directions	Bus: 134 or 43. Tube: Highgate tube, exit Muswell Hill Rd. Owner will collect from tube station on request.

Price	£70. Singles £45.
Rooms	2: 1 four-poster; 1 double.
Meals	Pubs/restaurants 300 yds.
Closed	Christmas & Boxing Day.
Directions	B1105 from Fakenham to Wells-next-the-Sea, then follow signs to beach/quay. House is 150 yds west of the quay.

Edwina & Nigel Roberts
29 Woodberry Crescent,
Muswell Hill,
London N10 1PJ

Tel	020 8365 3639
Mobile	07957 680521
Fax	020 8365 3639
Email	edwinakellerman@btinternet.com

Elizabeth & Dennis Woods
The Merchants House, 47 Freeman St
Wells-next-the-Sea,
Norfolk NR23 1BQ

Tel	01328 711877
Mobile	07760 466231
Email	denniswoods@talktalk.net
Web	www.the-merchants-house.co.uk

Entry 317   Map 4

Entry 318   Map 10

Norfolk

Norfolk

Fern Cottage

An elegant Georgian house a short walk from the bustling harbour and shops. Linda and Richard have thought of everything to make you happy. Peaceful bedrooms look onto the courtyard and have large beds, dear little fireplaces, good linen and modern art; bathrooms are light and fresh. A traditional English breakfast sets you up for walks, fishing, golfing and cycling (there's bike storage), a steam train to Walsingham or a day on the beach in your very own candy-striped hut. Birdwatchers will love it here, especially in autumn when the pink-footed geese arrive. *Minimum stay two nights. Beach hut £15.*

Glebe Farmhouse

After a wild walk on Holkham Beach, return to a house filled with warmth and colour. Life revolves around the big, square farmhouse kitchen: a painted dresser brimming with bright china, well-cushioned sofas, books, paintings, gentle fabrics, wooden floors and French windows to the garden. Mary, a painter, designer and thoughtful host, gives you a delicious breakfast here, or on the terrace in summer. Bedrooms are peaceful and cosy, with views to garden or fields and woodland. Mary and Jeremy have been doing B&B since renovating their traditional Norfolk farmhouse back in 1991.

Price	£70-£80. Singles £60.
Rooms	2 doubles.
Meals	Pubs/restaurants 2-5 minute walk.
Closed	Christmas & New Year.
Directions	B1105 (Fakenham); right into Polka Rd; over Station Rd to top of Standard Rd. Just after Cobblers Guest House, small alleyway. Gate on right leads to blue front door. Off street parking at rear.

Price	£70. Singles £40.
Rooms	2: 1 double, 1 twin/double. Extra fold-up bed for child.
Meals	Pub 5-minute walk.
Closed	Rarely.
Directions	A148 King's Lynn to Cromer, north onto B1355 just west of Fakenham. 6.5 miles to North Creake. Right after red phone box, then 300 yds. On right.

LInda & Richard Pearce
Fern Cottage,
Standard Road, Wells-next-the-Sea,
Norfolk NR23 1JU

Tel	01328 710306
Fax	01328 710874
Email	enquiries@ferncottage.co.uk
Web	www.ferncottage.co.uk

Mary & Jeremy Brettingham Smith
Glebe Farmhouse,
Wells Road, North Creake,
Fakenham, Norfolk NR21 9LG

Tel	01328 730133
Mobile	07818 041555
Email	enquiries@glebe-farmhouse.co.uk
Web	www.glebe-farmhouse.co.uk

Entry 319   Map 10

Entry 320   Map 10

Norfolk

1 Leicester Meadows

Up among 13 acres of wild meadow and woodland – not another building in sight. It's all so relaxed and unhurried: barn owls roosting in the outhouse, hens strutting the garden, geese pottering up from the pond. The 19th-century cottages, once the home of workers on the Holkham estate, have been imaginatively restored and enlarged. (Bob was an architect, Sara an art teacher; both are immensely friendly and helpful.) Polished wood and old brick are topped with bright rugs; paintings and ceramics engage the eye; steep stairs take you up to the bedrooms – one large, contemporary and elegant, the other cosy and fun.

Price	From £60. Singles from £45.
Rooms	2: 1 double; 1 double with separate bath.
Meals	Supper from £15. Pub 1 mile.
Closed	Rarely.
Directions	Off A148 near Fakenham; B1355 dir. Burnham Market. In S. Creake, left by flint bus shelter, right into Avondale Rd; 1 mile, taking left fork. At bottom of hill, house set back 100 yds on left.

	Bob & Sara Freakley
	1 Leicester Meadows, South Creake, Fakenham, Norfolk NR21 9NZ
Tel	01328 823533
Email	rf@freakley.com
Web	www.leicestermeadows.com

Entry 321   Map 10

Norfolk

Bagthorpe Hall

Close to bustling Burnham Market, yet here you are immersed in peaceful countryside. Tid is a pioneer of organic farming and good things from his 700 acres wing their way monthly to the farmers' market. Gina's passions are music, dance and gardens and she organises open days and concerts for charity. Theirs is a large, elegant house with a mural in the hall chronicling their family life. It's fascinating, and beautiful. Wonderful colours, good beds, generous curtains, excellent food – maybe fresh raspberries for breakfast. Birdwatching, boats, salt marshes and crab nets are a 15-minute drive. *Stabling available.*

Price	£70–£75. Singles £40.
Rooms	3: 1 double; 1 double with separate shower, 1 twin with separate bath.
Meals	Dinner £20–£25 (winter only). Pubs/restaurants 2 miles.
Closed	Rarely.
Directions	From King's Lynn for A148 to Fakenham. Left at East Rudham by Cat & Fiddle pub. 3.5 miles to Bagthorpe. Past farm on left, wood on right, white gates set back from trees. At top of drive.

	Gina Morton
	Bagthorpe Hall, Bagthorpe, Bircham, King's Lynn, Norfolk PE31 6QY
Tel	01485 578528
Mobile	07979 746591
Email	dgmorton@hotmail.com
Web	www.bagthorpehall.co.uk

Entry 322   Map 10

Norfolk

Lower Farm

This house reflects its farming owners – natural, laid-back, delightful. Enter a flagstoned hall with wooden settle, rosewood tallboy and pine doors stripped down by Amanda. The drawing room is shared but there are sofas in the bedrooms if you prefer privacy. These are more homely than lavish: two vast and high-ceilinged with good views from long windows, and the twin at the end of a long corridor. The garden is lovely and there are dogs and horses galore (stabling available); the walls bear the proof of success at point-to-points and shows. Breakfasts are ample.

Norfolk

Litcham Hall

For the whole of the 19th century this was Litcham's doctor's house; the red-brick Hall is still at the centre of the community. The big-windowed guest bedrooms look onto the stunning gardens with yew hedges, a lily pond and herbaceous borders. This is a thoroughly English home with elegant proportions – the hall, drawing room and dining room are gracious and beautifully furnished. The hens lay the breakfast eggs, the garden fills the table with soft fruit in season and John and Hermione are friendly and most helpful. There's a sitting room for guests. *Children & pets by arrangement.*

Price	£60. Singles £35.
Rooms	3: 2 doubles; 1 twin with separate bath/shower.
Meals	Pub/restaurant 800 yds.
Closed	Rarely.
Directions	From King's Lynn, A148 for Cromer. 3 miles after Hillington, 2nd of 2 turnings right to Harpley (no signpost) opp. Houghton Hall sign. 200 yds on; over x-roads, house 400 yds on left.

Price	£65-£85 . Singles by arrangement.
Rooms	3: 1 double, 1 twin; 1 twin with separate bath.
Meals	Occasional dinner, £25. Pub/restaurant 3 miles.
Closed	Christmas.
Directions	From Swaffham, A1065 north for 5 miles, then right to Litcham on B1145. House on left on entering village. Georgian red-brick with stone balls on gatepost.

Amanda Case
Lower Farm,
Harpley, King's Lynn,
Norfolk PE31 6TU
Tel   01485 520240
Fax   01485 520240

John & Hermione Birkbeck
Litcham Hall,
Litcham, King's Lynn,
Norfolk PE32 2QQ
Tel   01328 701389
Fax   01328 701164
Email   hermionebirkbeck@hotmail.com

Entry 323   Map 10

Entry 324   Map 10

Norfolk

Carrick's at Castle Farm

A comfortable, and jolly, mix of farmhouse B&B — rare-breed cattle, tractors, a large, warm-bricked house — and a rather swish interior. Both Jean and John are passionate about conservation and the protection of wildlife, and here you have absolute quiet for birdwatching, fishing, shooting or walking; recover in the drawing room with its books and lovely river views from long windows. Bedrooms are large, light and well thought-out with great bathrooms and binoculars, food is home grown or local, and there is coffee and cake, or wine, when you arrive. The pretty garden leads down to the River Wensum and a footpath.

Ethical Collection: Environment; Community; Food. See page 400 for details.

Price	From £75. Singles £55.
Rooms	3: 2 doubles;
	1 double, 1 twin both with separate bath (same party only).
Meals	Dinner, 3 courses, £20. BYO.
	Pub 0.5 miles.
Closed	Never.
Directions	From Norwich A47 to Dereham (don't go into Dereham). B1147 to Swanton Morley. In village take Elsing Road at Darby's pub; farm drive 0.5 miles on left.

	Jean Wright
	Carrick's at Castle Farm,
	Castle Farm, Swanton Morley,
	Dereham, Norfolk NR20 4JT
Tel	01362 637227/638302
Email	jean@castlefarm-swanton.co.uk
Web	www.carricksatcastlefarm.co.uk

Entry 325 Map 10

Norfolk

Kesmark House

Sheena and James continue to conserve their beautiful Georgian village house and garden. In the French bedroom — chintz, old armoire, carved bed — you lie in stylish comfort; the twin room is beamed, freshly decorated and very private. Delicious breakfast is served in the dining room, striking with old pamment floor and wood-burner; linger in comfort over the papers. The atmosphere is informal, your hosts relaxed. The listed house sits in two acres and you may picnic in the secluded top garden. Two traditional pubs in the village and the wonderful Norfolk coast an easy drive. *Stable Cottage used for overflow guests.*

Price	From £60. Singles £35.
Rooms	2: 1 double;
	1 twin with separate bath.
Meals	Pub 5 minute-walk.
Closed	Christmas.
Directions	B1147 north of Dereham to Swanton Morley. There, 500 yds after Angel Pub, house on right with white railings.

	Sheena & James Willis
	Kesmark House,
	Swanton Morley,
	Dereham, Norfolk NR20 4PP
Tel	01362 637663
Email	stay@kesmarkhouse.co.uk
Web	www.kesmarkhouse.co.uk

Entry 326 Map 10

Norfolk

Holly Lodge

The mock-medieval house and B&B gleams – from the tooled leather dining chairs to the pewter collection to the suit of armour, 'Dudley', at the foot of the stair. The three snug guest cottages flourish smart iron bedsteads and rugs on stone tiles, neat little shower rooms and tapestry-seat chairs, books, music, TV. Make the most of the Mediterranean garden with pond and decking in summer, the handsome conservatory and the utter peace. Your hosts are delightful – Jeremy who cooks three-course meals enthusiastically, ethically and with panache, and Canadian-raised Gill.

Travel Club Offer: see page 392 for details.

Price	£90-£120. Singles from £70-£100.
Rooms	3 cottages for 2.
Meals	Dinner, 3 courses with wine, £17.50. Pubs/restaurants 1 mile.
Closed	January.
Directions	From Fakenham A148, Fakenham-Cromer road; 6 miles; left at Crawfish pub. Signs to Thursford Collection, past village green; 2nd drive on left.

Jeremy Bolam
Holly Lodge,
Thursford Green,
Norfolk NR21 OAS

Tel	01328 878465
Email	info@hollylodgeguesthouse.co.uk
Web	www.hollylodgeguesthouse.co.uk

Entry 327   Map 10

Norfolk

The Old Vicarage

Norfolk at its best in this fine Georgian vicarage….huge skies, views that stretch forever, absolute peace. A curved staircase springs from the flagstoned inner hall lit by a cupola high above. Two traditional bedrooms (one with a view to Walsingham) have good beds and fine furniture, pretty china, fresh flowers. Enjoy hearty, home-produced breakfast in the sunlit dining room; wander through French windows to the garden. Sandy beaches, marsh walks and the seal colony are near; on your return a log fire and the lure of Rosie's scrumptious candlelit dinner will tempt you to stay put. *French spoken.*

Travel Club Offer: see page 392 for details.

Price	From £55. Ask for singles' rates.
Rooms	2: 1 twin/double; 1 double with separate bath.
Meals	Dinner, 2-3 courses, £18-£22. BYO. Pub 2 miles.
Closed	Christmas & New Year.
Directions	A148 Fakenham to Cromer for 6 miles. Left at Crawfish Inn into Hindringham, down hill & left before church, into Blacksmith's Lane. After 0.5 miles, first entrance beyond 30mph sign.

Rosie & Robin Waters
The Old Vicarage,
Blacksmith's Lane, Hindringham,
Norfolk NR21 0QA

Tel	01328 878223
Mobile	07747 688875
Fax	01328 878223
Email	watersrobin@hotmail.com

Entry 328   Map 10

Norfolk

Burgh Parva Hall

Sunlight bathes the Norfolk longhouse on summer afternoons; the welcome from the Heals is as warm. The listed house is all that remains of the old village of Burgh Parva, deserted after the Great Plague. It's a handsome house and warmly inviting... old furniture, rugs, books, pictures and Magnet the terrier-daschund. Large guest bedrooms face the sunsets and the garden annexe makes a sweet hideaway, especially in the summer. Breakfast eggs are from the garden hens, vegetables are home-grown, fish comes fresh from Holt and the game may have been shot by William. Settle down by the fire and tuck in.

Price	£60-£80. Singles from £35.
Rooms	3: 1 double, 1 twin; 1 twin with separate bath.
Meals	Dinner £22. BYO. Pub/restaurant 4 miles.
Closed	Rarely.
Directions	Fakenham A148 for Cromer. At Thursford B1354 for Aylsham. Just before Melton, speed bumps, left immed. before bus shelter; 1st house on right after farmyard.

Judy & William Heal
Burgh Parva Hall,
Melton Constable,
Norfolk NR24 2PU
Tel 01263 862569
Email judyheal@dsl.pipex.com

Entry 329   Map 10

Norfolk

Stable Cottage

In a privately owned village stands one of Norfolk's finest Elizabethan houses, Heydon Hall. In the Dutch-gabled stable block, fronted by Cromwell's Oak, is this cottage – fresh, sunny and enchanting. Each room is touched by Sarah's warm personality and love of country things; seagrass floors and crisp linen, toile de Jouy walls and pretty china. Bedrooms are cottagey and immaculate, there are fresh fabrics, baskets of treats in the bathrooms (one has a roll top bath) and delicious food on your plate. All this in a serene parkland setting: a rare treat. *Minimum stay two nights weekends in summer.*

Price	£80. Singles £45.
Rooms	2 twins/doubles.
Meals	Occasional dinner, 3 courses, £20. BYO. Pub 1 mile.
Closed	Christmas.
Directions	From Norwich, B1149 for 10 miles. 2nd left after bridge, for Heydon. 1.5 miles, right into village, over cattle grid, into park. Pass Hall on left, cottage in front of you; left over cattle grid and into stable yard.

Sarah Bulwer-Long
Stable Cottage,
Heydon Hall, Heydon,
Norfolk NR11 6RE
Tel 01263 587343
Mobile 07780 998742

Entry 330   Map 10

Norfolk

Incleborough House

A listed, mellow-bricked 17th-century house which faces a pretty, bird-filled, walled garden. Nick and Barbara have done a terrific restoration job and give you sumptuous bedrooms with huge beds, beautiful linen, super views, shining contemporary bathrooms, chocolates and wine. There's an elegant sitting room for tea and cakes, with an open fire and books to read. Breakfast at white linen-topped tables in the conservatory is a treat – try slow-baked marmalade ham with poached eggs. You are only 300 yards from the sea and the local walks are fabulous. *Min. stay two nights at weekends; check for late availability.*

Price	£150–£165. Singles £112.50–£123.75.
Rooms	3: 2 doubles, 1 twin/double.
Meals	Occasional dinner, with wine, £22.50. Restaurant 100 yds.
Closed	Never.
Directions	From Sheringham head for Cromer. In East Runton, 1st right into Felbrigg Road. House 200 yds on left behind oak trees.

Nick & Barbara Davies
Incleborough House,
Lower Common, East Runton,
Cromer, Norfolk NR27 9PG

Tel	01263 515939
Mobile	07738 241672
Email	enquiries@incleboroughhouse.co.uk
Web	www.incleboroughhouse.co.uk

Norfolk

The Old Rectory

Conservation farmland all around; acres of wild heathland busy with woodpeckers and owls; the coast two miles away. Relax in the spacious drawing room of this handsome 17th-century rectory and friendly family home, set in four acres of grounds. Fiona loves to cook and bakes her bread daily, food is delicious, seasonal and locally sourced, jams are homemade. Comfortable bedrooms have *objets* from diplomatic postings and the airy suite comes with mahogany furniture and armchairs so you can settle in with a book. Super views, three friendly dogs, tennis in the garden and masses of space.

Price	From £50. Singles £35.
Rooms	2: 1 suite; 1 double with separate bath & shower.
Meals	Dinner from £15. Pubs 2 miles.
Closed	Rarely.
Directions	From Norwich A1151 for Stalham. Just before Stalham, left to Happisburgh. Left at T-junc; 3 miles; 2nd left after E. Ruston church, signed by-way to Foxhill. Right at x-roads; 1 mile on right.

Peter & Fiona Black
The Old Rectory,
Ridlington,
Norfolk NR28 9NZ

Tel	01692 650247
Mobile	07799 133455
Email	blacks7@email.com
Web	www.oldrectory.northnorfolk.co.uk

Norfolk

Manor Farmhouse

A family buzz and candlelight in the farmhouse where you eat, peace in the 17th-century barn where you stay. All rooms lead off its charming, stylish, vaulted sitting room with cosy winter fire. You have a chunky four-poster and a tiny en suite shower on the ground floor, then two narrow staircases to two bedrooms upstairs – small, quirky, fun, with a tucked-up-in-the-roof feel. Come for a sunny courtyard garden, billiards in the stable, fresh flowers, lovely hosts, gorgeous food – and you may come and go as you please. Great value, a perfect rural retreat. *Children over seven welcome.*

Norfolk

Sloley Hall

A grand and gracious yellow-brick Georgian house with formal gardens and tree-studded parkland – only the swishing-tailed horses are missing. Of course there are flagstoned floors, Persian rugs, gleaming circular tables with vases of garden-grown flowers but your hosts aren't snooty – Barbara was married here and is charmingly easy-going and helpful. A huge light-flooded dining room is perfect for breakfast; the drawing room is comfy but uncluttered in pinks, with a marble fireplace and long views. Bedrooms are large and elegant with room for seats, and bathrooms warm and generous.

Travel Club Offer: see page 392 for details.

Price	From £50. Singles by arrangement.
Rooms	3: 1 double, 1 twin/double, 1 four-poster.
Meals	Dinner, 3 courses, £17.50. BYO. Pubs 1 mile.
Closed	Christmas & New Year.
Directions	From Norwich, A1151 & A149 almost to Stalham. Left for Walcott. At T-junc. left again. 1 mile on, right for H'burgh. Next T-junc., right. Next T-junc., left. Road bends right, look for house sign by wall.

David & Rosie Eldridge
Manor Farmhouse,
Happisburgh,
Norfolk NR12 0SA
Tel   01692 651262
Fax   01692 650220
Email   manorathappisburgh@hotmail.com
Web   www.northnorfolk.co.uk/manorbarn

Entry 333   Map 10

Price	£70–£90. Singles from £50.
Rooms	3: 1 suite; 1 double with separate bath; 1 twin with separate shower. Extra child bed available.
Meals	Pub/restaurant 2–4 miles.
Closed	Rarely.
Directions	From Norwich ring road, B1150 thro' Coltishall & Scottow. Right after Three Horseshoes pub (byway to Sloley); across staggered junc., 1st drive on right.

Mrs Barbara Gorton
Sloley Hall,
Norwich,
Norfolk NR12 8HA
Tel   01692 538582
Mobile   07748 152079
Email   babsgorton@hotmail.com
Web   www.sloleyhall.com

Entry 334   Map 10

Norfolk

Manor House

Sally looks after you beautifully in this elegant house on the edge of Halvergate marshes. Excellent walking – the Weavers Way runs past the farmhouse door – and there is good birdwatching; spot pink-footed geese in winter. Your sitting room is an open landing outside the bedroom with comfortable chairs, TV, books, guides and fresh flowers. Bedrooms are traditional and spotless with soft colours, splashes of colour from cushions and curtains and touches of luxury; mattresses are firm, bathrooms sparkle. Breakfast bacon and sausages are from the farm shop – wonderful – and jams and marmalades are homemade.

Price	£70-£90. Singles £40.
Rooms	2: 1 double with separate bath; 1 twin sharing bath (let to same party only).
Meals	Packed lunch £6.50. Pub 3 miles.
Closed	Christmas & New Year.
Directions	A47 towards Great Yarmouth. After Acle, right signed Halvergate. Into village, past Red Lion pub on right, take 3rd right signed Tunstall only. After 0.5 miles, farmhouse on left before the ruined church.

Sally More
Manor House,
Tunstall Road, Halvergate,
Norwich, Norfolk NR13 3PS

Tel	01493 700279
Fax	01493 700279
Email	smore@fsmail.net
Web	www.manorhousenorfolk.co.uk

Entry 335   Map 10

Norfolk

Washingford House

Tall octagonal chimney stacks and a Georgian façade give the house a stately air. In fact, it's the friendliest of places to stay: Paris and Nigel love entertaining and give you a delicious breakfast. The house, originally Tudor, is a delightful mix of old and new. Large light-filled bedrooms have loads of good books and views over the four-acre garden, a favourite haunt for local birds. Beyond, sheep graze equably on acres of green. Bergh Apton is a conservation village seven miles from Norwich and you are in the heart of it. *Children over 12 welcome.*

Price	£65-£75. Singles £35-£45.
Rooms	2: 1 twin; 1 single with separate bath.
Meals	Pubs/restaurants 4-6 miles.
Closed	Rarely.
Directions	A146 from Norwich to Lowestoft for 4 miles. Right after Gull Pub, signed Slade Lane. First left, then left at T-junc for 1 mile. Straight over x-roads; house on left past post office.

Paris & Nigel Back
Washingford House,
Cookes Road, Bergh Apton,
Norwich, Norfolk NR15 1AA

Tel	01508 550924
Mobile	07900 683617
Email	parisb@waitrose.com
Web	www.washingford.com

Entry 336   Map 10

Norfolk

The Buttery

At the end of a farm track, a little treasure: a thatch-and-flint octagonal dairy house just for you. Built on the Georgian and listed Berry Hall Estate, it has been perfectly restored by the best local craftsmen and is as neat as a new pin. You get a little kitchen and a fridge that Deborah stocks with delicious things for a full breakfast, a terracotta-tiled sitting room and a luxurious sofabed, a romantic mezzanine bedroom reached by a steep wooden stair, a jacuzzi bath and a sun terrace. Surrounded by birds, deer, sheep and peace, you may walk from the door into parkland and woods.

Norfolk

College Farm

Lavender has done B&B for years and looks after her stupendous listed house single-handedly. Over afternoon tea, she tells colourful stories of the house and her family's local history: from 1349 until the Dissolution of the Monasteries the house was a college of priests and there's stunning Jacobean panelling in the dining room. Bedrooms are big and lived-in, two of the bathrooms are tiny, all have lovely views over the garden with its pingos (ice age ponds). Come for history and architecture and friendly Lavender, and breakfast from the farm shop down the road. *Children over seven welcome.*

Travel Club Offer: see page 392 for details.

Price	£80-£95.
Rooms	Cottage with 1 double, sitting room & small kitchen.
Meals	Pub 10-minute walk.
Closed	Rarely.
Directions	From A47 Barnham Broom & Weston Longville x-roads, south towards Barnham Broom. After 150 yds, 1st farm track on right. Left at T-junc., left again, house on left.

Deborah Meynell
The Buttery,
Berry Hall, Honingham,
Norwich, Norfolk NR9 5AX
Tel   01603 880541
Fax   01603 880887
Email   thebuttery@paston.co.uk
Web   www.thebuttery.thesiliconworkshop.com

Entry 337   Map 10

Price	From £60. Singles £30.
Rooms	3: 1 twin, 1 twin/double; 1 double with separate bath. Extra shower available.
Meals	Afternoon tea included. Pub 1 mile.
Closed	Rarely.
Directions	From Thetford, A1075 north for Watton. After 9 miles, left to Thompson at 'Light Vehicles Only' sign. After 0.5 miles, 2nd left at red postbox on corner. Left again, house at end.

Lavender Garnier
College Farm,
Thompson,
Thetford,
Norfolk IP24 1QG
Tel   01953 483318
Fax   01953 483318
Email   collegefarm83@amserve.net

Entry 338   Map 10

Norfolk

Sallowfield Cottage

In the drawing room, gorgeous prints and paintings, unusual furniture and decorative lamps: Caroline's cottage is so crammed with family treasures it takes time to absorb the splendour. One bedroom, not huge but handsome, has a Regency-style canopied bed and decoration to suit the house (1850); the attic room is large and lovely but there are steep stairs. Drift into the fascinating garden to find hedged rooms and a jungly pond that slinks between the trees. Caroline, and her pets, love having guests and if you have friends living locally she can do lunch or dinner for up to ten. *Children over nine welcome.*

Price	£60. Singles £35.
Rooms	3: 1 double;
	1 double with separate bath,
	1 single with separate shower.
Meals	Lunch £10. Dinner from £20.
	Pub 2 miles.
Closed	Christmas & New Year.
Directions	A11 Attleborough-Wymondham.
	Take Spooner Row sign. Over
	x-roads by Three Boars pub. 1 mile;
	left at T-junc. to Wymondham for
	1 mile. Look for rusty barrel on left,
	turn into farm track.

Caroline Musker
Sallowfield Cottage,
Wattlefield, Wymondham,
Norfolk NR18 9NX

Tel	01953 605086
Mobile	07778 316616
Email	caroline.musker@tesco.net
Web	www.sallowfieldcottage.co.uk

Entry 339　Map 10

Norfolk

Le Grys Barn

Light pours into this 17th-century threshing barn – a jewel of a conversion in peaceful Norfolk. Julie lived in Hong Kong and sells jewellery from Bali. Her house glows with warmth and colour. Glass-topped tables increase the sense of space, Persian carpets beautify beech floors, golden buddhas rest in quiet corners. Across a courtyard, two private beamed and raftered bedrooms are stunningly equipped: guidebooks and glossies, easy chairs and Thai silk, music, flowers and mini fridge. Bathrooms have Italian tiles and breakfast, served on a Chinese altar table, is as delicious as all the rest.

Price	£70–£75. Singles from £45.
Rooms	2: 1 double, 1 twin/double.
Meals	Dinner, 3 courses, £20. BYO.
	Packed lunch available.
	Pub 5-minute drive.
Closed	Christmas & New Year.
Directions	From A140 at Long Stratton, take
	Flowerpot Lane (opp. Shell garage)
	to Wacton; at x-roads left by
	phone box, past swings; 500 yds to
	telegraph pole with sign: left turn
	up 'Private Rd', over cattle grid to
	end of lane.

Mrs Julie Franklin
Le Grys Barn,
Wacton Common, Long Stratton,
Norfolk NR15 2UR

Tel	01508 531576
Mobile	07770 794043
Email	jm.franklin@virgin.net
Web	www.legrys-barn.co.uk

Entry 340　Map 10

Norfolk

Rushall House

Plenty of treats to be had in this light and bright Victorian rectory: blue-shelled eggs for breakfast, homemade cake for tea, and radios, books and sofas in the double bedrooms. The wood-burner warm sitting room is classically decorated with a contemporary touch, airy bedrooms have pale walls, rich fabrics and a grand mix of colours and textiles (Jane's vintage furniture and fabrics are for sale in the courtyard studio). Walk or cycle after breakfast – it's good flat countryside and there are plenty of restorative pubs. Jane and Martin are relaxed hosts, and children will love collecting the eggs.

Ethical Collection: Food. See page 400 for details.

Price	From £65. Singles £40.
Rooms	3: 1 double; 1 double, 1 twin sharing bath/shower.
Meals	Dinner £23. BYO. Pubs/restaurants 0.5-3 miles.
Closed	Rarely.
Directions	Turn off A140 at r'bout to Dickleburgh; right at village store. After two miles pass Lakes Rd & Vaunces Lane, on right. Shortly after z-bend sign, house on right.

Martin Hubner & Jane Gardiner
Rushall House,
Dickleburgh Road, Rushall, Diss,
Norfolk IP21 4RX
Tel   01379 741557
Fax   01379 740148
Email   janegardineruk@aol.com
Web   www.rushallhouse.co.uk

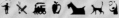

Entry 341   Map 10

Northamptonshire

Coton Lodge

Hidden at the end of a mile-long drive, a handsome, wisteria-clad farmhouse surrounded by enchanting gardens, ancient sycamores, horse chestnuts and limes. This is Joanne's childhood home to which she has returned with Peter – to run the farm and carry on the gardens her mother started 30 years ago. The elegant, early 19th-century rooms are filled with light and look out across the beautiful valley beyond. Bedrooms are softly decorated, utterly comfortable and spotless. Wake to birdsong and a delicious breakfast of waffles, fresh eggs from the farm and homemade jams. *Children over 12 welcome.*

Price	From £90. Singles from £70.
Rooms	3: 2 doubles, 1 twin.
Meals	Packed lunch £5. Pub 3 miles.
Closed	Rarely.
Directions	From M1 junc. 18 follow signs for Crick & W. Haddon. Bypass W. Haddon following signs to Guilsborough. After 0.5 miles fork right to Guilsborough, Coton Lodge 0.75 miles on right.

Joanne de Nobriga
Coton Lodge,
West Haddon Road, Guilsborough,
Northamptonshire NN6 8QE
Tel   01604 740215
Fax   01604 743515
Email   jo@cotonlodge.co.uk
Web   www.cotonlodge.co.uk

Entry 342   Map 8

Northamptonshire

Colledges House

Huge attention to comfort here, and a house full of laughter. Liz clearly derives pleasure from sharing her 300-year-old stone thatched cottage, immaculate garden, pretty conservatory and converted barn with guests. Bedrooms and bathrooms are luxurious and there is something special wherever you turn: a Jacobean trunk, a Bechstein piano, a beautiful bureau in the bathroom. Cordon Bleu dinners are elegant affairs – and great fun. Guests have said that staying here is "like staying with a good friend". Stroll around the conservation village of Staverton – delightful. *Children over eight & babes in arms welcome.*

Northamptonshire

The Vyne

Weighed down by wisteria, this 16th-century cottage rests in a honey-hued conservation village. There's not a straight line in the cosy oak-beamed cottage, its rooms filled with good antiques and eclectic art. The spacious twin is enchanting, tucked under the rafters, its beds decorated in willow-pattern chintz, its walls glinting with gilded frames; the double has a Georgian four-poster and a sampler-decorated bathroom that's a quick flit next door. Warm and charming, Imogen not only works in publishing but is a dedicated gardener and Cordon Bleu cook – enjoy supper in her sunny secluded garden. *Babies welcome.*

Travel Club Offer: see page 392 for details.

Price	£102–£106. Singles £65–£67.50.	Price	£75. Singles from £45.
Rooms	4: 1 double, 1 single. Cottage: 1 double, 1 twin.	Rooms	2: 1 twin; 1 four-poster with separate bath.
Meals	Dinner, 3 courses, £32. Pub 4-minute walk.	Meals	Supper £18. Dinner £28. BYO. Pub 2-minute walk.
Closed	Rarely.	Closed	Christmas & New Year.
Directions	From Daventry, A425 to Leamington Spa. 100 yds past Staverton Park Conference Centre, right into village, then 1st right. Keep left, & at 'Give Way' sign, sharp left. House immed. on right.	Directions	M40 exit 11. A422 to Northampton, left onto B4525. After 2 miles, left to Thorpe Mandeville. 3 miles, left to Culworth. After Culworth, right to Eydon.

Liz Jarrett
Colledges House,
Oakham Lane, Staverton, Daventry,
Northamptonshire NN11 6JQ

Tel	01327 702737
Mobile	07710 794112
Email	liz@colledgeshouse.co.uk
Web	www.colledgeshouse.co.uk

Imogen Butler
The Vyne,
High Street, Eydon, Daventry,
Northamptonshire NN11 3PP

Tel	01327 264886
Mobile	07974 801475
Fax	01327 260735
Email	imogen@ibutler2.wanadoo.co.uk

Entry 343   Map 8

Entry 344   Map 8

Northamptonshire

The Coach House

Sunlight and flower-scent fill this sprawling, rosy-brick home. Originally a coach house and stabling, it's now a series of elegant, light-filled ground-floor rooms around a central courtyard. Sarah's eye for colour and design shows in the clever mix of modern and traditional, gingham curtains, pretty fabrics and striking lampshades. Bedrooms ooze country-house luxury with antique lace pillowcases, thick towels, glossy magazines and doors to garden or courtyard. Relax here – or on the tennis court – after a day at Silverstone or Towcester races. And there's homemade bread for breakfast!

Northamptonshire

Bridge Cottage

Watch the cattle drinking peacefully at the river as you tuck into scrumptious breakfast. It was the setting that won Judy and Rod over and they've transformed a no-nonsense bungalow into a cottage full of light, sloping ceilings and unexpected character. A small, pretty garden borders the Willowbrook, with a decked terrace at the water's edge – just the spot to sit with a glass of wine or a cup of tea. Kingfishers flash by and you will probably see a red kite; your charming hosts have binoculars to borrow. Judy has only just begun B&B but does it with natural brilliance and loves every minute.

🧳 Travel Club Offer: see page 392 for details.

Price	£90. Singles from £45.
Rooms	2: 1 double, 1 twin.
Meals	Packed lunch on request. Pub/restaurant within 5 miles.
Closed	Rarely.
Directions	From A43 dual carriageway, A5 North for Hinckley. After 1.1 miles sharp left to Duncote. First house on left, 300 yds, 2nd gate.

Price	From £75. Singles from £40.
Rooms	3: 1 double, 1 twin; 1 double with separate bath.
Meals	Pub/restaurant 2 miles.
Closed	Rarely.
Directions	From south A1 to Peterborough junction. Take A605 signed Oundle & Northampton for 4 miles. At 1st r'bout right through Fotheringhay, then Woodnewton. House is first on left on bridge.

Sarah Baker Baker
The Coach House,
Duncote, Towcester,
Northamptonshire NN12 8AQ

Tel	01327 352855
Mobile	07875 215705
Email	sarahbb@3disp.co.uk

Judy Colebrook
Bridge Cottage, Oundle Road,
Woodnewton, Peterborough,
Northamptonshire PE8 5EG

Tel	01780 470779
Mobile	07979 644864
Email	enquiries@bridgecottage.net
Web	www.bridgecottage.net

🚶 🔊 🐈 🎨

Entry 345   Map 8

🚼 🍴 🔊 🐕 🐈

Entry 346   Map 9

Northumberland

Chain Bridge House

Livvy is a great cook, involved with the Cittaslow and Slow Food movements of Berwick – from the kitchen flow breakfasts, teas and dinners as seasonal, local and delicious as can be. The house, mid-19th century, is the last in England, and the Union Chain Bridge crosses an idyllic stretch of the Tweed; down river you may spot otters. There are books and log fires in the sitting room, a revolving summer house in the garden with views, white towels on heated rails, goose down duvets in lovely bedrooms... bliss. Babies, children, dogs – all get a generous welcome in this charming family home.

Price	£70-£75. Singles £40-£45.
Rooms	2: 1 double, 1 twin.
Meals	Dinner £25. Supper £15. Packed lunch from £5. Pubs/restaurants 5-7 miles.
Closed	Rarely.
Directions	A698; exit from A1 at East Ord, west of Berwick. After 1 mile, right for Horncliffe; follow signs for Honey Farm; past farm 200 yds; house on right.

Livvy Cawthorn
Chain Bridge House,
Horncliffe, Berwick-upon-Tweed,
Northumberland TD15 2XT

Tel	01289 386259
Fax	01289 386259
Email	info@chainbridgehouse.co.uk
Web	www.chainbridgehouse.co.uk

Entry 347 Map 16

Northumberland

West Coates

Slip through the gates of this Georgian townhouse and you're in the country. Two acres of leafy gardens, with shady or sunny spots to relax, belie the closeness of Berwick's centre. As surprising are the indoor pool and hot tub tucked in the corner. From the lofty ceilings and sash windows to the soft colours, gleaming furniture and handsome sporting prints, the house has a calm, ordered elegance. Bedrooms have antiques and garden views; two have roll top baths; fruit, homemade cakes, flowers welcome you. Warm, friendly Karen is a stunning cook, inventively using local produce and spoiling you.

Price	£90-£120. Singles from £50.
Rooms	3: 1 double, 1 twin/double; 1 twin/double with separate bath/shower.
Meals	Dinner £35. Pub/restaurant 10-min. walk.
Closed	Christmas & New Year.
Directions	From A1 take A6105 into Berwick. House 300 yds on left. Stone pillars at end of drive.

Karen Brown
West Coates, 30 Castle Terrace,
Berwick-upon-Tweed,
Northumberland TD15 1NZ

Tel	01289 309666
Mobile	07814 281973
Email	karenbrownwestcoates@yahoo.com
Web	www.westcoates.co.uk

Entry 348 Map 16

Northumberland

Broome

A totally surprising one-storey house, full of beautiful things. It is an Aladdin's cave and sits in the middle of a coastal village with access to miles of sandy beaches. The garden/breakfast room is its hub and has a country cottage feel; enjoy locally smoked kippers here, award-winning 'Bamburgh Bangers' and home-cured bacon from the village butcher. There's also a sun-trapping courtyard full of colourful pots for breakfasts in the sun. Guests have a cheerful sitting/dining room and bedrooms with fresh flowers and good books. Mary is welcoming and amusing and has stacks of local knowledge.

Northumberland

Hethpool

Spot wild goats on the hills of this valley, whose private roads are virtually car-free (vehicles are restricted). It's remote, rugged and breathtakingly beautiful. Inside, old family pieces, honeysuckle chintz, hunting gear, milling dogs – and Martin and Eildon who have lived here for years and look after you with ease. Bedrooms, old-fashioned rather than swish, share a sitting room; after one of Eildon's fine dinners, settle in in front of the fire. There's a 16th-century pele tower in the garden and the National Park beyond. Bring your horse and let your hosts be your guide!

Ethical Collection: Food. See page 400 for details.

Price	£75–£90. Singles £50–£60.	Price	From £70.
Rooms	2: 1 double, 1 twin, sharing separate bath/shower (2nd room let to same party only).	Rooms	2: 1 twin; 1 double with separate bath.
Meals	Pubs/restaurants 2-minute walk.	Meals	Dinner, 2-3 courses, £18.50–£25. Pub 8 miles.
Closed	November–March.	Closed	Rarely.
Directions	From Newcastle north on A1; right for Bamburgh on B1341. To village, pass 30mph sign & hotel; 1st right at Victoria Hotel. House 400 yds on right.	Directions	From Wooler A697 towards Coldstream; 2 miles left onto B6351. After 4 miles left to Hethpool; 1.5 miles, left at 'Private Drive' sign; 2nd on right.

	Mary Dixon Broome, 22 Ingram Road, Bamburgh, Northumberland NE69 7BT		**Eildon & Martin Letts** Hethpool, Wooler, Northumberland NE71 6TW
Tel	01668 214287	Tel	01668 216232
Mobile	07956 013409	Mobile	07710 767983
Email	mdixon4394@aol.com	Email	eildon@hethpoolhouse.co.uk
		Web	www.hethpoolhouse.co.uk

Northumberland

Bilton Barns

A solidly good farmhouse B&B whose lifeblood is still farming. The Jacksons know every inch of the countryside and coast that surrounds their 1715 home; it's a pretty spot. They farm 400 acres of mixed arable land that sweeps down to the coast yet always have time for guests. Dorothy takes pride in creating an easy and sociable atmosphere – three couples who were introduced to each other one weekend returned for a reunion! Bedrooms are big, carpeted, fresh and comfortable, a conservatory leads onto the garden and there's an airy guests' sitting room with an open fire and views to the sea.

Price	£60-£70. Singles £30-£40.
Rooms	3: 1 double, 1 twin, 1 four-poster.
Meals	Packed lunch from £4. Pub/restaurant 1.5 miles.
Closed	Christmas & New Year.
Directions	From Alnwick, A1068 to Alnmouth. At Hipsburn r'bout follow signs to station & cross bridge. 1st lane to left, 0.3 miles down drive.

Brian & Dorothy Jackson
Bilton Barns,
Alnmouth, Alnwick,
Northumberland NE66 2TB

Tel	01665 830427
Mobile	07939 262028
Email	dorothy@biltonbarns.com
Web	www.biltonbarns.com

Entry 351 Map 16

Northumberland

East Hepple Farmhouse

In the farmhouse sitting room, a wood-burner blazes away in winter. The double, too, has a sitting room, with an original cast-iron range and shelves groaning with books – bibliophile heaven. The peace is so deep in the Coquet valley that you may sleep until the whiff of sizzling local bacon hits your nostrils. Beds are firm, old pine pieces pretty, pillows feathery soft and views over the river to the Simonside hills abundant. Joan and Brian are expert at looking after you, will drive you to dinner and guide you the next day to the beaches, Cragside, Alnwick Castle and fabulous walking. To stay is a treat.

Price	£60-£65. Singles £40.
Rooms	2: 1 double & sitting room; 1 twin (let to same party only).
Meals	Packed lunch £3-£4. Pubs/restaurants 2.5 miles.
Closed	End of October to end of March.
Directions	West from Rothbury on B6341. In Hepple, pass church on left; next right, then immediate hard right into driveway.

Joan & Brian Storey
East Hepple Farmhouse,
Hepple, Rothbury,
Northumberland NE65 7LH

Tel	01669 640221
Mobile	07850 766049
Email	joanstorey@coquetdale.net
Web	www.easthepplefarmhouse.co.uk

Entry 352 Map 16

Northumberland

Thistleyhaugh

Enid thrives on hard work and humour, her passions are pictures, cooking and people and if she's not the perfect B&B hostess, she's a close contender. Certainly you eat well – local farm eggs at breakfast and their own beef at dinner. Choose any of the five large, lovely bedrooms and stay the week; they are awash with old paintings, silk fabrics and crisp white linen. But if you do stray downstairs, past the log fire and the groaning table, there are 720 acres of organic farmland to discover and a few million more of the Cheviots beyond that. Wonderful hosts, house and region.

Price	£75. Singles £50-£75.
Rooms	5: 4 doubles, 1 twin.
Meals	Dinner, 3 courses, £20. Pub/restaurant 2 miles.
Closed	Christmas, New Year & January.
Directions	Leave A1 for A697 for Coldstream & Longhorsley; 2 miles past Longhorsley, left at Todburn sign; 1 mile to x-roads, then right; on 1 mile over white bridge; 1st right, right again, over cattle grid.

Henry & Enid Nelless
Thistleyhaugh,
Longhorsley, Morpeth,
Northumberland NE65 8RG
Tel   01665 570629
Fax   01665 570629
Email   thistleyhaugh@hotmail.com
Web   www.thistleyhaugh.co.uk

Entry 353   Map 16

Northumberland

Lansdown House

The arched coach house doors to this 1600s house are still right on the pavement on the busy market town street. But nip down a side corridor and you could be in deep countryside; a delightfully long town garden and your own entrance give you independence, and bubbly Lesley is on hand to make sure you have all you need. Fab breakfasts (in bed if you want) set you up for miles of sandy beaches, cycling, shooting, riding, fly fishing and Alnwick Castle. Lazy lumps can just loll in a sumptuous bed admiring the Designers Guild wallpaper, the TV (flat-screen, naturally) and the fine pieces of furniture.

Travel Club Offer: see page 392 for details.

Price	£70-£80. Singles from £48.
Rooms	2: 1 double, 1 twin.
Meals	Dinner, 3 courses, £22.50. Packed lunch £5. Pubs/restaurants walking distance.
Closed	Rarely.
Directions	The house is on the main thoroughfare through Morpeth, on right heading north, next to Sour Grapes wine bar. Easy free parking.

Lesley Mantel
Lansdown House,
90 Newgate Street, Morpeth,
Northumberland NE61 1BU
Tel   01670 511129
Email   kitchendiva@gmail.com
Web   www.lansdownhouse.co.uk

Entry 354   Map 16

Northumberland

Shieldhall

The guest rooms are in the charming 18th-century farm buildings, each with its own entrance. Stephen and his sons make and restore antique furniture and rooms are named after the wood used within: Elm, Oak, Mahogany, Pine. Bathrooms are spacious, there's a cosy sitting room/library and you pop across the courtyard for meals in the main house – once home to the family of Capability Brown. Celia is friendly and attentive and loves cooking, so ingredients are often organic or locally sourced; there's also a secret bar and a small but interesting wine list. Peaceful, hospitable B&B – with fine views.

Price	£80. Singles £50.
Rooms	3: 1 double, 1 twin, 1 four-poster.
Meals	Dinner, 4 courses, £25. Pub 7 miles.
Closed	Rarely.
Directions	From Newcastle A696 for Jedburgh. 5 miles north of Belsay, right onto B6342. On left after 500 yds (turn into front courtyard).

Celia & Stephen Robinson-Gay
Shieldhall,
Wallington, Morpeth,
Northumberland NE61 4AQ
Tel   01830 540387
Fax   01830 540490
Email   robinson.gay@btconnect.com
Web   www.shieldhallguesthouse.co.uk

Entry 355   Map 16

Northumberland

The Hermitage

A magical setting, only three miles from Hadrian's wall. Through ancient woodland, up the long drive and over the burn to this beautiful Georgian house. Inside is supremely comfortable and elegant but still homely. Large, carpeted and delightful bedrooms are furnished with antiques, prints and superb beds; bathrooms have large roll top baths. There's a walled garden, and breakfasts (delicious) can be served on the terrace. Katie grew up in this lovely house, looks after you brilliantly and knows all there is to know about the area. *Guests back please by 11pm. Children over seven & babes in arms welcome.*

Price	From £80. Singles from £45.
Rooms	3: 1 double, 1 twin; 1 twin with separate bath.
Meals	Pub 2 miles.
Closed	October-February.
Directions	7 miles north of Corbridge on A68. Left on A6079 for 1 mile, then right through lodge gates with arch. House 0.5 miles down drive.

Simon & Katie Stewart
The Hermitage,
Swinburne, Hexham,
Northumberland NE48 4DG
Tel   01434 681248
Fax   01434 681110
Email   katie.stewart@themeet.co.uk

Entry 356   Map 16

Bog House

It's too quiet for some townies – and thank goodness! If you've had it with bustle, bury yourself in the depths of Northumberland, two miles from Hadrian's Wall. Here is an immaculate barn conversion that's mercifully free from the usual modern furniture; what you have is a contemporary, airy feel and an open-raftered space stuffed with antiques. Rosemary has created a stunning place. Breakfast sausages are local (organic where possible), the peace total and the welcome disarming; you have your own entrance and may come and go as you please. An indulgent, wonderful retreat.

Matfen High House

Bring the wellies! You are 25 miles from the border and the walking is a joy. Struan and Jenny are amusing company, love sporting pursuits and will drive you to Matfen Hall for dinner. The sturdy stone house of 1735 is a pleasant, pretty place to stay: the en suite bedrooms have fine fabrics and good pictures, the bathrooms are stocked with fluffy towels and the drawing room promises books and choice pieces. Breakfasts are superb (bacon and sausages from the farmer; bread, mustards and jams all Jenny's) and the countryside is stunning. Hadrian's Wall and the great castles (Alnwick, Bamburgh) beckon.

Price	£80–£90. Singles £45–£50.
Rooms	2: 1 twin, 1 double.
Meals	Dinner, 2 courses, £17–£20. Pubs/restaurants 15-minute drive.
Closed	Rarely.
Directions	A68; 5 miles north of Corbridge, right onto B6318. After 3.5 miles, left signed Moorhouse. On for 1 mile, right; left to Bog House after 1 mile. Last farm on left.

Rosemary Stobart
Bog House,
Matfen, Northumberland NE20 0RF

Tel	01661 886776
Mobile	07850 375535
Email	rosemary.stobart@btinternet.com
Web	www.boghouse-matfen.co.uk

Entry 357   Map 16

Price	£60–£70. Singles £30–£35.
Rooms	4: 1 double, 1 twin; 1 double, 1 twin sharing bath.
Meals	Packed lunch £4.50. Restaurant 2 miles.
Closed	Rarely.
Directions	A69 at Heddon on the Wall, onto B6318 past Robin Hood Inn; 500 yds, right to Moorhouse; right at next junction signed High House Brewey; past Hadrian Pet Hotel; 300 yds, right, opp. cottages.

Struan & Jenny Wilson
Matfen High House,
Matfen, Corbridge,
Northumberland NE20 0RG

Tel	01661 886592
Fax	01661 886847
Email	struan@struan.enterprise-plc.com

Entry 358   Map 12

Nottinghamshire

The Old Vicarage

Jillie's grandmother studied at the Slade and her paintings line the walls; glass and china adorn every surface. This wisteria-clad Victorian vicarage next to the 12th-century church was falling down when the Steeles bought it; now it's an elegant, traditional country home and popular with honeymoon couples. Long windows are generously draped, two of the bedrooms are spacious, baths have claw feet and a number of friendly cats and dogs wait to welcome you. Jerry bakes the bread and all the vegetables come from the garden. Mary Queen of Scots is reputed to have stayed at Langford as guest of the Earl of Shrewsbury!

Travel Club Offer: see page 392 for details.

Price	£70–£80. Singles £45–£50.
Rooms	3: 2 doubles, 1 twin.
Meals	Dinner, for special occasions, £25. Pub/restaurant 1.5 miles.
Closed	Rarely.
Directions	From A1, A46 to Lincoln & left onto A1133 for Gainsborough. Through Langford, 0.5 miles on, then left for Holme. House 100 yds on, on right, by church.

Jerry & Jillie Steele
The Old Vicarage,
Langford, Newark,
Nottinghamshire NG23 7RT
Tel   01636 705031
Email   jillie.steele@virgin.net
Web   www.langfordoldvicarage.co.uk

Entry 359   Map 9

Nottinghamshire

Wisteria Court

A listed, terraced cottage in Georgian Southwell – ideal for visiting the Minster. On the road but quiet at night, the modest cottage with a big-house feel is crisply elegant inside. Bedrooms, one with a cast-iron fireplace, another with a beautifully upholstered armchair, are small but charming. Good towels, pillows to die for and, in the shared sitting room, rich rugs and cushions. Perfectionist Lynn treats you to breakfast fruit salads, organic eggs, and bacon and honeycomb from the farm shop. The town is pretty and there are numerous castles and antique shops close by. *Children over 12 welcome.*

Ethical Collection: Food. See page 400 for details.

Price	£70.
Rooms	2: 1 double, 1 twin.
Meals	Pubs/restaurants 300 yds.
Closed	Rarely.
Directions	From A1 at Newark A617 towards Southwell. Left after Averham; 3 miles on, approach town, 'Minster spires' in view; sharp right turn, house 200 yds on left.

Lynn McKay
Wisteria Court,
58 Church Street, Southwell,
Nottinghamshire NG25 0HG
Tel   01636 815509
Mobile   07813 402864
Email   susan_lynn@btinternet.com

Entry 360   Map 9

Nottinghamshire

The Yellow House

A butter-yellow 30s semi in a quiet, tree-lined street. Suzanne, a well-travelled ex-model, and Misza her lovely dog, welcome you in. Colour schemes are cool, peaceful, with the occasional oriental touch. Your bedroom in the eaves – a charming, cossetting, cottagey hideaway with a good big bed – is crisply decorated in bold cream-and-olive florals, and has a good shower. Suzanne offers breakfast on the terrace in fine weather and has loads of info on walks. Nottingham's attractions are three miles away, the great oaks of Sherwood Forest are 12 miles north.

Price	£59.50. Singles £39.50.
Rooms	1 double.
Meals	Pubs 0.5 mile, restaurants 1 mile.
Closed	Rarely.
Directions	From A60 main Mansfield road going north, at junc. with Vale Pub right onto Thackerey's Lane; at r'bout straight on; after 100 yds right into Whernside Rd. Left at x-roads into Littlegreen Rd; house on left.

Suzanne Prew-Smith
The Yellow House,
7 Littlegreen Road,
Woodthorpe, Nottingham,
Nottinghamshire NG5 4LE
Tel   01159 262280
Email   suzanne.prewsmith1@btinternet.com
Web   www.theyellowhouse-nottingham.co.uk

Entry 361   Map 8

Oxfordshire

Uplands House

Come to be spoiled at this 'farmhouse' built in 1875 for the Earl of Jersey's son and completely renovated by this talented couple. It's elegant and sumptuously furnished with large, light bedrooms, crisp linen, thick towels, spoiling bathrooms and long bucolic views from the Orangery where you have tea and cake. Relax here with a book as the sounds and smells of the garden waft by, or chat to charming Poppy while she creates a delicious dinner. Breakfast is Graham's domain – try smoked salmon with scrambled eggs and red caviar. You're well placed for exploring but you may find it hard to leave.

Price	£90-£150. Singles £60-£90.
Rooms	3: 1 double, 1 twin/double, 1 four-poster.
Meals	Dinner, 2-4 courses, £20-£30. Pub 1.25 miles.
Closed	Rarely.
Directions	M40 junc.11; thro' Banbury, A422 thro' Wroxton, pass 'Warwickshire' & 'Upton House 200 yds' signs. Turn right after 10 yds down drive signed Uplands Farm; 1st entrance on right.

Poppy Cooksey & Graham Paul
Uplands House,
Upton, Banbury,
Oxfordshire OX15 6HJ
Tel   01295 678663
Mobile   07836 535538
Email   poppy@cotswolds-uplands.co.uk
Web   www.cotswolds-uplands.co.uk

Entry 362   Map 8

Oxfordshire

Buttslade House

A gorgeous ground-floor retreat for couples who need to catch up with each other. You get a smart, private bedroom across the courtyard from the 17th-century farmhouse with its barns and stables. A clever melody of ancient and contemporary style romps through your summer sitting room with ancestral portraits and modern Spanish art, antique sofas, fluorescent cushions and a comfortable wooden bed with a Rajasthan cover and feather pillows. Diana is fun and will pamper you or leave you, there's a blissful garden to stroll through, food is fresh and local and it's a hop to the village pub.

Price	£70. Singles £45.
Rooms	1 double & sitting room.
Meals	Dinner, 3 courses, £25. Lunch £7. Pub 200 yds.
Closed	Rarely.
Directions	From B4035 look for signs to Wykham Arms. Buttslade is 2nd house beyond pub, going down hill.

Diana Thompson
Buttslade House,
Temple Mill Road,
Sibford Gower, Banbury,
Oxfordshire OX15 5RX

Tel	01295 788818
Email	janthompson50@hotmail.com
Web	www.buttsladehouse.co.uk

Entry 363   Map 8

Oxfordshire

Minehill House

Bump your way up the track (mind the car!) to the top of a wild and windswept hill and a gorgeous family farmhouse with views for miles and young, energetic Hester to care for you. Little people will adore the ping-pong table and the trampoline; their parents will enjoy the well-polished flagstones, colourful oil paintings, wood-burning stove and seriously sophisticated food. Rest well in the big double room with Sanderson oak-leaved paper and stunning views, and a cubby-hole door through to extra twin beds; bathrooms are sparklingly clean and spacious. Bracing walks straight from the door.

Price	£70-£90. Singles from £45.
Rooms	1 double/family.
Meals	Dinner, 3 courses, from £30. Supper £15. Packed lunch available. Pubs 1-5 miles.
Closed	Christmas & New Year.
Directions	From Banbury B4035 to Brailes; after 10 miles take road signed Hook Norton; 0.5 miles, right onto unmarked uphill farm track to house.

Hester & Ed Sale
Minehill House,
Lower Brailes, Banbury,
Oxfordshire OX15 5BJ

Tel	01608 685594
Mobile	07890 266441
Email	ed_and_hester@lineone.net

Entry 364   Map 8

Oxfordshire

Buttermilk Stud

At the top of an avenue of limes, enveloped by 70 beautiful acres, is this rambling farmstead with orchards and vegetable gardens, wildlife, roses and foxgloves. George is a painter and the house is filled with vibrant art; Victoria looks after the three children and the small farm. Inside is a happy assemblage of family furniture, flowers from the garden, children, dogs and harmonious colours. Your bedroom is old-fashioned and comfortable, with beautiful views over rolling pasture. Outside are geese, horses, cows and chickens. And the marvellous Falkland Arms at Great Tew is an hour's stride across fields.

Price	£80. Singles £50.
Rooms	1 twin/double.
Meals	Packed lunch £10. Supper, 2 courses, £25. Dinner, 3 courses, £30. Pub 1 mile.
Closed	Rarely.
Directions	From Deddington B488 towards Chipping Norton. Through Hempton. After 1 mile right to South Newington. House on left after 1 mile.

Victoria Irvine
Buttermilk Stud,
Barford St Michael,
Banbury,
Oxfordshire OX15 0PL
Tel   01295 722929
Mobile   07803 907238
Email   buttermilk@btconnect.com

Entry 365   Map 8

Oxfordshire

Home Farmhouse

The house is charming, with low, wobbly ceilings, exposed beams, Inglenook fireplaces and winding stairs; the bedrooms, perched above their own staircases like crows' nests, are decorated with extravagant swathes of rich floral chintz. All rooms are unusual, old and full of character, but luxurious; lavish curtains embellish one bath. The family's history and travels are evident all over, the barn room has its own entrance and the Grove-Whites – who are super – run their B&B as a team. Two delightful dogs, too – Ulysses and Goliath. It's all so laid-back you'll find it hard to leave.

Price	£80. Singles £52.
Rooms	3: 2 twins/doubles, 1 double.
Meals	Dinner £27. Supper £18. Pub 100 yds.
Closed	Christmas.
Directions	M40 junc. 10, A43 for Northampton. After 5 miles, left to Charlton. There, left & house on left, 100 yds past Rose & Crown.

Rosemary & Nigel Grove-White
Home Farmhouse,
Charlton, Banbury,
Oxfordshire OX17 3DR
Tel   01295 811683
Fax   01295 811683
Email   grovewhite@lineone.net
Web   www.homefarmhouse.co.uk

Entry 366   Map 8

The Old Post House

Great natural charm in the 17th-century Old Post House: shiny flagstones, rich dark wood and mullion windows combine with luxurious fabrics, papers, colours and fine furniture. Bedrooms are big, with antique wardrobes, oak headboards and an old-fashioned feel. The walled gardens are lovely – rich with espaliered fruit trees and there's a pool for sunny evenings. Christine, a well-travelled ex-pat, has an innate sense of hospitality – as do her two Springer spaniels – and breakfasts are delicious. There's village traffic but your sleep should be sound, and Deddington is delightful. *Children over 12 welcome.*

Manor Farmhouse

Helen and John radiate pleasure and good humour. Blenheim Park is a short walk down the lane and this soft old stone house is perfect for any delusions of grandeur: good prints and paintings, venerable furniture, gentle fabrics, nothing cluttered or overdone. Shallow, curvy, 18th-century stairs lead past grandfather's bronze bust to the splendid double; the other small bedroom has its own challenging spiral stair to a cobbled courtyard. Breakfast is by the rough-hewn fireplace and the ancient dresser. Wander through the lovely garden in spring and summer; the village is palpably quiet.

Price	£80. Singles £52.
Rooms	3: 1 double, 1 twin/double, 1 four-poster.
Meals	Occasional dinner. Pubs/restaurants in village.
Closed	Rarely.
Directions	A4260 Oxford-Banbury. In Deddington, on right next to cream Georgian house. Park opposite.

Price	£68–£76. Singles from £50.
Rooms	2 doubles, sharing shower room.
Meals	Pub within walking distance.
Closed	Christmas.
Directions	A44 north from Oxford's ring road. At r'bout, 1 mile before Woodstock, left onto A4095 into Bladon. Last left in village; house on 2nd bend in road, with iron railings.

Christine Blenntoft
The Old Post House,
New Street, Deddington,
Oxfordshire OX15 0SP

Tel	01869 338978
Mobile	07713 631092
Fax	01869 338978
Email	kblenntoft@aol.com

Helen Stevenson
Manor Farmhouse,
Manor Road, Bladon, Woodstock,
Oxfordshire OX20 1RU

Tel	01993 812168
Fax	01993 812168
Email	helstevenson@hotmail.com
Web	www.oxlink.co.uk/woodstock/manor-farmhouse/

Entry 367 Map 8

Entry 368 Map 8

Oxfordshire

Caswell House

A handsome 15th-century manor house with an ancient orchard, walled gardens, smooth lawns and a moat brimming with trout. Guest wing quarters are spacious, beamed and comfortable, with views over the garden from leaded windows. Bedrooms are spoiling and large with the best linen, thick towels and warm bathrooms. Amanda and Richard are generous and easy-going – a game of snooker is a must! – and seasonal produce is sourced from the farm shop and cooked on the Aga. A great place to relax; for heartier souls there are 450 acres of rolling farmland.

Price	£80. Singles £60.
Rooms	3: 2 doubles, 1 twin.
Meals	Pubs/restaurants nearby.
Closed	Rarely.
Directions	A40 Burford to Oxford. Right after 1.8 miles to Brize Norton, left at staggered x-roads. Right at r'bout, left at mini-r'bout for Curbridge; on for 1.2 miles, house on right.

Mrs Amanda Matthews
Caswell House,
Caswell Lane, Brize Norton,
Oxfordshire OX18 3NJ
Tel 01993 701064
Mobile 07718 390867
Email stay@caswell-house.co.uk
Web www.caswell-house.co.uk

Entry 369 Map 8

Oxfordshire

Rectory Farm

Come for the happy buzz of family life. It's relaxed and informal and you are welcomed with tea and homemade shortbread by Mary Anne. The date above the entrance stone reads 1629 and bedrooms, light and spotless, have beautiful stone-arched and mullioned windows. The huge twin has ornate plasterwork and views over the garden and church; the double is cosier with a carved pine headboard; both have good showers and large fluffy towels. The pedigree North Devon cattle are Robert's pride and joy and his family has farmed here for three generations. It's a treat to stay. *Minimum stay two nights at weekends and high season.*

Travel Club Offer: see page 392 for details.

Price	£70-£75. Singles £50-£55.
Rooms	2: 1 double, 1 twin.
Meals	Pub 2-minute walk.
Closed	Mid-December-mid-January.
Directions	From Oxford, A420 for Swindon for 8 miles & right at r'bout, for Witney (A415). Over 2 bridges, immed. right by pub car park. Right at T-junc.; drive on right, past church.

Mary Anne Florey
Rectory Farm,
Northmoor, Witney,
Oxfordshire OX29 5SX
Tel 01865 300207
Mobile 07974 102198
Email pj.florey@farmline.com
Web www.oxtowns.co.uk/rectoryfarm

Entry 370 Map 8

Oxfordshire

Langsmeade House

Marianne has applied talent and her Dutch background to make her 1920s house irresistibly comfortable and perfect for house parties. There are two sitting rooms, velvet and tapestry sofas, wooden floors, panelling, excellent beds, some lovely Dutch furniture and lawns to loll on in the summer. Big-hearted Marianne imposes few rules, prepares terrific breakfasts and gives lifts in her London cab to Oxford's Park & Ride, the Ridgeway *and* to restaurants; she will collect you up until 1am! Traffic noise from the nearby M40 is constant – loud outside, audible inside – but we defy you not to be charmed.

Price	£80. Singles £45.
Rooms	3: 1 double;
	2 doubles sharing bath/shower
	(let to same party only).
Meals	Lunch £5. Dinner £17.50.
	Packed lunch £3.50. Pub 2 miles.
Closed	Rarely.
Directions	M40 from London, junc. 7 for
	Thame, right then left for Milton
	Common. Pass Belfry Hotel on
	right. House on left down 'No
	Through Road'.

	Mrs M Aben
	Langsmeade House,
	Milton Common, Thame,
	Oxfordshire OX9 2JY
Tel	01844 278727
Fax	01844 279256
Email	enquiries@langsmeadehouse.co.uk
Web	www.langsmeadehouse.co.uk

Entry 371   Map 8

Oxfordshire

71 Charlbury Road

An excellent Oxford address, traditionally comfortable, utterly peaceful, a 12-minute walk to the bus stop for town. Jacqueline, talented needlewoman, pianist and ex-stewardess, pays gentle attention to housekeeping and guests, yet never intrudes. Up carpeted stairs are comfy-cosy bedrooms with Vi-sprung mattresses and, in the double, a hand-made patchwork quilt. Spotless bathrooms are stocked with towels and bedroom windows face the garden; college playing fields stretch beyond. The sitting room has pale sofas, velvet armchairs, a harpsichord, a grand piano – let Jacqueline treat you to a little Chopin!

Price	£70. Singles £40.
Rooms	2: 1 single;
	1 double with separate bathroom.
Meals	Pubs/restaurants 0.5 miles.
Closed	Christmas, New Year & February.
Directions	North out of Oxford on A4165,
	Banbury Road, take 6th exit on
	right, Belbroughton Road. Left at
	the end into Charlbury Road; 2nd
	turning on right, first house on left.

	Jacqueline Burgess
	71 Charlbury Road,
	Oxford,
	Oxfordshire OX2 6UX
Tel	01865 511752
Email	jackiebjoyful@yahoo.com

Entry 372   Map 8

Oxfordshire

Cowdrays

Birdsong and sunlight find their way into every room and Margaret, genuinely welcoming, bends to the needs of all guests; the downstairs room is perfect for wheelchair-users. The house is down a quiet lane, there are chickens, geese, dogs and, in the lovely garden – a corner of which is Gertrude Jekyll-inspired – a tennis court. This is a homely, endearingly timeworn sort of place, neither smart nor stylish, but with good furniture, masses of books, clean bathrooms, a little sitting room... even a kitchen area in which to prepare a snack if you prefer not to walk to the historic village's pubs.

Price	From £70. Singles £35.
Rooms	5: 2 doubles;
	1 twin with separate shower;
	1 twin, 1 single sharing
	bath/shower.
Meals	Packed lunch £5. Pubs 7-min. walk.
Closed	Rarely.
Directions	Off A417, 3 miles from Wantage going east. Right into East Hendred; 3rd right into Orchard Lane; past pub; at x-roads, left into Cat St; house behind wall & gates.

	Margaret Bateman
	Cowdrays,
	Cat Street, East Hendred, Wantage,
	Oxford, Oxfordshire OX12 8JT
Tel	01235 833313
Mobile	07799 622003
Email	cowdrays@virgin.net
Web	www.cowdrays.co.uk

Entry 373   Map 4

Oxfordshire

Fyfield Manor

One of the most fabulous houses in Oxfordshire (once owned by Simon de Montfort) with vast water gardens created by the Browns. Through the grand wood-panelled hall enter a beamed dining room with high-backed chairs and brass rubbings; you breakfast (local, free-range, organic) through the 12th-century arch... or al fresco. Bedrooms are large, warm and light with snowy bed covers and views. Oxford Park & Ride is nearby, there's walking from the door and delightful Christine has wangled you a free glass of wine in the local pub if you walk or cycle. Superb. *Children over ten welcome.*

Ethical Collection: Environment.
See page 400 for details.

Travel Club Offer: see page 392 for details.

Price	From £70. Singles from £50.
Rooms	2: 1 twin/double;
	1 twin/double/family with separate bath.
Meals	Pubs within 1 mile.
Closed	Rarely.
Directions	M4 junc. 8/9; A4130 thro' Henley to Wallingford. Turn off for Benson; cont. thro' village 1 mile. Last house on right, behind 6 foot-high brick wall.

	Christine Brown
	Fyfield Manor,
	Benson, Wallingford,
	Oxfordshire OX10 6HA
Tel	01491 835184
Fax	01491 825635
Email	chris_fyfield@hotmail.co.uk
Web	www.fyfieldmanor.co.uk

Entry 374   Map 4

Oxfordshire

Hernes

The lovely rambling farmhouse has been in the family for over a century and has a warmly individual flavour. Pre-Raphaelite Aunt Connie looks down on you in the dimly-lit hall, the billiard room, with log-burning stove and comfortable chairs, is vast, and more ancestors keep an eye on you at breakfast. High-ceilinged bedrooms come without the usual arctic chill and have long views and country-house charm. The garden is wonderful, the surroundings peacefully rural and there's home-produced honey and marmalade for breakfast. Perfect for exploring Henley and some gorgeous *Vicar of Dibley* countryside.

Price	£97.50. Singles from £65. Single-night bank holiday surcharge.
Rooms	3: 1 twin/double, 1 four-poster; 1 double with separate bath.
Meals	Pub & restaurants 1 mile.
Closed	December-mid-January & occasionally.
Directions	Over lights in centre of Henley as far as Town Hall. Left through carpark; right onto Greys Rd for 2 miles; 300 yds after 30mph zone, 2nd drive on right; signed drive to main house.

	Richard & Gillian Ovey
	Hernes,
	Henley-on-Thames,
	Oxfordshire RG9 4NT
Tel	01491 573245
Fax	01491 574646
Email	governor@herneshenley.com
Web	www.herneshenley.com

Entry 375   Map 4

Oxfordshire

The Craven

Roses and clematis cover this pretty 16th-century thatched cottage where breakfast in the farmhouse kitchen is served at a long pine table by a dresser laden with china. Cosy beamed bedrooms have embroidered sheets and country views; the room on the ground floor with antique four-poster is charming, the room in the stable block has a Victorian half-tester and bathrooms promise gold taps and fluffy towels. More beams and pretty chintz sofas in the sitting room, where you sip tea or wine around a huge log fire. Carol's daughter Katie creates prize-winning dinners – and there are walks from the door.

Price	£75-£95.
Rooms	3: 2 doubles, 1 four-poster.
Meals	Dinner, 3 courses, from £24.50.
Closed	Rarely.
Directions	M4 junc. 14 to A338, then B4001. Thro' Lambourn, 1 mile north of village, fork left; 3 miles to Kingston Lisle, left to Uffington. Thro' village, right after church. House 0.3 miles out, on left.

	Carol Wadsworth
	The Craven,
	Fernham Road, Uffington,
	Oxfordshire SN7 7RD
Tel	01367 820449
Fax	01367 820351
Email	carol@thecraven.co.uk
Web	www.thecraven.co.uk

Entry 376   Map 3

Rutland

Old Rectory

Jane Austen fans will swoon. This elegant 1740s village house was used as Mr Collins's 'humble abode' by the BBC: you breakfast in the beautiful dining room that was 'Mr Collins's hall', and you can sleep in 'Miss Bennett's bedroom'. Victoria is the archetypal English woman – feisty, fun and gregarious – and looks after you beautifully with White Company linen in chintzy old-fashioned bedrooms and (not swish) bathrooms, fruit from the lovely garden and Aga-cooked bacon and eggs. You are near to some pleasant market towns and lovely walking and riding country. Don't forget the smelling salts!

Price	£80.
Rooms	2: 1 twin; 1 double with separate bath.
Meals	Pubs within 3 miles.
Closed	Rarely.
Directions	5 miles NE of Oakham, through Ashwell. Or 7 miles west of A1 from Stretton.

Victoria Owen
Old Rectory,
Teigh, Oakham,
Rutland LE15 7RT
Tel   01572 787681
Mobile   07717 223678
Email   torowen@btinternet.com

Entry 377   Map 9

Rutland

Old Hall Coach House

A rare and special setting; the grounds of the house meet the edge of Rutland Water, with far-reaching lake and church views. Inside: high ceilings, stone archways, antiques and a conservatory overlooking a year-round stunning garden and croquet lawn. Bedrooms are traditional with modern touches and comfortable; the double and single have super new bathrooms. Rutland is a mini-Cotswolds of stone villages and gentle hills, the lake encourages you to sail, fish, walk or ride, and Georgian Stamford, Burghley House and Belvoir Castle are nearby. Cecilie is a well-travelled, interesting host. *Minimum two nights at weekends.*

Price	From £90. Singles from £40.
Rooms	3: 1 double; 1 twin, 1 single, each with separate bath.
Meals	Dinner £30. Pub/restaurant 5-minute walk.
Closed	Occasionally.
Directions	From A1 Stamford bypass A606 for Oakham for 3 miles. Fork left for E. Weston; past village sign; 1st right, Church Lane; past church, right down hill; on right on left bend.

Cecilie Ingoldby
Old Hall Coach House,
Edith Weston, Oakham,
Rutland LE15 8HQ
Tel   01780 721504
Mobile   07767 678267
Email   cecilieingoldby@aol.com
Web   www.oldhallcoachhouse.co.uk

Entry 378   Map 9

Shropshire

Pinfold Cottage

Heart-warming B&B in a beautiful spot with lots of books, a parrot called Polly and vintage games and toys to add to the merry clutter. Walls are covered in illustrations and some lovely paintings, bedrooms are calm, simple and charming, but the biggest treat is Sue. Generous with her time, spirit and home cooking, she makes her own muesli with fruits and nuts from the garden. Natural sounds are provided by the well-fed birdlife and the trickle of the stream that meanders through the enchanting garden. Breakfasts are healthy and delicious and you'll revel in the peace. Superb value.

Price	£50. Singles £30.
Rooms	2: 1 double, 1 single, each with separate shower. Extra bath available.
Meals	Dinner, 3 courses, from £15. Packed lunch £7. Restaurant 0.5 miles.
Closed	Rarely.
Directions	From Oswestry, A483 from A5 for Welshpool. 1st left to Maesbury; 3rd right at x-roads with school on corner; 1st house on right.

	Mrs Sue Barr
	Pinfold Cottage,
	Newbridge,
	Maesbury, Oswestry,
	Shropshire SY10 8AY
Tel	01691 661192
Email	suebarr100@hotmail.com

Entry 379   Map 7

Shropshire

Top Farmhouse

The charming roadside house in little Knockin is 16th-century, magpie-gabled and rambling, the church and pound are 800 years old and Pam is theatrical and fun. Downstairs is attractive, warm and cosy, a lattice of beams dividing the dining room from the sitting room where wine and conversation flow. Upstairs, floors rise, fall and creak, and all is in apple-pie order: beds are of brass, oak and varnished pine, tea trays are filled with treats. A place with a huge heart to which the loyal return – and Pam's breakfasts are as generous as her spirit. Chirk and Powys castles are near. *Children over 11 welcome.*

Price	£65–£75. Singles from £35.
Rooms	3: 1 double, 1 twin, 1 double/family room.
Meals	Packed lunch available. Pub walking distance.
Closed	Rarely.
Directions	From Shrewsbury, A5 north. Through Nesscliffe & after 2 miles, left to Knockin. Through Knockin, past Bradford Arms. House 250 yds on left.

	Pam Morrissey
	Top Farmhouse,
	Knockin, Oswestry,
	Shropshire SY10 8HN
Tel	01691 682582
Mobile	07710 812712
Email	p.a.m@knockin.freeserve.co.uk
Web	www.topfarmknockin.co.uk

Entry 380   Map 7

Shropshire

Brimford House

Tucked under the Breidden Hills, farm and Georgian farmhouse have been in David's family for four generations. Views stretch all the way to the Severn; the simple garden does not try to compete. Bedrooms are spotless and fresh: a half-tester with rope-twist columns and Sanderson fabrics, a twin with Victorian wrought-iron bedsteads, a double with a brass bed and huge bathroom with roll top bath. Liz, friendly and helpful, serves you breakfast round the tulip-legged table: tuck into fresh farm eggs and homemade preserves. Farmhouse comfort, great value and walks from the door.

Travel Club Offer: see page 392 for details.

Price	£55–£70. Singles £40–£60.
Rooms	3: 2 doubles, 1 twin.
Meals	Packed lunch £4.50. Pub 3-minute walk.
Closed	Rarely.
Directions	From Shrewsbury A458 Welshpool road. After Ford, right onto B4393. Just after Crew Green, left for Criggion. House 1st on left after Admiral Rodney pub.

Liz & David Dawson
Brimford House,
Criggion, Shrewsbury,
Shropshire SY5 9AU
Tel   01938 570235
Mobile   07801 100848
Email   info@brimford.co.uk
Web   www.brimford.co.uk

Entry 381   Map 7

Shropshire

Meole Brace Hall

The Hathaways take B&B to a new state of excellence and love having guests in their heavenly house: Georgian and listed, with manicured gardens. It is the quintessence of English period elegance. Joan is a terrific cook who radiates courtesy and charm; Charles cheerfully assumes the role of 'mine host'. Their sumptuous home is rich with antiques, polished mahogany and eye-catching wallpapers and fabrics, and the Blue Room has an elegant half-tester bed. Summer breakfasts are taken in the conservatory, as is afternoon tea. A 20-minute stroll from Abbey and town, but it feels a million miles away.

Price	From £79. Singles from £59.
Rooms	3: 2 doubles, 1 twin.
Meals	Restaurants 1 mile.
Closed	Rarely.
Directions	A5 & A49 junc. (south of bypass), follow signs to centre. Over 1st mini r'bout, 2nd exit at next; 2nd left into Upper Rd; 150 yds on at bend, left & immed. right into Church Lane. Drive at bottom on left.

Joan Hathaway
Meole Brace Hall,
Shrewsbury,
Shropshire SY3 9HF
Tel   01743 235566
Fax   01743 236886
Email   hathaway@meolebracehall.co.uk
Web   www.meolebracehall.co.uk

Entry 382   Map 7

Shropshire

Upper Brompton Farm

Surround yourself with calming caramels, creams, beiges and golds in this Georgian farmhouse with a contemporary twist. Phillipa, an interior designer, has worked her magic here and it's all delightfully understated: a large comfortable sitting room with open fire and squishy sofas, bright bathrooms with thick towels, spoiling beds and linen, fresh flowers and gleaming furniture. Outside are acres of National Trust land, beautifully looked after, for walks, ambles and picnics. Food is scrumptious and generous; smoked kippers, scrambled eggs and homemade damson jam at breakfast, and farmhouse cooking for supper.

Price	£75–£90. Singles from £30.
Rooms	3 twins/doubles.
Meals	Packed lunch £5. Dinner £25. Restaurants 1.5 miles.
Closed	Christmas & New Year.
Directions	4 miles south of Shrewsbury on A458. In Cross Houses, left after petrol station, signed Atcham. Down lane & right to Brompton; follow to farm.

	Philippa Home
	Upper Brompton Farm,
	Cross Houses,
	Shrewsbury,
	Shropshire SY5 6LE
Tel	01743 761629
Mobile	07967 740838
Web	www.uppperbromptonfarm.co.uk

Entry 383   Map 7

Shropshire

Acton Pigot

Elegance abounds and yet there's a family farmhouse feel. The fine old house sits well on its ancient piece of ground, its sash windows looking across to the site of England's first parliament. The delightful Owens spoil you with afternoon tea before a log fire in the sitting room (and in the lovely garden in summer). Come for deep beds, soft lights, fine linen, hand-printed wallpaper and English oak in stair, beam and floor. Bedrooms are inviting and cosy. The two-acre garden hugs the house – a treat with rare plants, croquet lawn, shady spots and pool for summer. A restorative place run by special people.

Price	From £75. Singles £50.
Rooms	3: 1 double, 1 twin/double, 1 family room.
Meals	Pub 3 miles.
Closed	Christmas.
Directions	From A5 & Shrewsbury, onto A458 for Bridgnorth; 200 yds on, right to Acton Burnell. Entering Acton Burnell, left to Kenley; 0.5 miles, left to Acton Pigot; house 1st on left.

	John & Hildegard Owen
	Acton Pigot,
	Acton Burnell, Shrewsbury,
	Shropshire SY5 7PH
Tel	01694 731209
Mobile	07850 124000
Email	actonpigot@farming.co.uk
Web	www.actonpigot.co.uk

Entry 384   Map 7

Shropshire

Hannigans Farm

High on the hillside, a mile up the drive, the views roll out before you – stunning. Privacy and peace are yours in the converted dairy and barn across the flower-filled yard. Big, carpeted, ground-floor rooms have comfy beds and sofas; one has views that roll towards the setting sun. In the morning Fiona and Alistair, delightful, easy-going and fun, serve you home eggs, sausages from their own pigs and honey from their bees in the book-lined dining room of their farmhouse. Feel free to take tea in the garden with its little hedges and manicured lawns; you'll feel restored in this quiet Shropshire corner.

Shropshire

Jinlye

Wuthering Heights in glorious Shropshire – and every room with a view. There's comfort too, in the raftered lounge with its huge open fire, the swish dining room for fun breakfasts, the conservatory scented in summer – and the spacious bedrooms with their deep-pile carpets, new mattresses and sumptuous touches... expect faux-marble reliefs, floral sinks, boudoir chairs and spotless *objets*. Sheltered Jinlye sits in lush landscaped gardens surrounded by hills, rare birds, wild ponies and windswept ridges. Kate, Jan and their little papillon dogs look after you professionally and with ease.

Travel Club Offer: see page 392 for details.

Price	£70. Singles by arrangement.
Rooms	2 twins.
Meals	Pub 1.25 miles.
Closed	Rarely.
Directions	From Bridgnorth, A458 to Shrewsbury. 0.5 miles after Morville, right onto stone road & follow signs for 1 mile, to farm.

Price	£64–£86. Singles £54–£62.
Rooms	6: 3 doubles, 2 twins/doubles, 1 twin.
Meals	Packed lunch on request. Pubs 1 mile.
Closed	Christmas Day.
Directions	From Shrewsbury A49 to Church Stretton then right towards All Stretton. Once in All Stretton right, immed. past phone box, up a winding road, up the hill to Jinlye.

	Mrs Fiona Thompson
	Hannigans Farm,
	Morville,
	Bridgnorth,
	Shropshire WV16 4RN
Tel	01746 714332
Email	hannigansfarm@btinternet.com
Web	www.hannigans-farm.co.uk

	Jan & Kate Tory
	Jinlye,
	Castle Hill, All Stretton,
	Church Stretton, Shropshire SY6 6JP
Tel	01694 723243
Fax	01694 723243
Email	info@jinlye.co.uk
Web	www.jinlye.co.uk

Entry 385   Map 7

Entry 386   Map 7

Shropshire

Clun Farm House

These young owners make a great team. Susan gives you fabulous marmalade at breakfast and seasonal produce at dinner, Anthony helps you discover the secrets of the historic village and the heavenly hills. Both are enthusiastic collectors of country artefacts and have filled their listed, 15th-century farmhouse with eye-catching things; the cowboy's saddle by the old range echoes Susan's roots. Bedrooms have aged, oiled floorboards, fun florals and bold walls. Walk Offa's Dyke and the Shropshire Way; return to a cosy wood-burner, a warm smile and a delicious dinner. Brilliant value.

Price	From £70. Singles by arrangement.
Rooms	2: 1 double (& extra bunk-bed room); 1 twin/double with separate shower.
Meals	Dinner from £25. Packed lunch £3.50. Pubs/restaurants nearby.
Closed	Occasionally.
Directions	A49 from Ludlow & onto B4368 at Craven Arms, for Clun. In High St on left 0.5 miles from Clun sign.

Anthony & Susan Whitfield
Clun Farm House,
High Street, Clun,
Shropshire SY7 8JB

Tel	01588 640432
Mobile	07885 261391
Fax	01588 640432
Web	www.clunfarmhouse.co.uk

Entry 387 Map 7

Shropshire

The Birches Mill

Just as a mill should be, tucked in the nook of a postcard valley. It ended Gill and Andrew's search for a refuge from the city; it is a treat to share its seclusion and natural beauty where the only sounds are watery ones from the river. The fresh, breezy rooms in the 17th-century part have elegant brass beds, goose down duvets, fine linen and one has an original, very long, roll top bath; the new stone and oak extension blends beautifully and has become a large, attractive twin. Gill and Andrew are affable hosts, and have brought artistic flair to this stunning valley of meadowland and woods. *Children over 12 welcome.*

Travel Club Offer: see page 392 for details.

Price	£78-£86. Singles by arrangement.
Rooms	3: 1 double, 1 twin; 1 double with separate bath.
Meals	Packed lunch £6. Pub 3 miles.
Closed	November-March.
Directions	From Clun A488 for Bishops Castle. 1st left, for Bicton. 2nd left for Mainstone, then narrow winding lane for 1.5 miles. Up bank to farm, then 1st right for Burlow. House at bottom of hill on left by river.

Gill Della Casa & Andrew Farmer
The Birches Mill,
Clun, Craven Arms,
Shropshire SY7 8NL

Tel	01588 640409
Fax	01588 640409
Email	gill@birchesmill.fsnet.co.uk
Web	www.birchesmill.co.uk

Entry 388 Map 7

Shropshire

Hopton House

Karen looks after her guests with competence and care – she even runs courses on how to do B&B! Relax, unwind and enjoy the country views in this converted granary. Thanks to old beams, high ceilings and a new sun-filled dining/sitting room overlooking hills, there's a fresh uplifting feel. Bedrooms, warm, charming, just refurbished, have flat-screen TV, digital radio, good lighting and decanters of sherry; one has a balcony, another alder wood floors. Bathrooms are spoiling, breakfast promises Ludlow sausages, Hopton House hen eggs and homemade jams, dinner is local and home-grown. Perfect B&B.

Shropshire

Brick House Farm

From the roadside this looks unexceptional, but once through the gates and into the farmyard with strutting chickens you can see the black and white checked side of this 16th-century longhouse. David has kept the lovely wobbly walls and painted them simple white, left wooden beams exposed and found a hidden fireplace mentioned in Pevsner. Loll in the sitting room with its Victorian tiled floor, bright rugs and belting wood-burner, sleep soundly on smart mattresses, soak in a deep Villeroy & Boch bath, tuck into home-grown lamb for supper. The garden seeps into open countryside with peaceful, grazing horses.

Travel Club Offer: see page 392 for details.

Price	£75–£95. Singles from £55.
Rooms	3 doubles.
Meals	Dinner, 3 courses, £30. Light supper £12.50. Restaurant 3 miles.
Closed	23 December-2 January & occasionally.
Directions	A49 Craven Arms exit, B4368 west. After 1 mile, left signed Hopton Heath. At Hopton Heath x-roads, right over bridge, follow road right. House 2nd on left.

Price	£75.
Rooms	2: 1 double, 1 twin/double, each with separate bath.
Meals	Dinner, 3-4 courses, £25. BYO. Packed lunch £5.
Closed	Rarely.
Directions	On A4110, from Leintwardine; house 1st on left, with sandy coloured render, opposite church.

	Karen Thorne
	Hopton House,
	Hopton Heath, Craven Arms,
	Shropshire SY7 0QD
Tel	01547 530885
Mobile	07766 565737
Email	info@shropshirebreakfast.co.uk
Web	www.shropshirebreakfast.co.uk

	David Watson
	Brick House Farm,
	Adforton, Leintwardine,
	Craven Arms,
	Shropshire SY7 0NF
Tel	01568 770870
Email	info@adforton.com
Web	www.adforton.com

Entry 389   Map 7

Entry 390   Map 7

Shropshire

Upper Buckton

Hayden and Yvonne love their stunning location – which ensures a special stay. Bedrooms are large, with huge beds made to perfection, lovely linen and proper blankets; bathrooms sport robes and treats. Standing in lush gardens that slope peacefully down to millstream, meadows and river, the house has a motte and bailey castle site, a heronry, a point-to-point course and a ha-ha. Yvonne's cooking using local produce is upmarket and creative, Hayden's wine list is a treat – marvellous for walkers returning from a day in the glorious Welsh Borders. *Children by arrangement.*

Travel Club Offer: see page 392 for details.

Price	£76-£90. Singles £48-£55.
Rooms	3: 1 double; 2 twins/doubles, each with separate bath.
Meals	Dinner, 4 courses, £28. Pub/restaurant 5 miles.
Closed	Rarely.
Directions	From Ludlow, A49 to Shrewsbury. At Bromfield, A4113. Right in Walford for Buckton, on to 2nd farm on left. Large sign on building.

Hayden & Yvonne Lloyd
Upper Buckton,
Leintwardine,
Craven Arms, Ludlow,
Shropshire SY7 0JU

Tel	01547 540634
Fax	01547 540634
Email	ghlloydco@btconnect.com

Entry 391   Map 7

Shropshire

Walford Court

Come for a break from clock-watching and a spot of fresh air. Large bedrooms delight with feather and down on the comfiest mattresses, scented candles, books, games and double-end roll top baths – one under a west facing window. Aga-cooked breakfasts include eggs from 'the ladies of the orchard'; candlelit dinners may be served outside on fine evenings. Wander through apple, plum and pear trees, find a motte and bailey, strike out for a long hike. Craig and Debbie are thoughtful and hugely keen on wildlife (you get binoculars) and this is the perfect place to bring a special person – and a bottle of champagne.

Travel Club Offer: see page 392 for details.

Price	£65-£75. Singles £35.
Rooms	2: 1 double; 1 double & sitting room.
Meals	Dinner, 2-3 courses, £14-£20. Packed lunch £6. Lunch in the tea room. Pubs/restaurants 1-3 miles.
Closed	Christmas & Boxing Day.
Directions	A49 north of Ludlow; A4113 to Knighton. Thro' Leintwardine then right signed Knighton & Walford. In Walford, left signed Lingen & Presteigne, then immed. left. Signs to Walford Court Tea Room.

Debbie & Craig Fraser
Walford Court,
Walford,
Lentwardine, Ludlow,
Shropshire SY7 0JT

Tel	01547 540570
Email	enquiries@romanticbreak.com
Web	www.romanticbreak.com

Entry 392   Map 7

Shropshire

35 Lower Broad Street

You're almost at the bottom of the town, near the river and the bridge. Elaine's spotless terraced house is small and cosy; her office doubles as a sitting area for guests with leather armchairs and desk space for workaholics. Upstairs are two good-sized doubles with a country crisp feel, big beds and a pretty blue and white bathroom. Walkers, shoppers, antique- and-book hunters can fill up on homemade potato scones, black pudding, organic eggs and good coffee before striding out to explore. This is excellent value B&B: comfortable, clean and can be enjoyed without a car. Perfect for two couples.

Travel Club Offer: see page 392 for details.

Price	£65.
Rooms	2 doubles sharing bath & sitting room (let to same party only).
Meals	Pubs/restaurants 400 yds.
Closed	Rarely.
Directions	Right out of railway station, 200 yds to lights. Left onto Corve St, then up to top of hill. At lights, right & follow to Broad St; thro' arch into Lower Broad St. On right towards bottom.

Elaine Downs
35 Lower Broad Street,
Ludlow,
Shropshire SY8 1PH
Tel   01584 876912
Mobile   07970 151010
Email   a.downs@tesco.net

Entry 393   Map 7

Shropshire

Rosecroft

A pretty, quiet, traditional house with charming owners, well-proportioned rooms and an elegant sitting room. But there's not a trace of pomposity and breakfasts are huge enough to set you up for the day: Pimhill organic muesli, smoked or unsmoked local bacon, black pudding, delicious jams. The garden is a delight to stroll through – in summer you can picnic – and serious walkers are close to the Welsh borders. Bedrooms and bathrooms are polished to perfection, you have fresh flowers, homebaked cakes and biscuits when you arrive, the village has a super pub and Ludlow is five miles away. *Children over 12 welcome.*

Travel Club Offer: see page 392 for details.

Price	£70-£75. Singles £45-£50.
Rooms	2: 1 double; 1 double with separate bath.
Meals	Packed lunch £5. Pub 200 yds.
Closed	Rarely.
Directions	Between Ludlow & Leominster on A49, turn onto B4362 at Woofferton. After 1.5 miles, left into Orleton. Past school & small green, house on right, opp. vicarage.

Mrs Gail Benson
Rosecroft,
Orleton, Ludlow,
Shropshire SY8 4HN
Tel   01568 780565
Fax   01568 780565
Email   gailanddavid@rosecroftorleton.freeserve.co.uk
Web   www.stmem.com/rosecroft

Entry 394   Map 7

Shropshire

Shortgrove

Not a straight line inside or out — on this stunning, Elizabethan, timber-framed house. The approach, too, is intriguing, across the gated common, away from all roads; revel in seclusion and peace. The old English feel continues inside, where there's spaciousness, comfort and calm: expect cool colours, soft fabrics, plump armchairs, an inglenook for chilly nights. Cottagey bedrooms sit cosily under the eaves, their lovely leaded windows gazing on the two-acre garden and Shropshire beyond. Beryl — a cookery tutor and kind, generous hostess — dispatches delicious breakfasts from her Aga.

Price	From £90. Singles from £65.
Rooms	2: 1 twin; 1 double with separate bath.
Meals	Pub 1 mile.
Closed	Rarely.
Directions	Off A49, 1 mile south of Woofferton into School Lane. Immed. left at 2nd School Lane sign. Through gate onto common. Fork left where track divides and cont. to end of track.

	Beryl Maxwell
	Shortgrove,
	Brimfield Common,
	Ludlow,
	Shropshire SY8 4NZ
Tel	01584 711418
Web	www.shortgrove-ludlow-bb.co.uk

Entry 395   Map 7

Shropshire

Timberstone Bed & Breakfast

The house is young, engaging and fun — as are Tracey and Alex. She, once in catering, is a reflexologist and new generation B&Ber. Come for logs in winter, charming bedrooms under the eaves, a double ended or claw-foot bath, chunky beams with a modern feel, pale colours, white cotton… and the Bowen Technique (massage) in the garden studio or the relaxing sauna. In the warm guest sitting room — brimming with art — are books, kilims on oak boards, a wood-burner. Eggs come from their hens, breakfasts are special; have an excellent home-cooked supper or head for Ludlow and its clutch of Michelin stars.

Ethical Collection: Environment; Food.
See page 400 for details

Price	£75-£100. Singles £40-£60.
Rooms	4: 2 doubles; 1 twin, 1 family. Summerhouse: 1 double & kitchenette (summer only).
Meals	Dinner, 3 courses, £22. Pubs/restaurants 5 miles.
Closed	Rarely.
Directions	B4364 Ludlow-Bridgnorth. After 3 miles, right to Clee Stanton; on for 1.5 miles; left at signopst to Clee Stanton; 1st house on left.

	Tracey Baylis & Alex Read
	Timberstone Bed & Breakfast,
	Clee Stanton, Ludlow,
	Shropshire SY8 3EL
Tel	01584 823519
Mobile	07905 967263
Email	enquiry@timberstoneludlow.co.uk
Web	www.timberstoneludlow.co.uk

Entry 396   Map 7

Shropshire

Cleeton Court

A tiny lane leads to Cleeton Court, charming Ros and homemade cake. With views over meadows and heathland, the part 14th-century farmhouse feels immersed in countryside – rare peace. You have a private entrance to your rooms, and the use of the drawing room, prettily striped in yellow and cream, elegantly comfortable with sofas and log fire. Beamed bedrooms are delightfully furnished, one with a magnificent, chintzy four-poster and a vast bathroom; recline in the cast-iron bath, gaze on views from the window as you soak. Bring your boots: the walking is superb. *Children over five welcome.*

Somerset

Emmetts Grange

A superb landscape – the rugged real deal. And if you love huntin', shootin' and fishin' this is your place, high on the moor. At the end of a long drive, a listed country house; be greeted by a peacock (stuffed!) in the hall and a portrait of an ancestor in wig and ermine. Tom and Lucy have boys, dogs, ponies, hens, and raise Red Devon cattle; the Grange is their sideline. Bedrooms and bathrooms are large and comfortable with an old-fashioned feel but you are here for the outdoors: 900 acres of moorland asking to be discovered. Tom is the cook and, not surprisingly, is pretty keen on the local beef.

Price	From £70. Singles £45.
Rooms	2: 1 twin/double, 1 four-poster.
Meals	Pubs/restaurants 4 miles.
Closed	Christmas & New Year.
Directions	From Ludlow, A4117 for Kidderminster for 1 mile; left on B4364 for Cleobury North; on for 5 miles. In Wheathill, right for Cleeton St Mary; on for 1.5 miles; house on left.

Price	£70–£100. Singles from £40.
Rooms	4: 2 twin/double, 1 twin, 1 four-poster.
Meals	Dinner, 3 courses, £27. Pub 2 miles.
Closed	Christmas, New Year & occasionally.
Directions	M5 exit 27. A361 towards South Molton. 25 miles then right to A399 Ilfracombe. 1 mile, right towards Simonsbath. 6 miles, entrance to Grange on right.

Rosamond Woodward
Cleeton Court,
Cleeton St Mary, Ludlow,
Shropshire DY14 0QZ

Tel	01584 823379
Mobile	07778 903136
Email	roswoodward@talktalk.net
Web	www.cleetoncourt.co.uk

Tom & Lucy Barlow
Emmetts Grange,
Simonsbath, Minehead,
Somerset TA24 7LD

Tel	01643 831138
Mobile	07773 239797
Email	mail@emmettsgrange.co.uk
Web	www.emmettsgrange.co.uk

Entry 397   Map 7

Entry 398   Map 2

Somerset

North Wheddon Farm

Pootle through the vibrant green patchwork of Exmoor National Park and bowl down a pitted track to land in Blyton-esque bliss – a classic Somerset farmyard, crackling with geese and hens, round which is the gentleman farmer's house. Bedrooms are airy and calming with grand views, books, fresh flowers and small, but neat-as-a-pin bathrooms. Bring children and they will be in heaven, with eggs to collect and pigs to pat, or come just for yourself and a bit of indulgence. Food is 'River Cottage' style and much is home reared, the walking is fabulous for miles and kind Rachael sends you off with a thermos of tea.

Price	£60–£70. Singles £35.
Rooms	3: 1 double, 1 twin/double; 1 single with separate bath.
Meals	Dinner, 3 courses, £20. Cold/hot packed lunch £6.75-£9.75.
Closed	Rarely.
Directions	From Minehead A396 to Wheddon Cross. Pass pub on right & Moorland Hall on left. North Wheddon is next driveway on right.

Rachael Abraham
North Wheddon Farm,
Wheddon Cross,
Somerset TA24 7EX

Tel	01643 841791
Email	rachael@go-exmoor.co.uk
Web	www.go-exmoor.co.uk

Entry 399   Map 2

Somerset

Glen Lodge

High brick walls and tumbling gardens in the Victorian tanner's house give way to the warm embrace of a wood-burning stove and a giddy rush of intriguing artwork – one painting is by an elephant! Polished oak floors are dotted with oriental rugs, bedrooms are immaculate, bay windows gaze on the Bristol Channel. Meryl and David care about sustainable living – feast on American home baking and fruit from their 21 acres: all is recycled, composted and enjoyed. Surrounded by the woods and wilds of Exmoor National Park yet a short stroll from popular Porlock, you'll revel in comfort, warmth and their passion for life.

Travel Club Offer: see page 392 for details.

Price	£80. Singles £55.
Rooms	5: 1 double; 2 doubles sharing bath; 1 double, 1 twin both with separate bath.
Meals	Packed lunch £10. Dinner £28. Pub/restaurant 0.5 miles.
Closed	Christmas & New Year.
Directions	From Minehead, A39 to Porlock; on entering town, left at church into Parsons Street. At 'weak bridge' sign, left over bridge. Gate to house is in front.

Meryl Salter
Glen Lodge,
Hawkcombe, Porlock,
Somerset TA24 8LN

Tel	01643 863371
Mobile	07749 326009
Email	glenlodge@gmail.com
Web	www.glenlodge.net

Entry 400   Map 2

Somerset

Higher Orchard

A little lane tumbles down to the centre of lovely old Dunster (the village is a two minute-walk) yet here you have open views of fields, sheep and sea. Exmoor footpaths start behind the house and Janet encourages explorers, by bike or on foot; ever helpful and kind, she is a local who knows the patch well. The 1860s house keeps its Victorian features, bedrooms are quiet and simple and the double has a view to Blue Anchor Bay and Dunster castle and church. All is homely, with stripped pine, cream curtains, fresh flowers, garden fruit and home-laid eggs for breakfast. *Children & pets by arrangement.*

Ethical Collection: Environment.
See page 400 for details.

Travel Club Offer: see page 392 for details.

Price	£60. Singles from £35.
Rooms	3: 1 double, 2 twins/doubles.
Meals	Packed lunch from £3.50. Restaurants 2-minute walk.
Closed	Christmas.
Directions	From Williton, A39 for Minehead for 8 miles. Left to Dunster. There, right fork into 'The Ball'. At T-junc. at end of road, right. House 75 yds on right.

Mrs Janet Lamacraft
Higher Orchard,
30 St George's Street, Dunster,
Somerset TA24 6RS

Tel	01643 821915
Mobile	07896 464420
Email	lamacraft@higherorchard.fsnet.co.uk
Web	www.higherorchard.fsnet.co.uk

Entry 401 Map 2

Somerset

The Old Priory

The 12th-century priory leans against its church, has a rustic gate, a walled garden, a tumble of flowers. Both house and hostess are dignified, unpretentious and friendly. Here are old oak tables, flagstones, panelled doors, higgledy-piggledy corridors and large bedrooms in the softest colours. But a perfect English house in a sweet Somerset village needs a touch of pepper and relaxed, cosmopolitan Jane adds her own special flair with artistic touches here and there, and books and dogs for company. Dunster Castle towers above on the hill, walks start from the door.

Price	£75-£80. Singles by arrangement.
Rooms	3: 1 twin, 1 four-poster; 1 double with separate shower.
Meals	Restaurants/pubs 5-minute walk.
Closed	Christmas.
Directions	From A39 into Dunster, right at blue sign 'Unsuitable for Goods Vehicles'. Follow until church; house adjoined.

Jane Forshaw
The Old Priory,
Dunster,
Somerset TA24 6RY

Tel	01643 821540
Web	www.theoldpriory-dunster.co.uk

Entry 402 Map 2

Somerset

No.7

Feast on homemade biscuits, croissants and local whortleberry jam. Feast, too, on the views of the wooded valley. Then drink in the calm – TV-free! – of Lucy and Jean-Christophe's young, cosy, uncluttered 'cottage hotel': a peace punctuated only by the chimes of the ancient church. Bedrooms are light, not large, and airy, with goosefeather pillows, patchwork quilts and pretty iron beds – but mind your head on the beams. Bathrooms are immaculately white. Down the 17th-century spiralling wooden staircase to sofa and wood-burner below – or for a seat at a crisply white table for Jean-Christophe's delicious dinner.

Price	£65-£85. Singles from £45.
Rooms	3: 2 doubles;
	1 double with separate shower.
Meals	Dinner, 3 courses, £21.
	Afternoon tea from £5.
	Packed lunch from £5.50.
Closed	Christmas.
Directions	M5 exit 25. A358 towards Minehead, then A39 to Dunster. Thro' village past church, 200 yds; house on left.

Lucy Paget-Tomlinson
No.7,
7 West Street, Dunster,
Somerset TA24 6SN
Tel 01643 821064
Mobile 07736 375232
Email info@no7weststreet.co.uk
Web www.no7weststreet.co.uk

Entry 403   Map 2

Somerset

Wyndham House

The Vincents have made the house 'smile' again; charming and Georgian, it has views over Watchet's harbour and marina to Wales. The bedrooms are comfortable and traditional, the double looking onto a pretty courtyard, the twin to the Bristol Channel. Susan loves to cook: cake on arrival, biscuits in your room, a generous breakfast at the gleaming dining table, with her own preserves. The garden has palm trees, ponds, burgeoning borders and a revolving summer house; the steam railway runs just by, and on to the Quantock Hills. Watchet and its marina are being gently revived. *Children & dogs by arrangement.*

Price	From £70. Singles from £35.
Rooms	2: 1 twin;
	1 double with separate bath.
Meals	Pub/restaurants a short walk.
Closed	Christmas.
Directions	From railway station & footbridge in Watchet, up South Rd (for Doniford). After 50 yds, left into Beverly Drive. House 50 yds on left with gravel parking area.

Susan & Roger Vincent
Wyndham House,
4 Sea View Terrace,
Watchet,
Somerset TA23 0DF
Tel 01984 631881
Fax 01984 631881
Email rhv@dialstart.net

Entry 404   Map 2

Somerset

Hesperus Cottage

Deeply rural yet close to the M5, this 17th-century cottage slumps in a thickly wooded valley, with the river Tone rushing about at the end of the garden. Two bedrooms have their own entrance from a wooden terrace: find leather headboards, wooden floors, good lighting and a stash of glossy magazines on a chunky table. Indulge yourself in stone floored and tiled bathrooms with heaps of towels and Neal's Yard goodies, or render yourself comatose with a Swedish massage or some reiki. All this and an organic breakfast. Come to recharge your batteries and walk on the Quantock or Blackdown Hills.

Somerset

Causeway Cottage

Robert and Lesley are ex-restaurateurs, so guests heap praise on their food, most of which is sourced from a local butcher and fishmonger; charming Lesley also runs cookery courses. This is the perfect Somerset cottage, with an apple orchard outside and views to a lofty church across a cottage garden and a field. The bedrooms are light, restful and have a country-style simplicity with their green check bedspreads, white walls and antique pine furniture. A great hideaway for food-lovers with easy access to the M5 and a quiet, rural feel. Very special. *Children over ten welcome.*

Price	£70–£80. Singles £60.
Rooms	3: 1 single, 1 double + sofabed, 1 suite.
Meals	Pub 0.5 miles.
Closed	Rarely.
Directions	M5 junc. 26, A38 for Exeter. About 4 miles, right to Greenham; through Greenham to Appley & past primary school; after sign to Tracebridge, 0.25 miles, 1st drive on left.

Price	£70. Singles by arrangement.
Rooms	3: 1 double, 2 twins.
Meals	Supper from £20. Pub/restaurant 0.75 miles.
Closed	Christmas.
Directions	From M5 junc. 26, West Buckland road for 0.75 miles. 1st left just before stone building. Bear right; 3rd house at end of lane, below church.

Seb & Nicky Le Boedec-Lambley
Hesperus Cottage,
Tracebridge,
Wellington,
Somerset TA21 0HG

Tel	01823 672194
Email	info@hesperuscottage.com
Web	www.hesperuscottage.com

Lesley & Robert Orr
Causeway Cottage,
West Buckland, Wellington,
Somerset TA21 9JZ

Tel	01823 663458
Fax	01823 663458
Email	causewaybb@talktalk.net
Web	www.causewaycottage.co.uk

Entry 405   Map 2

Entry 406   Map 2

Somerset

Somerset

Rock House

Tucked away in an AONB, near the Quantocks and Exmoor, this elegant Georgian house hides behind a tall hedge in a sleepy village. Deborah greets her guests with impeccable manners and scrumptious biscuits; take tea in the drawing room where fresh flowers are beautifully arranged and there are books to read. Bedrooms are well-presented and full of thoughtful touches like fresh milk and a torch; bathrooms have generous towels and Molton Brown lotions. The Rock House fry-up will set you up for miles of walking, or a quick stroll to the top of the pretty garden with its croquet lawn. *Children & pets by arrangement.*

Bashfords Farmhouse

A feeling of warmth and happiness pervades the exquisite 17th-century farmhouse in the Quantock hills. The Ritchies love doing B&B even after 15 years, and there's a homely feel with splashes of style – well-framed prints, good fabrics, comfortable sofas. Rooms are pretty, fresh and large and look over the cobbled courtyard or open fields; the sitting room has an inglenook, sofas and books. Charles and Jane couldn't be nicer, know about local walks (the Macmillan Way runs past the door) and love to cook: local meat and game, tarte tatin, homemade bread and jams. A delightful garden rambles up the hill.

Price	From £80. Singles from £40.
Rooms	2: 1 twin; 1 double (extra single bed) with separate bathroom.
Meals	Pub in village.
Closed	Christmas.
Directions	M5 exit 25, signs to A358 Minehead. Left to Halse. Rock House in middle of village, 100 yds from pub.

Price	£65–£70. Singles £37.50–£40.
Rooms	3: 1 double; 1 double with separate shower; 1 twin with separate bath.
Meals	Dinner £27.50. Supper £22.50.
Closed	Rarely.
Directions	M5 junc. 25. A358 for Minehead. Leave A358 at West Bagborough turning. Through village for 1.5 miles. Farmhouse 3rd on left past pub.

Christopher & Deborah Wolverson
Rock House,
Halse, Taunton,
Somerset TA4 3AF

Tel	01823 432956
Mobile	07982 785889
Email	dwolverson@rockhousesomerset.co.uk
Web	www.rockhousesomerset.co.uk

Charles & Jane Ritchie
Bashfords Farmhouse,
West Bagborough,
Taunton,
Somerset TA4 3EF

Tel	01823 432015
Email	info@bashfordsfarmhouse.co.uk
Web	www.bashfordsfarmhouse.co.uk

Entry 407 Map 2

Entry 408 Map 2

Somerset

Tilbury Farm

The highest B&B in Somerset – up with the buzzards and the wind. Renovation is the Smiths' business and their conversion is exemplary. Reclaimed flags and seasoned oak enhance the natural beauty of the old farmhouse and barns; Pamela is a perfectionist, full of life and plans. Antiques on seagrass floors, dusky pink walls and crisp linen, a sitting room cosy with log fires in winter, a wonderfully monastic dining room for delicious breakfasts. And the setting is spectacular: 20 acres of fields and woodland, wildlife lake and spring. On a clear day you can see for 30 miles. *Children over ten welcome.*

Price	£60-£65. Singles £45-£50.
Rooms	3: 2 doubles, 1 twin.
Meals	Pubs 0.5 miles.
Closed	Rarely.
Directions	From Taunton, A358 north for Williton. Approx. 7 miles on, right for West Bagborough. Through village, up hill for 0.5 miles. Farm on left.

Mrs Pamela Smith
Tilbury Farm,
West Bagborough,
Taunton,
Somerset TA4 3DY
Tel   01823 432391

✂ 🐾

Somerset

Parsonage Farm

Breakfast beside the open fire is a feast: homemade bread and jam, eggs from the hens, juices from the orchard, pancakes and porridge from the Aga. This is an organic smallholding and your enthusiastic hosts have added an easy comfort to their 17th-century rectory farmhouse – quarry floors, log fires, books, maps and piano in the cosy sitting room. Suki, from Vermont, has turned a stable into a studio, and her pots and paintings add charm to the décor. Big bedrooms have fresh flowers and tranquil views. Wonderful walking and cycling in the Quantock Hills, and the new Coleridge Way starts down the lane.

Price	£55-£75. Singles £35-£50.
Rooms	3: 1 double (extra sofabed), 1 twin/double (extra pull-out bed); 1 double sharing bath.
Meals	Supper £10. Dinner, 2-3 courses, £20-£25.
Closed	Christmas Day.
Directions	A39 Bridgwater-Minehead. 7 miles on, left at Cottage Inn for Over Stowey; 1.8 miles; house on right after church.

Susan Lilienthal
Parsonage Farm,
Over Stowey, Nether Stowey,
Somerset TA5 1HA
Tel   01278 733237
Fax   01278 733511
Email   suki@parsonfarm.co.uk
Web   www.parsonfarm.co.uk

👤 ✂ 📷 🚂 🐾 📶 🐕 ✕

Somerset

Church House

Feel happy in this warm Georgian rectory with sweeping views over gardens, seaside homes and the dramatic Bristol channel. Tony and Jane are great fun, enormously generous and love what they do. Bedrooms are large, pristine and indulgent with goose down duvets as soft as a cloud, swish modern bathrooms, huge towels and thoughtful extras like fluffy hot water bottles and scrumptious biscuits. Breakfasts are a grand feast of eggs from their hens, organic sausages and homemade preserves, all served on delightful china at a long mahogany table. Take the whole house and be cosseted – great for large gatherings.

Price	From £80. Singles from £60.
Rooms	5: 4 doubles, 1 twin.
Meals	Pubs 400 yds.
Closed	Rarely.
Directions	M5 junc. 21, follow signs for Kewstoke. After Old Manor Inn on right, left up Anson Rd. At T-junc. right into Kewstoke Rd. Follow road for 1 mile; church on right; drive between church & church hall.

Jane & Tony Chapman
Church House, 27 Kewstoke Road,
Kewstoke, Weston-super-Mare,
Somerset BS22 9YD

Tel	01934 633185
Fax	01934 633185
Email	churchhouse@kewstoke.net
Web	www.churchhousekewstoke.co.uk

Entry 411   Map 2

Somerset

Rolstone Court Barn

A converted Victorian grainstore, full of light, good family furniture, portraits and interesting finds. It's down a narrow lane on the Somerset Levels – fabulous walking country – and has a big, Mendip-view garden. Two prettily decorated bedrooms are under the eaves, the other on the first floor, there's a lovely sitting room with open fire and a smart dining room for delicious breakfasts of organic bacon and sausages. Kathlyn, who extends her welcome to children and dogs, will collect from or deliver to Bristol airport, thus saving you airport parking. An attractive stopover for the Cornwall route.

Price	£70. Singles £45.
Rooms	3: 1 double; 1 double, 1 family room sharing bath/shower.
Meals	Pubs/restaurants 4 miles.
Closed	Rarely.
Directions	M5 junc. 21; north onto A370 towards Bristol. Take 2nd right to Rolstone, then 1st left into Balls Barn Lane. House 3rd & last.

Kathlyn Read
Rolstone Court Barn,
Rolstone, Hewish,
Weston-super-Mare,
Somerset BS24 6UP

Tel	01934 820129
Email	read@rolstone-court.co.uk
Web	www.rolstone-court.co.uk

Entry 412   Map 3

Somerset

Burrington Farm

Can this really be ten minutes from Bristol airport? High in the Mendips, it is blissfully quiet and rural, with fabulous views. A narrow lane, frothing with cow parsley in summer, takes you past the village church and square to Ros and Barry's 15th-century longhouse — and the kindest of welcomes. Inside are rugs and flagstones, books, paintings and fine old furniture. Guests have a cosy low-beamed snug and bedrooms are charming; you'll need to be nimble to negotiate ancient steps and stairs. Outside is a big, enchanting garden with arches festooned with clematis, honeysuckle and wisteria. *Airport pick-up offered.*

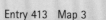 Travel Club Offer: see page 392 for details.

Price	From £60.
Rooms	3: 1 double; 2 doubles sharing bath (let to same party only).
Meals	Pub 5-minute walk.
Closed	Christmas.
Directions	A368 Bath-Weston-super-Mare, between Blagdon and Churchill. Take Burrington village sign, on to square with school on right. House 4th on left after Parish Rooms, immed. after Stable Cottage.

	Barry & Ros Smith Burrington Farm, Burrington, Somerset BS40 7AD
Tel	01761 462127
Mobile	07825 237144
Email	bookings@bedandburrington.co.uk
Web	www.bedandburrington.co.uk

Entry 413   Map 3

Somerset

Barton Drove Cottage

Come for the setting and the views — on a clear day you can see all the way to the Black Mountains. The pretty cottage extension is tucked into the hill so the first-floor drawing room opens directly to the terrace. All is polished and spotless inside and the bedrooms traditional: patterned rugs on soft carpets, goose down and crisp linen, fresh flowers, gleaming bathrooms and a loo with a view. Charming Sarah gives you bacon and sausages from Mendip piggies, eggs from her hens and soft fruit from the garden. Roe deer in the field, primroses in the woods, wonderful walking on Wavering Down.

Ethical Collection: Food. See page 400 for details.

Price	£65. Singles £35.
Rooms	2: 1 double; 1 twin with separate bath.
Meals	Supper £15. Packed lunch £5. Pubs within 3 miles.
Closed	Rarely.
Directions	From A38 0.5 miles up Winscombe Hill. When road begins to descend, left between houses onto unmade track. Cottage 100 yds on the left.

	Sarah Gunn Barton Drove Cottage, Winscombe Hill, Winscombe, Somerset BS25 1DJ
Tel	01934 842373
Mobile	07736 417363
Email	sarahgunn2000@hotmail.com
Web	www.bartondrovecottage.info

Entry 414   Map 3

Somerset

Harptree Court

One condition of Linda's moving to her husband's family home was that she should be warm! She is, and you will be, too. Linda has softened the 1790 house and imbued the rambling rooms with an upbeat elegance – they're sunny and sparkling with beds and windows dressed in delicate fabrics in perfect contrast to solid antique pieces. On one side of the soaring Georgian windows, 17 acres of parkland with ponds, an ancient bridge and carpets of spring flowers; on the other, the log-fired guest sitting room and extravagant bedrooms. An excellent breakfast sets you up to walk the grounds. Relaxing and easy.

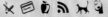 Travel Club Offer: see page 392 for details.

Price	£90-£110. Singles from £70.
Rooms	3: 2 doubles; 1 twin with separate bath.
Meals	Dinner, 2-3 courses, £17.50-£25. Pub 300 yds.
Closed	January.
Directions	Turn off A368 onto B3114 towards Chewton Mendip. After approx. 0.5 miles, right into drive entrance, straight after 1st x-roads. Left at top of drive.

Linda Hill
Harptree Court,
East Harptree, Bristol,
Somerset BS40 6AA

Tel	01761 221729
Mobile	07970 165576
Email	location.harptree@tiscali.co.uk
Web	www.harptreecourt.co.uk

✗ 🖪 🐗 📶 🐈 🐿️

Entry 415   Map 3

Somerset

Beryl

A lofty, mullioned, low-windowed home – yet light, bright and devoid of Victorian gloom. Every bedroom has a talking point… an extravagantly draped four-poster here, a vintage cot there, an original bath clad in mahogany reached by a tiny private stair. The flowery rooms in the attic have a 'gothic revival' feel, thanks to arched doorways. Holly, her daughter and her devoted staff serve delicious breakfasts in the sunny dining room, and drinks in the richly elegant drawing room. The old walled garden is full of flowers, roses, ancient figs and espaliered apples: the wonders of Wells lie just below.

Price	£75-£130.
Rooms	10: 3 doubles, 2 twins, 1 twin/double, 2 four-posters, 2 family rooms (1 with four-poster). 1 double with separate shower. Kitchenette.
Meals	Pubs/restaurants within 1 mile.
Closed	Christmas.
Directions	From Wells on Radstock Rd B3139. Follow signs to Horringtons; after church left into Hawkers Lane, next to bus pull in. At top of lane, past Beryl sign; 500 yds to main gate.

Holly Nowell
Beryl,
Wells, Somerset BA5 3JP

Tel	01749 678738
Fax	01749 670508
Email	stay@beryl-wells.co.uk
Web	www.beryl-wells.co.uk

♿ 🚹 ✗ 🖪 📶 🍷 🐕 🏊

Entry 416   Map 3

Somerset

Hillview Cottage

Don't tell too many of your friends about this place. It's an unpretentious ex-quarryman's cottage presided over by Catherine – a warm-spirited and cultured host who'll make fresh coffee, chat about the area, even show you around Wells Cathedral (she's an official guide). This is a comfy, tea-and-cakes family home with rugs on wooden floors, antique patchwork quilts, an old Welsh dresser in the kitchen and elevated views. The bedrooms have a French feel, and there's a sitting room with books and magazines. Walk from the door, or play tennis (on grass!) or croquet. Wonderful, modest and excellent value.

Somerset

Manor Farm

Come for ducks, cats, hens, pet sheep... a charming rural feel. Also, a magical view of the cathedral: you can stride to Wells across the fields. Ros is a geologist and keen walker, who looks after guests with immense kindness and is happy for folk to linger. Her house is ancient and much loved (massive low beams, creaking floorboards), packed with ornaments, pictures and a comfy mishmash of furniture; a log fire fills an inglenook in winter and the garden suite opens to a pretty corner of the garden (lit up in the evening). Delicious water comes from the spring, breakfast is a different treat each day.

Travel Club Offer: see page 392 for details.

Price	£70. Singles £35.	Price	£65–£90. Singles from £40.
Rooms	2: 1 twin/double, 1 twin sharing bathroom (2nd room let to same party only).	Rooms	4: 2 doubles, 1 suite; 1 twin/double with separate bath & shower.
Meals	Pubs 0.25 miles.	Meals	Packed lunch & light meals £4.50. Pub 1 mile.
Closed	Rarely.	Closed	November–February.
Directions	From Wells A371 to middle of Croscombe. Right at red phone box & then immed. right into lane. House up on left after 0.25 miles. Straight ahead into signed drive.	Directions	From Wells, A371 for Shepton Mallet for 1 mile; left onto B3139. In Dulcote, left at stone fountain. 4th on right after Manor Barn.

	Michael & Catherine Hay Hillview Cottage, Paradise Lane, Croscombe, Wells, Somerset BA5 3RN		**Rosalind Bufton** Manor Farm, Dulcote, Wells, Somerset BA5 3PZ
Tel	01749 343526	Tel	01749 672125
Mobile	07801 666146	Mobile	07732 600694
Email	cathyhay@yahoo.co.uk	Email	rosalind.bufton@talktalk.net
		Web	www.wells-accommodation.co.uk

Entry 417 Map 3   Entry 418 Map 3

Somerset

Claveys Farm

For the artistic seeker of inspiration: Fleur is a talented artist, Francis works for English Heritage, both have a passion for art, real food and lively conversation. Rugs are time-worn, panelling and walls are distempered with natural pigment, bedrooms are better than simple, beds have white linen. From the warm kitchen of this traditional farmhouse come delicious home-grown meals, breakfast eggs from the hens, oak-smoked bacon from Fleur's rare-breed pigs and homemade bread and jams. Acres of fields, footpaths and woodland await for long walks and Mells is a dream.

Price	£70. Singles £40.
Rooms	2: 1 double/family, 1 twin sharing separate bathroom.
Meals	Dinner, 3 courses, £25. BYO. Packed lunch £7. Pub/restaurant 0.5 miles.
Closed	Rarely.
Directions	At Mells Green on Leigh on Mendip road SW from Mells (NGR ST718452). Past red phone box; house last on right before speed de-restriction signs. If lost, Mells PO, by village pond, has map outside.

	Fleur & Francis Kelly
	Claveys Farm,
	Mells, Frome,
	Somerset BA11 3QP
Tel	01373 814651
Mobile	07968 055398
Email	bandb@fleurkelly.com
Web	www.fleurkelly.com/bandb

Entry 419   Map 3

Somerset

Broadgrove House

Down a long, private lane with views towards Alfred's Tower and Longleat, tranquillity: a 17th-century stone house with a walled cottage garden. Inside is just as special. Beams, flagstones and inglenook fireplaces have been sensitively restored; rugs, pictures, comfy sofas and polished antiques add warmth and serenity. The twin, at the end of the house, has its own sitting room. Breakfast on homemade and farmers' market produce before exploring Stourhead, Wells, Glastonbury. Sarah, engaging, well-travelled and a great cook, looks after guests and horses with enthusiasm. *Shooting available. Children by arrangement.*

Price	From £80. Singles £50.
Rooms	2: 1 twin & sitting room; 1 double with separate bath.
Meals	Pub/restaurant 1 mile.
Closed	Christmas.
Directions	Directions on booking.

	Sarah Voller
	Broadgrove House,
	Leighton, Frome,
	Somerset BA11 4PP
Tel	01373 836296
Mobile	07775 918388
Email	broadgrove836@tiscali.co.uk
Web	www.broadgrovehouse.co.uk

Entry 420   Map 3

Somerset

The Manor House

Tucked into a hamlet, the house oozes tranquillity. Late medieval, owned by Glastonbury monks, an architectural flourish at every turn: plasterwork ceiling, Jacobean staircase, Tudor fireplace, English country-house furnishings are gorgeously mixed with Indian textiles and antiques. Three bedrooms in a private wing share a boldly stylish bathroom and are prettily feminine with hand-crafted bedheads, antiques and rich fabrics. The garden delights with rose pergola, knot garden and fish pond. Local bread and organic meats for breakfast, and Harriet and Bryan cultured and engaging.

Price	£80. Singles £40.
Rooms	3: 2 doubles, 1 single all sharing bath (let to same party only).
Meals	Pub 2 miles.
Closed	15 December-15 January.
Directions	A361 Shepton Mallet-Glastonbury. At Pilton, turn between village stores and Crown Inn onto Totterdown Lane; 1 mile; right at T-junc. in W. Compton; next right 100 yds onto lane. On left.

	Harriet Ray
	The Manor House,
	West Compton,
	Shepton Mallet,
	Somerset BA4 4PB
Tel	01749 890582
Fax	01749 890582
Email	rayswestcompton@btinternet.com

✕ ⅓

Entry 421   Map 3

Somerset

Pennard House

Pennard has been in Susie's family since the 17th century – the cellars date from then and the superstructure is stately, lofty and Georgian. Multi-lingual Martin runs an antiques business from here and he and Susie obviously enjoy having guests in their home. You have the run of the library, drawing room, magnificent billiard room, 60-acre orchard, meadows, woods, grass tennis court and six acres of garden with a spring-fed pool (swim with the newts). Bedrooms are large and have good views; one is oval with a corner bath in the room. Although this is a big house it still feels warm and comfortably lived in.

🧳 Travel Club Offer: see page 392 for details.

Price	From £90. Singles from £45.
Rooms	3: 1 double, 1 twin; 1 twin/double with separate bath/shower.
Meals	Pub 2 miles.
Closed	Rarely.
Directions	From Shepton Mallet south on A37, through Pylle, over hill & next right to East Pennard. After 500 yds, right & follow lane past church to T-junc. at very top. House on left.

	Martin & Susie Dearden
	Pennard House,
	East Pennard, Shepton Mallet,
	Somerset BA4 6TP
Tel	01749 860266
Mobile	07770 751357
Fax	01749 860700
Email	susie.d@ukonline.co.uk

👤 ✕ 🗐 🚂 📶 ⅓ 🏊

Entry 422   Map 3

Somerset

Chalice Hill House

You can see St John's spire poking out over the treetops: vibrant Glastonbury buzzes just below. Fay's contemporary artistic flair mingles naturally with the classical frame of this Georgian house; grand mirrors, wooden floors, gentle colours and loads of books create an interesting feel. The bedrooms are enchanting, not at all understated; carved oak Slavic sleigh beds, embroidered Indian cotton bedspreads and views of the dovecote, wedding cake tree and Chalice Hill beyond. Weekend breakfasts are leisurely, served with panache (and optional chilli sauce!). Exotic, comfortable elegance – and a lovely hostess.

Somerset

Church Cottage

Partly clothed in English garden and with views to the church, this 400-year-old cottage has wooden beams, low ceilings and wonky walls. Ignore the modern house on the other side of the road and restore your senses with blue lias flagstones, neutral colours, soft cushions, a flash of Thompson gazelle skin, the whiff of woodsmoke and floppy roses on a scrubbed table. Caroline is artistic and rustles up a fine breakfast in her calm kitchen. Bedrooms are small and simple – pine furniture, cool colours; the Potting Shed is a private, generous nest for two. Miles of walking straight from the door.

 Travel Club Offer: see page 392 for details.

Price	£90. Singles £70.
Rooms	2: 1 double, 1 twin.
Meals	Pubs/restaurants 5-minute walk.
Closed	Rarely.
Directions	From top of Glastonbury High Street, right; 2nd left into Dod Lane. Past Chalice Hill Close; right into driveway.

Price	£65-£80.
Rooms	3: 2 doubles; 1 double with separate bath/shower.
Meals	Packed lunch available. Pubs 1 mile.
Closed	Rarely.
Directions	M5 exit 23 to A39. 7 miles; left to Shapwick. Cottage on left next to church.

Fay Hutchcroft
Chalice Hill House,
Dod Lane, Glastonbury,
Somerset BA6 8BZ

Tel	01458 830828
Mobile	07976 959409
Email	mail@chalicehill.co.uk
Web	www.chalicehill.co.uk

Caroline Hanbury Bateman
Church Cottage,
Station Road, Shapwick,
Bridgwater, Somerset TA7 9NH

Tel	01458 210904
Mobile	07875 598155
Email	caroline@shapwick.fsnet.co.uk
Web	www.profileskincare.co.uk/bnb/bnb.html

Entry 423   Map 3

Entry 424   Map 3

Somerset

Saltmoor House

An abundance of Georgian elegance and comfort: fresh flowers, beautiful pictures and Italianate murals, an 18th-century French mirror and Empire chairs, checks, stripes and toile de Jouy... all exist in perfect harmony. Gorgeous, light bedrooms have thick bathrobes and fat pillows; bathrooms thrill with roll top baths, soaps and scents. Elizabeth's cooking is sublime and imaginative and she uses plenty of home-grown produce. You are in the heart of the Somerset Moors and Levels, surrounded by mystical views and countryside of huge environmental significance: wonderful.

Price	From £110. Singles £55.
Rooms	3: 1 twin; 2 doubles, each with separate bath.
Meals	Dinner, 3-4 courses, £25-£30. BYO. Pub 5 miles.
Closed	Rarely.
Directions	M5, junc. 24; 5 miles via Huntworth to Moorland; 2 miles after Moorland, house on right after sharp right-hand bend.

	Crispin & Elizabeth Deacon Saltmoor House, Saltmoor, Burrowbridge, Bridgwater, Somerset TA7 0RL
Tel	01823 698092
Email	saltmoorhouse@aol.com
Web	www.saltmoorhouse.co.uk

Entry 425   Map 2

Somerset

Blackmore Farm

Come for atmosphere and architecture: the Grade I-listed manor-farmhouse is remarkable. Medieval stone walls, a ceiling open to a beamed roof, ecclesiastical windows, a fire blazing in the Great Hall. Ann and Ian look after guests and farm (900 acres plus dairy) with equal enthusiasm. Furnishings are comfortable not lavish, bedrooms are cavernous and the oak-panelled suite (with secret stairway intact) takes up an entire floor. Breakfast at a 20-foot polished table in the carpeted but baronial Great Hall, store your bikes in the chapel, visit the calves in the dairy. A rare place. *Farm shop on site.*

Price	£75-£85. Singles £45-£55.
Rooms	4: 1 double, 1 twin, 1 four-poster, 1 suite.
Meals	Pubs/restaurants 5-minute walk.
Closed	Rarely.
Directions	From Bridgwater, A39 west around Cannington. After 2nd r'bout, follow signs to Minehead; 1st left after Yeo Valley creamery; 1st house on right.

	Ann Dyer Blackmore Farm, Cannington, Bridgwater, Somerset TA5 2NE
Tel	01278 653442
Fax	01278 653427
Email	dyerfarm@aol.com
Web	www.dyerfarm.co.uk

Entry 426   Map 2

Somerset

Estate Farmhouse

A warm, interesting, artistic house with an owner to match. Jane has an eye for colour, material and form; coir matting sits stylishly with well-loved antiques and bedrooms feel fresh and new. Floorboards bend and creak, ceilings dip and wave, there are plump white duvets, pictures, prints and lots of well-thumbed books. The twin is the bigger, its bathroom comfortable and close. Breakfasts (some produce from their daughter's organic deli) are served at a long table in a charming dining room; the south-facing walled garden is perfect for a sundowner – just bring the ingredients. *Children by arrangement.*

Price	£70. Singles £55.
Rooms	2: 1 double; 1 twin with separate bath.
Meals	Pub 300 yds.
Closed	Christmas.
Directions	From Somerton Lake B3153 for Langport. Right after 2 miles for Pitney, just before Halfway Inn. Down to bottom of road; house last but one on right, with dark green railings.

	Jane Burnham Estate Farmhouse, Pitney, Langport, Somerset TA10 9AL
Tel	01458 250210

Entry 427   Map 3

Somerset

The Lynch Country House

Peace, seclusion and privacy at this immaculate Regency house in lush Somerset. First-floor bedrooms are traditionally grand, attic rooms are small but bright; those in the coach house have a more modern feel. Deep warm colours prevail, fabrics are flowery and carpets soft green. You'll feel as warm as toast and beautifully looked after. A stone stair goes right to the top where the observatory lets in a cascading light; the flagged hall, high ceilings, long windows and private tables at breakfast create a country-house hotel feel. A lovely garden has a pond, wildlife and a terrace to enjoy it from.

Price	£70–£100. Singles £60–£70.
Rooms	9: 1 double, 1 twin, 2 four-posters; 1 double (extra single bed) with separate bath. Coach house: 3 doubles, 1 twin.
Meals	Restaurants 5-minute walk.
Closed	Never.
Directions	From London, M3 junc. 8, A303. At Podimore r'bout A372 to Somerton. At junc. of North St & Behind Berry.

	Mr Roy Copeland The Lynch Country House, 4 Behind Berry, Somerton, Somerset TA11 7PD
Tel	01458 272316
Fax	01458 272590
Email	the_lynch@talk21.com
Web	www.thelynchcountryhouse.co.uk

Entry 428   Map 3

Somerset

Mill House

Peace and serenity on the Somerset Levels. The garden rolls into the fields and the stream flows (or rushes!) below the end of the listed Georgian millhouse into the Brue. This is where the family suite lies (a big double bed, a child's single, a sitting room with sofas). The double is carpeted, spacious and pretty in pinks and greens, views stretch for miles over the Levels and the comforts are entirely modern (pristine bathrooms, flat-screen TVs.) Aga-fresh breakfasts are brought to an elegant dining table, the marmalades are Rita's and you can fish without leaving the grounds. *Babies & children over ten welcome.*

Somerset

Rectory Farm House

A mile off a fairly main road but as peaceful as can be. Lavinia has showered love and attention on her early Georgian house and garden in a landscape that has changed little since the 18th century. Beams, sash windows, wood fires and high ceilings are the backdrop for gleaming family furniture, paintings and delightfully arranged flowers. Good-sized bedrooms in restful colours have starched linen, fluffy bathrobes and binoculars for watching wildlife; spot deer, badgers, foxes, hares, buzzards. Breakfast is so local it could walk to the table – and includes homemade marmalade and jams.

Price	£68-£88.
Rooms	2: 1 double, 1 family suite for 3 (& cot).
Meals	Pub 1 mile.
Closed	January.
Directions	A303; A37 towards Bristol; onto B3153 at Lydford. Right at Keinton Mandeville, down Coombe Hill; right at T-junc, bottom of hill. House 1st on right.

Price	From £90. Singles from £55.
Rooms	3: 1 double; 1 twin/double, 1 double sharing bath (let to same party only).
Meals	Dinner £30. Pub 0.5 miles.
Closed	Rarely.
Directions	From the east, exit A303 on to B3081 for Bruton. After 1 mile, left into Rectory Lane. House 0.25 miles on right.

	Michael & Rita Knight
	Mill House,
	Mill Road,
	Barton St David,
	Somerset TA11 6DF
Tel	01458 851215
Email	b&b@millhousebarton.co.uk
Web	www.millhousebarton.co.uk

	Michael & Lavinia Dewar
	Rectory Farm House,
	Charlton Musgrove, Wincanton,
	Somerset BA9 8ET
Tel	01963 34599
Mobile	07775 651868
Email	l.dewar@btconnect.com
Web	www.rectoryfarmhouse.com

✗ 🖃 🐾 ⚲

Entry 429   Map 3

✗ 🚂 🐦 ⚲

Entry 430   Map 3

Somerset

Lower Farm

The Good Life in the depths of Somerset, and a delightful family. The Dowdings have converted an old stone barn into a self-contained apartment with lime-washed walls and lovely bedrooms with views across the garden to fields. Perfect for a larger party – the cosy oak-floored sitting room comes with a wood-burner and extra beds. The whole place has a charmingly French feel – hens strut around the orchard, Charles grinds their own wheat for daily bread-making, kind Susie can bring you a delicious, organic breakfast: homemade apple juice and yogurt, local bacon, their own eggs. A place to do your own thing.

Ethical Collection: Environment; Food.
See page 400 for details.

Price	From £90.
Rooms	2: 1 double, 1 twin. Extra beds in shared sitting room; extra shower.
Meals	Pub 0.5 miles.
Closed	Rarely.
Directions	From junction of A371 and A359 towards Bruton. Right to Shepton Montague. At x-roads by pub follow sign to church and village hall. Sharp bend at church, house 100 yds on right. Park in yard behind house.

Charles & Susie Dowding
Lower Farm,
Shepton Montague,
Wincanton,
Somerset BA9 8JG
Tel	01749 812253
Email	enquiries@lowerfarm.org.uk
Web	www.lowerfarm.org.uk

Entry 431   Map 3

Somerset

Bratton Farmhouse

A gorgeous old (1600) house around which strut hens and happy Jacob sheep. Intelligent and generous Suellen has created contemporary, warm interiors and the bedrooms are a joy. One, in the main house, has oak-panelled walls, bucolic views and a vast bed with old French embroidered linen. Another, in a newly converted studio across the courtyard, gives you complete independence with your own stylish sitting room made cosy with a wood-burner; lovers can laze till late in a huge nest of feather and down. Good books and art surround you, breakfasts are delicious and imaginative, and walks are from the door.

 Travel Club Offer: see page 392 for details.

Price	From £80. Singles from £50.
Rooms	3: 1 twin/double & sitting room; 2 doubles, each with separate bath/shower.
Meals	Lunch £10. Dinner, 3 courses, £25. Packed lunch £5. Pub 2 miles.
Closed	Rarely.
Directions	A303 then A371 signed Wincanton & Castle Cary. Follow signs to Castle Cary. After approx. 2.5 miles, right to Bratton Seymour. House 0.4 miles on right.

Suellen Dainty
Bratton Farmhouse,
Bratton Seymour, Wincanton,
Somerset BA9 8BY
Tel	01963 32458
Mobile	07780 848567
Email	sdainty52@googlemail.com
Web	www.brattonfarmhouse.co.uk

Entry 432   Map 3

Somerset

Yarlington House

A mellow Georgian manor surrounded by impressive parkland, formal gardens, rose garden, apple tree pergola and laburnum walk. Your hosts are friendly and flexible, artists with an eye for detail; her embroideries are everywhere. Something to astound at every turn: fine copies of 18th-century wallpapers, 18th-century fabric around the canopied bed and a bedroom whose Regency striped wallpaper extends across the entire ceiling creating the effect of a Napoleonic tent. There are elegant antiques, proper 50s bathrooms, log fires, a heated pool (summer only). Surprising, unique. *Children by arrangement.*

Price	£120. Singles £60.
Rooms	2: 1 double, 1 twin.
Meals	Pubs/restaurants nearby.
Closed	August.
Directions	From Wincanton, 2nd left on A371, after Holbrook r'bout. Then 3rd right; 1st gateposts on left.

	Countess Charles de Salis Yarlington House, Wincanton, Somerset BA9 8DY
Tel	01963 440344
Fax	01963 440335
Email	carolyn.desalis@yarlingtonhouse.com
Web	www.yarlingtonhouse.com

Entry 433   Map 3

Somerset

The Dairy House

A captivating place, tucked under Cadbury Hill. What were once 17th-century stables have been transformed by perfectionist Emma. Step through a smoky-blue stable door into a little cottage – all yours. The sitting room has a grey slate floor, pale walls, interesting art and smart seagrass-covered stairs winding up to an airy, sloping-ceilinged bedroom. It is subtle, understated and beautifully restful. The cottage stands in its own pretty orchard but you're also welcome to explore Emma's gorgeous walled garden. Breakfast is served in the Dairy House. *Children over ten welcome.*

Travel Club Offer: see page 392 for details.

Price	£85. Singles £50.
Rooms	Cottage with 1 twin/double; sofabed; extra shower.
Meals	Pub/restaurant 1.5 miles.
Closed	Occasionally.
Directions	From Wincanton A303 west, exit Chapel Cross for Sparkford. Right for Sparkford, left for Little Weston. House 0.25 miles on left, sign on wooden gate.

	Emma & Graham Barnett The Dairy House, Little Weston, Sparkford, Somerset BA22 7HP
Tel	01963 440987
Email	grahambarnett@lineone.net

Entry 434   Map 3

Somerset

Barwick Farm House

A proper old-fashioned smallholding with Dorset sheep, hens, horses and all the attendant wildlife. Angela and Robin (charming, and passionate about the soil) have saved ancient elm floorboards, exposed the sandstone linterns of the original fireplaces, stuck to traditional materials, then limewashed the walls in vibrant colours. Roomy bedrooms have ironed cotton sheets and a comforting mishmash of styles; one bathroom is painted bubble-gum pink and has a free-standing bath with views over fields. Wake to birdsong and the sizzle of bacon; good walking and cycling start from the door.

Price	£60–£75. Singles from £35.
Rooms	2: 1 double, 1 family room.
Meals	Early Bird packed breakfasts also available. Restaurant 100 yds.
Closed	Rarely.
Directions	A37 to Dorchester; 0.25 miles outside Yeovil, 1st exit off r'bout (opp. Red House pub) following signs to Little Barwick House restaurant. Farmhouse in the fork of the road.

Angela Nicoll
Barwick Farm House,
Barwick, Yeovil, Somerset BA22 9TD

Tel	01935 410779
Mobile	07967 385307
Email	info@barwickfarmhouse.co.uk
Web	www.barwickfarmhouse.co.uk

Entry 435   Map 3

Somerset

Chinnock House

Fiona's flair has revived the grand little flax merchant's house – Regency, listed and buried down a tangle of lanes. She is charming and it's a delightful set-up. In the house, two big light bedrooms with high beds, thick eiderdowns and fine print wallpapers. In the coach house, two equally delightful sun-filled bedrooms and a super sitting room under the eaves with deep comfy sofas and chairs. Breakfast is at your hosts' gleaming dining table. You are surrounded by a glorious garden – French formality meets English profusion – in a hamlet that could be in France. *Children over eight welcome.*

Price	£70–£120. Singles from £42.
Rooms	4: 1 double; 1 twin with separate bath. Coach house: 2 twins, sharing bath.
Meals	Pubs/restaurants 1 mile.
Closed	Christmas & New Year's Eve.
Directions	Take either of two lanes off A30. Follow sign for West Chinnock but ignore left turn to W. Chinnock itself. House on right about 100m after M. Chinnock church on left.

Fiona Wynn-Williams
Chinnock House,
Middle Chinnock,
Crewkerne, Somerset TA18 7PN

Tel	01935 881229
Fax	01935 881066
Email	fionaww@btinternet.com

Entry 436   Map 3

Staffordshire

Slab Bridge Cottage

A 19th-century cottage in a quiet setting beside the Shropshire Union Canal. Bedrooms have floral curtains and all is spotless and homely, with open fires, polished copper, silver and brass, old oak furniture, pretty bathrooms, fresh flowers. Eat outside on the terrace overlooking the canal, or on the narrowboat on an evening cruise – but do book! Diana makes her own bread, biscuits, cakes and jams and has five much-loved llamas (very therapeutic), including baby Scrumpy. David cuts fresh vegetables and salads from the garden. On a good day the hens lay fresh eggs too.

Price	£65–£70. Singles £45–£50.
Rooms	2: 1 double with separate bath; 1 double with separate shower.
Meals	Dinner £20. Packed lunch £5. Pub 2 miles.
Closed	Christmas & New Year.
Directions	M6 junc. 12; A5 west to r'bout; straight on. 1 mile to Stretton x-roads, right then 1st left (Lapley Lane); 3 miles to small x-roads at white house; left. Cottage 0.5 miles, on right.

Diana Walkerdine
Slab Bridge Cottage,
Little Onn, Church Eaton,
Staffordshire ST20 0AU

Tel	01785 840220
Fax	01785 840220
Email	ddwalkerdine@btinternet.com

Entry 437   Map 8

Staffordshire

Manor House

A working rare-breed farm in an area of great beauty, a Jacobean farmhouse with oodles of history. Behind mullioned windows is a glorious interior crammed with curios and family pieces, panelled walls and wonky floors... hurl a log on the fire and watch it roar. Rooms with views have four-posters; one bathroom flaunts rich red antique fabrics. Chris and Margaret are passionate but understated hosts who serve perfect breakfasts (home-grown tomatoes, sausages and bacon from their pigs) and give you the run of a garden resplendent with plants, vistas, tennis, croquet, two springer spaniels and one purring cat. Heaven.

Price	£54–£60. Singles £34–£40.
Rooms	4: 3 four-posters, 1 double.
Meals	Pub/restaurant 1.5 miles.
Closed	Christmas.
Directions	From Uttoxeter, B5030 for Rocester. Beyond JCB factory, left onto B5031. At T-junc. after church, right onto B5032. 1st left for Prestwood. Farm 0.75 miles on right over crest of hill, thro' arch.

Chris & Margaret Ball
Manor House,
Prestwood, Denstone, Uttoxeter,
Staffordshire ST14 5DD

Tel	01889 590415
Mobile	07976 767629
Email	cm_ball@yahoo.co.uk
Web	www.4posteraccom.com

Entry 438   Map 8

Staffordshire

Martinslow Farm

High up in the Peaks, lost to the world, this listed 300-year-old farmhouse once sheltered donkeys... the accommodation has since stepped up a gear. The sitting room, as warm and engaging as Diana herself, is cosy with beams, log-burner and muted chintz. Peaceful bedrooms in the stable block (interconnecting for families) have a country feel: a rocking horse and equine curtains in the Stable (Diana and Richard love country pursuits, dogs and good company), mahogany beds in the Tack Room, carpets in both. Perfect tranquillity, a sheltered patio for great views, and delicious locally sourced food from Diana.

Staffordshire

Stoop House Farm

Step through a rosy arch from this enchanting 18th-century farmhouse: the view across garden, fields and valley will bowl you over. Inside, oak beams, heated flagged floors, a cast-iron range, a bedroom shot through with olive and gold. In this thriving conservation village (with lovely pub), the farm draws on the latest in green design, while two Andalusian horses share the grounds with sheep, pigs and poultry – expect superb eggs at breakfast! Your warm, lovely hosts, she a midwife, he a climber, share their passion for the outdoors with their guests – and the Peak District National Park lies at your feet.

Travel Club Offer: see page 392 for details.

Price	From £70.	Price	£60. Singles £45.
Rooms	Stables: 1 double, 1 twin.	Rooms	1 suite & sitting room.
Meals	Supper £25. Pub 5-minute walk.	Meals	Pub 1-minute walk.
Closed	Rarely.	Closed	Never.
Directions	A523 Leek-Ashbourne. At Winkhill, signs to Grindon. Over x-roads, left at T-junction; 300 yds; house on right below lane.	Directions	From Leek A523 towards Ashbourne. At crossroads left B5053. Thro' Onecote, up hill then 2nd right signed Butterton. Thro' village past shop on right, 200 yds, then right fork. House 2nd on right.

	Richard & Diana Bloor		**Andrea Evans**
	Martinslow Farm,		Stoop House Farm,
	Winkhill, Leek,		Butterton, Leek,
	Staffordshire ST13 7PZ		Staffordshire ST13 7SY
Tel	01538 304500	Tel	01538 304486
Fax	01538 304141	Mobile	07966 135979
Email	richard.bloor@btclick.com	Email	bnfrench@yahoo.co.uk
Web	www.dianabloor-apartments.co.uk		

Entry 439   Map 8

Entry 440   Map 8

Suffolk

The Old Vicarage

Up the avenue of fine old horse chestnut trees to find just what you'd expect from an old vicarage: a Pembroke table in the flagstoned hall, a log fire which warms the sitting room for tea and homemade cake, a refectory table sporting copies of *The Field...* an inviting sofa, a piano, hunting scenes and silver pheasants. Bedrooms are large, chintzy and handsomely furnished, and the double has hill views. Weave your way through the branches of the huge copper beech to the garden that Jane loves. She grows her own vegetables, and keeps hens and house with equal talent. *Children over seven welcome.*

Price	From £75–£80. Singles £45.
Rooms	2: 1 double; 1 twin, each with separate bath. Extra single room off twin.
Meals	Dinner £20. BYO. Packed lunch £6. Pub/restaurant 2 miles.
Closed	Christmas Day.
Directions	From Cambridge, A1307 for Haverhill. Left to Withersfield. At T-junc., left. Almost 3 miles on, high yew hedge; at 'Concealed Entrance' sign on left, sharp turn into drive.

	Jane Sheppard
	The Old Vicarage,
	Great Thurlow, Newmarket,
	Suffolk CB9 7LE
Tel	01440 783209
Mobile	07887 717429
Fax	01638 667270
Email	s.j.sheppard@hotmail.co.uk

Entry 441 Map 9

Suffolk

The Manse

Unmissable in its coat of rich red paint, the beamed, 16th-century Manse overlooks a historic village green. The owners will present you with a superb breakfast each day, plus homemade cakes or scones for tea, and a fresh posy of garden flowers. Robin, ex diplomatic service, has a passion for opera; Bridget organises the church choir. The guest quarters are completely private and deliciously cosy; there are polished antiques, fine porcelain and a wood-burning stove, a rose-tumbled garden for breakfast on fine days, and a chivalrous black labrador called Tristan, always happy to take guests for a walk.

Price	£65–£70. Singles from £40.
Rooms	1 twin/double & sitting room.
Meals	Pub/restaurant 2-minute walk.
Closed	Rarely.
Directions	From Bury St. Edmunds, A143 to Haverhill; left on to B1066 for Glemsford. 6 miles to Hartest; house on far side of green, opp. red telephone box. From Long Melford take A1092 towards Clare, then 1st right on to B1066.

	Bridget & Robin Oaten
	The Manse,
	The Green, Hartest,
	Suffolk IP29 4DH
Tel	01284 830226
Mobile	07910 857446
Email	robin@oatens.plus.com

Entry 442 Map 10

Suffolk

The Old Manse Barn

A loft-style apartment in sleepy Suffolk; this living/eating/sleeping space of blond wood, white walls and big windows has an urban feel yet overlooks countryside. Secluded from the main house, in a timber-clad barn, the style is thrillingly modern: leather sofas, glass dining table, stainless steel kitchenette. Floor lights dance off the walls while CD surround-sound creates mood. The fridge is well-stocked – homemade granola, local bread and ham – so breakfast when you want. There's peace for romance, solitude for work, a garden to sit in and friendly Sue to suggest the best pubs.

Price	£70.
Rooms	Studio with 1 double & kitchenette.
Meals	Pubs/restaurants within walking distance.
Closed	Rarely.
Directions	A134 for Bury St Edmunds & Sudbury; A1141 Lavenham, left after 1.4 miles for Cockfield & Stowmarket; house 1.2 miles on right.

Sue Jones
The Old Manse Barn,
Chapel Road, Cockfield,
Bury St Edmunds, Suffolk IP30 0HE

Tel	01284 828120
Mobile	07931 753996
Email	bookings@theoldmansebarn.co.uk
Web	www.theoldmansebarn.co.uk

Entry 443 Map 10

Suffolk

16 Bolton Street

Gillian and Bill have moved round the corner to Bolton Street and the welcome is as warm as ever. The house is 15th century; bustling Lavenham, part medieval, part Tudor, is one of England's showpiece towns. Heavy beams, low doorways, books, magazines and fresh flowers create a warm homely feel; steep oak stairs lead to fresh, cosy bedrooms where Gillian's patchwork and stitchwork abounds. Gillian likes nothing better than to spoil her guests with breakfasts of local sausages and bacon, potato cakes, tasty mushrooms and fresh fruit. A delightful, relaxed, generous place to stay. *Minimum stay two nights at weekends.*

Price	£80-£90.
Rooms	2: 1 twin/double, 1 double.
Meals	Packed lunch £6. Pubs/restaurants in Lavenham.
Closed	Rarely.
Directions	From the market square in Lavenham, pass The Great House Restaurant, then left into Bolton Street. Long pink house at bottom on right. Park outside to unload; Gillian will help with parking.

Bill & Gillian de Lucy
16 Bolton Street,
Lavenham,
Suffolk CO10 9RG

Tel	01787 249046
Mobile	07747 621096
Email	gdelucy@aol.com
Web	www.guineahouse.co.uk

Entry 444 Map 10

Suffolk

Milden Hall

Over five generations of Hawkins have lived in this seemingly grand 16th-century hall farmhouse with its smooth wooden floors, enormous windows and vast fireplaces. Bedrooms range from big to huge, are elegantly old-fashioned and filled with interesting tapestries, wall hangings and lovely furniture; it's a bit of a trek to the loo from the family room so you need to be nimble. Juliet is a passionate conservationist, full of ideas for making the most of the surrounding countryside, on foot or by bicycle. Expect delicious home-grown bacon, sausages, bantam eggs and fruit compotes for breakfast.

Ethical Collection: Environment; Food.
See page 400 for details.

Price	£60-£80. Singles from £40.
Rooms	3: 2 twins, 1 family room, all sharing bathroom.
Meals	Light supper £15. BYO. Pubs/restaurants 2-3 miles.
Closed	Rarely.
Directions	From Lavenham, A1141 for Monks Eleigh. After 2 miles, right to Milden. At x-roads, right to Sudbury on B1115. Hall's long drive 0.25 miles on left.

	Juliet & Christopher Hawkins Milden Hall, Milden, Lavenham, Suffolk CO10 9NY
Tel	01787 247235
Email	hawkins@thehall-milden.co.uk
Web	www.thehall-milden.co.uk

Entry 445   Map 10

Suffolk

Wood Hall

Susan greets you with the warmest of welcomes. Janus-like, her house looks both ways, Georgian to the front, and beamed Tudor behind. Breakfast on summer mornings on the terrace in the walled garden on homemade marmalade, jams and fruit compotes; in winter, settle beside the fire with a cup of tea. The bedrooms, one delicately floral, the other with cream walls, are elegant with padded headboards, thick curtains, armchairs, writing desks, candles, standard lamps, books and an ample tea tray. Wander through the garden to find a Victorian greenhouse with two types of vine. *Bridge classes offered to groups of four.*

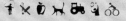 Travel Club Offer: see page 392 for details.

Price	From £85. Singles £50 (Sun-Thurs only).
Rooms	2: 1 double, 1 twin/double.
Meals	Pub 150 yds.
Closed	Christmas & New Year.
Directions	B1115 for Lavenham from Sudbury 3.5 miles; right to Little Waldingfield; house on left, 200 yds beyond The Swan. Parking at rear of house.

	Mrs Susan Nisbett Wood Hall, Little Waldingfield, Lavenham, Suffolk CO10 0SY
Tel	01787 247362
Email	susan@woodhallbnb.fsnet.co.uk
Web	www.thewoodhall.com

Entry 446   Map 10

Suffolk

Hill House

Nayland is a charming village and this apricot-coloured, listed house sits on a quiet lane. Enter an unusual tunnel hall with flagstones, rugs and fresh flowers, to find a beamed drawing room and an elegant dining room. It's all very Georgian with well-polished antiques, good art, and creamy colours dotted with bright chintz. Smart, fresh bedrooms have good views over the pretty garden and you get a choice of pillows. Pauline happily shares her home with you and provides generous breakfasts – in the garden in summer. Good farm markets and walks abound in Constable country. *Minimum stay two nights at weekends in summer.*

Suffolk

Nether Hall

The garden cascades with old English roses in summer. This is a charming 16th-century home in a valley made famous by John Constable; make the most of this delightful area. The River Box borders the garden, the house, barn and stables are old, the tennis court newer and inside is warmly enticing. Find elegance and period charm in uneven floors and ancient doors, little windows and wonky beams, woodsmoke from the inglenook, chintz and checks on the chairs. And there's a downstairs bedroom with its own entrance. Jennie immediately puts you at ease and is renowned for her breakfasts.

Travel Club Offer: see page 392 for details.

Price	From £70. Singles from £35.
Rooms	2: 1 twin/double; 1 double with separate bath.
Meals	Pub/restaurant short walk.
Closed	Christmas & New Year.
Directions	Enter village from A134 into Bear St. Past T-junction into Birch St. 100 yds turn left, house 70 yds uphill on right.

Price	£80–£85. Singles from £60.
Rooms	3: 1 double, 1 twin/double; 1 single with separate bath.
Meals	Pubs 1 mile.
Closed	Rarely.
Directions	3 miles from A12, on B1068 between Higham & Stoke by Nayland. On south side of road, 300 yds east of Thorington Street.

Mrs Pauline Heigham
Hill House,
Gravel Hill, Nayland,
Suffolk CO6 4JB
Tel   01206 262782
Email   heighamhillhouse@hotmail.com
Web   www.heighamhillhouse.co.uk

Patrick & Jennie Jackson
Nether Hall,
Thorington Street,
Stoke-by-Nayland, Suffolk CO6 4ST
Tel   01206 337373
Mobile   07799 560804
Fax   01206 337496
Email   patrick.jackson7@btopenworld.com

Entry 447   Map 10

Entry 448   Map 10

Suffolk

Priory House

A soft, 16th-century Suffolk combination of bricks and beams; drink in the peace of house and garden all day if you wish. The house is friendly and informal, with antique furniture, gleaming brass and William Morris-style floral sofas and chairs; the fascinating, heavily timbered dining room was once a cheese room where 'Suffolk Bang' was made. Expect white walls in the bedrooms and a wood-burning stove in the guest sitting room, along with books and comfy chairs. Plan your days with friendly Rosemary – the Southwold coast is half an hour away. *Children over ten welcome. Minimum stay two nights July-October.*

Price	From £70. Singles £40.
Rooms	3: 1 double; 1 double, 1 twin, each with separate bath.
Meals	Pubs/restaurants 8-minute walk.
Closed	Christmas week.
Directions	From Scole, A140, right onto A143 for Gt Yarmouth. After 7 miles, right at Harleston. B1116 to Fressingfield. Pass church & Fox & Goose on left. At top of hill, right, then left into Priory Rd.

Stephen & Rosemary Willis
Priory House,
Priory Road, Fressingfield, Eye,
Suffolk IP21 5PH

Tel	01379 586254
Fax	01379 586254
Email	willisbb@clara.co.uk

Entry 449   Map 10

Suffolk

Mulberry Hall

Delight in the characterful architecture and uneven tread of this handsome hall house of 1523; it was owned by Cardinal Wolsey and has Henry VIII's coat of arms above the fire. It rambles round corners, is rich in beams and beloved family pieces, and has two winding stairs. Penny, gentle and well-travelled, gives you tea and cakes in the drawing room and lights a log fire on chillier days. In the garden: old roses, pear pergola and mulberry tree; in the bedrooms: leaded windows, beamed walls, good beds. Homemade jam on home-baked bread when you wake, soft robes for the bath before bed.

Price	From £70. Singles from £40.
Rooms	2: 1 twin; 1 double with separate shower.
Meals	Supper £8-£12. Pubs/restaurants 5-8 miles.
Closed	Christmas-New Year.
Directions	5 miles west of Ipswich (off A1071). 300 yds into village on left next to farmyard but before phone box.

Penny Debenham
Mulberry Hall,
Burstall, Ipswich,
Suffolk IP8 3DP

Tel	01473 652348
Fax	01473 652110
Email	pennydebenham@hotmail.com

Entry 450   Map 10

Suffolk

Haughley House

A timber-framed, medieval manor in three acres of garden overlooking 30 acres of farmland. The attractive village is in a conservation area; your hosts: the Lord of the Manor and his wife. They also happen to be accomplished cooks and use the finest ingredients – their own beef, game and eggs, and vegetables and soft fruits from the kitchen garden. You'll find genuine country-house style here, tea and homemade cake on arrival, flowery wallpapers, much charm and sparkling shower rooms – there's even a stairlift. Ask Jeffrey to show you the manorial records and the priest hole. Aga-cooked breakfasts are a feast.

Price	From £90. Singles from £60.
Rooms	3: 2 doubles, 1 twin.
Meals	Dinner, 3 courses, £25.
Closed	Rarely.
Directions	From A14 exit 48, after 0.5 miles take right hand fork; house 100 yds on right.

Jeffrey & Caroline Bowden
Haughley House,
Haughley, Suffolk IP14 3NS
Tel   01449 673398
Fax   01449 673170
Email   bowden@keme.co.uk
Web   www.haughleyhouse.co.uk

Entry 451   Map 10

Suffolk

Church Farmhouse

Come for the good Suffolk light, peaceful views, lots of books and a relaxed atmosphere. The listed Elizabethan farmhouse sits in a quiet hamlet opposite an ancient thatched church with Southwold and the coast nearby. Restful, uncluttered bedrooms have fresh flowers and laundered linen; bathrooms are modern, well-lit and warm. No sitting room, but a delightful beamed dining room with a generous square table at which you may linger, or have tea in the pretty garden in summer. Sarah, well-travelled and entertaining, is a terrific cook.
Children over 12 welcome. Min. stay two nights at weekends in summer.

Price	From £70. Singles from £45.
Rooms	3: 1 double, 1 twin; 1 double with separate bath.
Meals	Dinner £25–£28. Pub/restaurants within 4 miles.
Closed	Christmas.
Directions	A12 for Wangford; left signed Uggeshall; house 1 mile on left before church.

Sarah Jupp
Church Farmhouse,
Uggeshall, Southwold,
Suffolk NR34 8BD
Tel   01502 578532
Mobile   07748 801418
Email   uggeshalljupp@btinternet.com
Web   www.uggeshall.fsnet.co.uk

Entry 452   Map 10

Suffolk

The Old Methodist Chapel

Atmosphere and architecture – easy to see what seduced Jackum and David into converting this listed Victorian chapel into a home. Bedrooms have their own entrance and are charming – one, with access to conservatory and courtyard garden, has pale walls, oak floors and beams; the flag-floored Retreat Room sports bright rugs and bedcovers from far-flung places. The chapel is comfortably, cosily cluttered and the Browns are easy-going. Potions and lotions by your bath, videos, DVDs and music in your room, books and flowers in every corner, and famous bacon from Peasenhall. *Minimum stay two nights at weekends.*

Price	£75-£90. Singles £50-£65.
Rooms	2: 1 twin, 1 double with separate bath.
Meals	Pubs/restaurants within walking distance.
Closed	Rarely.
Directions	From A12 in Yoxford, A1120 signed Peasenhall & Stowmarket. Chapel 200 yds on right.

Jackum & David Brown
The Old Methodist Chapel,
High Street, Yoxford, Suffolk IP17 3EU

Tel	01728 668333
Mobile	07810 432470
Email	browns@chapelsuffolk.co.uk
Web	www.chapelsuffolk.co.uk

Entry 453   Map 10

Suffolk

Sandpit Farm

Idyllic views of the wide Alde valley from this deeply comfortable, listed farmhouse. The river borders their 20 acres of beautiful meadows, orchard, gardens, tennis court, ponds and remains of brick-lined moat. Be charmed by family antiques and portraits, easy colour schemes, some beams and open fires, and every cossetting thing in the pretty bedrooms, one with its own sitting room. Susie and her Aga will cook a scrumptious breakfast of homemade and local produce. Near the coast, Snape for concerts, great birdwatching, walks and cycling. Peaceful and so relaxing. *Painting classes possible.*

Price	£65-£80. Singles from £45.
Rooms	2: 1 double, 1 twin.
Meals	Pub/restaurant 1.5 miles.
Closed	Rarely.
Directions	From A1120, Yoxford to Stowmarket, east to Dennington; take B1120, Framlingham. First left; house 1.5 miles on left.

Susie Marshall
Sandpit Farm,
Bruisyard, Saxmundham,
Suffolk IP17 2EB

Tel	01728 663445
Email	smarshall@aldevalleybreaks.co.uk
Web	www.aldevalleybreaks.co.uk

Entry 454   Map 10

Suffolk

Arch House

Arch House stands in three acres of garden, meadow and woodland by the river Hundred, home to the delightful and fun-loving Araminta and Hugh. He, a keen member of the Soil Association, shoots, fishes and grows his own veg; she is involved in the Healing Hands projects; both are fabulous cooks. They are also complementary therapists (book a treatment in advance!). The décor is traditional, the bedrooms colourful, and the casually elegant drawing/dining room has a boudoir grand piano you're most welcome to play. Trout, salmon or game for dinner; at breakfast, eggs from the hens. Wonderful value.

Price	£55-£70. Singles £30.
Rooms	2: 1 double, 1 twin with separate bath.
Meals	Dinner from £15. BYO. Pub 200 yds.
Closed	Rarely.
Directions	From A12, A1094 into Aldeburgh. Left at r'bout onto B1122 to Leiston. On left, 0.5 miles after Aldringham sign.

Araminta Stewart & Hugh Peacock
Arch House,
Aldeburgh Road, Aldringham,
Suffolk IP16 4QF

Tel	01728 832615
Mobile	07979 694779
Email	amintys@aol.com
Web	www.archhouse-aldeburgh.com

Entry 455   Map 10

Suffolk

Dunan House

You may get wild mushrooms for breakfast and new-laid eggs, homemade bread, jams and marmalade. This is a lovely place to stay, with an unusual, lively décor. Ann is a potter and her artistry is apparent everywhere: bedrooms are upbeat and attractive, with woven rugs and imaginative, decorative touches, and the double at the top has its own little sitting room and long views. Ann and Simon, an illustrator, are entertaining company. It is wonderfully close to town and sea with views over the marshes to the river Alde and beyond. *Minimum stay two nights at weekends; three nights on bank holidays.*

Price	From £75. Singles from £50.
Rooms	3: 1 twin/double, 1 double, 1 double with sitting room with single sofabed.
Meals	Pubs & restaurants 7-minute walk.
Closed	Christmas & New Year.
Directions	From A1094 drive towards town from r'bout. First right towards hospital, through 'Private Road' gate. House 100 yds on left, opp. tennis courts.

Mr Simon Farr & Ms Ann Lee
Dunan House,
41 Park Road, Aldeburgh,
Suffolk IP15 5EN

Tel	01728 452486
Email	dunanhouse@btinternet.com
Web	www.dunanhouse.co.uk

Entry 456   Map 10

Suffolk

The Old Butchers Shop

Artist Sarah has cleverly converted this old butcher's shop: you're right on the main street of an undisturbed brick and timber estuary village, a hop from the sea for birdwatching or walks, and Snape for music lovers. Bedrooms, not huge, are pretty and light with proper linen on supremely comfortable beds and views over the maturing garden or the street and fine Norman church. Two happy cats lie comatose in the drawing room with its gay kilims and bright checks, books jostle for space with pictures. Sarah is laid-back and fun and cooks a mean breakfast: homemade yogurt and stewed fruits, local kippers.

Suffolk

Melton Hall

There's more than a touch of theatre to this beautiful listed house. The dining room is opulent red; the drawing room, with its delicately carved mantelpiece and comfortable George Smith sofas, has French windows to the terrace. There's a four-poster in one bedroom, an antique French bed in another and masses of fresh flowers and books. The seven acres of garden include an orchid and wildflower meadow designated a County Wildlife Site. River walks, the coast and Sutton Hoo – the Saxon burial site – are close by. Cindy, her delightful children and their little dog, Snowball, give a great welcome.

Travel Club Offer: see page 392 for details.

Price	£65-£75. Singles from £45.
Rooms	3: 2 twins/doubles; 1 twin/double with separate bath/shower.
Meals	Pubs/restaurants within 5-min. walk.
Closed	Rarely.
Directions	From A12, signs to Orford. Left-hand bend after King's Head pub towards quay. House on opposite side of road with blue door. Park in Market Sq.

Price	£100-£120. Singles from £50.
Rooms	3: 1 double; 1 double, 1 single, sharing bath.
Meals	Dinner, 1-3 courses, £18-£36. BYO. Pubs/restaurants nearby.
Closed	Rarely.
Directions	From A12 Woodbridge bypass, exit at r'bout for Melton. Follow for 1 mile to lights; there, right. Immediately on right.

	Mrs Sarah Holland
	The Old Butchers Shop,
	111 Church Street, Orford, Woodbridge,
	Suffolk IP12 2LL
Tel	01394 450517
Fax	01394 459436
Email	sarah@oldbutchers-orford.co.uk
Web	www.oldbutchers-orford.co.uk

	Mrs Lucinda de la Rue
	Melton Hall,
	Woodbridge,
	Suffolk IP12 1PF
Tel	01394 388138
Mobile	07775 797075
Email	cindy@meltonhall.co.uk
Web	www.meltonhall.co.uk

Entry 457   Map 10

Entry 458   Map 10

Suffolk

The Hayloft

Romantics, walkers, birdwatchers and those who need to get away from it all will be in heaven. In the old hayloft is a self-contained and stunningly stylish apartment: a raftered sitting room with a sweeping oak floor, cream sofas and a window to trumpet the view. The bedroom is uncluttered and cosy with a big leather bed, gorgeous linen and feathered bedside lights. Continental breakfast is in the fridge (homemade jams, local honey, their own fruits in summer, home-baked rolls), there are ten idyllic acres of gardens, meadows and wildlife, and bikes to borrow. Farmers' markets and festivals abound.

Travel Club Offer: see page 392 for details.

Price	£120. Singles £80.
Rooms	Studio with 1 double & sitting room.
Meals	Restaurants 4 miles.
Closed	Christmas.
Directions	North of Woodbridge on A12, take road for Bredfield. At T-junc with B1078 (3 miles), left, then 1st right into Martins Lane. Farm House on right, gravel parking on left.

Adrian & Jane Stevensen
The Hayloft,
Valley Farm House, Clopton,
Woodbridge, Suffolk IP13 6QX

Tel	01473 737872
Mobile	07803 797897
Email	info@thehayloftsuffolk.co.uk
Web	www.thehayloftsuffolk.co.uk

Entry 459   Map 10

Suffolk

Grange Farm

The tennis court and garden are surrounded by a 12th-century listed moat – this is a glorious old place. Ancient stairs rise and fall all over the 13th-century house, there are sloping floors and honey-coloured beams and a lovely dining room that was once the dairy. Bedrooms are large, comfortable and traditional; the sitting room is cosy with baby grand, log fire, fresh flowers, books, puzzles and games, and the views are to a garden full of birds. Delightful Elizabeth spoils you with homemade cake, local honey, own bread and homemade marmalade for breakfast. Good value, great fun.

Travel Club Offer: see page 392 for details.

Price	£60. Singles £30.
Rooms	2: 1 twin/double, 1 twin, sharing bath.
Meals	Pub 2-mile walk.
Closed	December-March.
Directions	A1120 (Yoxford to Stowmarket) to Dennington. B1116 north for approx. 3 miles. Farm on right 0.9 miles north of Owl's Green & red phone box.

Elizabeth Hickson
Grange Farm,
Dennington, Woodbridge,
Suffolk IP13 8BT

Tel	01986 798388
Mobile	07774 182835
Web	www.grangefarm.biz

Entry 460   Map 10

Surrey

Greenaway

An enchanting cottage. People return time and again – for the house, the dovecote, the garden, the countryside, and Sheila and John. The sitting room is vast with restful rich colours and textures. A sturdy, turning oak staircase leads to the sweet bedrooms – and newly decorated bathrooms with roll tops; a peek at them all will only confuse you: each one is gorgeous. There's an ornate bedstead in the Chinese room and, in another, an oak bedstead and beams. An exceptional place and a delightful village with glorious walks on the Greensand Way, yet so close to London and the airports.

Price	£85–£95. Singles from £65.
Rooms	3: 1 double; 1 double, 1 twin, sharing bath.
Meals	Hotel restaurant 0.25 miles.
Closed	Rarely.
Directions	A3 to Milford, then A283 for Petworth. At Chiddingfold, Pickhurst Road off green. 3rd on left, with large black dovecote.

Sheila & John Marsh
Greenaway,
Pickhurst Road,
Chiddingfold,
Surrey GU8 4TS
Tel 01428 682920
Email jfmarsh@gotadsl.co.uk

🛉 ✗ 🖃 🚂 🐾

Entry 461 Map 4

Surrey

High Edser

Ancient wattle and daub, aged timbers and bags of character – it really does ramble. Built in 1532, High Edser sits in 2.5 acres of smooth lawns beyond which lie the village and the Surrey hills. But, unlike many houses of a certain age, this one is light and inviting and has the sort of family clutter that makes you feel at home. Bedrooms are full of character; kind Patrick and Carol leave you plenty of space to gently unfurl. The carved wooden fireplace in the stone-flagged dining room is spectacular, and there's a snug study just for guests. Very peaceful in an AONB, yet close to both airports.

Price	£65–£70. Singles £30–£40.
Rooms	3: 2 doubles, 1 twin, all sharing bath.
Meals	Pub/restaurant 300 yds.
Closed	Rarely.
Directions	From A3, 1st exit after M25, for Ripley. Through Ripley & West Clandon, over dual c'way (A246) onto A25. 3rd right to Shere. There, right to Cranleigh. House 5 miles on left, 1 mile past The Windmill.

Patrick & Carol Franklin Adams
High Edser,
Shere Road, Ewhurst,
Cranleigh, Surrey GU6 7PQ
Tel 01483 278214
Mobile 07775 865125
Email carol@highedser.co.uk
Web www.highedser.co.uk

🛉 ✗ 🔊 🐾 🍽

Entry 462 Map 4

Surrey

Lower Easing Farmhouse

A homely place with a lovely walled garden and super hosts; Gillian, who speaks French, German and Spanish, enjoys welcoming people from all over the world. The house, 16th to 19th century, has exposed timbers, books and bold colours. The dining room is red; the guest sitting room – with open fire and decorated with fascinating artefacts from around the world – is big enough for a small company meeting, or a wedding group. Your hosts, who are great fun, run an efficient and caring ship. In the walled garden, sipping tea, the distant rumble of the A3 reminds you how well placed you are for Gatwick and Heathrow.

Surrey

Old Great Halfpenny

It feels as rural as Devon, yet you are perfectly placed for airports and easy access to London. The 16th-century listed farmhouse sits on a country lane beneath the Pilgrim's Way. Beyond the pretty garden – Michael's passion – roll the North Downs and wooded hills with hardly a house in sight; there are fabulous walks right from the door. You have your own entrance with fairly steep steps to beautifully furnished bedrooms (Alison is an interior designer) with lovely fabrics and French antique beds. You will be treated to breakfast on the terrace in the summer and large log fires in winter. Special.

Travel Club Offer: see page 392 for details.

Price	From £70. Singles from £45.
Rooms	4: 1 twin/double; 1 twin/double with separate bath/shower; 2 singles sharing shower.
Meals	Pub 300 yds.
Closed	Occasionally.
Directions	A3 south. 5 miles after Guildford, Eashing signed left at service station. House 150 yds on left behind white fence.

Price	£75–£85. Singles £65.
Rooms	2 doubles, each with separate bath.
Meals	Pub 0.5 miles.
Closed	Rarely.
Directions	From London, exit A3 before Guildford, signed Burpham. Ring for detailed directions - 2 miles.

David & Gillian Swinburn
Lower Eashing Farmhouse,
Lower Eashing,
Godalming,
Surrey GU7 2QF

Tel 01483 421436
Fax 01483 421436
Email davidswinburn@hotmail.com

Michael & Alison Bennett
Old Great Halfpenny,
Halfpenny Lane, St Martha, Guildford,
Surrey GU4 8PY

Tel 01483 567835
Mobile 07768 745765
Fax 01483 303037
Email bennettbird@gmail.com

Entry 463   Map 4

Entry 464   Map 4

Surrey

Swallow Barn

A squash court and stables, once belonging to the next-door manor, have become a happy, homely house. Full of family memories and run by interesting and helpful people, it has a mature charm – and lovely trees in the garden, a paddock and a summer pool. Given the hushed tranquillity you are surprisingly close to the airports and the M25. The bedrooms are small but one has its own entrance, another the use of a sunny sitting room, the third a balcony; beds are firm and have super duvets, garden views are pretty and breakfasts are both generous and scrumptious. *Children over eight welcome.*

Price	£90. Singles £60.
Rooms	3: 1 double & sitting room, 1 twin; 1 twin with separate shower.
Meals	Pub/restaurant 0.75 miles.
Closed	Rarely.
Directions	From M25, exit 11, A319 into Chobham. Left at T–junc.; left at mini–r'about onto A3046. After 0.7 miles, right between street light & postbox. House 2nd on left.

	Joan & David Carey
	Swallow Barn,
	Milford Green, Chobham, Woking,
	Surrey GU24 8AU
Tel	01276 856030
Mobile	07768 972904
Email	swallowbarn@web-hq.com
Web	www.swallow-barn.co.uk

Entry 465   Map 4

Sussex

Redford Cottage

In a tiny village, a friendly home with much-loved books and very kind hosts. The immense inglenook dates back to 1510 and the garden suite opens to undulating lawns; it is cosy, old-worldly, floral and private, and its sitting room comes with a wood-burner. The barn has the woody spaciousness of a ski chalet and is perfect for friends... old rugs, new pine, games, views and (up steep open stairs) beds tucked under a sloped ceiling. The silence is filled with birdsong and you are surrounded by woodland, wildlife and the rolling South Downs. Breakfasts in the conservatory are a treat. *Min. stay three nights during Goodwood.*

Price	From £95. Singles from £65.
Rooms	3: 1 suite. Barn: 2 twins/doubles & sitting room.
Meals	Pubs/restaurants 2.5-4 miles.
Closed	Christmas.
Directions	On old A3, north from Petersfield, at Hill Brow right for Rogate, left after 300 yds to Milland. Follow lane through woods for 6 miles; right for Midhurst & Redford. On right, 150 yds beyond Redford sign.

	Caroline & David Angela
	Redford Cottage,
	Redford,
	Midhurst,
	Sussex GU29 0QF
Tel	01428 741242
Fax	01428 741242

Entry 466   Map 4

Sussex

The Quag

Buried in a birchwood, The Quag feels remote, yet Midhurst – "the second most attractive town in England" – is only two miles away. Feel private in your own space with spanking new bedroom, striking bathroom with chequerboard floor, wooden-floored sitting room, useful fridge and separate stairs to garden and pool. You breakfast in the main house at a long wooden table. Views are to the lawns that run romantically down to the stream, then across to the South Downs, from which are a maze of footpaths across common land. Mark works for Christie's and Loveday looks after you. A happy, relaxed atmosphere.

Price	From £80. Singles £50.
Rooms	1 twin & sitting room.
Meals	Pubs/restaurants nearby.
Closed	Occasionally.
Directions	A272 Midhurst-Petersfield; 2 miles from Midhurst, left signed Minsted. Count 7 telegraph poles, then 1st left. White house 1st on right.

	Loveday & Mark Wrey
	The Quag,
	Minsted,
	Midhurst,
	Sussex GU29 0JH
Tel	01730 813623
Email	beds@wrey.co.uk

Entry 467   Map 4

Sussex

Severals House

In a sunny clearing deep in the woods stands a mellow house in a garden filled with lavender. The Fairlies happened upon it years ago and fell in love with it. Originally two woodcutters' cottages – an old brick path still leads to the well – it was built in the year of Trafalgar. Jock is a rug weaver and a writer so there's a fine collection of books, and he and Serena are the loveliest hosts. The fresh-feeling, green and white bedroom is large, comfy and totally peaceful; breakfast includes Midhurst Royal sausages and homemade marmalade. Walk through a little garden gate into bird-filled woods.

Price	£80. Singles from £50.
Rooms	1 double.
Meals	Pubs/restaurants 1-2 miles.
Closed	Rarely.
Directions	From centre of Midhurst, A272 to Petersfield. 1 mile on, see Woolbeding on right; go past. Carry on A272; 300 yds on, left into wood. Blue 'Single Track Road' sign. House 300 yds on right.

	Serena & Jock Fairlie
	Severals House,
	Severals Wood,
	Midhurst,
	Sussex GU29 0LX
Tel	01730 812771

Entry 468   Map 4

Sussex

Amberfold

Down the secluded, wooded lane and through a stone archway to find a glorious terraced garden and a listed 17th-century house; the perfect hideaway. Bedrooms are in individual annexes so you can come and go as you please. Step in to vibrant colours and interesting art, large beds and fabulous linen, a refreshing lack of clutter and space for comfy armchairs; showers only do full pelt and towels are plentiful. Erling (who adores music and, clearly, gardening) is dedicated to your happiness, making this the perfect place to recharge the batteries in peace and quiet; breakfast on the terrace in summer.

Price	£75–£100. Singles £55–£75.
Rooms	2 doubles.
Meals	Pubs 1-4 miles.
Closed	Rarely.
Directions	From Midhurst, A286 for Chichester. After Royal Oak pub on left, Greyhound on right, on for 0.5 miles, left to Heyshott. On for 2 miles, do not turn off, look for house sign on left.

	Erling Sorensen
	Amberfold,
	Heyshott, Midhurst,
	Sussex GU29 0DA
Tel	01730 812385
Mobile	07802 415639
Email	erlingamberfold@aol.com
Web	www.amberfold.co.uk

Entry 469   Map 4

Sussex

West Marden Farm

Bowl down a gentle valley in the South Downs to find a 16th-century farmhouse with beautiful Sussex granaries and barn; the Edney family has farmed the land for generations. Your delightful, helpful hosts, committed to the environment, give you a sitting/dining room with a huge old fireplace, comfortable sofas, oak floor and French windows to the garden. Upstairs is a beamed bedroom with a luxurious feel and a fabulous bathroom (free-standing bath, swish shower) bursting with aromatic soaps and oils. Breakfasts are delicious, the walking is great, Goodwood is a 20-minute drive. *Minimum stay two nights weekends.*

Price	£85–£95.
Rooms	1 twin/double.
Meals	Pub 75 yds.
Closed	Christmas.
Directions	West Marden Farmhouse is in centre of village opposite Noredown Way.

	Carole Edney
	West Marden Farm,
	West Marden,
	Chichester,
	Sussex PO18 9ES
Tel	023 92 631761
Email	carole.edney@btinternet.com
Web	www.westmardenfarmhousebandb.co.c

Entry 470   Map 4

Sussex

Lordington House

Croquet on the lawn in summer, big log fires and woolly jumpers in winter, brilliant food all year round. On a sunny slope of the Ems valley, life ticks by peacefully as it has always done... The house is vast and impressive and a lime avenue links the much-loved garden with the AONB beyond. The 17th-century staircase is a glory, the décor is engagingly old-fashioned: Edwardian beds with firm mattresses and floral bedspreads, carpeted Sixties-style bathrooms, shepherdess wallpapers up and over wardrobe doors. A privilege to stay in a house of this age and character! *Children over five welcome. Dogs by arrangement.*

Price	From £90. Singles from £45.
Rooms	4: 1 double; 1 twin/double with separate bath/shower; 1 double, 1 single sharing bath/shower.
Meals	Dinner £20. Packed lunch from £5. Pub 1 mile.
Closed	Rarely.
Directions	Lordington (marked on some road maps) west side of B2146, 6 miles south of South Harting, 0.5 miles south of Walderton. Enter thro' white railings by letterbox; fork right after bridge.

Mr & Mrs John Hamilton
Lordington House,
Lordington,
Chichester,
Sussex PO18 9DX

Tel	01243 375862
Fax	01243 375862
Email	audreyhamilton@onetel.com

Entry 471   Map 4

Sussex

Church Gate

Janie has added a conservatory and sunny, friendly 'live-in' kitchen to her 1930s house. Smiling and bubbly, she greets with afternoon tea, rustles up tasty eggs at breakfast, and may even treat guests to home-baked bread or croissants, served on the terrace in summer. The house is adorned with Nigerian musical instruments and Janie's photographs from ex-pat days; the sun-streamed, practically furnished bedrooms are brightened with garden flowers. Polish your serve on the tennis court (bring the raquets), or set off for Chichester with its theatre and shops. Or pretty Itchenor, a mecca for sailors.

Ethical Collection: Food. See page 400 for details.

Travel Club Offer: see page 392 for details.

Price	From £80. Singles from £50.
Rooms	4: 1 double; 1 twin with separate bathroom. Cottage: 1 double, 1 twin & sitting room.
Meals	Pub within 4 miles.
Closed	Most of the winter months.
Directions	From A27 at Chichester take A286 Witterings; 5 miles; at r'bout bear right onto B2179. 0.5 miles turn right to Itchenor. 1 mile, house opp. church.

Mrs Janie Impey
Church Gate,
Itchenor,
Chichester,
Sussex PO20 7DL

Tel	01243 514700
Email	janie.allen@btinternet.com
Web	www.chichesterbandb.co.uk

Entry 472   Map 4

Sussex

Itchenor Park House

The Duke of Richmond reportedly built Itchenor Park for his French mistress in 1783. If he was hoping to hide her away, he succeeded – the listed Georgian house sits in beautiful formal gardens on a vast 700-acre farmed estate. It is remote, wonderfully tranquil, and a field path brings you to Chichester harbour for boat trips and sailing bustle. More walks to the beach and around the village. You stay in a graceful self-contained apartment in the cricket pavilion wing with private sitting room and use of the walled garden (breakfast is in the fridge). Your hosts are gracious and energetic people.

Price	£80. Singles from £40.
Rooms	1 twin/double & sitting room with sofabed & kitchenette.
Meals	Continental breakfast. Pub 5-minute walk.
Closed	Rarely.
Directions	A27 at Chichester onto A286 for the Witterings. At Birdham, right at garage onto B2179; 500 yds, right to Itchenor. Driveway on left past church, signed.

Susie Green
Itchenor Park House,
Itchenor,
Chichester,
Sussex PO20 7DN
Tel 01243 512221
Mobile 07718 902768
Email susie.green@lineone.net

Sussex

Crede Farmhouse

Walk through the characterful village of Bosham – for church, quay, history and boats. Lesley is vivacious and kind, Peter helps cook delectable Aga breakfasts. This flint house (1810) is fresh, peaceful and beautifully maintained: Farrow & Ball paints, elegant pictures, rococo-esque mirrors and lights. One bedroom is primrose, floral and white, with green views; the smaller double has a wrought-iron bed. Crackling fires in winter, an outdoor pool in summer, Chichester Theatre up the road and Portsmouth a 30-minute drive. A delightful place for harbour walks and Downland treks.
Minimum stay two nights in summer.

Price	From £80. Singles from £60.
Rooms	2: 1 double; 1 small double with separate bath.
Meals	Pubs/restaurants 5-minute walk.
Closed	Christmas.
Directions	From Chichester, A259 west for Bosham; through Fishbourne, past garden centre, left into Walton Lane. After sharp bend, right into Crede Lane; 200 yds to end of lane. On left, with white garage.

Mrs Lesley Hankey
Crede Farmhouse,
Crede Lane,
Bosham,
Sussex PO18 8NX
Tel 01243 574929
Email lesley@credefarmhouse.fsnet.co.uk

Sussex

The Well House

A delightful hideaway – your Normandy-styled annexe to a listed Georgian house leads into its own large garden and has a private entrance. In the 17th century it was a humble shelter but the thatch and beams are immaculate now. Marilyn's style reflects her warm personality – you have white bedding on a big brass bed, a rich rug on dark boards, small armchairs and an open stove, a hat stand for clothes and a fine chest of drawers. It's luxurious but cosy, with a shower room to match. An unspoilt beach, with dunes, is a seven-minute walk. Perfect. *Minimum stay two nights. Arrivals between 12 noon and 6pm.*

Sussex

Castle Cottage

However beautiful the countryside and the walks, you will be most enchanted by what your hosts have achieved. In birdsong woodland is a small house with a separate weather-boarded family barn and a cobbled conservatory. The barn's A-frame roof draws in the light and the front views, and there are perfect decorative touches: Persian carpets, dashing blue paints, a wrought-iron staircase, sculptures, handmade paper, superb lighting. The double in the house has the same magic. But the treehouse upstages all, high in a giant chestnut, with vast bed, veranda, sauna and shower room. Beautifully built... ineffable.

Price	From £85.
Rooms	1 double.
Meals	Pub/restaurants 2-10 minute walk.
Closed	Rarely.
Directions	A259 Littlehampton & Bognor. Left towards sea signed Climping Street & Beach. House 4th on right with private lay-by opposite.

Price	£110-£125.
Rooms	3: 1 double with separate bath/shower. Barn: 1 family suite. Treehouse: 1 double.
Meals	Pubs/restaurants 1.5 miles.
Closed	Rarely.
Directions	From Fittleworth, south on B2138. Right onto Coates Lane; 1 mile, then right onto 'private drive'. Right at castle, right again & immed. left.

Marilyn Craine
The Well House,
Climping Street, Climping,
Littlehampton, Sussex BN17 5RQ

Tel	01903 713314
Mobile	07866 060577
Email	info@baronshall.co.uk
Web	www.baronshall.co.uk

Alison Wyatt
Castle Cottage,
Coates Castle, Fittleworth,
Sussex RH20 1EU

Tel	01798 865001
Fax	01798 865032
Email	alison@castlecottage.info
Web	www.castlecottage.info

Entry 475   Map 4

Entry 476   Map 4

Sussex

Fitzlea Farmhouse

A wooded track leads to the beautiful, mellow, 17th-century farmhouse with tall chimneys and a cluster of overgrown outbuildings. Wood-panelled walls and ancient oak beams, a vast open fireplace, mullioned windows and deep sofas create an atmosphere of relaxed country-house charm. Maggie welcomes you to a delicious breakfast in her Aga-warm farmhouse kitchen; in spring, the scent of bluebells wafts through open doors. A winding staircase leads to comfortable timbered bedrooms which overlook fields, rolling lawns and woodland where you can stroll in peace. Heavenly. *Children by arrangement.*

Price	£50–£85. Singles by arrangement.
Rooms	3: 1 family room; 1 double, 1 twin, sharing bath.
Meals	Packed lunch available. Pubs/restaurants 2 miles.
Closed	Rarely.
Directions	Directions on booking.

Maggie Paterson
Fitzlea Farmhouse,
Selham,
Petworth,
Sussex GU28 0PS
Tel   01798 861429

Entry 477   Map 4

Sussex

Beauchamp Cottage

In the market town of Petworth, a tucked-away and very private retreat for two. The owners, who live nearby, have sensitively restored the little two-storey cottage with its brewery connections. Up the pine stair, under open rafters, is a light and airy sitting room with wooden floors and sofabed; downstairs, carved antique beds and fine linen, a super shower room and sweet garden views. Breakfast waits for you in the little kitchen with microwave and fridge; enjoy it on the patio. Petworth House (paintings, history, summer concerts in the park) is a mere stroll. *Off-street parking. Min. stay two nights preferred.*

Price	£85–£95.
Rooms	Cottage: 1 twin/double, sitting room & kitchen area.
Meals	Pubs/restaurants within 1.25 miles.
Closed	Christmas.
Directions	In Petworth, follow one-way system to end of East St. Straight onto Middle St; at T-junc. with High St, driveway opposite, thro' arch.

Dr David Parsons
Beauchamp Cottage,
c/o Fairfield House, High Street,
Petworth, Sussex GU28 0AU
Tel   01798 345110
Fax   01798 345110
Email beauchampcottage@btinternet.com

Entry 478   Map 4

Sussex

Highbridge Mill

Many humorous touches here – a 'No Diving' mat by the bath, a life-size family of pigs by the door – courtesy of Sue and Joffy, your mildly eccentric, extremely charming hosts. The old part of the house – attractive from the rear – was a flour mill (1810-1930) and there's a rusted wheel to prove it; the interiors are joyfully new. A red-Aga kitchen with wrought-iron chandelier, a ruby sitting room with an open fire, bedrooms with quilts and happy colours. Sue has cooked at various posh places and spoils you rotten; breakfast honey comes from the village via their own woodland bees. Huge fun.

Price	£80. Singles £50.
Rooms	2: 1 twin/double; 1 double with separate bath/shower.
Meals	Dinner, 3 courses, £40. Pubs within 10-minute drive.
Closed	1 December-1 April.
Directions	A23, then A272 for Haywards Heath. Pass Ansty Cross pub, downhill towards Cuckfield Rd. Drive to house on right opposite the r'bout sign.

	Sue Clarke
	Highbridge Mill,
	Cuckfield Road, Ansty,
	Sussex RH17 5AE
Tel	01444 450881
Mobile	07850 271606
Web	www.highbridgemill.com

Entry 479   Map 4

Sussex

Little Lywood

On the ground floor you feel nicely private; the bathroom is a couple of steps from your door. The softly-lit, unfussy room, which overlooks the drive and is well back from the road, has a pine dressing table, rattan chairs, matching curtains and duvet covers, and fresh flowers. You breakfast in the old part of this Elizabethan forester's cottage; a super dining room with small mullioned windows and ancient timbers – Jeannie and Nick will leave you to come and go as you please. Within easy reach of the Ashdown forest and Sussex's great gardens; the one here is lovely, too.

Price	£65. Singles £45.
Rooms	1 double with separate bath.
Meals	Pubs 2.5 miles.
Closed	Rarely.
Directions	From Haywards Heath, B2028 to Lindfield. House on left, 1.5 miles after passing church at north end of Lindfield.

	Jeannie & Nick Leadsom
	Little Lywood,
	Ardingly Road,
	Lindfield,
	Sussex RH16 2QX
Tel	01444 892571
Email	nick@nleadsom.plus.com

Entry 480   Map 4

Sussex

The Grange

There's a time-worn feel to this dreamy home. Books are stuffed into shelves, walls are decorated with years of paintings and wooden African hippos guard the stairs. A mainly Queen Anne rectory in a secluded spot beside the church, the house is beautifully old-fashioned with oak stairs, antique swords, an ancient tapestry and your own comfortable sitting room. The bedroom is light and traditional with an iron bedstead and lovely views over the paddock; a single room is next door. Bunny will look after you perfectly and there's wonderful walking in Pooh Bear country.

Price	From £70. Singles £40.
Rooms	1 double & sitting room.
Meals	Pubs 200 yds.
Closed	Occasionally.
Directions	In the centre of Hartfield, take road (Church Street) between The Haywagon & The Anchor pubs. Pass church on left; house is beyond church, on left.

Bunny & James Murray Willis
The Grange,
Hartfield,
Sussex TN7 4AG
Tel   01892 770259
Email   bunnymw@hotmail.co.uk

Sussex

Old Whyly

Rich colours, lush fabrics, deep sofas, fine oils – there's an effortless elegance to this manor house, once home to one of King Charles's Cavaliers. Bedrooms are atmospheric, one in French style, and the treats continue outside to a beautiful flower garden annually replenished with 5,000 tulips, a lake and orchard, a stunning swimming pool and new tennis court – fabulous. Dine under the pergola in summer; food is a passion and Sarah's menus are adventurous with a modern slant. Glyndebourne is close so make a party of it and take a divine 'pink' hamper with blankets or a table and chairs included.

Price	£90–£130. Singles by arrangement.
Rooms	3: 2 twins/doubles; 1 twin/double with separate bath.
Meals	Dinner, 3 courses, £30. Hampers £35. Pub/restaurant 1 mile.
Closed	Rarely.
Directions	0.5 miles past Halland on A22, south from Uckfield; 1st left off Shaw r'bout towards E. Hoathly; on for 0.5 miles. Drive on left with postbox; central gravel drive.

Sarah Burgoyne
Old Whyly,
East Hoathly,
Sussex BN8 6EL
Tel   01825 840216
Fax   01825 840738
Email   stay@oldwhyly.co.uk
Web   www.oldwhyly.co.uk

Sussex

Hailsham Grange

Come for elegance and ease. Noel welcomes you into his lovely Queen 'Mary Anne' home (1701-1705) – set back from the road in a town where they still hold two cattle markets a week. No standing on ceremony here, despite the décor: classic English touched with chinoiserie in perfect keeping with the house. Busts on pillars, swathes of delicious chintz, books galore and bedrooms a treat: a sunny double and a romantic four-poster. Summery breakfasts are served on the flagged terrace, marmalades and jams on a silver salver. The town garden, with its box parterre and bank of cherry trees, is an equal joy.

Sussex

Riverdale House

An acre of wild woodland and bewitching views over the Cuckmere valley – you can see why the Menzies family came here when they left London. The house, a stroll from the pretty village of Alfriston, is one of a pair of Victorian semis built for two brothers. Transformed inside, it's a fresh, stylish marriage of contemporary and period and is supremely comfortable. Musicians will enjoy the baby grand (Glyndebourne is eight miles) and there are books, toys and DVDs galore – even bikes with baby seats. Parents will seize upon the 'babysitting and lie-in' deal with gratitude. *Minimum stay two nights Easter-Oct.*

Travel Club Offer: see page 392 for details.

Price	£95-£120. Singles from £60.
Rooms	4: 1 double, 1 four-poster. Coach house: 1 double, 1 twin/double.
Meals	Pub/restaurants 300 yds.
Closed	Rarely.
Directions	From Hailsham High St, left into Vicarage Rd. House 200 yds on left. Park in coach yard.

Price	£80-£120. Family service £60.
Rooms	4: 2 doubles, 1 twin/double, 1 family suite.
Meals	Packed lunch £4.50. Pub/restaurant 0.25 miles.
Closed	24-26 December.
Directions	From A27 between Lewes & Polegate, right at r'bout signed Alfriston & Drusillas Park. Thro' village, past Deans Place Hotel. On right after 3rd 40mph sign.

	Mr Noel Thompson
	Hailsham Grange,
	Hailsham,
	Sussex BN27 1BL
Tel	01323 844248
Email	noel@hgrange.co.uk
Web	www.hailshamgrange.co.uk

	Rory & Pippa Menzies
	Riverdale House,
	Seaford Road, Alfriston,
	Sussex BN26 5TR
Tel	01323 871038
Email	info@riverdalehouse.co.uk
Web	www.riverdalehouse.co.uk

Entry 483   Map 5

Entry 484   Map 5

Sussex

Ocklynge Manor

On the top of a hill overlooking Eastbourne, a charming 18th-century house. Once a commandery for the Knights of St John of Jerusalem, it was later home of children's illustrator Mabel Lucie Attwell. Now it is the home of Wendy, talented maker of breads, cakes and jams, immaculate seamstress and delightful hostess. Creamy carpeted bedrooms create a mood of relaxed indulgence and are full of thoughtful touches: dressing gowns, DVDs, your own fridge. The day starts with a superb breakfast overlooking the lovely walled garden, and ends in a pretty chintz sitting room just for guests.

Price	£70-£80. Singles from £45.
Rooms	3: 1 twin, 1 family suite for 3; 1 double with separate shower.
Meals	Pub 5-minute walk.
Closed	Rarely.
Directions	From Eastbourne General Hospital, over r'bout on A2021. 1st right to Kings Ave; house at top.

Wendy Dugdill
Ocklynge Manor,
Mill Road, Eastbourne,
Sussex BN21 2PG
Tel   01323 734121
Mobile   07979 627172
Email   ocklyngemanor@hotmail.com
Web   www.ocklyngemanor.co.uk

Entry 485   Map 5

Sussex

Globe Place

A listed 17th-century house beside the church in a tiny village, ten minutes from Glyndebourne. Alison – a former chef to the Beatles – is a great cook and can provide you with a delicious and generous hamper, and tables and chairs too. Willie is a former rackets champion who gives tennis coaching; there's a court in the large, pretty garden, and a pool. Relax by the inglenook fire in the drawing room after a walk on the Cuckoo Trail or the South Downs, then settle down to a great supper – local fish, maybe, with home-grown vegetables. An easy-going, fun and informal household. *Children over 12 welcome.*

Price	£80. Singles £45.
Rooms	4: 2 doubles, 2 singles sharing baths (singles for same party).
Meals	Dinner £25. BYO. Hamper £30-£32.50. Pub 10-minute drive.
Closed	Christmas.
Directions	From Boship r'bout on A22, A267. 1st right to Horsebridge & immed. left to Hellingly. Follow road past the church, left into Mill Lane. House next to church. Parking at top of drive.

Alison & Willie Boone
Globe Place,
Hellingly,
Sussex BN27 4EY
Tel   01323 844276
Mobile   07870 957608
Email   aliboone@globeplace.plus.com

Entry 486   Map 5

Sussex

Fox Hole Farm

Whitewashed, carpeted and beamed, a wood-burner twinkling in its inglenook, the pretty tile-hung farmhouse is as cosy as can be. Come for stacks of woody character, a rolling hillside real farm setting and lovely hosts whose kindness goes beyond the call of duty. There are woodpeckers in the glorious cottage garden, nightingales in the wood and low-beamed bedrooms with latch cupboards, mellow boards and latticed windows that reveal sheep and hill views. Enjoy a really lovely breakfast (excellent bacon, eggs straight from the hens) after which you can set off for a two-mile woodland walk to Battle.

Price	From £62. Singles from £45.
Rooms	3: 2 doubles, 1 triple.
Meals	Restaurant 1.5 miles.
Closed	24 December-1 February.
Directions	From Battle on A271, 1st right on B2096. After 0.75 miles, right into drive.

Paul & Pauline Collins
Fox Hole Farm,
Kane Hythe Road, Battle,
Sussex TN33 9QU

Tel	01424 772053
Fax	01424 772053
Email	foxholefarm@kanehythe.orangehome.co.uk

Entry 487   Map 5

Sussex

Wellington House

A stroll away from the gardens of Great Dixter is a warm, comfortable, charming B&B. Behind the Victorian red-brick façade the Brogdens have worked an informal magic, giving guests a cosy sitting room and two big peaceful bedrooms above. These are creamy-walled and carpeted, with comfy mattresses, antique bed linen, pristine shower rooms and good toiletries. Fanny is passionate about food, bakes her own bread, grows her own peaches – a treat; Vivian is a charmer. Visit Bodiam by river boat, comb Camber Sands, explore Rye, revel in Dixter… and return to tea and homemade cakes in the garden.

Travel Club Offer: see page 392 for details.

Price	From £75. Singles £50.
Rooms	2 doubles.
Meals	Supper, 3 courses, from £18 (min. 4). Pubs within 2 miles.
Closed	Christmas & New Year.
Directions	Follow brown tourist signs in Northiam village for Great Dixter House & Gardens to Dixter Rd. House at main road end, next to opticians.

Fanny & Vivian Brogden
Wellington House,
Dixter Road, Northiam, Rye,
Sussex TN31 6LB

Tel	01797 253449
Mobile	07989 928236
Email	fanny@frances14.freeserve.co.uk

Entry 488   Map 5

Sussex

Boonshill Farm

A glorious farmhouse down a cinder track with a duck pond, brick and weatherboard outbuildings, flouncing flower beds and charming Lisette, a garden designer from London who has achieved something different. Large bedrooms have original wide wood flooring, old garden gates for headboards, reclaimed windows as beautiful mirrors, comfortable chairs, pale colours and views across green fields. Outside are acres of lawns, a wildflower garden, chickens and handsome Berkshire pigs; breakfast here is special. You're ten minutes from the cobbled streets of Rye with its smart shops, and the walking's great, too.

Price	£80. Singles £50. Child £10.
Rooms	2: 1 double, 1 twin. Extra child bed.
Meals	Pub 1 mile.
Closed	Rarely.
Directions	Grove Lane opposite The Bell in Iden. Down lane for 1 mile, then left immediately before oast house, down track. Boonshill is at end of track, on left, white gate.

Lisette Pleasance
Boonshill Farm,
Grove Lane, Iden, Rye,
Sussex TN31 7QA
Tel   01797 280533
Mobile   07706 054787
Email   boonshillfarm@yahoo.co.uk
Web   www.boonshillfarm.co.uk

Entry 489   Map 5

Sussex

Willow Tree House

A 500-yard trot from the centre, this is excellent town B&B. Simon and Wendy have overhauled a fine Georgian house and give you smart, spacious bedrooms — here and there an exposed brick wall or a rustic beam — with calm, neutral colours, comfy beds and snazzily tiled shower rooms. The breakfast room is like a small hotel with separate tables smartly dressed; there are homegrown tomatoes in the summer, homemade jams and all else is locally sourced. Free on-site parking, an honesty bar and a quiet garden at the back are welcome extras. *Minimum stay two nights bank holidays & Rye Fawkes Festival.*

Price	£80–£120. Singles £70–£85.
Rooms	6: 5 doubles, 1 twin. (Extra child beds available.)
Meals	Pubs/restaurants 500 yds.
Closed	Rarely.
Directions	500 yds from town centre; 1.5 miles from Rye Harbour. On-site parking.

Simon Crumpler
Willow Tree House,
113 Winchelsea Road, Rye,
Sussex TN31 7EL
Tel   01797 227820
Email   info@willow-tree-house.com
Web   www.willow-tree-house.com

Entry 490   Map 5

Warwickshire

Hardingwood House

Close to Stratford and with a theatrical, Tudor feel. Denise, warm and delightful, spoils guests with big bedrooms, dressing rooms, good linen and deep gold-tapped baths. There are books, flowers, antique clocks and plush sofas; tapestry and velvet curtains frame leaded windows; dark timbers and reds and pinks abound. The 1737 barn is immaculate inside and out: the kitchen gives onto a stunning patio, while bedrooms have views to garden or fields. Much rural charm, yet close to Birmingham – and there's a self-catering cottage for two if you like your independence. *Advance booking essential.*

Price	£75. Singles £50.
Rooms	3: 1 double, 2 twins.
Meals	Pub 1 mile.
Closed	Rarely.
Directions	M6 junc. 4; A446 for Lichfield. Into right lane & 1st exit towards Coleshill. From High St, turn into Maxstoke Lane. After 4 miles, right. 1st drive on left.

Mrs Denise Owen
Hardingwood House,
Hardingwood Lane,
Fillongley, Coventry,
Warwickshire CV7 8EL

Tel	01676 542579
Fax	01676 541336
Email	denise@hardingwoodhouse.fsnet.co.uk

Entry 491   Map 8

Warwickshire

Park Farm House

Fronted by a circular drive, the warm red-brick farmhouse is listed and old – it dates from 1655. Linda is friendly and welcoming, a genuine B&B pro, giving you an immaculate guest sitting room filled with pretty family pieces. The bedrooms sport comfortable mattresses, mahogany or brass beds, blankets on request, bathrobes, flowers, magazines, DVDs. A haven of rest from the motorway (morning hum only) this is in the heart of a working farm yet hugely convenient for Birmingham, Warwick, Stratford, Coventry. You may get their own beef at dinner and the vegetables are home-grown.

Price	£75. Singles from £45.
Rooms	3: 2 doubles, 1 twin.
Meals	Dinner, 3 courses, from £25. Supper £18. Pub/restaurant 1.5 miles.
Closed	Rarely.
Directions	M6 & M69 exit 2; B4065 through Ansty to Shilton; left at lights then next left. Over small m'way bridge and right to Barnacle; through village. Left at brick wall signed Spring Road. House at end.

Linda Grindal
Park Farm House,
Barnacle, Shilton,
Coventry,
Warwickshire CV7 9LG

Tel	0247 6612628
Fax	0247 6616010
Web	www.parkfarmguesthouse.co.uk

Entry 492   Map 8

Warwickshire

Mows Hill Farm

From the flagstoned kitchen, peep through the stable door at the cattle munching in their stalls – perfect for nature lovers! The place has been in the family for generations and the late-Victorian farmhouse has a warm, uplifting feel. Lynda and Edward have completely redecorated: the sitting and dining rooms are elegant and comfortable, the family room (with shower) is a symphony of lavender and white, the double room dramatic cream and navy. You get a proper farmhouse breakfast in the new, warm conservatory – homemade bread and jams, home-reared bacon, just-laid eggs – and field views reach out from every window.

Price	£80. Singles from £50.
Rooms	2: 1 family room; 1 double with separate bath.
Meals	Pub/restaurant 3 miles.
Closed	Rarely.
Directions	A3400 Hockley Heath; B4101 (Spring Lane); left into Umberslade Rd. At 2nd triangle, keep right & onto Mows Hill Rd; 0.25 miles on right.

Mrs Lynda Muntz
Mows Hill Farm, Mows Hill Road,
Kemps Green, Tanworth in Arden,
Warwickshire B94 5PP

Tel	01564 784312
Mobile	07919 542501
Email	mowshill@farmline.com
Web	www.b-and-bmowshill.co.uk

Entry 493   Map 8

Warwickshire

Salford Farm House

Beautiful within, handsome without. Thanks to subtle colours, oak beams and lovely old pieces, Jane has achieved a seductive combination of comfort and style. A flagstoned hallway and an old rocking horse, ticking clocks, beeswax, fresh flowers: this house is well-loved. Jane was a ballet dancer, Richard has green fingers and runs a fruit farm nearby – you may expect meat and game from the Ragley Estate and delicious fruits in season. Bedrooms have a soft, warm elegance and flat-screen TVs, bathrooms are spotless and welcoming, views are to garden or fields. Wholly delightful.

Price	£85. Singles £52.50.
Rooms	2 twins/doubles.
Meals	Dinner £25.
Closed	Rarely.
Directions	A46 from Evesham or Stratford; exit for Salford Priors. On entering village, right opp. church, for Dunnington. House on right, approx. 1 mile on, after 2nd sign on right for Dunnington.

Jane & Richard Beach
Salford Farm House,
Salford Priors, Evesham,
Warwickshire WR11 8XN

Tel	01386 870000
Email	salfordfarmhouse@aol.com
Web	www.salfordfarmhouse.co.uk

Entry 494   Map 8

Warwickshire

Cross o' th' Hill Farm

Stratford in 12 minutes on foot, down a footpath across a field: from the veranda you can see the church where Shakespeare is buried. There's been a farm on this rural spot since before Shakespeare's time but part of the house is Victorian. Built around 1860, it's full of light, with wall-to-ceiling sash windows, glass panelling in the roof, large uncluttered bedrooms and smart, newly decorated bathrooms. The garden, full of trees and birds, dates from the same period – there's even a sunken croquet lawn. Decima grew up here; she and David are gentle hosts, and passionate about art and architecture.

Ethical Collection: Food. See page 400 for details.

Price	£80-£83. Singles £60-£63.
Rooms	3: 2 doubles;
	1 double with separate bath.
Meals	Pubs/restaurants 20-minute walk.
Closed	20 December-February.
Directions	From Stratford south on A3400 for
	0.5 miles, 2nd right on B4632 for
	Broadway Rd for 500 yds. 2nd drive
	on right for farm.

Decima Noble
Cross o' th' Hill Farm,
Broadway Road, Stratford-upon-Avon,
Warwickshire CV37 8HP
Tel	01789 204738
Mobile	07973 971067
Email	decimanoble@hotmail.com
Web	www.crossothhillfarm.com

Entry 495 Map 8

Warwickshire

Drybank Farm

Behind the high, worn, red-brick facia of the farmhouse lies a cool, impressive hall, where Angela – beautifully organised and helpful – welcomes you. Honey coloured beams, lush fabrics and jugs of fresh flowers make for a perfectly serene feel, and the countrified bedrooms and bathrooms are superb. If it's action you're after, your host will flawlessly arrange shooting, quad biking, horse riding – whatever you wish. Family horses Roger and Jack will be waiting for you at the end of the day, as will a deep bath, French soaps, fluffy dressing gowns ('his' and 'hers') and a feather duvet. Wonderful!

Price	From £76. Singles £55.
Rooms	3: 1 double, 1 twin/double, 1 suite.
Meals	Packed lunch from £9.
	Pub 0.5 miles.
Closed	Christmas.
Directions	A422 from Stratford to Ettington;
	thro' village, past Chequers pub on
	left. Right at x-roads; house on left
	over brow of hill.

Angela Winter
Drybank Farm, Fosseway,
Ettington, Stratford-upon-Avon,
Warwickshire CV37 7PD
Tel	01789 740476
Mobile	07966 332299
Email	drybank@btinternet.com
Web	www.drybank.co.uk

Entry 496 Map 8

Warwickshire

Blackwell Grange

Come for sheep-dotted views from mullioned windows and profound peace. The mellow stone farmhouse is homely in an old-fashioned way; there are flagstones, beams, floorboards that creak, and a guest sitting room stuffed with books, magazines, old sofas and an open fire. The best bedroom is in the house, cosy with afternoon sun, well-loved furniture and touches of chintz; the annexe room is on the ground floor and suitable for wheelchair users. Breakfast on eggs from the bantams (Lavender Perkin) who strut the summer lawns in the charming garden; take back some home-grown lamb for the freezer.

Price	From £75-£80. Singles from £45.
Rooms	3: 2 twins/doubles, 1 single.
Meals	Pubs 1-1.5 miles.
Closed	Rarely.
Directions	From Stratford-upon-Avon, A3400 for Oxford. After 5 miles, right by church in Newbold on Stour & follow signs to Blackwell. Fork right on entering Blackwell. Entrance beyond thatched barn.

	Liz Vernon Miller
	Blackwell Grange,
	Blackwell, Shipston-on-Stour,
	Warwickshire CV36 4PF
Tel	01608 682357
Fax	01608 682856
Email	sawdays@blackwellgrange.co.uk
Web	www.blackwellgrange.co.uk

Entry 497   Map 8

Warwickshire

The Old Manor House

Jane, a Cordon Bleu cook, runs her 16th- and 17th-century house with huge energy and efficiency. The A-shaped double in the main part of the house has ancient beams, oak furniture and a lovely bathroom; a newly decorated twin and a single in the other wing are private and self-contained, with a large and elegant drawing and dining room for all visitors to share. Breakfasts are carefully prepared here and the river Stour flows through the beautiful landscaped garden. In warm weather enjoy a drink on the terrace surrounded by old, scented roses; dinner will be excellent and locally sourced. *Children over seven welcome.*

Price	From £85-£90. Singles from £45.
Rooms	3: 1 double with separate bath; 1 twin, 1 single sharing bath (2nd room let to same party only).
Meals	Dinner from £25. Restaurants nearby.
Closed	Rarely.
Directions	From Stratford, A422 for Banbury. After 4 miles, right at r'bout onto A429 for Halford. There, 1st right. House with black & white timbers straight ahead after 150 yds.

	Jane Pusey
	The Old Manor House,
	Halford, Shipston-on-Stour,
	Warwickshire CV36 5BT
Tel	01789 740264
Mobile	07786 467916
Email	info@oldmanor-halford.fsnet.co.uk
Web	www.oldmanor-halford.co.uk

Entry 498   Map 8

Warwickshire

Oxbourne House

Hard to believe the house is new, with its beamed ceilings, fireplaces and antiques. Bedrooms are fresh, crisp, cosy and cared for, the family room with an 'in the attic' feel; lighting is soft, beds excellent, bath and shower rooms attractive and warm, and views far-reaching. In the garden are tennis, sculpture and Graeme's rambler bedecked pergola. Wake to birdsong and fresh eggs from village ducks and hens; on peaceful summer nights, watch the dipping sun. Posy and Graeme are hugely likeable and welcoming and the village pub is just down the road. A most comforting place to stay. *Dogs by arrangement.*

Travel Club Offer: see page 392 for details.

Price	£60-£80. Singles from £45.
Rooms	3: 1 double, 1 family room for 3; 1 twin/double with separate bath.
Meals	Dinner from £20. Pub 2-minute walk.
Closed	Rarely.
Directions	A422 from Stratford-upon-Avon for Banbury. After 8 miles, right to Oxhill. Last house on right on Whatcote Road.

Graeme & Posy McDonald
Oxbourne House,
Oxhill, Warwick,
Warwickshire CV35 0RA
Tel	01295 688202
Mobile	07753 661353
Email	graememcdonald@msn.com
Web	www.oxbournehouse.co.uk

Entry 499   Map 8

Warwickshire

Shrewley Pools Farm

A charming, eccentric home and fabulous for families, with space to play and animals to see: sheep, bantams and pigs. A fragrant, romantic garden, too, and a fascinating house (1640), all low ceilings, aged floors and steep stairs. Timbered passages lead to large, pretty, sunny bedrooms (all with electric blankets) with leaded windows and polished wooden floors and a family room with everything needed for a baby. In a farmhouse dining room Cathy serves sausages, bacon, pork, game and lamb from the farm, can do gluten-free breakfasts and is happy with teas for children. Buy a day ticket and fish in the lake.

Travel Club Offer: see page 392 for details.

Price	From £55. Singles from £40.
Rooms	2: 1 family room (& cot), 1 twin.
Meals	Packed lunch £4. Child's high tea £4. Pub/restaurant 1.5 miles.
Closed	Christmas.
Directions	From M40 junc. 15, A46 for Coventry. Left onto A4177. 4.5 miles to Five Ways r'bout. 1st left, on for 0.75 miles; signed, opp. Farm Gate Poultry: track on left.

Cathy Dodd
Shrewley Pools Farm,
Five Ways Road, Haseley, Warwick,
Warwickshire CV35 7HB
Tel	01926 484315
Mobile	07818 280681
Email	cathydodd@hotmail.co.uk
Web	www.shrewleypoolsfarm.co.uk

Entry 500   Map 8

Warwickshire

Woolscott House

Scrunch across gravel to the tall, prosperous, well-kept Georgian house – a showcase for Juliet, interior designer. Warm and enthusiastic, she looks after dogs, guests, garden with equal talent. Bedrooms up steep stairs are not huge but madly comfortable, all rich textiles and subtle colours, family pieces and interesting pictures. Bed linen is divine, views are rural (the odd sheep), one bath is befriended by Venetian glass fish, another is reached down a flight of well-clad stairs. There are bags of sofas, books, magazines, a chatty parrot. In summer, dip in the pool or wave a tennis racquet. You'll love it.

Price	£80. Singles £60.
Rooms	2: 1 double, 1 twin each with separate bath.
Meals	Pub/restaurant 0.5 miles.
Closed	Christmas.
Directions	A426 Rugby-Dunchurch; A45 towards Daventry. After 1 mile, right to Grandborough. 1.25 miles, then round sharp right-hand bend; house 3rd on left.

	Juliet Eckersley Woolscott House, Woolscott, Rugby, Warwickshire CV23 8DB
Tel	01788 522154
Email	cjpdce@inweb.co.uk

Entry 501   Map 8

Warwickshire

Marston House

A generous feel pervades this lovely family home; Kim's big friendly kitchen is the hub of the house. She and John are easy-going and kind and there's no standing on ceremony. Feel welcomed with tea on arrival, delicious homemade breakfasts, oodles of interesting facts about what to do in the area. The house is big and sunny; old rugs cover parquet floors, soft sofas tumble with cushions and sash windows look onto the smart garden packed with interesting plants and birds. Bedrooms are roomy, traditional and supremely comfortable. A special place with a big heart and great walks straight from the house.

Ethical Collection: Community; Food. See page 400 for details.

Travel Club Offer: see page 392 for details.

Price	£85-£100. Singles from £60.
Rooms	3: 1 double, 1 twin/double, each with separate bath; 1 twin/double with separate shower.
Meals	Kitchen supper £25. Dinner £30 (min. 4). Pub 5-minute walk.
Closed	Rarely.
Directions	M40 exit 11. From Banbury, A361 north for 7 miles; at Byfield village sign, left into Twistle Lane; on to Priors Marston; 5th house on left with cattle grid, after S-bend (3 miles from A361).

	Kim & John Mahon Marston House, Byfield Road, Priors Marston, Southam Warwickshire CV47 7RP
Tel	01327 260297
Fax	08703 835445
Email	kim@mahonand.co.uk
Web	www.ivabestbandb.co.uk

Entry 502   Map 8

Wiltshire

Oaklands

It was the first house in Warminster to have a bathroom. The bathrooms have multiplied since and the interiors have had a recent (delightful) makeover; easy to see why this lovely spacious 1880s house has been in the family forever. Andrew, retired headmaster, and Carolyn, quietly charming, are used to catering for large numbers and serve delicious breakfasts in an elegant room. Bedrooms, most comforting and welcoming, overlook churchyard and trees; fresh fabrics, soft colours, cosy bathroom, family antiques. Deep comfort, lovely people, a big garden for summer and Bath not too far away.

Price	£65–£85. Singles from £55.
Rooms	2: 1 double, 1 twin/double (rooms can interconnect).
Meals	Occasional dinner (min. 4). Pub/restaurant 3 miles.
Closed	Christmas & rarely.
Directions	From Warminster centre direction Salisbury. On right, opp. end of St John's churchyard.

Carolyn & Andrew Lewis
Oaklands,
88 Boreham Road,
Warminster,
Wiltshire BA12 9JW

Tel 01985 215532
Mobile 07850 158302
Email apl1944@yahoo.co.uk

Entry 503 Map 3

Wiltshire

The Duck Yard

Independence with your own terrace, your own entrance and your own sitting room. Peaceful too, at the end of the lane, with a colourful cottage garden, a summerhouse and roaming bantams. Unflappable Harriet makes wedding cakes, looks after guests and cheerfully rustles up fine meals at short notice; breakfasts promise delicious homemade bread. Your carpeted bedroom and aquamarine bathroom are tucked under the eaves; below is a sitting room cosy with wood-burner, books and old squashy sofas, leading to a terrace. Good for walkers – maps are supplied and you may even borrow a dog.

Price	£70. Singles £50.
Rooms	1 twin/double & sitting room.
Meals	Dinner, 3 courses, £25. Packed lunch £7. Pub 2 miles.
Closed	Christmas & New Year.
Directions	A303 to Wylye, then for Dinton. After 4 miles left at x-roads, for Wilton & Salisbury. On for 1 mile, down hill, round sharp right bend, signed Sandhills Rd. 1st low red brick building on left. Park in space on left.

Harriet & Peter Combes
The Duck Yard,
Sandhills Road, Dinton, Salisbury,
Wiltshire SP3 5ER

Tel 01722 716495
Mobile 07729 777436
Fax 01722 716163
Email harriet.combes@googlemail.com

Entry 504 Map 3

Wiltshire

Baverstock Manor

Instantly gracious – the 15th-century honey stone that lights up in sunlight, the Jacobean wing, the climbing roses, the solidity… Inside it is creaky, friendly, artistic, full of well-worn antiques and lovely faded rugs. There are posies of primroses and large bowls of roses, deep recesses guarding porcelain, walls hung with Indian rugs and eclectic art, baskets brimful of bathroom oils. The spacious, stylish double comes in creams and greens, its window seat overlooking the enchanting garden, the family room is more vibrant, with a cute little single room attached. A country-house delight. *Children over eight welcome.*

Price	£80. Singles £40.
Rooms	3: 1 double with separate bath; 1 twin/double, 1 single sharing bath.
Meals	Dinner, £25. Packed lunch £6. Pubs within 4 miles.
Closed	December–January.
Directions	From Salisbury, A36 to Wilton, then A30 (to Shaftesbury). After 3 miles, in Barford St Martin, right onto B3089; after 2 miles, right to Baverstock; after 0.75 miles stone gateway on right, on S-bend.

	Tim & Belinda Hextall
	Baverstock Manor,
	Dinton, Salisbury,
	Wiltshire SP3 5EN
Tel	01722 716206
Mobile	07818 000589
Fax	01722 716510
Email	bhextall@googlemail.com

Entry 505   Map 3

Wiltshire

Little Langford Farmhouse

A rare treat to have your milk fresh from the cow – the Helyers have pedigree cattle. The bedrooms of this rather grand Victorian-gothic farmhouse are large and pretty with period furniture and crisp linen; there are impressive countryside views, a baby grand and a billiard room. Everything is elegant and polished yet cosy, and terrace doors are thrown open for delicious al fresco breakfasts in summer. The farm, part of which is an SSSI, is treasured for its glorious walks, wild flowers and butterflies, and the Helyers are immensely welcoming. *Minimum stay two nights at weekends. Children by arrangement.*

Price	£72–£77. Singles £55–£65.
Rooms	3: 1 double, 1 twin/double; 1 twin with separate shower.
Meals	Pub/restaurant 1.75 miles.
Closed	Christmas & New Year.
Directions	Exit A303 at A36 junc; follow signs for Salisbury. 2 miles; right for The Langfords. In Steeple L., right for Hanging L. At T-junc. opp. village hall, left for Little Langford. House 0.75 miles on left.

	Patricia Helyer
	Little Langford Farmhouse,
	Little Langford, Salisbury,
	Wiltshire SP3 4NP
Tel	01722 790205
Fax	01722 790086
Email	bandb@littlelangford.co.uk
Web	www.littlelangford.co.uk

Entry 506   Map 3

Wiltshire

Dowtys

A stunning setting and a recently converted farmhouse up a long drive, with fabulous views over the Nadder valley. Peaceful bedrooms are generously sized, very private – one ground-floor bedroom has its own garden room – and have rafters and beams, antiques, smart bathrooms, excellent beds. The guest sitting room has a contemporary feel with frameless windows, open fireplace, sliding oak patio windows and underfloor heating. Relax on the terrace, sit beneath the espaliered limes in the immaculate garden, dip into the National Trust woods. Footpaths start from the gate and the wildlife is abundant.

Price	£65-£75. Singles from £45.
Rooms	3: 1 double; 1 double, 1 twin both with separate bath/shower.
Meals	Packed lunch on request. Pub 0.25 miles.
Closed	Christmas & New Year.
Directions	B3089 approaching Dinton from east (Barford St Martin). Take 1st turn right after village sign & 30mph, signed Wylye. 100 yds; 1st right up Dowtys Lane to house.

Mrs Di Verdon-Smith
Dowtys,
Dowtys Lane, Dinton,
Salisbury,
Wiltshire SP3 5ES
Tel   01722 716886
Email   dowtys.bb@gmail.com
Web   www.dowtysbedandbreakfast.co.uk

Entry 507   Map 3

Wiltshire

Old Stoke

As pretty as thatched cottages come. This lovely old farmhouse is edged by an AONB filled with birdsong and wildlife, yet you are close to Salisbury. Guests have a book-filled sitting room with Dorset cream walls and pretty chairs and sofas to collapse onto: upstairs are fresh bedrooms with bright fabrics on headboards and window cushions, feathery beds and sparkling bathrooms. Tracie is charming and cooks well; good wholesome food using eggs from her own hens, vegetables from the garden and delicious flapjacks or cake for tea. Stroll down the fecund garden to a meadow and the river. *Children over eight welcome.*

Price	£50-£65. Singles £35-£40.
Rooms	2: 1 twin/double; 1 double with separate bath.
Meals	Dinner £15-£20. Packed lunch £6. Pub 1 mile.
Closed	December-February.
Directions	SW from Salisbury on A354; right at Coomb Bissett dir. Bishopstone. 2nd left after White Hart, signed Stoke Farthing. In hamlet, sharp bend to right, 2nd house on left. Parking to left of house.

Tracie Pickford
Old Stoke,
Stoke Farthing,
Broadchalke,
Salisbury,
Wiltshire SP5 5ED
Tel   01722 780513
Email   traciepickford@hotmail.co.uk

Entry 508   Map 3

Wiltshire

85 Exeter Street

You are so central here that you can wander into town on foot (having parked by the house or walked from the station). Susan's Georgian house, facing the cathedral close, is on a main road but the bedrooms sit very quietly at the back and the upstairs drawing room has a lovely view of the spire. Enjoy a good breakfast of fresh fruit, local bacon and sausages, and homebaked bread downstairs at one big table. Bedrooms are simple and traditional: William Morris curtains, a five-foot bed and a shower cabinet in one, a single bed with a spare roll-out bed in the other. Good, solid city B&B. *French & German spoken.*

Wiltshire

Bolhays

Fresh flowers and the smell of irresistible freshly baked bread fill the rooms of this smartly cosy Victorian villa. Sisters Bar and Sue have kept period details – pine doors, marble fireplaces – but updated the look with Farrow & Ball paints and oatmeal carpets. Bedrooms are light and restful with white and brass bedsteads, bed linen is impeccable and bathrooms sparkle. The breakfast room overlooks the pretty, pocket-handkerchief garden and there's a very comfy front parlour to come back to. A treat to be in the centre of Salisbury, staying with such lovely, easy-going people. *Children over 12 welcome.*

Travel Club Offer: see page 392 for details.

Price	From £75. Singles from £50.
Rooms	2: 1 double; 1 single/twin with separate bath/shower.
Meals	Pubs & restaurants nearby.
Closed	Rarely.
Directions	Ring road round Salisbury to south of city; past r'bout to Southampton; at next r'bout (Exeter St r'bout), 3rd exit on to Exeter St (signed Old George Mall). No 85 near city centre. Park opp. house; ask for permit on arrival.

	Susan Orr-Ewing
	85 Exeter Street,
	Salisbury,
	Wiltshire SP1 2SE
Tel	01722 417944
Mobile	07904 814408
Email	info@85exeterstreet.co.uk
Web	www.85exeterstreet.co.uk

Entry 509   Map 3

Price	£65. Singles £45.
Rooms	2: 1 double; 1 double with separate bathroom.
Meals	Pubs/restaurants 5-minute walk.
Closed	Rarely.
Directions	From r'bout where A345 meets A36 on north. side of Salisbury, take City Centre exit. Wyndham Rd 2nd left.

	Bar Barbour & Sue Lemin
	Bolhays,
	48 Wyndham Road, Salisbury,
	Wiltshire SP1 3AB
Tel	01722 320603
Email	info@bolhays.com
Web	www.bolhays.com

Entry 510   Map 3

Wiltshire

The Priory

This is a good city apartment in a partly Jacobean house on the main street, suitable for those who prefer independence. A conservatory-style bedroom – overlooking a quiet garden – has acres of floral curtain, bulging book shelves, gleaming furniture, two single beds and a large sofa; the bathroom is old fashioned but spotless. The Credlands give you breakfast in their Aga-warmed kitchen at a large table. Not sophisticated but a good, unusual base if you're visiting Salisbury, and you can do it all on foot. Ask to see the fireplace in the drawing room; it's stunning. *Minimum stay two nights. Free parking.*

Price	From £75-£80. Singles from £60.
Rooms	1 twin.
Meals	Pub/restaurant 100 yds.
Closed	Rarely.
Directions	Enter town's one-way system. From north side of Market Sq, right into Brown St. Through 2 sets of lights; house on left, set back from road.

Michael & Sarah Credland
The Priory,
95 Brown Street,
Salisbury,
Wiltshire SP1 2BA

Tel	01722 502337
Email	credland@btopenworld.com
Email	www.thepriorybedandbreakfast.co.uk

🚶 ✗ 🚂 📶 🐕

Entry 511   Map 3

Wiltshire

The Mill House

In a tranquil village next to the river is a house surrounded by water meadows and wilderness garden. Roses ramble, marsh orchids bloom and butterflies shimmer. This 12-acre labour of love is the creation of Diana, now in her 80s, and her son Michael. Their home, the time-worn 18th-century miller's house, is packed with country clutter – porcelain, teddy bears, ancestral photographs above the fire – while bedrooms are quaint, old-fashioned and flowery, with firm, comfy beds. The family has lived here over 46 years and have been doing B&B for 26 of them. *Children over eight welcome.*

Price	From £80. Singles from £55.
Rooms	5: 3 doubles, 1 family room; 1 twin with separate bath.
Meals	Pub 5-minute walk.
Closed	Never.
Directions	From A303 take B3083 at Winterbourne Stoke to Berwick St James. Go through village, past Boot Inn & church. Turn left into yard just before the sharp left bend. Coming from A36 (B3083), house 1st on right.

Diana Gifford Mead & Michael Mertens
The Mill House,
Berwick St James, Salisbury,
Wiltshire SP3 4TS

Tel	01722 790331
Fax	01722 790753
Web	www.millhouse.org.uk

✗

Entry 512   Map 3

Wiltshire

The Manor

Isabel is a delight and a great cook (she used to run a chalet in the Swiss Alps), happy to chat by the Aga as she rustles up huge breakfasts. She has decorated her beautifully converted home in style: bedrooms are prettily papered in pale pink and blue, mattresses are of the finest quality. Breakfast is eaten at a polished oak table, glazed doors thrown open to the garden in summer. This is a treat of a 17th-century brick-and-flint manor in a beguiling spot by the river Avon; good walking and plenty of wildlife.

Price	£80. Singles from £45.
Rooms	2 twins/doubles.
Meals	Pub/restaurant 2-minute walk.
Closed	Rarely.
Directions	From Upavon towards Andover on A342. Manor 3rd house on right & last before bridge.

	Isabel Green
	The Manor,
	Upavon, Pewsey,
	Wiltshire SN9 6EB
Tel	01980 635115
Mobile	07919 278334
Email	themanorupavon@hotmail.co.uk
Web	www.themanorupavon.co.uk

Entry 513   Map 3

Wiltshire

Puckshipton House

An intriguing name, Puckshipton: it means Goblin's Barn. The house is deep in the lush countryside of the Vale of Pewsey, reached by a long tree-lined drive. You stay in the Georgian end, with a private entrance that leads to a Regency-blue hall. Rooms are stylish and uncluttered, an attractive mix of old and new with good beds, crisp linen and bathrooms that are cossetting, one with a roll top bath. The dining and sitting rooms have wood-burners both. James, a forester, and Juliette have young children, a walled garden and a thatched hen house from which to fetch your breakfast egg.

Price	£80. Singles £50.
Rooms	2: 1 four-poster; 1 twin/double with separate bath/shower.
Meals	Pubs & restaurant 5-minute drive.
Closed	Christmas.
Directions	Devizes A342 towards Rushall; left to Chirton, right to Marden & through village. On for 0.25 miles; right into private drive.

	Juliette & James Noble
	Puckshipton House,
	Beechingstoke,
	Pewsey,
	Wiltshire SN9 6HG
Tel	01672 851336
Email	noble.jj@gmail.com
Web	www.puckshipton.co.uk

Entry 514   Map 3

Wiltshire

Upper Westcourt

Long views down Pewsey Vale, a stroll to the pub, bedrooms looking onto a beautiful garden. This is a relaxed, light-filled house surrounded by farmland that stretches away to Somerset, between Pewsey Downs and Martinsell Hill. Inside are rich curtains, polished old furniture, photographs and paintings; bedrooms and bathrooms are sunny with florals, pictures and books; drawing room sofas demand to be sunk into before a winter log fire; breakfasts may include fresh fruits and tomatoes from the garden. Come for traditional good taste and charming, welcoming, well-organised hosts.

Price	£70-£80. Singles £45.
Rooms	3: 1 twin/double; 1 twin, 1 single sharing separate bath (single let to same party).
Meals	Pubs within walking distance.
Closed	Christmas & Easter
Directions	A346 or A338 to Burbage. In High St, turn west to Westcourt, over bypass. At sharp left bend, right; 300 yds on left.

Peter & Carolyn Hill
Upper Westcourt,
Burbage, Marlborough,
Wiltshire SN8 3BW

Tel	01672 810307
Mobile	07979 650472
Email	prhill@onetel.com
Web	www.upperwestcourt.co.uk

Entry 515   Map 3

Wiltshire

Westcourt Farm

Rozzie and Jonny left London to restore a medieval, Grade II* cruck truss hall house (beautifully) and wildflower meadows, hedgerows and ponds. They are delightful people, and eager to welcome you. Rooms are freshly decorated, crisp yet traditional; the country furniture is charming, the crucks and trusses a carpenter's delight. Bedrooms have comfortable beds and fine linen, bathrooms are spot-on, there's a lovely dining room and a barn for corporate meetings. Encircled by footpaths and fields, Westcourt is the oldest house in a perfect village, two minutes from an excellent pub.

Price	£80. Singles £40.
Rooms	2: 1 twin with separate bath; 1 double with separate shower.
Meals	Pub/restaurant in village.
Closed	Christmas & New Year.
Directions	A338 Hungerford-Salisbury; after 4 miles signed Shalbourne; through village & fork left at pub; 150 yds, 2nd drive on right.

Jonny & Rozzie Buxton
Westcourt Farm,
Shalbourne,
Marlborough,
Wiltshire SN8 3QE

Tel	01672 871399
Email	info@westcourtfarm.com
Web	www.westcourtfarm.com

Entry 516   Map 3

Wiltshire

Fisherman's House

Watch ducks shoot the rapids of the Kennet River as it swooshes past the lawns of this exquisitely decorated home. It looks every inch a doll's house, but Jeremy and Heather add a deft human touch. The elegance of excellent breakfasts taken in the conservatory is balanced by the comforting hubbub emanating from the family kitchen. There's a guests' sitting room with an open fire and, upstairs, ornately and generously decorated bedrooms. Time slips by effortlessly here, many people come to visit the crop and stone circles and Marlborough is a hop away.

Price	£80. Singles £40.
Rooms	4: 2 doubles sharing bath (2nd room let to same party only); 1 twin, 1 single sharing bath.
Meals	Lunch/packed lunch from £3. Pub 500 yds.
Closed	Christmas.
Directions	From Hungerford, A4 for Marlborough. After 7 miles, right for Stitchcombe, down hill (bear left at barn) & left at T-junc. On entering village, house 2nd on left.

Jeremy & Heather Coulter
Fisherman's House,
Mildenhall, Marlborough,
Wiltshire SN8 2LZ

Tel	01672 515390
Fax	01672 519009
Email	heathercoulter610@btinternet.com
Web	www.fishermanshouse.co.uk

Entry 517   Map 3

Wiltshire

Blue Barn

Jackie's gorgeous home is along a byway and surrounded by a lovely garden and paddocks with sweeping views. Through an avenue of trees you glimpse the stunning timber-framed green oak farmhouse. You have independence in your own annexe with a light and airy L-shaped sitting room, tartan sofa, lots of pictures, comfy chairs and a French daybed for an extra guest. Jackie brings your locally sourced breakfast here and you eat round a farmhouse table. The twin bedroom is fresh and pretty with rose-covered chintz headboards; the shower room spotless. You are right on the Ridgeway for fabulous walking.

Price	£70. Singles from £55.
Rooms	1 twin for 2-4 & sitting room. Extra beds available.
Meals	Pub 3 miles.
Closed	Never.
Directions	A346 Marlborough-Swindon. Turn for Ogbourne St George. Right after Crown Inn, continue to 'No Through Road' sign. At Ridgeway, left, then continue until Blue Barn.

Jacqueline Palmer
Blue Barn,
Ogbourne St George, Marlborough,
Wiltshire SN8 2NT

Tel	01672 841082
Mobile	07770 975965
Email	jax@capalmer.co.uk
Web	www.blue-barn.co.uk

Entry 518   Map 3

Wiltshire

Glebe House

The rogues' gallery of photographs up the stairs says it all: Glebe House is quirky and fun. Friendly Ginny spoils guests rotten with pressed linen and sociable dinners served on Wedgewood china. Charming, cosy and comfortable are the bedrooms, one with an Indian theme; delightful is the drawing room with its landscape oils, Bechstein piano and rugs from all over Asia; settle into a coral sofa and roast away by the fire. Breads, marmalades and jams are homemade, beautiful views shoot off down the valley, the garden trills with hundreds of birds and Mr Biggles (the grey parrot) chats by the Aga.

Travel Club Offer: see page 392 for details.

Price	From £65. Singles from £40.
Rooms	2: 1 double, 1 twin.
Meals	Dinner, 3 courses, from £23.
Closed	Christmas.
Directions	From Devizes-Chippenham A342. Follow Chittoe & Spye Park. On over crossroads onto narrow lane. House 2nd on left.

Bill & Ginny Scrope
Glebe House,
Chittoe, Chippenham,
Wiltshire SN15 2EL

Tel	01380 850864
Mobile	07767 608841
Email	gscrope@aol.com
Web	www.glebehouse-chittoe.co.uk

Entry 519   Map 3

Wiltshire

The Limes

Through the electric gates, past the gravelled car park and the pretty, box-edged front garden and you arrive at the middle part of a 1620 house divided into three. The beams, stone mullions and leaded windows are charming, and softly spoken Ellodie is an exceptional hostess. Light bedrooms have pretty curtains and fresh flowers, tiled bathrooms have good soaps and thick towels, logs glow in the grate, and breakfasts promise delicious Wiltshire bacon, prunes soaked in orange juice and organic bread. You are on the busy main road leading out of Melksham – catch the bus to Bath from right outside the door.

Travel Club Offer: see page 392 for details.

Price	£56-£80. Singles £40.
Rooms	3: 1 doubles, 2 twins/doubles.
Meals	Dinner £18-£22. BYO. Packed lunch £5. Pub 1.5 miles.
Closed	Rarely.
Directions	Leave Melksham on A365 to Bath. After Victoria Motors, sharp right at school sign, brown gates will open slowly. Park on right, follow path to house.

Ellodie van der Wulp
The Limes,
Shurnhold House,
Shurnhold, Melksham,
Wiltshire SN12 8DG

Tel	01225 790627
Mobile	07974 366892

Entry 520   Map 3

Wiltshire

The Coach House

In an ancient hamlet a few miles north of Bath, an impeccable conversion of an early 19th-century barn. Bedrooms are fresh and cosy with sloping ceilings; the drawing room is elegant with porcelain and chintz, its pale walls the ideal background for striking displays of fresh flowers. Sliding glass doors lead to a south-facing patio… then to a well-groomed croquet lawn bordered by flowers, with vegetable garden, tennis court, woodland and paddock beyond. Helga and David are delightful and there's lots to do from here; the splendours of Bath, Castle Combe and plenty of good golf courses are all near.

Wiltshire

Manor Farm

Farmyard heaven in the Cotswolds. A 17th-century manor farmhouse in 550 arable acres; horses in the paddock, dozing dogs in the yard, tumbling blooms outside the door and a perfectly tended village, with duck pond, a short walk. Beautiful bedrooms are softly lit, with muted colours, plump goose down pillows and the crispest linen. Breakfast in front of the fire is a banquet of delights, tea among the roses is a treat, thanks to charming, welcoming Victoria. This is the postcard England of dreams, with Castle Combe, Lacock, grand walking and gardens to visit. *Children over 12 welcome.*

Travel Club Offer: see page 392 for details.

Price	£60–£75. Singles from £35.
Rooms	2: 1 double with separate bath/shower; 1 twin/double let to same party only.
Meals	Dinner, 3 courses, from £20. Pubs/restaurants 1 mile.
Closed	Rarely.
Directions	From M4 junc. 17, A350 for Chippenham. A420 to Bristol (east) & Castle Combe. After 6.3 miles, right into Upper Wraxall. Sharp left opp. village green; at end of drive.

Price	From £75. Singles from £40.
Rooms	3: 2 doubles; 1 twin with separate bath.
Meals	Pub 1 mile. Wild venison suppers by special arrangement.
Closed	Christmas.
Directions	From M4 A429 to Cirencester (junc. 17). After 200 yds, 1st left for Grittleton; there, follow signs to Alderton. Farmhouse near church.

Helga & David Venables
The Coach House,
Upper Wraxall,
Chippenham,
Wiltshire SN14 7AG

Tel	01225 891026
Email	david@dvenables.co.uk
Web	www.upperwraxallcoachhouse.co.uk

Victoria Lippiatt-Onslow
Manor Farm,
Alderton, Chippenham,
Wiltshire SN14 6NL

Tel	01666 840271
Mobile	07721 415824
Email	victoria.lippiatt@btinternet.com
Web	www.themanorfarm.co.uk

Entry 521   Map 3

Entry 522   Map 3

Wiltshire

Alcombe Manor

Down a maze of magical lanes discover this hamlet and its 17th-century manor house: a deeply romantic hideaway with panelling, wooden floors, a couple of medieval windows, deep sofas, log fires, a galleried hall, shelves of books and plenty of places to sit. A fine oak staircase leads to large, light bedrooms, reassuringly old-fashioned; carpeted floors creak companionably and every ancient leaded window has a dreamy garden view... five acres of English perfection, no less, with topiary and a stream dashing through. Your hosts are kind and helpful, the peace is palpable, and you are just five miles from Bath.

Price	From £75. Singles £50.
Rooms	3: 2 twins, each with separate bath/shower; 1 single sharing bath.
Meals	Occasional dinner. Pubs nearby.
Closed	Rarely.
Directions	M4 junc. 17; A4 to Bath through Box; right for Middle Hill & Ditteridge; 200 yds, left signed Alcombe. Up hill for 0.5 miles, fork right; 200 yds on left.

	Simon & Victoria Morley
	Alcombe Manor,
	Box, Corsham,
	Wiltshire SN13 8QQ
Tel	01225 743850
Mobile	07887 855634
Email	morley@alcombemanor.co.uk

Entry 523   Map 3

Wiltshire

Manor Farm

The road through the sleepy Wiltshire village brings you to a Queen Anne house with a *petit château* feel, enfolded by a tranquil garden with tulip meadow, groomed lawns and... hens! Inside is as lovely; watercolourist Clare is a perfectionist behind the scenes and is charming. The bedroom is elegant and cosy, its soft-painted panelled walls hung with good pictures, its sash windows beautifully dressed. Scrumptious, all-organic breakfasts are served in a butter-yellow kitchen; the eclectically furnished drawing room, shared among guests, has a real fire and a delightful lived-in, family feel.

Price	£80. Singles by arrangement.
Rooms	1 double.
Meals	Pub 200 yds.
Closed	Christmas & New Year.
Directions	M4 exit 17. North on A429 for Malmesbury, right on B4042. Right after 3 miles to Little Somerford. Past pub, right at crossroads, 50 yds on, house behind tall wall.

	Clare Inskip
	Manor Farm,
	Little Somerford, Malmesbury,
	Wiltshire SN15 5JW
Tel	01666 822140
Mobile	07970 892344
Email	clareinskip@hotmail.com

Entry 524   Map 3

Wiltshire

Bullocks Horn Cottage

Up a country lane to this hidden-away house which the Legges have turned into a haven of peace and seclusion. Liz loves fabrics and mixes them with flair, Colin has painted a colourful mural – complete with macaws – in the conservatory. Bedrooms are quiet with lovely views, the sitting room with log fire has large comfy sofas, and the garden, which has been featured in various magazines, is exceptional. Home veg and herbs and local seasonal food are used at dinner which, in summer, you can eat in the cool shade of the arbour, covered in climbing roses and jasmine. *Minimum stay two nights July/August.*

Price	From £75. Singles from £35.
Rooms	2: 1 twin; 1 twin with separate bath.
Meals	Dinner £20-£25. BYO. Pub 1.5 miles.
Closed	Christmas & Easter.
Directions	From A429, B4040 through Charlton, past Horse & Groom. 0.5 miles, left signed 'Bullocks Horn No Through Road'. On to end of lane. Right; 1st on left.

	Colin & Liz Legge Bullocks Horn Cottage, Charlton, Malmesbury, Wiltshire SN16 9DZ
Tel	01666 577600
Email	legge@bullockshorn.clara.co.uk
Web	www.bullockshorn.co.uk

Entry 525   Map 3

Worcestershire

Harrowfields

Tucked just off the high street this compact cottage is surprisingly stylish with contemporary colours and old beams, great books and a cosy feel. Bedrooms large enough to lounge in are delightful (one even has a wood-burner) with crisp, jump-on-me beds, sound systems, super bathrooms, pump-action lotions, antique pine furniture and garden views. Susie and Adam (who cooks) are natural and charming, hens cluck in the garden, breakfast is local and seasonal, you can walk for miles or just to the pub. Young, romantic couples will be in heaven here; uncork the wine, light the fire, turn up the music.

Price	£60-£65. Singles from £45.
Rooms	2: 1 double; 1 double with separate shared bath.
Meals	Pubs in village.
Closed	Rarely.
Directions	Enter Eckington from Bredon (M5 junc. 9). Turn 1st right by village shop. House on left before Anchor pub.

	Susie Alington & Adam Stanford Harrowfields, Cotheridge Lane, Eckington, Worcestershire WR10 3BA
Tel	01386 751053
Email	susie@harrowfields.co.uk
Web	www.harrowfields.co.uk

Entry 526   Map 8

Worcestershire

Bidders Croft

Completely rebuilt in 1995 from 200-year-old bricks, this solid house has a hand-carved mahogany hall pillar, oak-framed loggias and an enormous conservatory where you eat overlooking the garden, orchard, field and the Malvern Hills. Traditional bedrooms with padded headboards and skirted dressing tables are warm and comfortable; bathrooms are spick and span. Bill and Charlotte give you a log fire, books and magazines in the sitting room, an Aga-cooked breakfast and candlelit dinner with home-grown vegetables and fruit. The hills beckon walkers, the views soar and you're near the Malvern theatres.

Worcestershire

Old Country Farm

Ella's passion for this remote, tranquil place – and the environment in general – is infectious. She believes the house was once home to a Saxon chief. Certainly, it has beams dating from 1400; now it's a rambling mix of russet stone and colour-washed brick, with a warm and delightfully cluttered kitchen, wooden floors, lovely rugs. Friendly, low-ceilinged bedrooms are simple and rustic. Ella's parents collected rare plants and the garden is full of hellebores and snowdrops; roe deer and barn owls flit about in the surrounding woods. A wonderful retreat for nature lovers, birdwatchers and walkers.

Travel Club Offer: see page 392 for details.

Price	£79-£89. Singles £49-£55.
Rooms	2: 1 twin with separate bath, 1 double with separate shower.
Meals	Dinner, 4 courses, £29.50 (for min. 4). Pub/restaurant 250 yds.
Closed	Christmas & New Year.
Directions	From Upton-upon-Severn, A4104 dir. Little Malvern & Ledbury. After 3 miles, pass Anchor Inn on right; drive is 250 yds on left, house signed.

Price	£60-£90. Singles £35-£55.
Rooms	3: 1 double; 1 double with separate bath; 1 double with separate shower.
Meals	Pubs/restaurants 3 miles.
Closed	Rarely.
Directions	From Worcester A4103 for 11 miles; B4220 for Ledbury. After leaving Cradley, left at top of hill for Mathon, right for Coddington; house 0.25 miles on right.

Bill & Charlotte Carver
Bidders Croft,
Welland, Malvern,
Worcestershire WR13 6LN

Tel	01684 592179
Mobile	07778 750600
Email	carvers@biddersscroft.com
Web	www.biddersscroft.com

Entry 527 Map 8

Ella Grace Quincy
Old Country Farm,
Mathon, Malvern,
Worcestershire WR13 5PS

Tel	01886 880867
Email	ella@oldcountryhouse.co.uk
Web	www.oldcountryhouse.co.uk

Entry 528 Map 8

Worcestershire

Home Farm

A half-moated farmhouse in a magical spot: the timbered part — 14th-century and listed — peeps through the trees as you approach. Gorgeous in summer (terrace, tennis, gardens, ducks) but light, relaxing and spacious all year round: antiques, soft colours and an open fire in the guest sitting room, fresh fabrics and carpeted comfort in the bedrooms, and peaceful views to the Abberley Hills and beyond. Roger and Anne are generous hosts and give you local bacon at breakfast and stewed fruits and jam from their plums. Make time for Great Witley, the most stunning baroque church in England. *Children over ten welcome.*

Price	£75–£85. Singles £45–£50.
Rooms	3: 1 twin; 1 single, 1 twin each with separate bath/shower.
Meals	Pubs within 5 miles.
Closed	Christmas & New Year.
Directions	On entering Great Witley from Worcester on A443, left onto B4197 to Martley; after 0.25 miles 1st right on sharp left-hand bend by grass triangle & chevrons; up hill 1st house on right.

	Roger & Anne Kendrick
	Home Farm,
	Great Witley, Worcester,
	Worcestershire WR6 6JJ
Tel	01299 896825
Email	anniekendrick@hotmail.com
Web	www.homefarmbandb.com

Entry 529   Map 8

Yorkshire

Village Farm

Tucked behind the houses and shops, this was once the village farm with land stretching to the coast; the one-storey buildings overlooking a courtyard are now large immaculate bedrooms in gorgeous colours with luxurious touches. Baths are deep, beds crisply comfortable, heating is underfoot. Delicious breakfasts are served at wooden tables in a light room with a contemporary feel; wicker sofa and chairs, terracotta floors, white walls. Justin and Alison are friendly but give you complete privacy; stride the cliffs, watch birds at Flamborough Head or make for Spurn Point — remote and lovely.

Price	£70. Singles from £39.95.
Rooms	3: 2 doubles, 1 twin.
Meals	Pubs/restaurants within 2 miles.
Closed	Rarely.
Directions	A165 Beverley to Bridlington. At Beeford x'roads, right onto B1249 to Skipsea. There, pass church on left, at x'roads, straight across to Back Street. On right, opp. pub.

	Justin & Alison Thorn
	Village Farm,
	Skipsea, Yorkshire YO25 8SW
Tel	01262 468479
Mobile	07813 612803
Email	villagefarmskipsea@yahoo.com
Web	www.villagefarmskipsea.co.uk

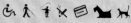

Entry 530   Map 13

Yorkshire

Manor Farm

Pass the stables into the scullery and the sweet smell of saddles and tack; enter a warm kitchen where muslin-wrapped hams hang to dry. This is special: a thriving and immaculate working farm with a relaxed, artistic owner. Low-ceilinged bedrooms are stuffed with colour, old armchairs and thick rugs, books and rose china. There's a garden room for summer breakfasts – home-baked bread and muesli from the Side Oven Bakery, hen and duck eggs from the farm – and a charming garden tucked deep in the wedge of Thixendale. Wonderful for those seeking a remote escape. *Preferably bookings by telephone.*

Price	From £70. Singles from £35.
Rooms	2: 1 twin & sitting room; 1 double sharing bath (let to same party).
Meals	Packed lunch £7.50. Pub in village.
Closed	Rarely.
Directions	Left at top of Garrowby Hill A166; 4 miles to Thixendale. Thro' village, farm on left. 10 miles from Malton, through Birdsall on unclassified roads.

Gilda & Charles Brader
Manor Farm,
Thixendale, Malton,
Yorkshire YO17 9TG

Tel	01377 288315
Fax	01377 288315
Email	info@manorfarmthixendale.co.uk
Web	www.manorfarmthixendale.co.uk

Entry 531   Map 13

Yorkshire

Low Penhowe

With the Turners at the helm, you are on a safe ship. They see to everything so perfectly – the crispness of the breakfast bacon, the freshness of the eggs from their hens, the homemade bread, the bowls of flowers, the fire in the guest drawing room. Traditional, comfortable bedrooms face south and overlook the garden – lap up the views in summer while birds soar and twitter, Christopher's Highland cattle peer over the fence and the chickens strut and scratch. Castle Howard and the North Yorks Moors are in front of you and all around are abbeys, castles, rivers, ruins and woods. *Children over ten welcome.*

Ethical Collection: Community; Food.
See page 400 for details.

Travel Club Offer: see page 392 for details.

Price	£72-£90. Singles £60.
Rooms	2: 1 double; 1 twin/double with separate bath.
Meals	Packed lunch £6. Pubs 1.5 miles.
Closed	Christmas & New Year.
Directions	A64 at Whitwell on the Hill, right for Kirkham. Over crossing & Derwent, pass Kirkham Priory & Stone Trough Inn. Right at T-junc, left for Burythorpe, over x-roads, 700 yds; right up drive.

Christopher & Philippa Turner
Low Penhowe,
Burythorpe, Malton,
Yorkshire YO17 9LU

Tel	01653 658336
Mobile	07900 227000
Email	lowpenhowe@btinternet.com
Web	www.bedandbreakfastyorkshire.co.uk

Entry 532   Map 13

Portobello Farm

Among a flurry of geese and hens discover this old farmhouse with pretty sash windows, varied floor levels and huge kitchen hung with dried flowers, pots, platters and paintings. All has a warm, bohemian feel with floor stencils, oak furniture, books, vibrant art and a log-burning stove in the sitting room. Bedrooms have traditional iron beds, patchwork quilts, painted floors, small shower rooms (and a quirky bathroom with stone walls). The garden slips away to fields where sheep slowly munch; Lynne gives you the heartiest of breakfasts at a round table in the hallway and you're 20 minutes from York. Wonderful.

Crown House

Scarborough… bracing walks, salty air, fresh fish and buckets and spades. But the Firths have one of those charming listed houses in respectable South Cliff, moments from the Esplanade. Inside, good proportions, light rooms with lovely bathrooms and contemporary furniture. Barbara, thoughtful and fun, serves great breakfasts (and juices just-squeezed) at a good oval table that seats up to ten. Bedrooms are cream, stylish and restful. Coastline and castles by day, home baking on your return, books and CDs to borrow, cats to admire, and a theatre just down the road.

 Travel Club Offer: see page 392 for details.

Price	From £65. Singles £45.
Rooms	3: 2 doubles;
	1 twin with separate bath.
Meals	Pubs 3-6 miles.
Closed	Christmas & New Year.
Directions	Take unclassified road from Norton to Stamford Bridge & Pocklington. 1st turn right after 30mph sign, lane signed Menethorpe; 1 mile along farm drive, signed.

Price	From £80.
Rooms	3 doubles.
Meals	Supper £15. Dinner £25.
	Packed lunch available.
	Restaurants 10-minute walk.
Closed	Christmas to end of January.
Directions	From station, A165 signed Filey. Right over Valley Bridge, left at end; immed. right on Belmont Road. At green, right again; left into Crown Terrace.

	Lynne Cole
	Portobello Farm,
	Welham, Norton, Malton,
	Yorkshire YO17 9QY
Tel	01653 658518
Email	portobello.farm@tiscali.co.uk
Web	www.portobellofarm.co.uk

	Barbara Firth
	Crown House,
	6 Crown Terrace, Scarborough,
	Yorkshire YO11 2BL
Tel	01723 375401
Mobile	07736 626289
Email	barbara@crownhousescarborough.co.uk
Web	www.crownhousescarborough.co.uk

Entry 533   Map 13

Entry 534   Map 13

Yorkshire

Foulsyke Farmhouse

The pretty village of Scalby is on the edge of the North Yorkshire Moors, close to Scarborough with its sweeping bays and Whitby – a great little town to explore. Jayne and John do perfect B&B, give you afternoon tea, a heart-warming breakfast with eggs from the hens and sausages from the butcher, and charming cosy bedrooms with a country-cottage feel. Your sitting room is packed with magazines, books and maps; plan your walking or cycling routes here. Leave the car and take the bus to Scarborough – John will happily collect – or you can get the bus by the duck pond!

Price	£56. Singles £33.
Rooms	3: 1 twin/double, 2 doubles.
Meals	Light supper £6. Packed lunch £5. Tea room open weekends & bank holidays. Pubs 0.5 miles.
Closed	Never.
Directions	A171 Scarborough-Whitby. 0.5 miles past entrance to Scalby, left onto Barmoor Lane (signed Suffield & Harwood Dale). House 1st right after pond.

Jayne Pickup
Foulsyke Farmhouse,
Barmoor Lane, Scalby, Scarborough,
Yorkshire YO13 0PG

Tel	01723 507423
Mobile	07789 445109
Email	jaynepickup@btinternet.com
Web	www.foulsykefarmhouse.co.uk

Entry 535   Map 13

Yorkshire

Holly Croft

Huge kindness and thoughtful touches (hot water bottles, lifts to the pub, cake and tea on arrival) make this home special. The décor is Edwardian plush – wallpapers striped and floral, curtains lavish – the comfort indisputable. The double has an elaborate floral-and-rose headboard with matching drapes, there are bathrobes in fitted wardrobes, big showers and generous breakfasts – own jams, Yorkshire teas, kippers if you choose – are served round the polished mahogany table. After a bracing clifftop walk return to a homely sitting room overlooking the garden. Whitby is 20 minutes away.

Travel Club Offer: see page 392 for details.

Price	From £70. Singles from £45.
Rooms	2: 1 twin; 1 double with separate bath.
Meals	Evening meal by prior arrangement (min 4 people). Pub 600 yds.
Closed	Rarely.
Directions	A171 from Scarborough to Whitby; at Scalby x-roads, by tennis courts, take road on right. Signed 500 yds on right.

John & Christine Goodall
Holly Croft,
28 Station Road, Scalby, Scarborough,
Yorkshire YO13 0QA

Tel	01723 375376
Mobile	07759 429706
Email	christine.goodall@tesco.net
Web	www.holly-croft.co.uk

Entry 536   Map 13

Grinkle Lodge

It's peaceful at this gothic Victorian stone house, which stands on the northern flank of the fabulous moors. Pretty gardens are home to wildlife, and free-range chickens provide eggs for breakfast. Inside find fresh flowers, country rugs, Sanderson wallpapers and hand-painted murals. Janette is an artist: one bedroom has a vine-clad ceiling, another a seascape between 'marbled' columns. Polished wood, fine linen and gorgeous views abound. Tim gives you delicious dinners at mahogany tables, perhaps Whitby crab, rack of local lamb, Yorkshire rhubarb and ginger crumble. *Minimum stay two nights with half board at weekends.*

Brickfields Farm

Down a long, quiet track but just a stone's throw from bustling Kirkbymoorside, this is a walker's paradise. Friendly Janet provides maps and information and sends you off to the North York Moors with a tasty breakfast, served at separate tables in the conservatory overlooking sheep and guinea fowl. Bedrooms are in the main house or in the long low barn and all are lovely; a French vintage bed, antiques, heavy curtains and sprung mattresses, fresh flowers and a hidden fridge. Bathrooms have big, open showers, thick towels and generous lotions and bubbles. And there's a smart new sitting room for guests.

Price	£80–£92.		Price	£60–£90.
Rooms	3: 2 doubles, 1 twin.		Rooms	6: 1 double, 1 twin, 4 suites.
Meals	Dinner £22.		Meals	Pub/restaurant 1 mile.
Closed	Rarely.		Closed	Rarely.
Directions	From A171 Whitby to Guisborough road travelling north, take right turn to Grinkle and Easington. After 2 miles take right turn. Signed.		Directions	A170 east from Thirsk to Kirkbymoorside; continue past roundabout for 0.5 miles. Right into Kirkby Mills, signed. House 1st right along small lane.

Tim & Janette Boskett
Grinkle Lodge,
Snipe Lane, Grinkle, Whitby,
Yorkshire TS13 4UD
Tel   01287 644701
Email   grinklelodge@yahoo.co.uk
Web   www.grinklelodge.co.uk

Janet Trousdale
Brickfields Farm,
Kirkby Mills, Kirkbymoorside,
Yorkshire YO62 6NS
Tel   01751 433074
Email   janet@brickfieldsfarm.co.uk
Web   www.brickfieldsfarm.co.uk

Yorkshire

No 54

The welcome tea and homemade cakes set the tone for your stay; this is a happy place. No 54 was once two cottages on the Duncombe estate; now it's a single house and Lizzie has made the most of the space. Buttermilk walls, be-rugged flagged floors, country furniture, open fires and a stylish lack of clutter. A single-storey extension has been fashioned into three extra bedrooms around a secluded courtyard. Thoughtful extras – a Roberts radio, fresh milk, hot water bottles – make you feel looked after, and the breakfasts will fuel the most serious of walks. Make a house party and bring your friends!

Price	£80. Singles from £35.
Rooms	4: 2 doubles, 1 twin; 1 single with separate shower.
Meals	Dinner, 2-3 courses, £28-£35. Restaurants 10-minute walk.
Closed	Christmas & New Year.
Directions	A170 to Helmsley; right at mini r'bout in centre, facing The Crown; house 500 yds along A170, on right.

Lizzie Would
No 54,
Bondgate, Helmsley,
Yorkshire YO62 5EZ

Tel	01439 771533
Mobile	07774 292149
Email	lizzie@no54.co.uk
Web	www.no54.co.uk

Entry 539   Map 13

Yorkshire

Sproxton Hall

Drive through a stone archway into an old courtyard: the 17th-century beamed farmhouse, once attached to Rievaulx Abbey, is still part of a working farm – complete with rare-breed Belted Galloways. Inside, a handsome grandfather clock and a genuine welcome from Margaret and Andrew. The guests' sitting and dining rooms have 18th-century country antiques and the bedrooms are traditional and comfortable, with lovely views; the double has a half-tester with floral canopy. Sensible, hearty breakfasts prepare you for a day on the peaceful North Yorkshire Moors. *Children over ten welcome.*

Price	£74-£80. Singles £46.
Rooms	3: 1 twin, 1 double; 1 twin with separate bath & shower.
Meals	Pubs/restaurants 1-3 miles.
Closed	Christmas & New Year.
Directions	From Thirsk A170 for 12 miles. Right onto B1257 (1 mile before Helmsley); 50 yds on, left by church. House at end of 'No Through Road'.

Margaret & Andrew Wainwright
Sproxton Hall,
Sproxton, Helmsley,
Yorkshire YO62 5EQ

Tel	01439 770225
Email	sproxtonhall@btinternet.com
Web	www.sproxtonhall.co.uk

Entry 540   Map 13

Yorkshire

Shallowdale House

Phillip and Anton have a true affection for their guests so you will be treated like angels. Sumptuous bedrooms dazzle in yellows, blues and limes, acres of curtains frame wide views over the Howardian Hills, bathrooms are gleaming and immaculate. Breakfast on the absolute best; fresh fruit compote, dry-cured bacon, homemade rolls – and walk it off in any direction straight from the house. Return to an elegant drawing room, with a fire in winter, and an enticing library. Dinner is out of this world and coffee and chocolates are all you need before you crawl up to bed. Bliss. *Children over 12 welcome.*

Price	£95–£115. Singles £75–£85.
Rooms	3: 2 twins/doubles; 1 double with separate bath/shower.
Meals	Dinner, 4 courses, £35.
Closed	Christmas & New Year.
Directions	From Thirsk, A19 south, then 'caravan route' via Coxwold & Byland Abbey. 1st house on left, just before Ampleforth.

Anton van der Horst & Phillip Gill
Shallowdale House,
West End, Ampleforth,
Yorkshire YO62 4DY

Tel   01439 788325
Fax   01439 788885
Email   stay@shallowdalehouse.co.uk
Web   www.shallowdalehouse.co.uk

✕ ▱ ◊ 🐾

Entry 541   Map 12

Yorkshire

The Old Rectory

The house was a rectory first, then the residence of the Bishops of Whitby. Both Turner and Ruskin stayed here and probably enjoyed as much good conversation and comfort as you will. Bedrooms are pretty, traditional and with grand views; the drawing room is classic country house – the sort that foreigners envy – with a fine Venetian window and an enticing window-seat. The elegant, deep pink dining room looks south over a garden of rare old trees. Wander at will to find an orchard, a tennis court and a croquet lawn. Breakfast is generous and thoughtful. *Children over eight welcome.*

Price	From £66. Singles from £40.
Rooms	2: 1 double with separate bath & dressing room; 1 twin with separate bath & shower.
Meals	Pub opposite.
Closed	Rarely.
Directions	Take A168 (Northallerton road) off A19; over r'bout; left into village; house opp. pub, next to church.

Tim & Caroline O'Connor-Fenton
The Old Rectory,
South Kilvington,
Thirsk,
Yorkshire YO7 2NL

Tel   01845 526153
Mobile   07981 329764
Email   ocfenton@talktalk.net

✕ 🐾 📷

Entry 542   Map 12

Yorkshire

Hunters Hill

The moors lie behind this solid, stone farmhouse, five yards from the National Park, in farmland and woodland with fine views... marvellous walking country. The house is full of light and flowers; bedrooms are pretty but not overly grand. The attractive sitting room has deeply comfortable old sofas, armchairs and fine furniture, while rich colours, hunting prints and candles at dinner give a warm and cosy feel. The Orr family has poured a good deal of affection into this tranquil house and the result is a home that's happy, charming and remarkably easy to relax in... Wonderful.

Price	£80. Singles from £50.
Rooms	2: 1 twin/double; 1 twin/double with separate bath.
Meals	Dinner, 3 courses, £30. Pub/restaurant 500 yds.
Closed	Rarely.
Directions	From A170 to Sinnington. On village green, keep river on left, fork right between cottages, sign to church. Up lane, bearing right up hill. House past church beyond farm buildings.

The Orr Family
Hunters Hill,
Sinnington,
York,
Yorkshire YO62 6SF
Tel 01751 431196
Email ejorr@tiscali.co.uk

✗ ☙ ⋈

Entry 543   Map 13

Yorkshire

Cundall Lodge Farm

Ancient chestnuts, crunchy drive, sheep grazing, hens free-ranging. This four-square Georgian farmhouse could be straight out of Central Casting. And there's tea and oven-fresh cake to welcome. Homely rooms of damask sofas and pretty wallpaper have views to Sutton Bank's White Horse or the river Swale. Bedrooms are comfy with family furnishings and inviting chairs. This is a working farm with typical farmers' breakfast: free-range eggs, homemade jams and local cured bacon. The garden and river walks guarantee peace. David and Caroline are sociable and generous. *Children over ten welcome.*

Travel Club Offer: see page 392 for details.

Price	£70-£85.
Rooms	3: 2 doubles; 1 twin/double.
Meals	Packed lunch £5. Pubs/restaurants 2 miles.
Closed	Christmas & January.
Directions	Exit junc. 49 A1(M) onto A168 (Thirsk). Turn off 1st junc. for Cundall. Turn right at the Crab & Lobster. 2 miles on left.

Caroline Barker
Cundall Lodge Farm,
Cundall, York,
Yorkshire YO61 2RN
Tel 01423 360203
Mobile 07773 494260
Email info@lodgefarmbb.co.uk
Web www.lodgefarmbb.co.uk

✗ ▦ 🚜 ⚲

Entry 544   Map 12

Yorkshire

North Dockenbush

An 1800s farmhouse transformed into a handsome B&B with a modern vibe. Animal skins and displays of flowers gleam in the mirrored light of chandeliers; dark red walls flicker in firelight. Sink into Siberian goose down, wake to waterfall showers and Molton Brown treats. Oliver loves country pursuits, housekeeper Jackie provides the feminine touch (and biscuits!) – both radiate energy. Breakfast bacon and eggs are farmyard fresh while port rounds off hearty British meals. Dogs and horses share the stables and the estate, close to Harrogate, is a walker's paradise: you're on the doorstep of the Yorkshire Dales.

Price	£90. Singles £65.
Rooms	5: 3 doubles; 2 doubles sharing bath (let to same party only).
Meals	Dinner, 4 courses and half bottle of wine, £30 (min. 4 people). Pub/restaurant 2 miles.
Closed	Christmas.
Directions	Leave Harrogate on A61 (Ripon road). At 2nd r'bout, right onto B6156 to Knaresborough. Left into Brereton, follow past sign for village only, then next right on corner.

Oliver Whiteley
North Dockenbush,
Brearton, Harrogate,
Yorkshire HG3 3DF

Tel	01423 797650
Mobile	07712 677654
Email	oliver@northdockenbush.co.uk
Web	www.northdockenbush.co.uk

Entry 545   Map 12

Yorkshire

Braythorne Barn

Absolute independence here with your own entrance; inside are paintings, fine furniture, colourful fabrics and rugs. Beams and floors are light oak, windows and doors hand-crafted and sunlight dances around the rooms. Trina has given the bedroom a Scandinavian stripes-and-gingham feel. The bathroom is spotless, the sitting room – all yours – generously furnished. Walk the Priests Way, from Bolton Abbey to Knaresborough. Chickens in the field and great breakfasts – perhaps brandy-soaked fruit compote… this is a rural idyll with a contemporary twist. *Children over 12 welcome. Minimum stay two nights.*

Price	£75–£85. Singles from £55.
Rooms	2: 1 twin & sitting room; 1 double with separate bath.
Meals	Packed lunch £6. Pubs/restaurants 2-4 miles.
Closed	Rarely.
Directions	From Pool-in-Wharfedale, A658 over bridge towards Harrogate. 1st left to Leathley; right opp. church to Stainburn (1.5 miles). Bear left at fork; house next on left.

Petrina Knockton
Braythorne Barn,
Stainburn, Otley,
Yorkshire LS21 2LW

Tel	0113 2843160
Mobile	07866 372488
Email	trina@home-relocation.co.uk
Web	www.braythornebarn.co.uk

Entry 546   Map 12

Yorkshire

Sunnybank

A Victorian gentleman's residence just a short walk up the hill from the centre of bustling *Last of the Summer Wine* Holmfirth, still with its working Picturedrome cinema (touring bands too), arts and folk festivals, restaurants and shops. Peter and Anne look after you beautifully. Big peaceful bedrooms are a fresh mix of contemporary, Art Nouveau and Art Deco pieces, caramel cream velvets and silks, spoiling bathrooms and lovely views. A huge Yorkshire breakfast will set you up for a lazy stroll round the charming gardens, or a brisk yomp through rural bliss. *Minimum stay two nights at weekends.*

Price	£65-£90. Singles from £55.
Rooms	3: 2 doubles, 1 twin/double (with extra single bed).
Meals	Supper snacks £10. Packed lunch £10. Pubs/restaurants 500 yds.
Closed	New Year & occasionally.
Directions	A6024 signed Glossop out of Holmfirth centre. Take right in between Ashley Jackson Studio & Worthingtons into Upperthong Lane. House on drive on right just past church.

Peter & Anne White
Sunnybank,
78 Upperthong Lane,
Holmfirth,
Yorkshire HD9 3BQ
Tel   01484 684857
Email   info@sunnybankguesthouse.co.uk
Web   www.sunnybankguesthouse.co.uk

X 🖻 🚒 🐾 📶 🐕 🐈 ♿

Entry 547   Map 12

Yorkshire

Field House

You drive over bridge and beck to this listed, 1713 farmhouse – expect comfort, homeliness and open fires. Pat and Geoff love showing guests their hens, horses, goats and lambs, and will tell you about the 14 circular walks or lend you a torch so you can find the pub across the fields! Ramblers will be in heaven – step out of the front door, past the lovely walled garden and you're in rolling, Bronte countryside. Good big bedrooms are in farmhouse style, one bathroom has a roll top bath, another a 70s blue suite, and Geoff's breakfasts are generous in the finest Yorkshire manner.

Ethical Collection: Community; Food. See page 400 for details.

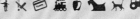 Travel Club Offer: see page 392 for details.

Price	£58-£66. Singles £34-£42.
Rooms	3: 1 double, 1 twin; 1 twin with separate bath/shower.
Meals	Dinner from £10. Packed lunch available. Pub/restaurant 200 yds.
Closed	Rarely.
Directions	1 mile from Halifax on A58 Leeds road. Turn between Stump Cross Inn car park & Clarence Smith's carpet shop. 100 yds to gates.

Pat & Geoff Horrocks-Taylor
Field House,
Staups Lane, Stump Cross, Halifax,
Yorkshire HX3 6XW
Tel   01422 355457
Mobile 07933 325046
Email   enquiries@fieldhouse-bb.co.uk
Web   www.fieldhouse-bb.co.uk

🏃 X 🖻 🚒 🐾 🐕 🐈 🚜

Entry 548   Map 12

Thurst House Farm

This solid Pennine farmhouse, its stone mullion windows denoting 17th-century origins, is English to the core. Your warm, gracious hosts give guests a cosy and carpeted sitting room with an open fire in winter; bedrooms are equally generous, with inviting brass beds, antique linen and fresh flowers. Outside: clucking hens, two friendly sheep and a hammock in a garden with beautiful views. Tuck into homemade bread, marmalade and jams at breakfast, and good traditional English dinners, too – just the thing for walkers who've trekked the Calderdale or the Pennine Way. *Children over eight welcome.*

Price	£80. Singles by arrangement.
Rooms	2: 1 double, 1 family room.
Meals	Dinner, 4 courses, £25. Packed lunch £5. Restaurants within 0.5 miles.
Closed	Christmas & New Year.
Directions	Ripponden on A58. Look for brown Beehive sign and then right up Royd Lane 100 yds before lights; right at T-junc. opp. Beehive Inn; on for 1 mile. House on right, gateway on blind bend, reverse in.

David & Judith Marriott
Thurst House Farm,
Soyland, Ripponden,
Sowerby Bridge,
Yorkshire HX6 4NN
Tel   01422 822820
Mobile 07759 619043
Email   thursthousefarm@bushinternet.com

Entry 549   Map 12

Holme House

A delightful Georgian house in bustling Hebden Bridge: with its artists, musicians, book shops, real ale pubs and commitment to Fair Trade, it's the Totnes of the Pennines. Perfect if you enjoy the outdoor life – walks along the Calder Valley start from the door – but prefer to be based in town. Inside, you will be spoiled with classic proportions, a light-filled hallway, sometimes local art and a comfortable sitting room with leather sofas. Fresh flowers, chocolates, great beds and cool, creamy colours encourage you to linger in bed, but Sarah's locally sourced breakfasts will set you up for anything.

Price	£70-£85. Singles £55.
Rooms	3: 2 doubles, 1 twin.
Meals	Packed lunch from £7.50. Pubs/restaurants 100 yds.
Closed	Christmas Day & Boxing Day.
Directions	On corner of New Road (main road thro' town) & Holme Street. Car park on left as you turn into Holme Street, thro' black railings.

Sarah Eggleston
Holme House,
New Road, Hebden Bridge,
Yorkshire HX7 8AD
Tel   01422 847588
Fax   01422 847354
Email   mail@holmehousehebdenbridge.co.uk
Web   www.holmehousehebdenbridge.co.uk

Entry 550   Map 12

Yorkshire

Ponden House

Bump your way up to Brenda's sturdy house, high on the wild Pennine Way. The spring water makes wonderful tea and the house hums with interest and artistic touches. Comfy sofas are jollied up with throws, there are homespun rugs and hangings, paintings, plants and a piano. Feed the hens, plonk your boots by the Aga, chat with your lovely leisurely hostess as she turns out fab home cooking; food is a passion. Bedrooms are exuberant but cosy, it's great for walkers and there's a hot tub under the stars (bookable by groups in advance). Good value with a lived-in, homely feel.

Price	£60-£65. Singles £30-£45.
Rooms	3: 2 doubles; 1 twin sharing bath.
Meals	Occasional dinner, 3 courses, £16. Packed lunch £5. Pub/restaurant 3 miles.
Closed	Rarely.
Directions	From B6142 for Colne. Pass through Stanbury village, cont. past Old Silent Inn. Access is either via Ponden Mill or Ponden reservoir.

Brenda Taylor
Ponden House,
Stanbury,
Haworth,
Yorkshire BD22 0HR
Tel   01535 644154
Email   brenda.taylor@pondenhouse.co.uk
Web   www.pondenhouse.co.uk

Entry 551   Map 12

Yorkshire

Pickersgill Manor Farm

A sparkling welcome, immaculate bedrooms, spectacular views. So you'll forgive the ramshackle yard: this is a working farm! The handsome new farmhouse stands high on the moors, criss-crossed by the Millennium Way. Lisa seduces you with Italian coffee and homemade cake, then shows you the rest: big wooden sleigh beds in lovely big rooms; a guest sitting room with books, games and wood-burning stove; Neal's Yard potions, stacks of white towels. Delicious breakfasts are for walkers – sausages from their pigs, eggs from their hens – and are fun. If you time it right, you'll be cuddling new-born lambs.

Price	£70. Singles £45.
Rooms	3: 2 doubles, 1 family.
Meals	Supper £10. Packed lunch £5. Pub/restaurant 1.5 miles.
Closed	Rarely.
Directions	A65 from Ilkley, then A6034 to Silsden Moor. On top of hill right into Cringles Lane. After 1.5 miles, left into Low Lane. After 0.5 miles, left when you see B&B sign.

Lisa Preston
Pickersgill Manor Farm,
Low Lane,
Silsden Moor,
Yorkshire BD20 9JH
Tel   01535 655228
Email   pickersgillmanorfarm@tiscali.co.uk
Web   www.pickersgillmanorfarm.co.uk

Entry 552   Map 12

Yorkshire

Knowles Lodge

Chris's father built this timber-framed house in 1938 on 18 acres of glorious hillside. It's a comfortable, comforting place to stay. Honey walls and polished floors give the sitting room a light, airy feel, cheerful throws on deep sofas make it cosy, and there are fine views of the River Wharfe and Dales Way through endless windows. Bedrooms are attractive with sprightly fabrics and fresh flowers; draw back the curtains and have your morning cuppa looking at those views. You're superbly well looked after, you can even get married here. Great walking and trout fishing, and the solitude a balm. *Children over seven welcome.*

Yorkshire

Austwick Hall

Feast on fabulous views of the Yorkshire Dales from this centuries-old hall. Michael and Eric welcome you into an astonishingly luxurious interior: log fire, stone floors, sweeping staircase... stained-glass sunlight beams in over the gallery. Oil paintings, old lamps (a secret passage!) bring the atmosphere alive. Bedrooms are silky antique chic, all chandeliers and Persian rugs; luxuriate in the Blue Room's roll top bath. There are heady sights and scents in the verdant grounds and breathtaking hikes in the Three Peaks. Enchanting, opulent, quirky, comfortable – the hall and your hosts. *Min. stay two nights at weekends.*

Travel Club Offer: see page 392 for details

Price	£90. Singles £55.
Rooms	3: 2 doubles, 1 twin.
Meals	Packed lunch £5. Pubs/restaurants within 2 miles.
Closed	Never.
Directions	From Skipton A59 to Bolton Abbey. At r'bout, B6160 for Burnsall. 3 miles after Devonshire Arms, right imm. after Barden Tower for Appletreewick. Down hill, over bridge, up hill & on for 0.75 miles. Cross bridge; imm. on left.

Price	£95-£155. Singles £85-£145.
Rooms	4: 2 doubles, 1 four-poster, 1 suite.
Meals	Packed lunch £5. Dinner, 5 courses, £30. Pub/restaurant 0.5 miles.
Closed	Never.
Directions	1 mile off A65, midway between Kendal & Skipton. Follow sign for Austwick, through village. House on left halfway up hill towards the moors (marked 'No Through Road').

	Pam & Chris Knowles-Fitton
	Knowles Lodge,
	Appletreewick, Skipton,
	Yorkshire BD23 6DQ
Tel	01756 720228
Fax	01756 720381
Email	pam@knowleslodge.com
Web	www.knowleslodge.com

	Michael Pearson & Eric Culley
	Austwick Hall,
	Austwick,
	Settle,
	Yorkshire LA2 8BS
Tel	01524 251794
Email	austwickhall@austwick.org
Web	www.austwickhall.co.uk

Entry 553　Map 12

Entry 554　Map 12

Yorkshire

Brandymires

The Wensleydale hills lie framed through the windows of the time-warp bedrooms; no TV, no fuss, just calm. In the middle of the National Park, this is a glorious spot for walkers. Gail and Ann bake their own bread and make jams and marmalade, and their delicious, well-priced dinners are prepared with fresh local produce and served at your own table. Two bedrooms, not in their first flush of youth, have four-posters; all have the views. If you're arriving by car, take the 'over-the-top' road from Buckden to Hawes for the most stunning countryside. *Minimum stay two nights. Children over eight welcome.*

Ethical Collection: Food. See page 400 for details.

Travel Club Offer: see page 392 for details.

Price	£52. Singles £31.
Rooms	3: 1 twin, 2 four-posters, all sharing 2 bath/shower rooms.
Meals	Dinner, 4 courses, £18.50 (not Thurs). Pubs/restaurant 5-minute walk.
Closed	November–February.
Directions	300 yds off A684, on road north out of Hawes, signed Muker & Hardraw. House on right.

Gail Ainley & Ann Macdonald
Brandymires,
Muker Road,
Hawes,
Yorkshire DL8 3PR
Tel   01969 667482

Entry 555   Map 12

Yorkshire

Mallard Grange

Perfect farmhouse B&B. Hens, cats, sheepdogs wander the garden, an ancient apple tree leans against the wall, guests unwind and feel part of the family. Enter the rambling, deep-shuttered 16th-century farmhouse, cosy with well-loved family pieces, and feel at peace with the world. Breakfast is generous – homemade muffins, poached pears with cinnamon and a sizzling full Monty. A winding steep stair leads to big, friendly bedrooms, two cheerful others await in the outhouses and Maggie's enthusiasm for this glorious area is as genuine as her love of doing B&B. *Minimum stay two nights at weekends.*

Travel Club Offer: see page 392 for details.

Price	£75–£90. Singles from £60.
Rooms	4: 1 double, 3 twins/doubles.
Meals	Pubs/restaurants 10-minute drive.
Closed	Christmas & New Year.
Directions	B6265 from Ripon for Pateley Bridge. Past entrance to Fountains Abbey. House on right, 2.5 miles from Ripon.

Maggie Johnson
Mallard Grange,
Aldfield, Ripon,
Yorkshire HG4 3BE
Tel   01765 620242
Mobile   07720 295918
Email   maggie@mallardgrange.co.uk
Web   www.mallardgrange.co.uk

Entry 556   Map 12

Yorkshire

Lawrence House

A classically comfortable house run with faultless precision by John and Harriet – former wine importer and interior decorator respectively. The house is listed, and Georgian, the garden is formal, flagged and herbaceous, the position – by the back gate to Studley Royal, overlooking long meadow and parkland – is supreme. There's a linen-sofa'd drawing room just for guests, and the promise of a very good dinner. Bedrooms and bathrooms are in a private wing: light, well-proportioned, full of special touches. And Fountains Abbey awaits your discovery. *Golf, riding & clay pigeon shooting can be arranged.*

Price	£110. Singles £70.
Rooms	2: 1 twin/double, 1 twin.
Meals	Dinner £30. Pub/restaurant 1 mile.
Closed	Christmas & New Year.
Directions	A1 to Ripon. B6265 & Pateley Bridge road for 2 miles. Left into Studley Roger. House last on right.

John & Harriet Highley
Lawrence House,
Studley Roger, Ripon,
Yorkshire HG4 3AY

Tel	01765 600947
Fax	01765 609297
Email	john@lawrence-house.co.uk
Web	www.lawrence-house.co.uk

Yorkshire

Park House

The soundtrack could be *Perfect Day*: a scenic drive, delicious cake on arrival, undisturbed peace in the converted estate cottages – partly built with stone from next door's stunning Cistercian Jervaulx Abbey, owned by your hosts. Antique gems stand out among leather bucket chairs, splashes of colour brighten a neutral palette, guest bedrooms are luxurious. Try Carol's bacon, egg and maple crumpets for breakfast – the menu lists local suppliers. Leave pets and children at home but take boots and binoculars for the glorious scenery of Nidderdale: an AONB and a fitting backdrop to a perfect country stay.

Price	From £70. Singles from £45.
Rooms	3: 2 doubles, 1 twin.
Meals	Packed lunch £3-£5. Pub 1.25 miles.
Closed	Never.
Directions	House is midway between Masham & Leyburn, about 25 minutes off A1. Full directions given on booking.

Ian & Carol Burdon
Park House,
Jervaulx, Ripon,
Yorkshire HG4 4PH

Tel	01677 460184
Mobile	07730 983439
Email	ba123@btopenworld.com
Web	www.jervaulxabbey.com

Yorkshire

Mill Close

Country-house B&B in a tranquil spot among fields and woodland; spacious, luxurious and with your own entrance through a flower-filled conservatory. Beds are large and comfortable, there's a grand four-poster with a spa bath, and candle scones for flickering light. Be spoiled by handmade chocolates, fluffy robes, even your own 'quiet' fridge. A blue and cream sitting room has an open fire – but you are between the National Park and the Dales so walks are a must. Start with one of Patricia's famous breakfasts: bacon and sausages from the farm, smoked haddock or salmon, homemade jams. Bliss.

Travel Club Offer: see page 392 for details.

Price	£80-£90. Singles £45-£65.
Rooms	3: 2 doubles, 1 four-poster.
Meals	Pubs/restaurants 2 miles.
Closed	Christmas & New Year.
Directions	Follow the brown tourist signs from the village of Patrick Brompton on A684. Farm is 1 mile from village.

Patricia Knox
Mill Close,
Patrick Brompton, Bedale,
Yorkshire DL8 1JY
Tel   01677 450257
Email   pat@millclose.co.uk
Web   www.millclose.co.uk

Entry 559   Map 12

Yorkshire

Lovesome Hill Farm

Who could resist home-reared lamb followed by sticky toffee pudding? This is a working farm and the Pearsons the warmest people imaginable; even in the mayhem of the lambing season they greet you with homemade biscuits and Yorkshire tea. Their farmhouse is as unpretentious as they are: chequered tablecloths, cosy and simple bedrooms (four in the old granary, one in the cottage) with garden and hill views, and a proper Victorian-style sitting room. The A167 traffic hum mingles with the odd sheepdog bark; you are brilliantly placed for the Moors and Dales. Good for walkers, families, business people.

Travel Club Offer: see page 392 for details.

Price	£64-£70. Singles £35-£42. Gate Cottage: £70-£80.
Rooms	5: 1 twin, 1 double, 1 family room, 1 single. Gate Cottage: 1 double.
Meals	Dinner, 2-3 courses, £15-£20. BYO. Packed lunch for walkers. Pub 4 miles.
Closed	Rarely.
Directions	From Northallerton, A167 north for Darlington for 4 miles. House on right, signed.

John & Mary Pearson
Lovesome Hill Farm,
Lovesome Hill, Northallerton,
Yorkshire DL6 2PB
Tel   01609 772311
Email   pearsonlhf@care4free.net
Web   www.lovesomehillfarm.co.uk

Entry 560   Map 12

Yorkshire

Millgate House

The perfect hideaway, tucked quietly off the main square. One moment you are on a town pavement facing a sober Georgian front; the next, in a lofty room, elegant with Adam fireplace, fine mouldings, period furniture and myriad prints and paintings. Bedrooms and bathrooms are similarly splendid, with wooden shutters, cast-iron baths and dramatic Swale valley views; breakfasts are generous and superb. As if this were not enough, there is the most enchanting walled garden adorned with hostas, clematis, old roses – a feast for the senses in spring and summer. Tim and Austin are engaging hosts.

Price	£95-£120. Singles £85.
Rooms	3: 1 double, 1 twin; 1 double with separate bath/shower.
Meals	Restaurant 250 yds.
Closed	Never.
Directions	Next door to Halifax Building Society in the centre, opp. Barclays at bottom of Market Place. Green front door with small brass plaque.

	Austin Lynch & Tim Culkin
	Millgate House,
	Richmond, Yorkshire DL10 4JN
Tel	01748 823571
Mobile	07738 298721
Email	oztim@millgatehouse.demon.co.uk
Web	www.millgatehouse.com

Entry 561   Map 12

Yorkshire

Hill Top

Books, magazines, bath essences, biscuits by the bed – and the charming, warm and artistic Christina. Her pretty, listed, limestone farmhouse dates from 1820 and is deceptively big. Ivory walls are a perfect foil for some good furniture and paintings; the sitting room overlooks the charming garden and has a cosy fire. Bedrooms are comfy and conventional; food is fresh, interesting and as homemade as possible. Far-reaching views over rolling countryside in this AONB where waterfalls, moorland and castles beckon. Handy for Scotland or the south. *Babes in arms & children over seven welcome.*

Price	£70. Singles £35.
Rooms	2: 1 twin; 1 twin sharing bath (let to same party only).
Meals	Dinner, 2-3 courses, £15-£20. Pub/restaurant 1.5 miles.
Closed	Christmas & New Year.
Directions	From Scotch Corner west on A66. Approx. 7 miles on, down hill. Left to Newsham. Through village; 2nd left opp. sign on right for Helwith. House on right, name on gate.

	Christina Farmer
	Hill Top,
	Newsham, Richmond,
	Yorkshire DL11 7QX
Tel	01833 621513
Email	plow67@tiscali.co.uk

Entry 562   Map 12

Yorkshire

Dunsa Manor

Come when there are drifts of snowdrops up the drive. A ha-ha divides the lawns, terraces and paddock from the 600 acres of farmland (arable, dairy, sheep). Built by Ignatius Bonomi in 1841, the listed house has been in the family for 140 years. Spacious reception rooms face south to the hills; equally good-sized bedrooms are furnished with Edwardian and Victorian pieces and 20th-century basins. Outside is a charming new terrace for a fine day with planted pergola and views. Perfect peace and countryside for walking and riding; hire a horse or bring your own, return to an excellent dinner.

Price	£80. Singles £55.
Rooms	2: 1 double with separate bath; 1 family room with separate shower.
Meals	Dinner, 2 courses, £27.50. Pub 3 miles.
Closed	Rarely.
Directions	Off A66 west of Scotch Corner. Left at sign for Dalton, 1.75 miles, into narrow country lane. Dunsa Manor is approx. 200 yds on left. 1st drive on left.

Shaheen Burnett
Dunsa Manor,
Dalton, Richmond,
Yorkshire DL11 7HE

Tel	01325 718251
Mobile	07817 028237
Email	shaheenburnett@btinternet.com
Web	www.dunsamanor.com

Entry 563   Map 12

Yorkshire

Cliffe Hall

What remains is the Victorian section of an earlier mansion, embellished by Richard's family in 1858. Inside is a beautifully proportioned and charming family home: huge reception rooms, plasterwork ceilings, acres of sofas, family portraits, cases of books. Bedrooms are traditional and uncontrived, bathrooms carpeted and twin beds super-comfy; large windows look onto the glorious grounds (anyone for tennis?) and a croquet lawn that runs down to the Tees where you fish for trout. Soft, timeless grandeur, visiting thesps, a sweet dog and a hostess who is as special as her house.

Ethical Collection: Food. See page 400 for details.

Travel Club Offer: see page 392 for details.

Price	£80. Singles £40.
Rooms	2 twins, each with separate bath.
Meals	Pub 1 mile.
Closed	10 December–1 January.
Directions	From A1, exit onto B6275. North for 4.2 miles. Into drive (on left before Piercebridge); 1st right fork.

Caroline & Richard Wilson
Cliffe Hall,
Piercebridge, Darlington,
Yorkshire DL2 3SR

Tel	01325 374322
Mobile	07785 756380
Fax	01325 374947
Email	petal@cliffehall.co.uk

Entry 564   Map 12

Scotland

Aberdeenshire

Woodend House

Elegant riverside living at a fishing lodge by the river Dee – one of the most magnificent settings in Scotland. Outside, a wild, wonderful garden; inside, beautiful wallpapers, fabrics and rugs. The dining hall leads to the kitchen with an Aga, the drawing room has dreamy river views, the large bedrooms ooze comfort and more fabulous views, and the bathrooms have old cast-iron baths and fine toiletries. Breakfast and dinner are local, seasonal and first-class. All this, and a fishing hut and a secure rod room for salmon and sea trout fishing in season. *Minimum stay two nights.*

Aberdeenshire

Lys-na-Greyne House

Peace, tranquillity and a natural welcome – one of the loveliest places in this book. Expect a sweeping stair, sun-streamed rooms, log fires, a country-house feel and the most comfortable beds in Scotland. Your room may be huge – two are; one with a dressing room and a balcony, all with family antiques, bathrobes, fine linen, Spode china… and views of river, field, forest and hill where osprey and lapwing glide. Meg picks flowers and organic veg from the garden and her food is delicious; David is an enthusiastic naturalist and can advise on walking and wildlife. Nearby, golf, fishing and castles by the hatful.

Travel Club Offer: see page 392 for details.

Price	£100. Singles £75.
Rooms	3: 1 double, 1 twin; 1 twin with separate bath.
Meals	Dinner, 4 courses, £30. Packed lunch £5-£10. Pub 2 miles.
Closed	Christmas, New Year & occasionally.
Directions	Directions on booking.

Price	£90. Singles from £45.
Rooms	3: 1 twin/double; 2 twins/doubles with separate bath/shower. Extra shower available.
Meals	Supper £25. Pub/bistro 15-minute walk.
Closed	Rarely.
Directions	From Aboyne, A93 west for Braemar. Just before 30mph sign, left down Rhu-na-Haven Rd. House 400 yds on, 4th gateway on right.

Miranda & Julian McHardy
Woodend House,
Trustach, Banchory,
Aberdeenshire AB31 4AY
Tel   01330 822367
Mobile   07812 142728
Email   miranda.mchardy@woodend.org
Web   www.woodend.org

David & Meg White
Lys-na-Greyne House,
Rhu-na-Haven Road,
Aboyne,
Aberdeenshire AB34 5JD
Tel   01339 887397
Fax   01339 886441
Email   meg.white@virgin.net

Entry 565   Map 19

Entry 566   Map 19

Aberdeenshire

Lynturk Home Farm

The stunning drawing room, with pier-glass mirror, ancestral portraits and enveloping sofas, is reason enough to come, while the food, served in a candlelit, deep-sage dining room, is delicious, with produce from the farm. You're treated very much as friends here and your hosts are delightful. It's peaceful, too, on the Aberdeenshire Castle Trail. The handsome farmhouse has been in the family since 1762 and you can roam the surrounding 300 acres of rolling hills. Inside, good fabrics and paints, hunting prints and some lovely family pieces. "A blissful haven," says a reader. *Fishing, shooting & golf breaks.*

Price	From £80. Singles £50.
Rooms	3: 2 twins/doubles; 1 double with separate bath.
Meals	Dinner, 4 courses, £25. Pub 1 mile.
Closed	Rarely.
Directions	20 miles from Aberdeen on A944 (towards Alford); thro' Tillyfourie, then left for Muir of Fowlis & Tough; after Tough, 2nd farm drive on left, signed.

John & Veronica Evans-Freke
Lynturk Home Farm,
Alford,
Aberdeenshire AB33 8DU

Tel	01975 562504
Mobile	07773 389793
Fax	01975 563517
Email	lynturk@hotmail.com

Entry 567   Map 19

Aberdeenshire

Ford of Clatt

A perfect, and peaceful, retreat for writers, artists and anybody wishing to hide away. Lucy and her family have a lovely, 19th-century former drovers' inn with an atmosphere of quiet serenity, tucked in below the Correen hills. Your bedroom is a warm, comfortable sanctuary with family photos, a spotted teapot, books and fresh flowers on antique tables; chill out on a striped sofa stool, watch the view from the cane chairs by the window or loll in a roll top with L'Occitane soaps. Breakfast is hearty, perfect for walkers, and there are interesting megalithic standing stones; Lucy offers massage to yomp-weary limbs.

Price	£60. Singles £42.
Rooms	1 twin/double.
Meals	Packed lunch on request. Pub/restaurants within 2 miles.
Closed	Rarely.
Directions	From Aberdeen A96. 7 miles after Invervrie left at Oyne fork. After Oyne, left to Clatt. After Leslie T-junc, house on corner on right; turn into courtyard.

Lucy Aykroyd
Ford of Clatt,
Clatt, Huntly,
Aberdeenshire AB54 4PJ

Tel	01464 831115
Mobile	07732 749833
Email	me@lucyaykroyd.co.uk
Web	www.fordofclatt.co.uk

Entry 568   Map 19

Aberdeenshire

Old Mayen

Follow narrow lanes crowded by beech trees and hedges, through high rolling hills and fast flowing rivers to this beautiful house perched next to a farm and overlooking the unspoilt valley below. You get classic country-house style in elegant bedrooms, spoiling bathrooms, a book-filled sitting room, cut flowers and a delicious candlelit dinner by a roaring fire. Fran and Jim are infectiously enthusiastic and kind; breakfasts are a moveable feast (outside in good weather) and the garden hums with birds. A fine retreat for tired and jaded souls – and there are castles, distilleries and gardens to visit.

Aberdeenshire

Balwarren Croft

Thirty acres at the end of a farm track, a field of Highland cattle, mixed woodland, ancient dykes, a lochside full of birdlife, a herb garden with over 200 varieties and a burn you may follow down the hill. Hazel and James, warm, friendly, quietly passionate about green issues, came to croft 25 years ago. The whole place is a delight: cathedral roof, shiny wooden floors, cashmere blankets, sparkling bathrooms, log fires, delicious breakfasts (home eggs, jams and chutneys) and dinners a treat. A beautiful, uplifting place in an area steeped in mystery – and peace. *Courses in dry stone walling & all things herbal.*

Travel Club Offer: see page 392 for details.

Price	£80. Singles £45.
Rooms	2: 1 double; 1 double with separate shower.
Meals	Dinner £25. Supper £18. Packed lunch £8.
Closed	Rarely.
Directions	From A96, A97 to Banff. After crossing river Deveron (9 miles), left onto B9117; 3 miles, on left behind thick beech hedge.

Price	£68–£74. Singles £40–£46.
Rooms	2: 1 twin; 1 double.
Meals	Dinner, 3 courses, £22. Pub/restaurant 10 miles.
Closed	Rarely.
Directions	North from Aberchirder on B9023. Right at Lootcherbrae (still B9023); 2nd left for Ordiquhill. After 1.7 miles, right at farm track opp. Aulton Farm; last croft up track.

	James & Fran Anderson Old Mayen, Rothiemay, Huntly, Aberdeenshire AB54 7NL
Tel	01466 711276
Fax	01466 711276
Email	oldmayen@tiscali.co.uk

	Hazel & James Watt Balwarren Croft, Ordiquhill, Cornhill, Aberdeenshire AB45 2HR
Tel	01466 751688
Fax	01466 751688
Email	balwarren@tiscali.co.uk
Web	www.balwarren.com

Entry 569   Map 19

Entry 570   Map 19

Angus

Newtonmill House

The house and grounds are in apple-pie order; the owners are charming and unobtrusive. This is a little-known part of Scotland, so explore the glens, discover deserted beaches and traditional fishing villages, and play a round or two of golf on one of the many good courses nearby. Return to a cup of tea in an elegant sitting room, then a proper supper of seasonal, local and home-grown produce. Upstairs are crisp sheets, soft blankets, feather pillows, fresh flowers, homemade fruit cake and sparkling, warm bathrooms with thick towels; you are beautifully looked after here.

Travel Club Offer: see page 392 for details.

Price	£96. Singles £58.
Rooms	2: 1 twin; 1 double with separate bath.
Meals	Dinner from £28. Supper from £18. BYO. Packed lunch £10. Pub 2 miles.
Closed	Christmas.
Directions	Aberdeen-Dundee A90, turning marked Brechin/Edzell B966. Heading towards Edzell, Newtonmill House is 1 mile on left, drive marked by pillars and sign.

Rose & Stephen Rickman
Newtonmill House,
By Brechin,
Angus DD9 7PZ
Tel   01356 622533
Mobile   07793 169482
Email   rrickman@srickman.co.uk
Web   www.newtonmillhouse.co.uk

Entry 571   Map 19

Angus

Ethie Castle

Amazing. A listed Pele tower that dates to 1300 and which once was home to the Abbot of Arbroath, murdered in St Andrews on Henry VIII's orders. His private chapel remains, as does his secret stair. As for the rest of the house: turret staircases, beautiful bedrooms, a 1500s ceiling in the Great Hall, a Tudor kitchen with a walk-in fireplace that burns night and day. Kirstin and Adrian are experts at breathing new life into old houses and have already started to reclaim the garden. Lunan Bay, one of Scotland's most glorious beaches, is at the end of the road. There's a loch too.

Price	From £95. Singles from £75.
Rooms	3: 1 four-poster; 1 twin/double, 1 double, each with separate bath/shower.
Meals	Dinner, 4 courses with wine, £30. Packed lunch up to £10. Pub/restaurant 3 miles.
Closed	Rarely.
Directions	North from Arbroath on A92; right after Shell garage for Auchmithie; left at T-junc.; on for 2 miles; at BT phone box, private road to Ethie Barns in front.

Adrian & Kirstin de Morgan
Ethie Castle,
Inverkeilor, Arbroath,
Angus DD11 5SP
Tel   01241 830434
Fax   01241 830432
Email   kmydemorgan@aol.com
Web   www.ethiecastle.com

Entry 572   Map 16+19

Argyll & Bute

Sithe Mor House

Terrific views from this lovely house on the shores of Loch Awe; its own bay and jetty below, acres of sky above and a winning pair at the helm. Patsy ensures all runs smoothly and John, a former oarsman of repute and the first man to row each way across Scotland, sweeps you along with joie de vivre. With ornate plasterwork, antlers and oils, lofty domed ceilings in the bedrooms and loch views, this 1880s house combines a baronial feel with massive luxury in bathrooms, beds and fabrics. Stay for dinner, borrow a kilt, marvel at the Oxford and Cambridge boat race memorabilia. *Minimum stay two nights.*

Price	£100–£110. Singles £60–£75.
Rooms	2: 1 double, 1 twin/double.
Meals	Dinner, 4 courses, £35. Restaurants & pub 0.5–3 miles.
Closed	Rarely.
Directions	A82 from Glasgow; A85 from Tyndrum. At Taynuilt, left onto B845 to Kilchrenan village. After 1 mile, single track 'No Through Road' to Taychreggan. House is last on left.

Patsy & John Cugley
Sithe Mor House,
Kilchrenan, Loch Awe,
Argyll & Bute PA35 1HF

Tel	01866 833234
Mobile	07748 522783
Email	patsycugley@tiscali.co.uk
Web	www.sithemor.com

Entry 573   Map 17

Argyll & Bute

Dun Na Mara

Twenty paces from the door, past the standing stone, a sweep of private beach and – on a clear day – dazzling views to Mull. The Arts & Crafts house has been given a minimalist makeover by Mark and Suzanne – ex-architects and friendly, caring, interesting hosts. The result is a luminous interior of low-slung beds, quilted throws, cream bucket chairs, sensual bathrooms, colourful cushions and sea views from three bedrooms. Breakfast on banana and walnut porridge, kedgeree, the full Scottish works; end the day with sherry in the sitting room, magazines, DVDs, beautiful art and books. *Children over 12 welcome.*

Price	£90–£105. Singles £50–£65.
Rooms	7: 5 doubles, 2 singles.
Meals	Pubs 3 miles.
Closed	December–January.
Directions	North from Oban on A828; over Connel Bridge; north for two miles; house signed left just after lay-by, before Benderloch village.

Mark McPhillips & Suzanne Pole
Dun Na Mara,
Benderloch, Oban,
Argyll & Bute PA37 1RT

Tel	01631 720233
Email	stay@dunnamara.com
Web	www.dunnamara.com

Entry 574   Map 17

Argyll & Bute

Barndromin Farm

Jamie and Morag run the farm – and three children, two collies, one kelpie, a clutch of hens and Frank the cat. It's a busy home, and a happy one, that opens its arms to guests. Bedrooms are carpeted and comfy, with flowery duvets and pretty family pieces, there's a big red sofa in the drawing room and a polished table for breakfast – tuck into croissants, bacon, sausages, black pudding, farm eggs. As for the views: the farmhouse, in the family for 100 years, is set on the hillside overlooking the glassy loch. Fish, walk, ride, spot grouse, sheep, cows, deer, red squirrels and rare butterflies. Gorgeous.

Price	From £70.
Rooms	3: 1 double, 1 twin, 1 double with private bath.
Meals	Pub/restaurant 4-6 miles.
Closed	Never.
Directions	6 miles south of Oban on A816 to Lochgilphead. Take 2nd entrance on left 200 yds after Knipoch Hotel.

Jamie & Morag Mellor
Barndromin Farm,
Knipoch, By Oban,
Argyll PA34 4QS
Tel 01852 316297
Mobile 07775 741617
Email mogsmellor@hotmail.co.uk
Web www.knipochbedandbreakfast.com

Argyll & Bute

Glenmore

A pleasing buzz of family life and no need to stand on ceremony. The house was built in 1854 but it's the later 30s additions that set the style: carved doorways, red-pine panelling, Art Deco pieces, oak floors, elaborate cornicing and a curvy stone fireplace. Alasdair's family has been here for 140 years and much family furniture remains. One of the huge doubles is arranged as a suite with a single room and a sofabed; bath and basins are chunky 30s style with chrome plumbing. From the organic garden and the house there are magificent views of Loch Melfort with its bobbing boats; you're free to come and go as you please.

Price	£70-£90. Singles £40-£50.
Rooms	2: 1 family suite; 1 double with separate bath/shower.
Meals	Pub 0.5 miles, restaurant 1.5 miles.
Closed	December & January.
Directions	From A816 0.5 miles south of Kilmelford; a private tree lined avenue leads to Glenmore. House signed from both directions. Go past Lodge House at bottom of drive; follow drive for 0.25 miles to big house.

Melissa & Alasdair Oatts
Glenmore,
Kilmelford, Oban,
Argyll & Bute PA34 4XA
Tel 01852 200314
Mobile 07786 340468
Email oatts@glenmore22.fsnet.co.uk
Web www.glenmorecountryhouse.co.uk

Argyll & Bute

Melfort House

Enter a wild landscape of hidden glens, ancient oak woods and rivers that tumble to a blue sea. Find a Georgian-style, beautifully renovated house with views straight down the loch, exquisite furniture, designer fabrics, oak flooring and original paintings and prints. Bedrooms are sumptuous, with superb views (especially the Loch room with its Art Deco bathroom in veridian green), soft carpets, warmth and comfort. Yvonne and Matthew (who cooks) are brilliant at looking after you; breakfast on fresh fruit, Stornoway black pudding, tattie scones fresh from the Aga – even chilli omelettes! Argyll at its finest.

Price	£85–£115. Singles from £65. £15 for sofabed.
Rooms	3: 1 double, 2 twins/doubles.
Meals	Dinner, 3 courses, from £26. Packed lunch £7. Pub/restaurant 400 yds.
Closed	Rarely.
Directions	From Oban take A816 south, signed Campbeltown. After 14 miles, go thro' Kilmelford, then right to Melfort. Follow road & bear right after bridge.

	Yvonne & Matthew Anderson
	Melfort House,
	Kilmelford, By Oban,
	Argyll & Bute PA34 4XD
Tel	01852 200326
Mobile	07718 930007
Email	relax@melforthouse.co.uk
Web	www.melforthouse.co.uk

Argyll & Bute

Corranmor House

A radiant setting on the Ardfern peninsula. Barbara and Hew are as generous and committed to their guests as they are to the 400-acre farm, where they rear sheep and geese. The drawing room started life as a 16th-century bothy (you'd never guess!), the red dining room sparkles with silver, they enjoy dining with guests and the food is delicious: goose, mutton, lamb, or fish from local landings. Bedrooms are exceptionally private – the double across the courtyard, the suite with the log-fired sitting room. Wander and admire; the eye always comes to rest on the water and boats of Loch Craignish and the Sound of Jura.

Price	£80. Suite £80–£135. Singles £45.
Rooms	2: 1 double & sitting room; 1 family suite & sitting room.
Meals	Lunch £15. Dinner, 3 courses and cheese, £30; with lobster £45. Pubs/restaurants 0.75 miles.
Closed	1 December–3 January; 4th week of August.
Directions	From A816, B8002 to Ardfern, & thro' village; 0.75 miles past church, long white house high on right. Right by Heron's Cottage, up drive.

	Hew & Barbara Service
	Corranmor House,
	Ardfern,
	Lochgilphead,
	Argyll & Bute PA31 8QN
Tel	01852 500609
Fax	01852 500609
Email	corranmorhouse@aol.com

Argyll & Bute

The Lodge

You are in Campbell country! Follow the rambling road around Loch Fyne to this elegant Victorian shooting lodge with an ancient oak woodland in its grounds. Enter a grand, enormously high ceilinged entrance hall, horned animals keeping watch from their lofty mantle. The house is a treasure trove... of mahogany bookcases and portraits in gold frames, candelabras, tapestries and open period fireplaces. Fall asleep over a copy of Dickens (no TV signal here!) beneath a coronet canopy, wake refreshed for a highland stroll with a hamper from Loch Fyne Oysters: pâté, smoked salmon, oatcakes, a bottle of wine.

Price	£80. Singles £60.
Rooms	1 double with separate bath.
Meals	Packed lunch or hamper £15-£20. Restaurants 5 miles. Oyster bar 7 miles.
Closed	Rarely.
Directions	From Glasgow on A83, left on A815 to St Catherine's. Train station: Arrochar, 11 miles.

Mr & Mrs Michael Thorndyke
The Lodge,
St Catherine's,
Loch Fyne,
Argyll & Bute PA25 8AZ
Tel 01499 302208
Email lauri.thorndyke@btinternet.com

🛉 ✗ 🐕

Entry 579   Map 14

Argyll & Bute

Achamore House

No traffic jams here, tucked between the mainland and Islay. Despite its grandeur – turrets, Arts & Crafts doors, plasterwork ceilings – Achamore is not stuffy and neither is Don, your American host. A coastal skipper, he can take you to sea, or over to other islands in his diesel catamaran. Find warm wood panelling and light-washed rooms, huge bedrooms with shuttered windows, oversize beds, heavy antiques; all have iPods and music. You get the run of the house – billiard room, library, large lounge, TV room (great for kids). With 50 acres of gardens and a quiet beach it's ideal for big parties or gatherings.

💼 Travel Club Offer: see page 392 for details.

Price	£90-£130. Singles from £35.
Rooms	9: 2 doubles, 1 family room; 2 doubles sharing bath; 2 twins/doubles sharing bath; 2 singles sharing bath.
Meals	Pub/restaurant 1 mile.
Closed	Rarely.
Directions	Uphill from ferry landing, turn left at T-junc.; 1 mile, stone gates on right, signed; house at top of drive.

Don Dennis
Achamore House,
Isle of Gigha,
Argyll & Bute PA41 7AD
Tel 01583 505400
Fax 01583 505 387
Email gigha@atlas.co.uk
Web www.achamorehouse.com

🛉 ✗ 📧 🚂 🐕 🚲

Entry 580   Map 14

Ayrshire

Langside Farm

Your hosts' gentle intelligence and humour is reflected in their home – the main part dates back to 1745 – with long views to the east. Inside, a well-proportioned Georgian elegance, fresh contemporary artwork (some Elise's) and a snug Aga kitchen. Deep red sofas, pale striped walls, books and lamps draw you in; pretty bedrooms have a period feel and vary in style. Local (much organic) produce promises fine breakfasts and suppers; water comes from a private spring. There's good walking and golf nearby. Chat in the kitchen, sit by the fire, make yourselves truly at home.

Price	£59-£79. Singles from £36.50.
Rooms	3: 1 twin/double, 1 twin, 1 four-poster.
Meals	Packed lunch £5.50. Supper £15. Dinner £24.50. Pubs/restaurants 5-10 minute drive.
Closed	November, January & February.
Directions	0.7 miles from Dalry end of B784. B784 links B780 Dalry to Kilbirnie road to A760 Kilbirnie to Largs road.

Nick & Elise Quick
Langside Farm,
Dalry,
Ayrshire KA24 5JZ
Tel   01294 834402
Fax   08700 569380
Email   mail@langsidefarm.co.uk
Web   www.langsidefarm.co.uk

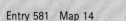

Entry 581   Map 14

Ayrshire

The Carriage House

An avenue of limes, 250 acres of parkland, rhododendrons, wellingtonia – what a view to wake to! Luke's family have owned the estate and castle for 900 years. Their stylishly converted Carriage House, with its ochre walls, cobbled courtyard and drawing room, is full of light and comfortable good taste; polished floors, handsome antiques, family photographs, contemporary fabrics. Aga-cooked breakfasts are taken in a huge kitchen with hand-crafted fittings. Tennis court, swimming pool, country walks: this is an elegant place to unwind. The Borwicks are confident and keen hosts.

Price	£90. Singles £55.
Rooms	3: 1 double, 1 twin/double, 1 single/twin.
Meals	Pubs/restaurants 3-7 miles.
Closed	Rarely.
Directions	From Beith enter Dalry on A737. First left (signed Bridgend Industrial Estate); uphill through houses, past farm on right at top of hill. First right into Blair Estate.

Luke & Caroline Borwick
The Carriage House,
Blair, Dalry,
Ayrshire KA24 4ER
Tel   01294 833100
Mobile 07831 301294
Email   blairenterprises@btconnect.com
Web   www.blairestate.com

Entry 582   Map 14

Ayrshire

Heughmill

Five acres of fields and lawn with free-range hens that kindly donate for breakfast and huge views to the sea. The house is just as good, surrounded by old stone farm buildings, with climbing roses and a small burn tumbling through. Inside, a lovely country home with tapestries in an airy hall, an open fire in the sitting room and a terrace that sits under a vast sky. Country-house bedrooms are stylishly homely. Two have the view, one has an old armoire, another comes with a claw-foot bath; all have delightful art. Julia sculpts, Mungo cooks breakfast on the Aga. Rural Ayrshire waits, yet you are close to the airport.

Price	£65-£80.
Rooms	3: 2 twins/doubles, 1 twin.
Meals	Pubs within 2 miles.
Closed	Christmas & New Year.
Directions	3 miles south of Kilmarnock, turn east down B730 for Tarbolton. After 0.75 miles, right onto narrow road signed Ladykirk. House is 250 yds on right.

Mungo & Julia Tulloch
Heughmill,
Craigie,
By Kilmarnock,
Ayrshire KA1 5NQ
Tel   01563 860389
Web   www.stayprestwick.com

Entry 583   Map 14

Clackmannanshire

Kennels Cottage

Live the dream: tour Scotland by classic car. Sandy does Triumphs, Austin Healeys, convertible Beetles. Tanya spoils you, with big crisp beds, huge white towels, elegant blinds, orchids and oriental touches. The old gamekeeper's cottage is a stunningly fresh, stylish and immaculate place, all white walls, white sofas, books, paintings and the odd flash of gold. In the morning, feast on local bacon, Fair Trade coffees and eggs from their hens served at one convivial table. Take a picnic to the garden, wander through what was the Dollarbeg estate, replete with pheasant and deer... totally unwind.

Price	£70-£80. Singles £50.
Rooms	3 doubles.
Meals	Packed lunch £10. Pub 2 miles.
Closed	January & February.
Directions	From Dollar take B913 towards Blairingone. House 2 miles from Dollar just before Blairingone.

Tanya Worsfold & Sandy Stewart
Kennels Cottage,
Dollarbeg, Dollar,
Clackmannanshire FK14 7PA
Tel   01259 742186/742476
Fax   01259 743716
Email   tanya.worsfold@btinternet.com
Web   www.guesthousescotland.co.uk

Entry 584   Map 15

Dumfries & Galloway

Knockhill

Fabulous Knockhill: stunning place, stunning position, a country house full of busts and screens, oils and mirrors, chests and clocks, rugs and fires. In the intimate drawing room stuffed with treasures, floor-to-ceiling windows look down the wooded hill. Fine stone stairs lead to country-house bedrooms that are smart yet homely: headboards of carved oak or padded chintz, books and views. Come for a grand farming feel and delicious Scottish meals; the Morgans are the most unpretentious and charming of hosts. Mellow, authentic, welcoming – an enduring favourite.

Price	£80–£84. Singles £54.
Rooms	2: 1 twin; 1 twin with separate bath.
Meals	Dinner £26. Pub 5 miles.
Closed	Rarely.
Directions	From M74 junc. 19 B725 for Dalton. Look out for signpost by church in Ecclefechan to Hoddam Castle. After 1.2 miles right at x-roads for Lockerbie. 1 mile on, right at stone [not whitewashed] lodge cottage. At top of long drive.

Yda & Rupert Morgan
Knockhill,
Lockerbie, Dumfries & Galloway
DG11 1AW
Tel   01576 300232
Fax   01576 300818
Email   morganbellows@yahoo.co.uk

Entry 585   Map 15

Dumfries & Galloway

Applegarth House

Here is an old peaceful manse at the top of the hill, right next door to the church, with a 12th-century motte; the views from the pretty garden stretch for miles around. The house is a good size, with original pine floors and sweeping stairs. Off the large and light landing are three bedrooms with warm carpets, shuttered windows and glorious garden and country views. Let the tawny owls lull you to sleep then wake to freshly stewed fruits and excellent porridge. There are paths to wander through the flower beds, statues to admire and endless wildlife; a perfect stop off point for a trip north or south.

Price	£80–£84. Singles from £54.
Rooms	3: 2 twins; 1 double with separate bath.
Meals	Dinner £26. BYO. Hotel restaurant 1.5 miles.
Closed	Rarely.
Directions	M74 junc. 17 to Lockerbie, B7076 for Johnstonebridge. 1st right after 1.5 miles; after 100 yds left over m'way bridge. After 1 mile, right at T-junc., then 2nd left to church. Next to church.

Frank & Jane Pearson
Applegarth House,
Lockerbie, Dumfries & Galloway
DG11 1SX
Tel   01387 810270
Fax   01387 811701
Email   jane@applegarthtown.demon.co.uk

Entry 586   Map 15

Dumfries & Galloway

Craigadam

A 1703 house set in 700 acres, where pheasants strut proudly up the drive. The farmhouse becomes a 'country house' inside: a sitting room with three vast sofas and numerous chairs, a dining table that seats 26, seven rooms in the stables, three more in the house, a billiard room and an honesty bar. Delightful, energetic Celia pulls it all together and creates a house-party feel. The food and wines are fabulous and the lamb, venison, partridge and duck come from the family's organic farm. Retire to a themed bedroom (Scottish, African, Chinese), a deep soak and a comfortable bed.

Price	From £88. Singles on request.
Rooms	10 suites.
Meals	Dinner £25. Pub 2 miles.
Closed	Christmas & New Year.
Directions	A75, then north on A712 towards Corsock. After 2 miles, Craigadam signed on right.

Mrs Celia Pickup
Craigadam,
Castle Douglas, Dumfries & Galloway
DG7 3HU

Tel	01556 650100
Fax	01556 650100
Email	inquiry@craigadam.com
Web	www.craigadam.com

Entry 587 Map 15

Dumfries & Galloway

Chipperkyle

Sink into the sofas without worrying about creasing them; this beautiful Scottish-Georgian family home has not a hint of formality, and the sociable Dicksons put you at your ease. Sitting and dining rooms connect through a large arch; there are family pictures, rugs on wooden floors and a log fire. Upstairs: a cast-iron bed dressed in good linen, striped walls, flowered curtains, lots of books and windows with views – this wonderful house just gets better and better. There are 200 acres, dogs, cats, donkeys and hens, and you can walk, play golf, visit gardens, sail or cycle – in magnificent countryside.

Price	£92.
Rooms	2: 1 double; 1 twin with separate bath/shower. Cot available.
Meals	Dinner available for groups. Pub 3 miles.
Closed	Christmas.
Directions	A75 Dumfries ring road for Stranraer. Approx. 12 miles to Springholm & right to Kirkpatrick Durham. Left at x-roads, after 0.8 miles, up drive on right by white lodge.

Willie & Catriona Dickson
Chipperkyle,
Kirkpatrick Durham, Castle Douglas,
Dumfries & Galloway DG7 3EY

Tel	01556 650223
Mobile	07917 730009
Email	special_place@chipperkyle.co.uk
Web	www.chipperkyle.co.uk

Entry 588 Map 11

Dumfries & Galloway

Chlenry Farmhouse

A wonderful approach, private and peaceful. Beyond the romantic old buildings in the glen and the rushing burn, the handsome house comes into view. It is a big traditional farmhouse full of old-fashioned comfort and fresh flowers, with charming owners and friendly dogs. In peaceful bedrooms, solid antiques jostle with tasselled lampshades, silk flowers and magazines on country matters; there are proper big bath tubs and suppers for walkers. Meals can be simple or elaborate, often with game or fresh salmon; gardens and golf courses wait to be discovered.

Dunbartonshire

Blairbeich Plantation

Past swaying birches to a Swedish wonderland in the woods. It is a beautiful fusion of antique and modern and a mini-loch laps three feet from its walls. There are light stone floors and cathedral ceilings and delightful ground-floor bedrooms that look onto the loch — an enclave of wilderness that universities come to study. Despite all this it is the interior that knocks you flat: Malla — relaxed, friendly, a fine cook — has covered every inch with something spectacular and the sitting room is a private art gallery. Mosaic showers, orchids, woodpeckers... and curling on the loch in winter. Fabulous.

Travel Club Offer: see page 392 for details.

Price	£70. Singles from £45.
Rooms	3: 1 twin with separate bath; 1 double, 1 twin sharing bath.
Meals	Supper, £17.50. Dinner, 4 courses, £30. Packed lunch £6. Pub 1.5 miles.
Closed	Christmas, New Year & occasionally.
Directions	A75 for Stranraer. In Castle Kennedy, right opp. Esso station. Approx. 1.25 miles on, after right bend, right signed Chlenry. Down hill, 300 yds on left.

David & Ginny Wolseley Brinton
Chlenry Farmhouse,
Castle Kennedy, Stranraer,
Dumfries & Galloway DG9 8SL

Tel	01776 705316
Mobile	07704 205003
Email	wolseleybrinton@aol.com
Web	www.chlenryfarmhouse.com

Entry 589   Map 14

Price	£70–£100. Singles from £60.
Rooms	2 doubles.
Meals	Dinner, 4 courses, £35. Pub/restaurant 1.5 miles.
Closed	Rarely.
Directions	From west, A811 into Gartocharn; 1st right (School Road); 1 mile up to T-junction, then left; house on right, signed.

Malla Macdonald
Blairbeich Plantation,
Gartocharn,
Loch Lomond,
Dunbartonshire G83 8RR

Tel	01389 830257
Email	macdonald@blairbeich.com
Web	www.blairbeich.com

Entry 590   Map 14

Dunbartonshire

Finglen House

The Campsie Hills rise behind (climb them and you can see Loch Lomond), the Fin Burn takes a two-mile tumble down the hill into the garden, and herons and wagtails can be spotted from the breakfast table. All this 40 minutes from Glasgow. Sabrina's designer flair gives an easy, graceful comfort to the whole house: good beds in stylish rooms, proper linen, French touches, eclectic art, cast-iron baths and cream-painted wooden floors. A fresh, elegant drawing room with log fire is yours to share. Douglas, a documentary film maker, knows the Highlands and Islands well; he and Sabrina are fun and good company.

Price	£80. Singles £50.
Rooms	2: 1 double;
	1 double with separate bath.
Meals	Pub 5-minute drive.
Closed	Christmas & New Year.
Directions	A81 from Glasgow right on A891 at
	Strathblane. 3 miles on, in
	Haughhead, look for a wall & trees
	on left, & turn in entrance signed
	Schoenstatt. Immed. left to house.

	Sabrina & Douglas Campbell
	Finglen House,
	Campsie Glen,
	Dunbartonshire G66 7AZ
Tel	01360 310279
Mobile	07774 820454
Email	sabrina.campbell@btinternet.com
Web	www.finglenhouse.com

Entry 591   Map 15

Edinburgh & the Lothians

Lochmill House

Susan is delightful and kind and spoils you rotten. Her home-baking is wicked (expect a feast for breakfast), her green fingers produce fresh flowers from a pretty, peaceful garden all year round, and she's hot on Scottish history so can help you make the best of your stay. The house is modern and on the edge of town, a mile or so from the M9 and very easy for Edinburgh and Glasgow. Big lovely rooms swim with light, there's a smart multi-windowed sitting room to relax in and a spotless country-cosy bedroom with wicker chairs and crisp linen. *Children over 12 welcome.*

Price	£75. Singles £40.
Rooms	1 twin.
Meals	Occasional supper/dinner.
	Packed lunch £6.
	Pub & restaurants 0.5 miles.
Closed	Christmas & occasionally.
Directions	From west M9, junc 4. From east
	M9 junc. 3, then A803 into
	Linlithgow. There, north onto
	A706 for Bo'ness & 0.2 miles on
	left. Follow to very end of road.

	Mr & Mrs W Denholm
	Lochmill House,
	3 Lade Court,
	Linlithgow,
	West Lothian EH49 7QF
Tel	01506 846682
Mobile	07759 959414
Email	susanedenholm@hotmail.com

Entry 592   Map 15

24 Saxe Coburg Place

A ten-minute walk – or an even quicker bus ride – from the centre of Edinburgh, this 1827 house stands in a quiet, no-through road with a communal garden in the centre. There's a garden level entrance to three simple and luxurious bedrooms with extra long beds, good lighting, handsome antiques and spotless bathrooms – one with Paris metro tiling in white and green. Most excitingly you can nip over the street in your bathrobe to the Victorian Baths for a swim, sauna or workout in the gym; all before a delicious, generous continental breakfast in the hall, or on the pretty terrace in summer. Marvellous.

7 Gloucester Place

A cantilevered staircase in walnut and mahogany, a soaring hand-painted cupola: the classic Georgian townhouse is five minutes from Princes Street. Rooms are cosy yet immaculate, sprinkled with paintings and decorative things from travels to far-flung places. Bedrooms are comfy, traditional and well-stocked with books and radio (and there are Z-beds for children). Bag the south-facing double with its stunning Art Deco bathroom and garden views. Naomi is pretty relaxed and happy to chat to you about the local music and art scene, or to leave you in peace. An interesting and hospitable place to unwind.

Price	£75–£120. Singles £40–£55.
Rooms	3: 1 double, 1 twin/double, 1 single.
Meals	Continental breakfast. Restaurants/pubs 5-minute walk.
Closed	Rarely.
Directions	From George St, down Frederick St. Over 3 sets of lights, left at bottom of hill. Right up Clarence St; at junction, over to Saxe Coburg St. Saxe Coburg Place is at end. Ask about parking.

Price	£90–£110. Singles from £50.
Rooms	3: 1 double; 1 double with separate bath; 1 double with separate shower. Extra child beds.
Meals	Pubs/restaurants 300 yds.
Closed	Christmas & rarely.
Directions	From George St (city centre), down Hanover St, across Queen St at lights. Left into Heriot Row, right onto India St, then left.

Diana McMicking
24 Saxe Coburg Place,
Edinburgh EH3 5BP

Tel	0131 315 3263
Mobile	07979 351717
Email	diana@saxecoburgplace.co.uk
Web	www.saxecoburgplace.co.uk

Naomi Jennings
7 Gloucester Place,
Edinburgh EH3 6EE

Tel	0131 225 2974
Mobile	07803 168106
Email	naomijennings@hotmail.com
Web	www.stayinginscotland.com

21 India Street

Portraits of the Macpherson clan beam down upon you at delicious breakfast served in a sunny and elegant dining room. In this house of great character you are cared for by Zandra, who offers guests the Laird's Room with its half-tester and the (smaller) Patio Room with its own front entrance. And it's just a hop and a skip up the majestic cobbled streets of New Town to Princes Street and the centre. Zandra plays the Scottish harp, loves to cook, has two beautiful black labs and has written about her life as wife of a clan chieftain – read up about it all in the spacious drawing room.

11 Belford Place

Guests love Susan's modern townhouse above the Water of Leith. A golden retriever wags his welcome in the wooden-floored entrance, a picture-lined staircase winds upward. Outside, New Zealand flax bursts into flower while herons and foxes share an exquisite sloping garden. Handsome rooms offer china cups and floral spreads; dazzling bathrooms have Molton Brown goodies. Taste Stornoway black pudding at the gleaming breakfast table – there are simple suppers and box lunches if you're on the trot. You hear owls at night yet you're a hop from the city, with free parking and a bus stop nearby. *Min. stay two nights in August.*

Travel Club Offer: see page 392 for details.

Price	£95–£127.50. Singles £60–£85.
Rooms	2: 1 double, 1 twin.
Meals	Restaurants close by.
Closed	Rarely.
Directions	Down South Queensferry Rd; left at Y-junc; at 2nd Y-junc. left into Craig Leith Rd. Thro' Stockbridge, over lights at bridge; 3rd right into Royal Circus; sharp right thro' Circus Gdns; left into India St.

Price	£70–£120.
Rooms	3: 1 double, 2 twins/doubles.
Meals	Supper £10. Packed lunch £10. Pub 200 yds, restaurants 10-min. walk.
Closed	Christmas.
Directions	From city centre go to Belford Road; Belford Place is 1st left after Travelodge Hotel. House is down hill opposite Edinburgh Sports Club. Free parking. No 13 bus goes past top of lane.

Mrs Zandra Macpherson of Glentruim
21 India Street,
Edinburgh EH3 6HE

Tel	0131 225 4353
Mobile	07817 334940
Email	zandra@twenty-one.co.uk
Web	www.twenty-one.co.uk

Lady Susan Kinross
11 Belford Place,
Edinburgh EH4 3DH

Tel	0131 332 9704
Mobile	07712 836399
Email	suekinross@blueyonder.co.uk
Web	www.edinburghcitybandb.com

Entry 595   Map 15

Entry 596   Map 15

12 Belford Terrace

Leafy trees, a secluded garden, a stone wall and, beyond, a quiet riverside stroll. Hard to believe that Edinburgh's galleries, theatres and restaurants are a few minutes' walk. This Victorian end terrace, beside Leith Water, oozes an easy-going elegance, helped by Carolyn's laid-back but competent manner. Ground-floor bedrooms – she lives at 'garden level' – are big and creamy with stripy fabrics, antiques, sofas and huge windows. (The single has a *Boys Own* charm.) Carolyn spoils with crisp linen, books and biscuits and a delicious, full-works breakfast. After a day in town, relax in the garden.

2 Fingal Place

An elegant house on a Georgian terrace. The leafy park lies opposite (look upwards to Arthur's Seat). Bustling theatres, shops and the university are a stroll away, yet this is a very quiet house. Your hostess is a Blue Badge Guide and will help plan your trips – or cater for celebrations and graduations with lunch and dinner; it's entirely flexible. Bedrooms are downstairs at garden level and have antique beds, spotless bathrooms and seductive linen; one looks onto a lovely patio garden. Noodle the Llasa Apso and Gillian's cat are equally welcoming. *Parking metered until 5.30pm weekdays.*

Travel Club Offer: see page 392 for details.

Price	£60–£100. Singles from £40.	Price	£80–£115 (£90–£130 during Festival). Singles from £55 (from £65 during Festival).
Rooms	3: 1 double, 1 twin/double; 1 single with separate shower.	Rooms	2: 1 twin (with single room attached), 1 twin.
Meals	Pub/restaurants within 10-minute walk.	Meals	Pubs/restaurants 100 yds.
Closed	Christmas.	Closed	22–27 December.
Directions	From Palmerston Place through 2 sets of lights, downhill on Belford Rd past Menzies Belford Hotel. Immediately left is Belford Terrace.	Directions	From centre of Edinburgh (West End), Lothian Rd to Tollcross (clock) & Melville Drive. At 2nd major lights, right into Argyle Place; immed. left into Fingal Place.

	Carolyn Crabbie 12 Belford Terrace, Edinburgh EH4 3DQ		**Gillian Charlton-Meyrick** 2 Fingal Place, The Meadows, Edinburgh EH9 1JX
Tel	0131 332 2413		
Mobile	07785 303396	Tel	0131 667 4436
Fax	0131 332 0224	Mobile	07880 705022
Email	carolyncrabbie@blueyonder.co.uk	Email	gcmeyrick@fireflyuk.net

Entry 597 Map 15

Entry 598 Map 15

20 Blackford Road

A 20-minute stroll from the Royal Mile is a substantial Victorian house with relaxed hosts and a touch of old-world luxury. From a cushioned window seat you gaze onto a lovely wildlife-filled walled garden where you can eat out on a warm day; breakfasts, though not the full Monty, are superb. Bedrooms, one up, one down, are tranquil and serene, with delicately papered walls and lush toile de Jouy; the drawing room, with cream sofas, soft lights, drinks tray and beautiful books, is elegant yet cosy. Lucas the rescue greyhound completes the picture – of a happy, charming place to stay. *Min. stay two nights in August.*

Price	£70–£90. Singles £60.
Rooms	2: 1 double/twin, 1 twin, each with separate bath.
Meals	Restaurants 500 yds.
Closed	Christmas & New Year.
Directions	A720 city bypass, take Lothianburn exit to city centre. Continue for 2.5 miles on Morningside Rd; right into Newbattle Terrace; 2nd left into Whitehouse Loan. Immed. right into Blackford Road. House at end on left.

	John & Tricia Wood
	20 Blackford Road, Edinburgh EH9 2DS
Tel	0131 447 4233
Mobile	07930 452945
Email	jwood@dsl.pipex.com

Entry 599　Map 15

1 Albert Terrace

A warm-hearted home with a lovely garden, an American hostess and two gorgeous Siamese cats. You are 20 minutes by bus from Princes Street yet the guests' sitting room overlooks pear trees and clematis and the rolling Pentland Hills. Cosy up in the winter next to a log fire; in summer, take your morning paper onto the terrace above the sunny garden. Books, fresh flowers, interesting art and ceramics and – you are on an old, quiet street – utter, surprising peace. Bedrooms are colourful, spacious and bright, one with an Art Deco bathroom and views over the garden. Clarissa is arty, easy, generous and loves having guests.

Price	£75–£85. Singles £35–£45.
Rooms	3: 1 double; 1 double, 1 single sharing bath.
Meals	Pubs/restaurants nearby.
Closed	Rarely.
Directions	From centre of Edinburgh, A702 south, for Peebles. Pass Churchill Theatre (on left), to lights. Albert Terrace 1st right after theatre.

	Clarissa Notley
	1 Albert Terrace, Edinburgh EH10 5EA
Tel	0131 447 4491
Email	canotley@aol.com

Entry 600　Map 15

Craigbrae

Half a mile down a narrow winding lane and you wash up at the old stone farmhouse, with huge windows overlooking fields and a cooperage across the yard. The house has been recently renovated so there's a lovely new bathroom in New England style and bedrooms that ooze tranquillity and thoughtful touches. Your hosts are hospitable and great fun; the drawing room is warm, cosy and homely; there are books, china, family pieces and good oils. Edinburgh is 15 minutes by train from the village, the airport 12 minutes by taxi or car. And there's a pretty garden that catches the sun.

Inveresk House

Cromwell stayed here, and plotted his siege of Edinburgh Castle; the house oozes history. The magnificent main rooms are furnished with ornate antiques, squashy sofas in chintzes, flowers, gilt, mirrors, seriously gorgeous rugs and Alice's own vibrant art. Bedrooms and bathrooms, on the expected scale, come with vintage radiators, huge beds, good old-fashioned comfort. Musicians will be happy – there are two baby grands. Come for Inveresk (a conservation village), golf (the course at Musselburgh is the oldest in the world), interesting conversation and history by the hatful. Edinburgh is a bus hop away.

Price	£70-£90. Singles from £35.
Rooms	3: 1 double; 2 twins/doubles sharing 2 bath/shower rooms.
Meals	Pubs/restaurants 2 miles.
Closed	Christmas.
Directions	Please ask for directions when booking.

Price	£100-£140. Singles £65.
Rooms	3: 1 double, 1 twin, 1 family room.
Meals	Pubs/restaurants in Musselburgh.
Closed	Rarely.
Directions	From Edinburgh, A199 (A1) to Musselburgh. There, signs to Inveresk. At top of Inveresk Brae, sharp right into cul-de-sac. 2nd opening on right, opp. gates with GM on them, bear right past cottages to house.

Louise & Michael Westmacott
Craigbrae,
Kirkliston,
Edinburgh EH29 9EL
Tel   0131 331 1205
Fax   0131 319 1476
Email   louise@craigbrae.com
Web   www.craigbrae.com

Alice & John Chute
Inveresk House,
3 Inveresk Village, Musselburgh,
East Lothian EH21 7UA
Tel   0131 665 5855
Mobile   07951 818560
Email   chute.inveresk@btinternet.com
Web   www.invereskhouse.com

Edinburgh & the Lothians

Letham House

Sweep down the rhododendron-lined drive to enter a magical, secret world. This fine, early 17th-century mansion has elegant staircases, resplendent fabrics, gleaming antiques and roaring fires; generous, people-loving Barbara and Chris just want you to enjoy it all. They give you complete privacy and tranquillity in stunning south-facing bedrooms; the views over mature trees and impeccable parkland are the stuff of dreams. Eat robustly, sleep peacefully, indulge yourself in gorgeous bathrooms; this is a nurturing retreat. You won't want to leave, but there are beaches and golf nearby; Edinburgh is beyond.

Price	£90–£150. Singles £55–£75.
Rooms	5: 2 doubles, 2 twins/doubles; 1 suite with separate bath.
Meals	Dinner, 3 courses, £30. Packed lunch £10. Guest kitchen. Pubs/restaurants 1 mile.
Closed	Rarely.
Directions	From A1 south, exit at Oak Tree junction. Follow signs for Haddington (B6471). Immed. right after 40mph signs, through large stone pillars. Straight down drive.

Barbara Sharman
Letham House,
Haddington,
East Lothian EH41 3SS
Tel   01620 820055
Mobile 07974 375775
Email   stay@lethamhouse.com
Web   www.lethamhouse.com

Entry 603   Map 15

Edinburgh & the Lothians

Eaglescairnie Mains

Wildlife thrives: eight acres of conservation headland have been created and wildflower meadows planted on this 350-acre working farm… you'd never guess Edinburgh is so close. The Georgian farmhouse sits in lovely gardens, its peace interrupted by the odd strutting pheasant. There's a traditional conservatory for summery breakfasts, a perfectly proportioned drawing room (coral walls, rich fabrics, log fire) for wintery nights, and beautiful big bedrooms full of books. Barbara is warm and charming, Michael's commitment to the countryside is wide-ranging, and the atmosphere is gracious and unhurried.

Ethical Collection: Environmen; Community.
See page 400 for details.

Price	£55–£75. Singles from £35.
Rooms	3: 2 doubles, 1 twin.
Meals	Pub 1 mile.
Closed	Christmas.
Directions	From A1 at Haddington B6368 south for Bolton & Humbie. Right immed. after traffic lights on bridge. 2.5 miles on through Bolton, at top of hill, fork left for Eaglescairnie. Entrance 0.5 miles on left.

Barbara & Michael Williams
Eaglescairnie Mains,
Gifford, Haddington,
East Lothian EH41 4HN
Tel   01620 810491
Fax   01620 810491
Email   williams.eagles@btinternet.com
Web   www.eaglescairnie.com

Entry 604   Map 16

Edinburgh & the Lothians

Glebe House

Gwen has lavished a huge amount of time and love on her 1780s manse. The perfect Georgian family house with all the well-proportioned elegance you'd expect, it is resplendent with original features – fireplaces, arched glass, long windows – that have appeared more than once in interiors magazines. Bedrooms are light, airy and hung with generous swathes of fabric. The sea is a stone's throw away and golfers have 21 courses to choose from. There's also a fascinating sea bird centre close by – yet you are 30 minutes from Edinburgh! Regular trains take you to the foot of the castle.

Price	£100. Singles by arrangement.
Rooms	3: 1 double, 1 twin, 1 four-poster.
Meals	Restaurants 2-minute walk.
Closed	Christmas.
Directions	From Edinburgh, A1 for Berwick. Left onto A198, follow signs into North Berwick. Right into Station Rd signed 'The Law', to 1st x-roads; left into town centre; house on left behind wall.

Gwen & Jake Scott
Glebe House,
Law Road, North Berwick,
East Lothian EH39 4PL

Tel	01620 892608
Mobile	07973 965814
Email	gwenscott@glebehouse-nb.co.uk
Web	www.glebehouse-nb.co.uk

Entry 605   Map 16

Fife

Blair Adam

If staying in a place with genuine Adam features is special, how much more so in the Adams' family home! They've been in this corner of Fife since 1733: John laid out the walled garden, son William was a prominent politician, Sir Walter Scott used to come and stay… you may be similarly inspired. The house stands in a swathe of parkland and forest overlooking the hills and Loch Leven, with big, friendly, light-flooded rooms filled with intriguing contents. The pretty bedroom is on the ground floor and you eat in the private dining room or with the family in the kitchen – you choose.

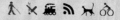 Travel Club Offer: see page 392 for details.

Price	From £90. Singles from £50.
Rooms	1 twin.
Meals	Dinner £20. Restaurants 5 miles.
Closed	December–January.
Directions	From M90 exit 5, take B996 south for Kelty. Right for Maryburgh, through village, right through pillars onto drive, under motorway via tunnel, then up to house.

Keith & Elizabeth Adam
Blair Adam,
Kelty,
Fife KY4 0JF

Tel	01383 831221
Mobile	07986 711099
Fax	01383 839971
Email	adamofblairadam@hotmail.com

Entry 606   Map 15

Fife

Fife

Ladywell House

Up the farm track to the large stone manse — once holiday home of Frances Shand Kydd. Duncan and Camilla invite you in to a big elegant hall and smart spotless bedrooms above, where cool neutrals mix with rich flashes of colour, crisp linen hugs squishy goose down, shutters open to wide views — and Diana's room stays largely untouched. In the drawing room are flamboyant curtains and huge cream sofas, an honesty tray and Camilla's clever jewellery for sale. Duncan cooks a locally sourced breakfast as generous as all the rest; for the evening there's Falkland, with its shops, cobbles and delicious places to dine.

Fincraigs

Immersed in delightful, forgotten countryside, this 18th-century farmhouse, once the factor's house, has an air of great comfort and warmth; Felicity and Tom make you feel instantly at home. There's a sunny drawing room with open fire and old family pieces, and a guest sitting area upstairs. Two pretty bedrooms have lovely linen and fine views over the garden and rolling hills. Fincraigs' ten acres, presided over by roaming hens and ducks, include an orchard and walled garden; expect fabulous home cooking and Tom's delicious wines. Fishing villages, the Tay estuary, East Neuk, Dundee and St Andrews are close by.

 Travel Club Offer: see page 392 for details.

Price	£60-£80. Singles from £45.
Rooms	3: 1 double, 1 twin; 1 twin with separate bath.
Meals	Pub 10-minute walk.
Closed	Rarely.
Directions	A92 north; 1st exit at 'New Inn' r'bout, signed Falkland. 2.5 miles just before village, farm road on left signed Ladywell House. Then 1st right through black gates.

Price	From £80. Singles from £40.
Rooms	2: 1 double; 1 twin with separate bath.
Meals	Dinner, 3 courses, from £25. Pubs 3-5 miles.
Closed	Occasionally.
Directions	From A92 heading north, left after Rathillet, at Balmerino/Gauldry sign. Fincraigs 1 mile from main road on left.

Duncan & Camilla Heaton Armstrong
Ladywell House,
Falkland,
Fife KY15 7DE

Tel	01337 858414
Mobile	07931 304436
Email	duncan@tullochscott.co.uk
Web	www.ladywellhousefife.co.uk

Felicity & Tom Gilbey
Fincraigs,
Kilmany,
Cupar,
Fife KY15 4QQ

Tel	01382 330256
Mobile	07971 627813
Email	anyone@fincraigs.freeserve.co.uk

Entry 607   Map 15

Entry 608   Map 15 +19

Fife

The Cottage

You have to be desperate to go to this wee B&B. If it's full, you could try next door: the owners, flushed with success from their first venture, carried on to build ten in a row. There's no view but this place is for lovers of privacy; indeed, most visitors tend to be fairly insistent about not sharing with other guests – a tug on the old handle may elicit a sharp 'no!' from within. The chic gold and turquoise exterior belies the rather spartan look within: a bare bulb and one seat to hover over. Ladies and gents are both welcome but not together – and as it's so popular, you may have to queue.

Price	A penny.
Rooms	1 single.
Meals	Meals not advised.
Closed	Probably.
Directions	Follow your nose.

Miss P Daily
The Cottage,
Slacksdown Lane,
Flushing PI5 5EE

Entry 609   Map 1212

Fife

18 Queen's Terrace

So peaceful that it's hard to imagine that you're in the heart of St Andrews and a mere ten-minute walk from the Royal & Ancient golf club. Jill's stylish and traditional home shows off her artistic flair; the light, restful drawing room and elegant dining room are full of character, sunlight and flowers. Large bedrooms have especially comfortable beds, crisp linens, whisky and water, and poetry and prose on bedside tables. An enchanting place – and Jill, friendly and generous, is a mine of information on art, gardens and walks; sit on the terrace in summer and admire the water garden. *Children over 12 welcome.*

Price	From £85. Singles £65–£70.
Rooms	4: 3 doubles, 1 twin.
Meals	Dinner, 3 courses with wine, £20–£35.
Closed	Rarely.
Directions	Into St Andrews on A917; pass Old Course Hotel. Right at 2nd mini r'bout, left through arch at 2nd mini r'bout. 250 yds, right into Queens Gardens. Right at T-junc. On left opp. church.

Jill Hardie
18 Queen's Terrace,
St Andrews,
Fife KY16 9QF

Tel	01334 478849
Fax	01334 470283
Email	stay@18queensterrace.com
Web	www.18queensterrace.com

Entry 610   Map 15 +19

Fife

Kinkell

An avenue of beech trees patrolled by guinea fowl leads to the house. If the sea views and the salty smack of St Andrews Bay air don't get you, step inside and have your senses tickled. The elegant drawing room has two open fires, rosy sofas, a grand piano – gorgeous. Bedrooms and bathrooms are immaculate, sunny and warm. There's great cooking too; Sandy and Frippy excel in the kitchen and make full use of local produce. From the front door head down to the beach, walk the wild coast, jump on a quad bike, try your hand at clay pigeon shooting. All this and wonderful hosts. *Minimum stay two nights wedding bookings.*

Price	£80. Singles from £50.
Rooms	3 twins/doubles.
Meals	Dinner £25. Restaurants in St Andrews, 2 miles.
Closed	Rarely.
Directions	From St Andrews, A917 for 2 miles for Crail. Driveway in 1st line of trees on left after St Andrews.

Sandy & Frippy Fyfe
Kinkell,
St Andrews,
Fife KY16 8PN
Tel   01334 472003
Fax   01334 475248
Email fyfe@kinkell.com
Web   www.kinkell.com

Entry 611   Map 16 +19

Fife

Falside Smiddy

The old smithy sits right on a bend (peaceful at night) but city dwellers won't mind. Saved from dereliction by Rosie and musical, chatty Keith, it is a home you are invited to share. Expect fresh flowers, maps on walls, books, boots and interesting ephemera – not for style seekers but this place is interesting and different. Small rooms have homemade biscuits and hat stands for clothes, bath and shower rooms are spotlessly clean. Rosie cooks a truly good breakfast and turns berries into jams, and the wood-burner makes winters cosy. Lovely walks from the door to the sea and you are close to golf courses.

Price	£56-£65. Singles £40.
Rooms	2 twins.
Meals	Pub 2 miles. St Andrews 4 miles.
Closed	Occasionally.
Directions	From St Andrews, A917 for Crail. After 4 miles, ignore turning for Boarhills, & continue to small river. Over bridge; house 2nd on left.

Rosie & Keith Birkinshaw
Falside Smiddy,
Boarhills,
St Andrews,
Fife KY16 8PT
Tel   01334 880479
Email rosiebirk@btinternet.com

Entry 612   Map 16 +19

Highland

The Grange

A Victorian townhouse with its toes in the country: the mountain hovers above, the loch shimmers below and whales have been sighted from the breakfast table. Bedrooms, one in a turret, another with a terrace, are large, luscious, warm and inviting – all crushed velvet, beautiful blankets and immaculate linen. Bathrooms are breathtaking and ooze panache. Expect neutral colours, decanters of sherry, a carved wooden fireplace, a Louis XV bed. Thoughtful breakfasts are served at glass-topped tables with flowers and white china; Joan's warm vivacity and love of B&B makes her a wonderful hostess.

Highland

Tigh An Dochais

A contemporary, award-winning, 'see-through' house on a narrow strip of land between the road and the rocky shoreline, with stunning views across Broadford bay and the mountains beyond. Full-length windows and a cathedral ceiling allow light to flood in to an oak-floored sitting room with a wood-burner and super modern art. Downstairs are bedrooms with crisp white linen, tartan throws and modern bathrooms with underfloor heating. Neil is passionate about local food; try black pudding from Stornoway at breakfast, good fish and game for supper. Step straight onto the beach here, or stride out for the hills.

Travel Club Offer: see page 392 for details.

Price	£98-£110.
	Singles 10% off room rate.
Rooms	3 doubles.
Meals	Restaurants 12-minute walk.
Closed	Mid-November to Easter.
Directions	A82 Glasgow-Fort William; there, right up Ashburn Lane, next to Ashburn guesthouse. On left at top.

Price	£70-£80. Singles £55-£65.
Rooms	3: 2 doubles, 1 twin/double.
Meals	Dinner, 4 courses, £22-£25. BYO. Packed lunch £5. Pub/restaurant 200 yds.
Closed	Rarely.
Directions	Leave Skye Bridge & follow A87 to Broadford. After 6 miles pass Hebridean Hotel on left, house is 200 yds further up A87 on right.

	Joan & John Campbell
	The Grange,
	Grange Road, Fort William,
	Inverness-shire PH33 6JF
Tel	01397 705516
Email	info@thegrange-scotland.co.uk
Web	www.thegrange-scotland.co.uk

	Neil Hope
	Tigh An Dochais,
	13 Harrapool,
	Isle of Skye IV49 9AQ
Tel	01471 820022
Email	hopeskye@btinternet.com
Web	www.skyebedbreakfast.co.uk

Entry 613   Map 17

Entry 614   Map 17

Highland

The Berry

Drive through miles of spectacular landscape then bask in the final approach down a winding single-track road to the hamlet of Allt-Na-Subh – just five houses by the stunning loch. Joan, who paints, is friendly and kind, and her Rayburn-warmed kitchen the hub of this croft-style modern house. Inside is fresh and light with simple bedrooms – one up, one down; the sitting room has open fires and south-facing views. Eat fish straight from the boats, stride the hills and spot golden eagles, red deer and otters. The perfect place for naturalists and artists, or those seeking solace. *Skye is a 20-minute drive.*

Price	£60. Singles from £30.
Rooms	2: 1 double with separate shower; 1 double sharing bath.
Meals	Dinner, 3 courses with wine, £28. Packed lunch £7. Pub 20-minute drive.
Closed	Rarely.
Directions	From A87 at Dornie follow signs for Killilin, Conchra & Salachy. House 2.7 miles on left.

Joan Ashburner
The Berry,
Allt-Na-Subh,
Dornie,
Kyle of Lochalsh,
Highland IV40 8DZ
Tel   01599 588259

Entry 615   Map 17

Highland

Tanglewood House

Down a steep drive through stunning landscape to this modern, curved house on the shore of Loch Broom – and distant views of the old fishing port of Ullapool. The drawing room is filled with antique rugs, fine fabrics, original paintings, flowers and a grand piano; bask in the views from the floor-to-ceiling window. Bedrooms are delightful: bold colours, crisp linen, proper bath tubs with fluffy towels. Anne gives you just-squeezed orange juice and eggs from her hens for breakfast, and delicious dinners; explore the wild garden then stroll to the rocky private beach for a swim in the loch. Superb. *Minimum stay two nights.*

Price	£82–£96. Singles £66–£73.
Rooms	3: 1 double, 2 twins.
Meals	Dinner, 4 courses, £33. BYO. Pubs in village 0.5 miles.
Closed	Christmas & New Year.
Directions	On outskirts of Ullapool from Inverness on A835, left immed. after 4th 40mph sign. Take cattle grid on right & left fork down to house.

Anne Holloway
Tanglewood House,
Ullapool,
Ross-shire IV26 2TB
Tel   01854 612059
Email   info@tanglewoodhouse.co.uk
Web   www.tanglewoodhouse.co.uk

Entry 616   Map 17

Highland

Invergloy House

A peaceful, no-smoking home run by Margaret, a professional musician and James, a retired chemical engineer. It is a converted coach house with stables in the beautiful Great Glen and sits in 50 wild lochside acres of rhododendron, woodland and wonderful trees. Bedrooms are traditional, warm and welcoming; views of Loch Lochy and the mountains from the big picture window in the guest drawing room are spectacular. Walk to the private shingle beach on the loch, spot the wild roe deer in the grounds, savour the secluded peace and quiet. *Children over eight welcome.*

Price	From £72. Singles £46.
Rooms	2: 1 double, 1 twin.
Meals	Restaurants 2-5 miles.
Closed	Christmas & New Year.
Directions	From Spean Bridge north on A82. After 5 miles, house signed on left.

Margaret & James Cairns
Invergloy House,
Spean Bridge,
Inverness-shire PH34 4DY
Tel 01397 712681
Email cairns@invergloy-house.co.uk
Web www.invergloy-house.co.uk

Entry 617   Map 18

Highland

The Old Ferryman's House

This former ferryman's house is small, homely and delightful, and just yards from the river Spey with its spectacular mountain views. Explore the countryside or relax in the garden with a tray of tea and homemade treats; there are plants tumbling from whisky barrels and baskets. The sitting room is cosy with a wood-burning stove and lots of books (no TV). Generous Elizabeth, a keen traveller who lived in the Sudan, cooks delicious and imaginative meals: wild salmon, herbs from the garden, heathery honeycomb, homemade bread and preserves. An unmatched spot for explorers, and very good value.

Price	£55. Singles £27.50.
Rooms	3: 1 double, 1 twin, 1 single, sharing 1 bath & 2 wcs.
Meals	Dinner, 3 courses, £19.50. BYO. Packed lunch £6.
Closed	Occasionally in winter.
Directions	From A9, follow main road markings through village, pass golf club & cross river. From B970 to Boat of Garten; house on left, just before river.

Elizabeth Matthews
The Old Ferryman's House,
Boat of Garten,
Inverness-shire PH24 3BY
Tel 01479 831370
Fax 01479 831370

Entry 618   Map 18

Highland

Craigiewood

The best of both worlds: the remoteness of the Highlands (red kites, wild goats) and Inverness just four miles. The landscape surrounding this elegant cottage exudes a sense of ancient mystery augmented by these six acres – home to woodpeckers, roe deer and glorious roses. Inside, maps, walking sticks, two cats and a lovely, family-home feel – what you'd expect from delightful owners. Bedrooms, old-fashioned and cosy, overlook a garden reclaimed from Black Isle gorse. Gavin runs garden tours and can take you off to Inverewe, Attadale, Cawdor and Dunrobin Castle. Warm, peaceful, special.

Highland

Wemyss House

The peace is palpable, the setting overlooking the Cromarty Firth is stunning. Take an early morning stroll and spot buzzards, pheasants, rabbits and roe deer. The deceptively spacious house with sweeping maple floors is flooded with light and fabulous views, big bedrooms are warmly decorated with Highland rugs and tweeds, there's Christine's grand piano in the living room, Stuart's handcrafted furniture at every turn, and a sweet rescue dog called Bella. Aga breakfasts include homemade bread, preserves and eggs from happy hens. Dinners are delicious, Christine and Stuart are wonderful hosts and readers are full of praise.

Travel Club Offer: see page 392 for details.

Price	£70-£80. Singles £40.
Rooms	2 twins.
Meals	Pub 2 miles.
Closed	Christmas & New Year.
Directions	A9 north over Kessock Bridge. At N. Kessock junc. filter left to r'bout to Kilmuir. After 0.25 miles, right to Kilmuir; follow road uphill, left at top, then straight on. Ignore 'No Through Road' sign, pass Drynie Farm, follow road to right; house 1st left.

	Araminta & Gavin Dallmeyer
	Craigiewood,
	North Kessock, Inverness,
	Inverness-shire IV1 3XG
Tel	01463 731628
Mobile	07831 733699
Email	2minty@craigiewood.co.uk
Web	www.craigiewood.co.uk

Entry 619   Map 18

Price	From £80.
Rooms	3: 2 doubles, 1 twin.
Meals	Dinner £30.
	Restaurants 15-minute drive.
Closed	Rarely.
Directions	From Inverness, A9 north. At Nigg r'bout, right onto B9175. Through Arabella; left at sign to Hilton & Shandwick; right towards Nigg; past church; 1 mile, right onto private road. House on right.

	Christine Asher & Stuart Clifford
	Wemyss House,
	Bayfield, Tain,
	Ross-shire IV19 1QW
Tel	01862 851212
Mobile	07759 484709
Email	stay@wemysshouse.com
Web	www.wemysshouse.com

Entry 620   Map 18

Highland

Loch Eye House

A serene place for walkers, golfers, naturalists – and anyone who enjoys sociable dinner at an elegant table where mahogany gleams and wine glasses sparkle. It was Lucinda's dream to live here – she has childhood memories of skating on the loch; now the handsome, sunny house (15th century at the back, 1870 at the front) is exquisitely furnished and filled with fresh flowers. Bedrooms have perfect proportions and harmonious colours, bathrooms are immaculate, one with loch views: spot rare birdlife as you soak. The lawns sweep towards the loch and every view is sublime.

Price	£90. Singles £45.
Rooms	3: 1 double; 1 double, 1 twin, sharing bath.
Meals	Dinner, 3 courses, £30.
Closed	Occasionally.
Directions	A9 for Tain, then B9165 for Fearn. 1st left for Loandhu, then 1.5 miles & on left.

Lucinda Poole
Loch Eye House,
Fearn,
Ross-shire IV20 1RS

Tel	01862 832297
Fax	01862 832914
Email	loofy@ndirect.co.uk

Highland

Linsidecroy

Heaven in the Highlands with stunning valley and mountain views. The house, built in 1863 was part of the Duke of Sutherland's estate; Robert, a factor, first set eyes on it 20 years ago and now it is home. A sublime renovation gives you walls of books, valley views and an open fire in the airy drawing room. Super bedrooms come with rugs, crisp linen, books galore and fresh flowers. There are two terraces, one for breakfast, one for pre-dinner drinks; all around you Davina's remarkable garden is taking shape. You can fish and walk, play some golf, or head north to Tongue through Britain's wildest land. Magical.

Price	£80. Singles £50.
Rooms	2: 1 double, 1 twin.
Meals	Hotel 6 miles.
Closed	Christmas, Easter & occasionally.
Directions	A836 west out of Bonar Bridge. After 4 miles, left onto A837. Cross Shin river, then right towards Rosehall & Lochinver, 1.5 miles, double wooden gates on right. House is 150 yds up drive.

Robert & Davina Howden
Linsidecroy,
Invershin, Lairg,
Sutherland IV27 4EU

Tel	01549 421255
Mobile	07776 259768
Email	howden@linsidecroy.wanadoo.co.uk

Highland

St Callan's Manse

Fun, laughter and conversation flow in this warm, relaxed and happy home. You share it with prints, paintings, antiques, sofas and amazing memorabilia – and three dogs, nine ducks, 14 hens and 1,200 teddy bears of every shape, size and origin. Snug bedrooms have pretty fabrics, old armoires, sheepskin rugs, tartan blankets. Caroline cooks delicious breakfasts and dinners; Robert, a fund of knowledgeable anecdotes, can arrange just about anything. All this in incomparable surroundings: glens, forests, buzzards, deer and the odd golden eagle. A gem. *2.5% credit card charge. Dogs by arrangement.*

Price	£80. Singles £65.
Rooms	2: 1 double with separate bath; 1 double with separate shower.
Meals	Dinner, 2-4 courses, £14.50-£25. BYO. Pub/restaurant in village, 1.5 miles.
Closed	Occasionally.
Directions	From Inverness, A9 north. Cross Dornoch bridge. 14 miles on, A839 to Lairg. Cross small bridge in Rogart; sharp right uphill, for St Callan's church. House 1.5 miles on, on right, next to church.

Robert & Caroline Mills
St Callan's Manse,
Rogart, Sutherland IV28 3XE

Tel	01408 641363
Fax	01408 641313
Email	robert@robertmills.me.uk
Web	www.miltonbankcottages.co.uk

Entry 623   Map 21

Highland

Thrumster House

A Victorian's laird's house in 12 acres of sycamore-wooded estate. Drive south a mile to the 5,000-year-old neolithic remains of the Yarrow Archeological Trail for brochs, round houses and long cairns, then back to the big old house, "steamboat gothic" in the words of an American guest. The vaulted hall gives an ecclesiastical feel, with fires burning at both ends and a grand piano on the landing (it gets played wonderfully). Big bedrooms have mahogany dressers, brass beds, floral wallpapers, lots of books. Islay and Catherine look after guests well and conversation flows. There's free trout fishing too.

Price	£80. Singles £45.
Rooms	2: 1 double; 1 twin with separate bath.
Meals	Dinner, 3 courses with wine, £30.
Closed	Rarely.
Directions	A99 north through Ulbster. After 2 miles, pass church & 'Yarrow Archaeological Trail' sign, then 1st left (200 yds) & up drive to house.

Islay MacLeod
Thrumster House,
Thrumster, Caithness KW1 5TX

Tel	01955 651387
Fax	01955 651733
Email	islay.macleod@btinternet.com
Web	www.thrumster.co.uk

Entry 624   Map 21

Moray

Inverugie

A handsome Georgian house with lofty porticos, generous bays, tall windows and impressive drive. The feel is solid and traditional inside: velvet sofas in sage-green and rose, floral curtains at pelmetted windows, touches of Art Deco... toile de Jouy in the double, cream padded headboards and new beds in the twin. The large dining and drawing rooms look over ancient woodland, pasture land and grazing sheep; beyond, beaches, castles, standing stones and rivers rich with salmon and trout. Lucy is a dynamo – finding time for riding, fieldsports, three young children and you; she even grinds her own flour for your bread.

Price	£60-£70.
Rooms	2: 1 twin/double; 1 double with separate bath.
Meals	Dinner £25. Pub 8 miles.
Closed	Christmas & New Year.
Directions	To Forres on A96, through Kinloss on B9089 to College of Roseisle village & over B9013. Veer right (for Duffus) & 1.3 miles on, left to Keam Farm. Past farm, house at end of road through stone pillars.

	Lucy Mackenzie
	Inverugie,
	Hopeman,
	Moray IV30 5YB
Tel	01343 830253
Email	machadodorp@compuserve.com
Web	www.inverugiehouse.co.uk

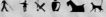

Moray

Westfield House

Sweep up the drive to the grand home of an illustrious family: Macleans have lived here since 1862. Inside: polished furniture and burnished antiques, a tartan-carpeted hall, an oak stair hung with ancestral oils. John farms 500 acres while Veronica cooks sublimely; dinner is served at a long candelabra'd table, with vegetables from the vegetable garden. A winter fire crackles in the guest sitting room, old-fashioned bedrooms are warm and inviting (plump pillows, fine linen, books, lovely views), the peace is deep. A historic house in a perfect setting, run by the most charming people.

Price	£80. Singles from £40.
Rooms	3: 1 twin; 1 twin with separate bath & shower; 1 single with separate bath.
Meals	Dinner, 3 courses, £25. Pub 3 miles.
Closed	Rarely.
Directions	From Elgin, A96 west for Forres & Inverness; after 2.5 miles, right onto B9013 for Burghead; after 1 mile, signed right at x-roads. Cont. to 'Westfield House & Office'.

	John & Veronica Maclean
	Westfield House,
	Elgin,
	Moray IV30 8XL
Tel	01343 547308
Fax	01343 551340
Email	veronicamaclean@hotmail.com

Moray

Blervie

The Meiklejohn coat of arms flies from the flagpole, an apple's throw from the orchard in which King Malcolm met his death. Blervie is a small 1776 mansion, "a restoration in progress", its finely proportioned rooms crammed with fresh flowers and splendid things to catch the eye. A large dresser swamped in china, a piano in the hall, books everywhere and the sweet smell of burnt beech from grand marble fireplaces. Big bedrooms have comfy old sofas at the feet of four-posters; bathrooms are eccentrically old-fashioned. Fiona and Paddy enjoy country pursuits and like to dine with their guests.

Price	£80.
Rooms	2: 1 four-poster; 1 four-poster with separate bath. Extra single bed.
Meals	Dinner, 4 courses, £28.
Closed	Christmas & New Year.
Directions	From A96 to Forres. South at clocktower, straight across r'bout onto B9010. Pass hospital; 1 mile on, left at Mains of Blervie sign. Right at farm.

Paddy & Fiona Meiklejohn
Blervie,
Forres,
Moray IV36 2RH
Tel   01309 672358
Email   meiklejohn@btinternet.com

Entry 627   Map 18

Perth & Kinross

Grenich Steading

Perched above silvery Loch Tummel is Lindsay's award-winning renovation of a once derelict barn. Inside, blue-and-white Portuguese tiles, seagrass matting and a wood-burning stove. You get a kitchen, dining and sitting room so you can self-cater too (minimum one week). Gaze upon mountain-to-loch views, walk in the unspoilt glen or visit the theatre at Pitlochry. Lindsay loves nurturing both garden and guests; her two Scottish deerhounds are welcoming too. The sunsets are fabulous, and there's so much to do you'll barely be inside. *Children over eight welcome. Min. stay two nights weekends May-October.*

Price	£70. Singles £50.
Rooms	2: 1 double; 1 twin sharing bath & sitting room (2nd room let to same party only).
Meals	Dinner by arrangement, Oct to Mar only, £26 inc. wine. Pub 0.75 miles.
Closed	Christmas & New Year.
Directions	From A9 north of Pitlochry, turn for Killiecrankie. Left onto B8019 for Tummel Bridge for 7 miles to Loch Tummel Inn. House, signed, 0.75 miles on, then up forestry track on right for 0.5 miles.

Lindsay Morison
Grenich Steading,
Strathtummel,
Pitlochry,
Perth & Kinross PH16 5RT
Tel   01882 634332
Mobile   07900 362179

Entry 628   Map 15 +18

Perth & Kinross

Beinn Bhracaigh

Here is a solid Victorian villa, with later wings, built for an Edinburgh family in the 1880s, when Pitlochry was hailed as the Switzerland of the North. Ann and Alf, generous hosts, have swept through with the cream paint and all is spanking new. Expect soft lighting, gleaming wooden floors, silk flowers, bowls of pot pourri and scented candles. The lounge is comfy and has an honesty bar with over 50 malt whiskies, good-sized bedrooms have excellent mattresses, padded head boards and views to the Tummel Hills, bathrooms are all new with thick towels and lovely lotions. Breakfast is a huge, imaginative feast.

Price	£60-£90. Singles from £45.
Rooms	10: 4 doubles, 6 twins/doubles.
Meals	Dinner £22.50-£30 (for groups only, by arrangement). Pubs/restaurants within 10-minute walk.
Closed	23-28 December.
Directions	From A9, turn for Pitlochry. Under railway bridge, then right at scout hut & up East Moulin Road. 2nd left into Higher Oakfield; house almost immediately on left.

Ann & Alf Berry
Beinn Bhracaigh,
14 Higher Oakfield, Pitlochry, Perth,
Perth & Kinross PH16 5HT
Tel 01796 470355
Mobile 07708 668436
Email info@beinnbhracaigh.com
Web www.beinnbhracaigh.com

Entry 629 Map 15 +18

Perth & Kinross

Rock House

Prepare to fall hopelessly in love. Hard to know here, high above Loch Tay, whether the views are more beautiful outside or in. The cathedral ceiling in the sitting room allows light to soar upwards, there's a striking collection of modern art and an unfussy style: white sofas, painted furniture, and, here and there, a bit of quirky fun or a perfect antique. Sleep deeply in beds piled with linen cushions, soft woollen throws and cotton ticking, wake to grape and mint salad, Irish bread, kedgeree or anything else you want... Roland and Penny are passionate about their house, the land, and real food.

Price	£100. Singles £80.
Rooms	2 doubles.
Meals	Dinner, 2-3 courses, £20-£30. Packed lunch £10. Pub/restaurant 2.2 miles.
Closed	Rarely.
Directions	From Aberfeldy, A827 dir. Kenmore. At Loch Tay where main road turns sharp right, cont. along narrow road signed Acharn. Follow loch side for 2.2 miles. At top of hill, house on right.

Roland & Penny Kennedy
Rock House,
Achianich, Kenmore, Aberfeldy,
Perthshire PH15 2HU
Tel 01887 830336
Fax 01887 830214
Email rockhouse@lochtay.co.uk
Web www.lochtay.co.uk

Entry 630 Map 15 +18

Craighall Castle

The view from the balcony that circles the drawing room is simply stunning, and the deep gorge provides the fabulous walks where you might glimpse deer, red squirrels and otters. Nicky and Lachie, ever welcoming, battle to keep up with the demands of the impressive home that has been in the family for 500 years. Any mustiness or dustiness can be forgiven, as staying here is a memorable experience. Nothing is contrived, sterile or luxurious, and there's so much drama and intrigue it could be the setting for a film. Breakfast is served in the 18th-century library, and there's a Regency drawing room, too.

Mackeanston House

They grow their own organic fruit, make their own preserves, bake their own bread. Likeable and energetic – Fiona a wine buff and talented cook, Colin a tri-lingual guide – your hosts are hospitable people whose 1690 farmhouse combines informality and luxury in peaceful, central Scotland. Light-filled bedrooms have soft carpets, pretty fabrics, fine antiques; one has a canopied bed, a double shower (with a seat if you wish it) and a bath that overlooks fields. In the conservatory with views to Stirling Castle you may dine on salmon from the Teith and game from close by. *Local & battlefield tours.*

Price	£80. Singles £45.
Rooms	2: 1 four-poster; 1 twin (extra single bed) with separate bath.
Meals	Restaurant 3 miles.
Closed	Christmas & New Year.
Directions	From Blairgowrie, A93 for Braemar for 2 miles. Just before end of 30mph limit, sharp right-hand bend, with drive on right. Follow drive for 1 mile.

Price	£92–£98. Singles £56–£59.
Rooms	2: 1 double, 1 twin/double.
Meals	Dinner £28. Pub 1 mile.
Closed	Christmas.
Directions	From M9, north, junc. 10 onto A84 for Doune. After 5 miles, left on B826 for Thornhill. Drive on left after 2.2 miles, right off farm drive.

Nicky & Lachie Rattray
Craighall Castle,
Blairgowrie,
Perth & Kinross PH10 7JB

Tel	01250 874749
Fax	01250 874749
Email	lrattray@craighall.co.uk

Fiona & Colin Graham
Mackeanston House,
Doune, Stirling,
Perth & Kinross FK16 6AX

Tel	01786 850213
Mobile	07921 143018
Email	enquiries@mackeanstonhouse.co.uk
Web	www.mackeanstonhouse.co.uk

Perth & Kinross

Old Kippenross

Pink since 1715 (a signal to Jacobites that the house was a safe haven), Old Kippenross rests in a wooden valley overlooking the river Allan – spot herons, dippers and otters. The Georgian part was built above the 500-year-old Tower House, and its rustic white-vaulted basement embraces dining room and sitting room, strewn with soft sofas and Persian rugs. Upstairs there are deeply comfortable sash-windowed bedrooms and warm, well-equipped bathrooms stuffed with towels. Sue and Patrick (who is an expert on birds of prey) are welcoming; breakfast and dinner are delicious. *Children over ten welcome. Dogs by arrangement.*

Price	£90. Singles from £60.
Rooms	2: 1 double, 1 twin.
Meals	Dinner £27. BYO. Pub 1.5 miles.
Closed	Rarely.
Directions	M9 exit 11, B8033 for Dunblane. 500 yds, right over dual c'way, thro' entrance by stone gatehouse. Down drive, 1st fork right after bridge. House along gravelled drive.

Sue & Patrick Stirling-Aird
Old Kippenross,
Dunblane,
Perth & Kinross FK15 0LQ

Tel	01786 824048
Fax	01786 824482
Email	kippenross@hotmail.com

Entry 633   Map 15

Scottish Borders

Over Langshaw Farm

A peaceful place in the rolling hills of the Scottish Borders, with an inspiring commitment to organic food and good husbandry. The energy here goes into Friesians and ewes, homemade farmhouse ice creams, bonny brown hens and guests. So, a cheery place for families and walkers, with unsophisticated bedrooms, old-fashioned bathrooms and a guest sitting room with a log fire and white shutters. Plus all the nooks and crannies you'd expect from a 1700s house, and a sweet smiling welcome from Sheila. She and Martyn have detailed walking maps and could not be more helpful. Authentic – and with views to die for.

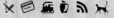 Travel Club Offer: see page 392 for details

Price	£65. Family room £75. Singles £35.
Rooms	2: 1 double; 1 family room with separate bath.
Meals	Dinner from £20. Packed lunch from £5. Pubs/restaurants 4-5 miles.
Closed	Never.
Directions	North from Galashiels, A7 past Torwoodlea golf course & right to Langshaw. After 2 miles, right at T-junc., then left at Earlston sign in Langshaw. White house, in trees, signed at farm road.

Sheila & Martyn Bergius
Over Langshaw Farm,
Galashiels,
Scottish Borders TD1 2PE

Tel	01896 860244
Fax	01896 860668
Email	overlangshaw@btconnect.com

Entry 634   Map 15

Scottish Borders

Fauhope House

Near to Melrose Abbey and the glorious St Cuthberts' Walk, this solid 1890s house is immersed in bucolic bliss. Views soar to the Eildon Hills through wide windows with squashy seats; all is elegant, fire-lit, fresh and serene. Bedrooms are warm with deeply coloured walls, thick chintz, pale tartan blankets and soft carpet; bathrooms are modern and pristine. Breakfast is served with smiles at a flower-laden table and overlooking those purple hills. A short walk through the garden and over a footbridge takes you to the interesting town of Melrose, with shops, restaurants and its own theatre.

Price	From £80. Singles from £55.
Rooms	3 twins/doubles.
Meals	Pub/restaurant 0.5 miles.
Closed	Rarely.
Directions	From A7, through Gattonside; at end of village, at sign on left 'Monkswood', immed. left; right up drive.

Ian & Sheila Robson
Fauhope House,
Gattonside, Melrose,
Scottish Borders TD6 9LY

Tel	01896 823184
Mobile	07816 346768
Fax	01896 820188
Email	fauhope@bordernet.co.uk

Entry 635   Map 15

Scottish Borders

Skirling House

An intriguing house with 1908 additions, impeccably maintained. The whole lovely place is imbued with the spirit of Scottish Arts & Crafts, augmented with Italianite flourishes. Colourful blankets embellish chairs; runners soften flagged floors; the carvings, wrought-ironwork and rare Florentine ceiling are sheer delight. Upstairs, a more English comfort holds sway: carpets and rugs, window seats and wicker, fruit and flowers. Bob cooks the finest local produce, Isobel shares a love of Scottish contemporary art and both look after you beautifully. Outside: 25,000 newly planted trees and grand walks from the door.

Price	£110–£120. Singles £60.
Rooms	5: 3 doubles, 1 twin, 1 twin/double.
Meals	Dinner £32. Pubs/restaurants 2 miles.
Closed	Christmas & January-February.
Directions	From Biggar, A702 for Edinburgh. Just outside Biggar, right on A72 for Skirling. Big wooden house on right opp. village green.

Bob & Isobel Hunter
Skirling House,
Skirling, Biggar,
Scottish Borders ML12 6HD

Tel	01899 860274
Fax	01899 860255
Email	enquiry@skirlinghouse.com
Web	www.skirlinghouse.com

Entry 636   Map 15

Scottish Borders

Lessudden

A treat to stay in a great and historic tower house in the heart of the Scottish Borders. Your generous hosts give you big cosy bedrooms with private bathrooms and a spacious sitting room with fine old rugs, heaps of books and a log fire. Memorable meals are served at a polished oak refectory table beneath the gaze of Sir Walter Scott's uncle and aunt; they lived here, he was a frequent visitor. The 1680s white-stone stairwell is unique, the décor is traditional and homely, the living is relaxed and Alasdair and Angela care for their guests as open-heartedly as they do their cats, dogs, horses and hens.

Price	From £70. Singles from £50.
Rooms	2: 1 double; 1 twin with separate bathroom.
Meals	Dinner, 3-4 courses, £25. Pub 0.5 miles.
Closed	Rarely.
Directions	North on A68 to St Boswells. Right opp. Buccleuch Arms Hotel, on through village; left up drive immed. beyond turning to golf course.

	Alasdair & Angela Douglas-Hamilton
	Lessudden,
	St Boswells,
	Scottish Borders TD6 0BH
Tel	01835 823244
Fax	01835 823244
Email	alasdaird@lineone.net
Web	www.lessudden.com

Entry 637   Map 16

Scottish Borders

New Belses Farm

Once lost by Lord Lothian in a game of backgammon, this Georgian farmhouse is safe in current hands. Delightful Helen divides her time between between helping on the farm, gardening and caring for sundry pets, fan-tail doves, hens (fox permitting), family and guests. Bedrooms glow in a harmony of old paintings, lush chintzes and beautiful antiques; beds are extra long, towels snowy white. It's like home, only better. Discover great Border towns, stunning abbeys, fishing on the Tweed. Enjoy an excellent dinner locally then back to plump sofas by the log fire. Heaven.

Price	From £80.
Rooms	2: 1 double, 1 twin.
Meals	Pubs/restaurants 3.5-5 miles.
Closed	Christmas.
Directions	From Jedburgh, A68 for Edinburgh. Left after 3.5 miles to Ancrum; B6400 Ancrum to Lilliesleaf road; right after 4 miles, down drive (signed).

	Peter & Helen Wilson
	New Belses Farm,
	Ancrum, Jedburgh,
	Scottish Borders TD8 6UR
Tel	01835 870472
Mobile	07710 277020
Fax	01835 870482
Email	wilson699@totalise.co.uk

Entry 638   Map 16

Stirling

The Moss

Rozie loves fishing and Jamie keeps bees; they live in a charming listed house full of lovely things and are great hosts. Outside are 28 acres where deer prune the roses, pheasants roam and a garden seat sits with its toes in the water. Generous bedrooms are very private in their own wing and have big beds with feather pillows, books, flowers and long views to pastures and moorland. Expect walking sticks and the bell of HMS Tempest in the porch, rugs in the hall and smart sofas in the log-fired drawing room. Breakfast comes fresh from the Aga and is delivered to a big oak table, from which there are yet more views.

Price	£80. Singles £40.
Rooms	3: 1 twin; 2 doubles sharing bath (2nd room let to same party only).
Meals	Pubs/restaurants within 2 miles.
Closed	Rarely.
Directions	4 miles west of Blanefield. Half a mile after Beech Tree Inn turn left off A81. After 300 yds, over bridge, 1st entrance on left.

Jamie & Rozie Parker
The Moss,
Killearn,
Stirling G63 9LJ
Tel   01360 550053
Mobile   07787 123599
Email   themoss@freeuk.com

Entry 639   Map 15

Stirling

Blairhullichan

So much to do here in the National Park: woodland walks, cycle tracks, your own fishing bay on the edge of Loch Ard, a private island to wade out to for picnics. The tranquil house sits high on a slope with fabulous loch views from the drawing room, comfortable with window bay, big fireplace and stacks of books. Reassuringly old-fashioned bedrooms have new mattresses and crisp linen; bathrooms have good towels and lotions. Be charmed by the 'Highlands in miniature' – plus resident labradors and welcoming Bridget, who gives you a grand breakfast and the best of her local knowledge. *Minimum stay two nights.*

Price	£75–£80. Singles £40.
Rooms	3: 1 double with sitting room, 1 twin; 1 double with separate bath/shower.
Meals	Dinner, with wine, £25–£35. Restaurant 10 miles.
Closed	Mid-December-mid-February.
Directions	A81 to Aberfoyle; at Bank of Scotland, B829 to Kinlochard; 4.5 miles, pass Macdonald Hotel into village. Left at shop; road becomes unpaved, pass new wooden house on right. On left, signed.

John & Bridget Lewis
Blairhullichan,
Kinlochard,
Aberfoyle,
Stirling FK8 3TN
Tel   01877 387341
Email jablewis@aol.com
Web   www.blairhullichan.net

Entry 640   Map 15

Stirling

Cardross

Dodge the lazy sheep on the long drive to arrive (eventually!) at a sweep of gravel and lovely old Cardross, in a gorgeous setting with its 15th-century tower. Bang on the enormous old door and either Archie or Nicola (plus labradors and Jack Russells) will usher you in. And what a delight it is; light and space, long views, exquisite furniture, wooden shutters, towelling robes, fresh flowers, crisp linen, a cast-iron period bath – and that's just the bedrooms. It all feels warm, kind and generous, the drawing room is vast, the house is filled with character and the Orr Ewings can tell you all the history.

Western Isles

Kinloch

Meander across the flower-filled machair to the wide open spaces of South Uist – home to waders, hen harriers, corncrakes and talkative Wegg. The house, built 20 years ago, is comfy with books, photos, easy chairs, pictures and angling paraphernalia. Bedrooms – the upstairs double the best – have patchwork and pine and a general junk-shop chic; views across the loch are enormous, sunrises are spectacular. Wegg loves cooking, especially barbecued fish and game; his breakfasts and dinners are sociable occasions and you are surrounded by a clever acre of garden. Nature lovers will adore it. *Shoes off at the front door!*

Price	£90–£100. Singles £50–£55.
Rooms	2: 1 twin; 1 twin with separate bath.
Meals	Occasional dinner. Pubs/restaurants 2.5-6 miles.
Closed	Christmas & New Year.
Directions	A811 Stirling-Dumbarton to Arnprior; B8034 towards Port of Menteith; 2 miles, then cross Forth over humpback bridge. Drive with yellow lodge 150 yds from bridge on right. 1st exit on right from drive.

Price	£66. Singles £33.
Rooms	3: 1 twin/double; 1 twin/double, 1 single sharing owner's bathroom.
Meals	Dinner £17. Packed lunch £6. Restaurant 5 miles.
Closed	Rarely.
Directions	30 mins from Benbecula airport; 30 mins from Lochboisdale ferry; 45 mins from Lochmaddy.

Sir Archie & Lady Orr Ewing
Cardross,
Port of Menteith, Kippen,
Stirling FK8 3JY
Tel   01877 385223
Mobile   07734 504057
Email   adoewing@cardrossestate.demon.co.uk
Web   www.cardrossholidayhomes.com

Wegg Kimbell
Kinloch,
Grogarry,
Isle of Uist HS8 5RR
Tel   01870 620316
Email   wegg@kinlochuist.com
Web   www.kinlochuist.com

Western Isles

Airdabhaigh

A rare 'undiscovered' corner of Britain... moody hills, lochs and acres of treeless blowy shores are wildly atmospheric. Miles of white sandy beaches too, and vast skies. Flora is inspirational; she's involved in Community Arts and runs dyeing and weaving workshops – a unique island experience. Wood panelling, thick walls, a peat fire, a warm kitchen, the wind whistling outside – and now, just below the house, a restored thatched shieling for writing, reading, painting. Sweet bedrooms are a haven of warmth and simplicity. It's utterly peaceful, 100% authentic, a step back in time. *Ask about creative workshops.*

Price	£40. Singles £22.
Rooms	2: 1 double, 1 twin sharing shower.
Meals	Pub/restaurant within walking distance.
Closed	Rarely.
Directions	From Lochmaddy ferry, left on A867 for 8.6 miles to T-junc. Left on A865 for 2.4 miles (ignore signs to Carinish), then right at church. Up track. House 1st on left.

Flora Macdonald
Airdabhaigh,
Uppertown, Carinish, North Uist,
Western Isles HS6 5HL

Tel	01876 580611
Mobile	07748 935204
Email	floraidh@hebrides.net
Web	www.calanas.co.uk

Entry 643   Map 20

Western Isles

Broad Bay House

In a wild landscape, 21st-century sophistication and style. Built in 2007, the house rises on graceful flights of decking above the beach. On an otherwise deserted shore, there is a villa right next door – but it disappears the moment you're inside. A stunning hall leads to a vaulted living room, whose windows face the waves on three sides... wow! More intimate boutique hotel than B&B – subtle lighting, oak doors, original art – Broad Bay has been designed with sheer, unadulterated comfort in mind. Ian and Marion are considerate, generous, flexible hosts and the food, served at candlelit tables, is heavenly.

Price	£129–£170.
Rooms	4: 2 doubles, 2 twins/doubles.
Meals	Dinner, 3 courses, £30. Packed lunch £7–£10. Pub/restaurant 7 miles.
Closed	Rarely.
Directions	A867 from Stornoway towards Barvas & Ness. On edge of Stornoway, right onto B895. After 6 miles, house on right, between Back & Gress.

Ian Fordham
Broad Bay House,
Back,
Stornoway,
Isle of Lewis HS2 0LQ

Tel	01851 820990
Email	ian@ianfordham.com
Web	www.broadbayhouse.co.uk

Entry 644   Map 20

Wales

Anglesey

Cleifiog

Liz moved here for the view: you can see why. The creamy Georgian monks' hospice, later an 18th-century customs house, looks across to the coast of Snowdonia; the masts of Beaumaris Bay chink in the wind. As well as being a keen gardener and needlework collector, Liz paints; pursuits that inform the mellow restoration and decoration of this house. Big, bright, elegant rooms, are sprinkled with tapestries, antique samplers and fresh flowers. Be charmed by the welcome, the soft linens, the ample breakfasts and the wonderful soft sea air. *Children over four welcome. Minimum stay two nights at weekends.*

Price	£75–£95. Singles £45–£65.
Rooms	3: 1 twin/double, 1 twin, 1 suite.
Meals	Pub/restaurant 200 yards.
Closed	Christmas & New Year.
Directions	A55 over Britannia Bridge to Anglesey. A545 to Beaumaris. Past 2 left turns, house is 5th on left facing the sea. Bus stop outside.

Liz Bradley
Cleifiog,
Townsend, Beaumaris, Anglesey
LL58 8BH

Tel	01248 811507
Email	liz@cleifiogbandb.co.uk
Web	www.cleifiogbandb.co.uk

Entry 645   Map 6

Anglesey

North Stack

Perched on the extreme north-westerly tip of Wales, high on a cliff overlooking the Irish sea, this 200-year-old fog signal station in an RSPB Reserve is special indeed. You must leave your car in the warden's car park and be taken in a 4x4 across the mountain. Once there, do not expect shops and restaurants, just fabulous views from the dining room, great food, quiet cosy sitting areas, wonderful walks (perhaps to the lighthouse and its little café), seagulls flying at your level and you may spot a dolphin. Bedrooms are simple and attractive with pine furniture and views to the sea. *Application for brochure essential.*

Price	£75. Singles £45.
Rooms	2: 1 double with separate shower; 1 twin sharing bath.
Meals	Dinner, 3 courses, £25. BYO.
Closed	October–March.
Directions	On Holyhead seafront, take upper road on left. After 2 bridges, Warden's House at Breakwater Country Park on left. Phone to be collected. If coming by train or ferry, ring from station.

Philippa Jacobs
North Stack,
c/o 4 Lower Park Street, Holyhead,
Anglesey LL65 1DU

Tel	01407 761252
Mobile	07772 324461
Email	northstack@hotmail.com

Entry 646   Map 6

Carmarthenshire

The Drovers

The ice-cream pink Georgian townhouse looks good enough to eat – as do the leek and cheese cakes; Jill is a superb cook. A fabulous Welsh hospitality pervades this B&B, along with antiques, gas log fires and peaceful, cosy rooms. Downstairs areas are spacious, with a rambling hotel feel; sunny bedrooms are laced with books and floral wallpapers; bathrooms come in contemporary white and cream, stocked with spoiling towels. Over breakfast (relaxed, delicious, locally sourced) you gaze through deep sash windows onto the town square; order a packed lunch and head for the hills. *Min. stay two nights weekends in high season.*

Price	£65–£70. Singles from £45.
Rooms	3: 2 doubles, 1 twin/double.
Meals	Dinner, 3 courses, £20. Packed lunch £5. Inns 50 yds.
Closed	Christmas & New Year.
Directions	In town centre, opposite fountain.

Mrs Jill Blud
The Drovers,
9 Market Square, Llandovery,
Carmarthenshire SA20 0AB
Tel   01550 721115
Email jillblud@aol.com
Web   www.droversllandovery.co.uk

Carmarthenshire

Mount Pleasant Farm

Sheep bleat, cats bask, and the views to the Black Mountain are breathtaking: your bedroom view is one of the best in this book. Sue and her daughter are warm and delightful and Sue is a brilliant cook – only the best local lamb and beef will do. The veg is organic and the eggs (bright orange!) are from up the hill; vegetarians are spoiled too. After dinner there's snooker, a log fire, a cosy sofa; then a seriously comfortable bed in a room with a lovely country-house feel. Aberglasney and the National Botanic Gardens are nearby, coastal walks less than an hour away. *Children over 12 welcome. 1.5 hours from Pembroke Dock.*

Price	£64. Singles £32–£38.
Rooms	3: 1 twin/double, 1 single, sharing bath (2nd room let to same party only); 1 twin/double.
Meals	Dinner, 3 courses with wine, £17.50. Packed lunch £7.50.
Closed	Christmas.
Directions	A40 Llandovery-Llandeilo. At Llanwrda, right for Lampeter (A482). Out of village, 1st right after mounted pillar box in lay-by on left. Over bridge & up hill; 1st left. House 1st on right.

Sue, Nick & Alice Thompson
Mount Pleasant Farm,
Llanwrda,
Carmarthenshire SA19 8AN
Tel   01550 777537
Fax   01550 777537
Email rivarevivaluk@aol.com

Carmarthenshire

Mandinam

On a heavenly bluff on the edge of the Beacons, beneath wheeling red kites and moody Welsh skies, lies Mandinam, the 'untouched holy place'. Delightful artistic Marcus and Daniella are its guardians, the farm is now mostly conservation land and they look after you as friends. Be charmed by bold rugs on wooden floors, weathered antiques, lofty ceilings, shutters, fires... and scrumptious meals in a red dining room. The rustic coach house studio, with hillside terrace and wood-burner, is for dreamers; the serene four-poster room has underfloor heating. Watch the sun go down before dinner, revel in the peace.

Ethical Collection: Environment; Community; Food. See page 400 for details.

Travel Club Offer: see page 392 for details.

Price	£70-£80. Singles by arrangement.
Rooms	2: 1 studio twin/double, 1 four-poster.
Meals	Lunch or picnic from £7.50. Dinner £25. Pub 2.5 miles.
Closed	Christmas.
Directions	Left at Llangadog village shop; 50 yds; right for Myddfai. Past cemetery, 1st right for Llanddeusant; 1.5 miles, thro' woods on left.

Daniella & Marcus Lampard
Mandinam,
Llangadog,
Carmarthenshire SA19 9LA
Tel   01550 777368
Email info@mandinam.co.uk
Web   www.mandinam.co.uk

Entry 649 Map 7

Carmarthenshire

Plas Alltyferin

Wisteria-wrapped and delightfully creaky in parts, this Georgian family house comes with 270 secluded acres in the handsome Towy Valley, close to the superb gardens of Aberglasney and The National Botanical Gardens. The dining room, where you breakfast, has the original panelling; the bedrooms have an old-fashioned charm. Not the place for you if you like spotlessness and state-of-the-art plumbing, but the views across the ha-ha to the Norman hill fort are timelessly lovely and the welcome is heartfelt. Gerard and Charlotte are the easiest, kindest and dog-friendliest of hosts. *Children over ten welcome.*

 Travel Club Offer: see page 392 for details.

Price	£50-£70. Singles £35-£40.
Rooms	2: 1 twin; 1 twin with separate bathroom.
Meals	Pubs/restaurants within 2 miles.
Closed	Rarely.
Directions	From Carmarthen A40 east to Pont-ar-gothi. Left before bridge & follow narrow lane for approx. 2 miles keeping to right-hand hedge. House on right, signed. Call for precise details.

Charlotte & Gerard Dent
Plas Alltyferin,
Pont-ar-gothi, Nantgaredig,
Carmarthenshire SA32 7PF
Tel   01267 290662
Fax   01267 290662
Email dent@alltyferin.co.uk
Web   www.alltyferin.co.uk

Entry 650 Map 6

Carmarthenshire

Sarnau Mansion

Listed and Georgian, the house has its own water supply. Play tennis and revel in 16 acres of beautiful grounds complete with pond, walled garden and woodland with nesting red kites. Bedrooms are simply furnished in heritage colours; bathrooms are big. The oak-floored sitting room with chesterfields has French windows onto the garden, the dining room is simpler with separate tables and there's good, fresh home cooking from Cynthia. One mile from the A40, you can hear a slight hum of traffic if the wind is from that direction. You are 15 minutes from the National Botanic Garden of Wales. *Children over five welcome.*

Price	£60–£70. Singles £45.
Rooms	3: 2 doubles, 1 twin.
Meals	Dinner, 3 courses, around £20. BYO. Pub 1 mile.
Closed	Rarely.
Directions	From Carmarthen A40 west for 4 miles. Right for Bancyfelin. After 0.5 miles, right into drive on brow of hill.

Cynthia & David Fernihough
Sarnau Mansion,
Llysonnen Road, Bancyfelin,
Carmarthenshire SA33 5DZ

Tel	01267 211404
Fax	01267 211404
Email	fernihough@so1405.force9.co.uk
Web	www.sarnaumansion.co.uk

Entry 651   Map 6

Ceredigion

Broniwan

Carole and Allen have created a model organic farm, and it shows. They are happy, the cows are happy and the kitchen garden is the neatest in Wales. With huge warmth and a tray of Welsh cakes they invite you into their cosy, ivy-clad house of natural browns, reds and the odd vibrant flourish of local art. Another passion is literature; call to arrange a literary weekend. Plentiful birdlife in the wonderful garden with views to the Preseli hills adds an audible welcome from tree-creepers, redstarts and wrens. The National Botanic Garden of Wales and Aberglasney are nearby, the coastal paths a quick drive.

Price	£60–£64. Singles £35.
Rooms	2: 1 double; 1 double with separate bath.
Meals	Dinner £20. BYO.
Closed	Rarely.
Directions	From Aberaeron, A487 for 6 miles for Brynhoffnant. Left at B4334 to Rhydlewis; left at Post Office & shop, 1st lane on right, then 1st track on right.

Carole & Allen Jacobs
Broniwan,
Rhydlewis, Llandysul,
Ceredigion SA44 5PF

Tel	01239 851261
Fax	01239 851261
Email	broniwan@btinternet.com
Web	www.broniwan.com

Entry 652   Map 6

Ceredigion

Ffynnon Fendigaid

Arrive through rolling countryside – birdsong and breeze the only sound – to this old farmhouse; within moments you will be sprawled on a leather sofa admiring modern art and wondering how a little bit of Milan arrived here along with Huw and homemade cake. A place to come and pootle, with no rush; you can stay all day to pick gently through the gardens, or opt for hearty walking. Either way your bed is big, the colours are soft, the bathrooms are luxurious and the food is local – try all the Welsh cheeses. Wide beaches are minutes away, red kites and buzzards soar above you. Pulchritudinous.

Price	£60–£70. Singles from £35.
Rooms	2 doubles.
Meals	Dinner, 3 courses, £16. Packed lunch £6. Pub 1 mile.
Closed	Rarely.
Directions	From A487 Cardigan & Aberystwth coast road, take B4334 at Brynhoffnant towards Rhydlewis. 1 mile to junction where road joins from right & lane to house on left.

Huw Davies
Ffynnon Fendigaid,
Rhydlewis, Llandysul,
Ceredigion SA44 5SR

Tel	01239 851361
Mobile	07974 135262
Email	ffynnonf@btinternet.com
Web	www.ffynnonf.co.uk

Entry 653   Map 6

Conwy

Pengwern Country House

The steeply wooded Conwy valley snakes down to this stone and slate gabled property set back from the road in Snowdonia National Park. Inside has an upbeat traditional feel: a large sitting room with floor-to-ceiling bay windows and pictures by the Betws-y-Coed artists who once lived here. Settle with a book by the wood-burner; Gwawr and Ian know just when to chat and when not. Bedrooms have rough plastered walls, colourful fabrics and super bathrooms, one with a double-ended roll top and views of Lledr Valley. Breakfast on fruits, yogurts, herb rösti, soda bread – gorgeous. *Min. stay two nights at weekends in summer.*

Price	£68–£82. Singles from £50.
Rooms	3: 1 double, 1 four-poster, 1 twin/double.
Meals	Pubs/restaurants within 1.5 miles. Packed lunch £5.
Closed	Christmas & New Year.
Directions	From Betws-y-Coed, A5 towards Llangollen for 1 mile. Driveway on left, opposite small stone building.

Gwawr & Ian Mowatt
Pengwern Country House,
Allt Dinas,
Betws-y-Coed,
Conwy LL24 0HF

Tel	01690 710480
Email	gwawr.pengwern@btopenworld.com
Web	www.snowdoniaaccommodation.co.uk

Entry 654   Map 7

Conwy

Rhiw Goch

Come to relax in this 17th-century longhouse overlooking the magnificent Lledr valley: the only sound is the wind rustling through the trees and birdsong. Inside is bright and cosy, filled with books and comfy places to squirrel yourself away in; jolly rugs and wooden floors, simple white walls, a wood-burner and a piano if you want to play. Bedrooms have beige carpets, good beds and plenty of space, there are fabulous views from every window and breakfasts are generous. Abigail has created a gorgeous garden with lots of seating areas; secret pathways and high places look over Snowdonia. *Minimum stay two nights preferred.*

Price	£70. Singles from £35.
Rooms	2: 1 double, 1 family room, sharing bath.
Meals	Pubs 5-minute drive.
Closed	Christmas & New Year.
Directions	A470 Betws-y-Coed to Dollgelleau for 3 miles; right, 200 yds after sign for Ponty Pant r'way stn; follow lane to top of hill. Cont. round to right, past green shed to house beyond.

Abigail King
Rhiw Goch,
Pont y Pant,
Dolwyddelan,
Conwy LL25 0PQ
Tel 01690 750231

Entry 655   Map 7

Flintshire

Golden Grove

Huge, Elizabethan and intriguing – Golden Grove was built by Sir Edward Morgan in 1580. The Queen Anne staircase, oak panelling, faded fabrics and fine family pieces are enhanced by jewel-like colour schemes: rose-pink, indigo, aqua. In summer the magnificent dining room is in use; in the winter the sitting room fire counters the draughts. The two Anns are charming and amusing, dinners are delicious and the family foursome tend the garden — beautiful, productive and well-kept. They also find time for a nuttery and a sheep farm as well as their relaxed B&B. Many return to this exceptional place.

Price	£100. Singles £65.
Rooms	3: 1 double; 1 double, 1 twin, each with separate bath.
Meals	Dinner £28.
Closed	November-February.
Directions	Turn off A55 onto A5151 for Prestatyn. At Texaco before Trelawnyd, right. Branch left immed. over 1st x-roads; right at T-junc. Gates 170 yds on left.

Ann & Mervyn and Ann & Nigel Steele-Mortimer
Golden Grove,
Llanasa, Holywell,
Flintshire CH8 9NA
Tel 01745 854452
Email golden.grove@lineone.net

Entry 656   Map 7

Flintshire

Plas Penucha

Swing back in time with polished parquet, tidy beams, a huge Elizabethan panelled lounge with books, leather sofas and open fire – a cosy spot for tea in winter. Plas Penucha – 'the big house on the highest point in the parish' – has been in the family for 500 years. Airy, old-fashioned bedrooms have long views across the garden to Offa's Dyke and one has a shower in the corner. The L-shaped dining room has a genuine Arts & Crafts interior; outside, rhododendrons and a rock garden flourish. Beyond is open countryside and St Asaph, with the smallest medieval cathedral in the country.

Gwynedd

Lympley Lodge

The solid Victorian exterior belies a surprising interior. Welcoming Patricia, a former restorer, has brought together a gorgeous collection of furniture, while her meticulous paintwork adds light and life to her seaside home. Above is the Little Orme; below, across the main coast road, the sweep of Llandudno Bay. Bedrooms strike the perfect balance between the practical and the exotic; all have crisp linen, rich fabrics, fresh flowers, lovely views. There's an elegant sitting room for guests, a stunning dining room with a Renaissance feel and breakfasts full of local and homemade produce. Wonderful.

Travel Club Offer: see page 392 for details.

Price	From £60. Singles from £32.
Rooms	2: 1 double, 1 twin.
Meals	Dinner £18.50. Packed lunch £4. Pub 3 miles.
Closed	Rarely.
Directions	From Chester, A55, B5122 left for Caerwys. 1st right into High St. Right at end. 0.75 miles to x-roads & left, then straight for 1 mile. House on left, signed.

Price	£80. Singles £50–£55.
Rooms	3: 1 double, 1 twin; 1 double with separate bath.
Meals	Restaurants/pubs 5-minute drive.
Closed	Mid-December to end of January.
Directions	From Llandudno Promenade, turn right and follow B5115 (Colwyn Bay) up the hill. Pass right turn for Bryn Y Bia. House entrance (board on side of building) on right.

	Mrs Nest Price
	Plas Penucha,
	Peny Cefn Road, Caerwys, Mold,
	Flintshire CH7 5BH
Tel	01352 720210
Email	info@plaspenucha.co.uk
Web	www.plaspenucha.co.uk

	Patricia Richards
	Lympley Lodge,
	Colwyn Road, Craigside, Llandudno,
	Gwynedd LL30 3AL
Tel	01492 549304
Email	patricia@lympleylodge.co.uk
Web	www.lympleylodge.co.uk

Entry 657 Map 7

Entry 658 Map 7

Gwynedd

Abercelyn Country House

The 1729 rectory comes with rhododendron-rich grounds, an immaculate kitchen garden and a mountain stream. In spite of the rugged setting Abercelyn is a genteel retreat. Shutters gleam, logs glow and bedrooms are spacious and light with smart bathrooms and luscious views. You are well looked after: the drawing room overflows with outdoor guides, Ray orchestrates adventure trips to Snowdonia National Park and Lindsay cooks a great breakfast with eggs from their own hens. Bala Lake is a ten-minute stroll – or you can strike off round it for the whole 14 miles – bracing indeed! *Guided walks & canoeing.*

Ethical Collection: Environment; Community; Food. See page 400 for details.

Travel Club Offer: see page 392 for details.

Price	£70-£80. Singles £50.
Rooms	3: 2 doubles, 1 twin/double.
Meals	Pub 10-minute drive. Restaurant 15-min walk; free return taxi service.
Closed	Rarely.
Directions	On A494 Bala-Dolgellau road, 1 mile from centre of Bala, opp. Llanycil Church.

Ray & Lindsay Hind
Abercelyn Country House,
Llanycil, Bala, Gwynedd LL23 7YF

Tel	01678 521109
Mobile	07762 609069
Email	info@abercelyn.co.uk
Web	www.abercelyn.co.uk

Entry 659   Map 7

Gwynedd

Dolgadfa

Gasp at the beauty of the road to Dolgadfa, every bend revealing yet another perfect frame of southern Snowdonia – the gentle prelude to the ragged peaks. The youthful Robertsons' slice of this bliss is unexpectedly luxurious. The deep limpid river winds past the listed guest barn where bedrooms – one with stone steps straight onto the riverside garden – are fresh and country-cosy, with gingham curtains and all the trimmings. A bright living room with roaring fire, sofas and Welsh oak floor is yours, and Louise does a fine breakfast. For a couple or a party, a superb place. *Fishing & shooting available.*

Price	£70-£80. Singles £50.
Rooms	3: 1 double, 1 twin; 1 double with separate bath.
Meals	Pub/restaurant in village, 1 mile.
Closed	Christmas.
Directions	B4401; after Llandrillo, 2nd right. Single track road; over bridge; at T-junc. left, on for 1.5 miles; 2nd farmhouse on left. White gate.

Louise Robertson
Dolgadfa,
Llandderfel, Bala,
Gwynedd LL23 7RE

Tel	07708 249537
Email	dolgadfa@btinternet.com
Web	www.dolgadfa.co.uk

Entry 660   Map 7

Gwynedd

Bryniau Golau

Under clear skies, there are few more soul-lifting views: the long lake and miles of Snowdonia. Each generous room is beautifully furnished – traditional with a contemporary twist, and more glorious views to the garden and lake. Katrina, friendly and adaptable, spoils you with open fires in the sitting room, goose down duvets on the beds, spa baths for all, underfloor heating and scrumptious breakfasts that set you up for the day. Linger on the lawn, perhaps with a drink as the sun sets, and try your hand at fly fishing or white water rafting. A wonderful place for a house party – and the walking is superb.

Price	£80–£90. Singles £55–£65.
Rooms	3: 2 four-posters, 1 twin/double.
Meals	Supper available. Pubs/restaurants within 2 miles.
Closed	Rarely.
Directions	From Bala B4391; 1 mile, B4403 Llangower. Pass Bala Lake Hotel; look for sign showing left turn; 20 yds after tree, sign on right; left up hill, over cattle grid; 1st on right.

	Katrina le Saux Bryniau Golau, Llangower, Bala, Gwynedd LL23 7BT
Tel	01678 521782
Email	katrinalesaux@hotmail.co.uk
Web	www.bryniau-golau.co.uk

Entry 661   Map 7

Gwynedd

The Old Rectory – on the lake

The drive to get here is fantastic and the approach truly beautiful – The Old Rectory waits for you on the other side of the lake. The owners are full of enthusiasm for their fabulous B&B and spoil guests rotten – comfy beds with smooth Egyptian cotton sheets, luxurious baths, WiFi and satellite TV in the rooms and fresh home-cooked meals. Fabulous photos of the lake in its many moods decorate the dining room walls, there's an open fire in the sitting room and binoculars for birdwatching in the bedrooms. Woods and water for walking and fishing, and views from every window over the large, lovely, luminous lake.

Price	£90. Singles £60.
Rooms	3: 2 doubles, 1 twin.
Meals	Dinner £22.50.
Closed	Rarely.
Directions	A470 from Dolgellau. A487 from Cross Foxes Inn, then B4405 (signposted Tywyn). Follow along lakeside; turn right at head of lake and cont. 0.25 miles. House illuminated by blue lights at night.

	Ricky Francis The Old Rectory – on the lake, Talyllyn, Gwynedd LL36 9AJ
Tel	01654 782225
Mobile	07919 190445
Email	enquiries@rectoryonthelake.co.uk
Web	www.rectoryonthelake.co.uk

Entry 662   Map 7

Gwynedd

Y Goeden Eirin

An education in Welsh culture, and a stylish spot from which to explore the country. Against the backdrop of wild Snowdonia, surrounded by 20 acres of rough grazing, house and setting have an open seaside feel. Inside presents a cosy picture: Welsh-language and English books share the shelves, paintings by contemporary Welsh artists enliven the walls, an arty 70s décor mingles with sturdy Welsh oak in the bedrooms and bathrooms are chic. Wonderful food is served alongside the Bechstein in the beamed dining room – the welcoming, thoughtful Eluned and John have created an unusually delightful space.

Ethical Collection: Environment; Food.
See page 400 for details.

Travel Club Offer: see page 392 for details.

Price	£70-£90. Singles from £50.
Rooms	3: 2 doubles, 1 twin.
Meals	Dinner, 3 courses, £28. Packed lunch £12. Pub/restaurant 1 mile.
Closed	Christmas-New Year & occasionally.
Directions	From Caernarfon onto Porthmadog & Pwllheli road. A487 thro' Bontnewydd, left at r'bout, signed Dolydd. House 0.5 miles on right, before garage on left.

Dr John & Mrs Eluned Rowlands
Y Goeden Eirin,
Dolydd, Caernarfon,
Gwynedd LL54 7EF
Tel 01286 830942
Mobile 07708 491234
Email john_rowlands@tiscali.co.uk
Web www.ygoedeneirin.co.uk

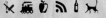

Entry 663   Map 6

Gwynedd

Plas Tan-yr-allt

Who shot Shelley in the drawing room? The poet fled in 1813, the mystery unsolved. The listed house has a colourful history, irresistible to the owners who have just finished a glorious restoration: roll top baths, deep luscious colours, underfloor heating, handsome furniture. *The Daily Telegraph* said Tanny exemplifies "contemporary country-house style"… and there's country-house cooking too. Nick uses local ingredients, and guests eat together at an impressive oak and slate table for dinner – a convivial treat. Wonderful views stretch from the terrace and gardens over the estuary and bay.

Price	£120-£175. Singles £100-£140.
Rooms	6: 3 doubles, 1 twin, 2 four-posters.
Meals	Dinner, 3 courses, £38.50 (Wed-Sun). Pubs/restaurants 10-minute walk.
Closed	2 weeks in January/February.
Directions	Leave Tremadog on A498 for Beddgelert. Signed on left after 0.5 miles. House at top of hill.

Michael Bewick & Nick Golding
Plas Tan-yr-allt,
Tremadog,
Porthmadog,
Gwynedd LL49 9RG
Tel 01766 514545
Email info@tanyrallt.co.uk
Web www.tanyrallt.co.uk

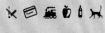

Entry 664   Map 6

Gwynedd

The Old Rectory

In the heart of the Lleyn Peninsula, an immaculate Georgian rectory in its own grounds. There are gardens to relax in, a horse in the paddock and wonderful art on the walls – Gabrielle has created delightful interiors. Seagrass floors and toile de Jouy, big mirrors and family antiques, a log fire for cool evenings, a guest drawing room with sofas and books... the mood is one of easy elegance and you can come and go as you please. Gabrielle rides, Roger sails and both are relaxed and charming hosts. The area is stunning, walks start from the door; no wonder guests return. *Pets by arrangement. Min. two nights bank holidays.*

Price	From £90. Singles from £60.
Rooms	3: 1 twin/double, 2 doubles.
Meals	Packed lunch £6.50. Pub/restaurant 2 miles.
Closed	Christmas.
Directions	From Pwllheli, A499 to r'bout. Right onto A497 Nefyn & Boduan road for 3 miles; left opp. church; house set back, on right.

Gabrielle & Roger Pollard
The Old Rectory,
Boduan, Pwllheli,
Gwynedd LL53 6DT

Tel	01758 721519
Fax	01758 721519
Email	thepollards@theoldrectory.net
Web	www.theoldrectory.plus.com

Entry 665   Map 6

Monmouthshire

Allt-y-bela

A beautiful and ancient house, built between 1420 and 1599, kicking off an early Renaissance architectural buzz and now perfectly restored for the 21st century. It is reached down a narrow lane in its own private and secluded valley. Here is made-to-measure pampering among soaring beams and period furniture. A log-warmed dining room for private meals delivered by two clever chefs, and a big farmhouse kitchen if you want to be more involved. Bedrooms soothe with limewashed walls, fabulous beds, no TV, stunning art, and proper bathrooms that glow in wood. And now the garden is being created... *Minimum stay two nights.*

Price	£125.
Rooms	2 doubles.
Meals	Farmhouse supper £30. Any other meals by arrangement. Pubs/restaurants 3 miles.
Closed	Rarely.
Directions	A449 towards Usk, then B4235 to Chepstow. After 200 yds, unsigned right turn. Follow for 0.5 miles; left into 'No Through Road', follow for 2 miles.

Louise & Alison Barber
Allt-y-bela,
Llangwm Ucha,
Usk,
Monmouthshire NP15 1EZ

Tel	01291 672872
Email	bb@alltybela.co.uk
Web	www.alltybela.co.uk

Entry 666   Map 7

Monmouthshire

The Nurtons

After following the twists and turns of the glorious Wye valley, what a pleasure to be greeted by Adrian and Elsa. The façade of their history-rich home is Victorian, the interior rambling and intriguing, the site ancient. A flagged area conceals a sacred 'healing bath' and, at the back, are two simple B&B suites with private sitting areas inside and out: a double is in the main part of the house. The plantsman's garden reflects a passion for all things organic; you breakfast generously – not on bacon and eggs, but fresh fruits, homebaked bread, delicious muesli, honey from their bees. Tranquil and sincerely green.

Ethical Collection: Environment; Food.
See page 400 for details..

Price	From £65. Singles from £35.
Rooms	3: 1 double, 1 double & sitting room & child bed, 1 twin & sitting room & sofabed.
Meals	Evening platter £30 (for 2). Packed lunch £5. Pub 0.75 miles.
Closed	Rarely.
Directions	A466 just north of Tintern village, drive to house is opp. the Old Station-Tintern.

	Adrian & Elsa Wood
	The Nurtons,
	Tintern,
	Monmouthshire NP16 7NX
Tel	01291 689253
Email	info@thenurtons.co.uk
Web	www.thenurtons.co.uk

Entry 667   Map 7

Monmouthshire

Penpergwm Lodge

On the edge of the Brecon Beacons, a large and lovely Edwardian house. Breakfast round the mahogany table, relax in the warmly inviting sitting room with piano and real fire. The Boyles have been here for years and pour much of their energy into three beautiful acres of parterre and potager, orchard and flowers. Bedrooms are gloriously traditional – ancestral portraits, big windows, good chintz – with garden views; bathrooms are a skip across the landing. A pool and tennis for the sporty, two summer houses for the dreamy, a good pub you can walk to. Splendid, old-fashioned B&B.

Price	£65–£75. Singles £40.
Rooms	2 twins, each with separate bath.
Meals	Pub within walking distance.
Closed	Rarely.
Directions	A40 to Abergavenny; at big r'bout on SE edge of town, B4598 to Usk for 2.5 miles. Left at King of Prussia pub, up small lane; house 200 yds on left.

	Catriona Boyle
	Penpergwm Lodge,
	Abergavenny,
	Monmouthshire NP7 9AS
Tel	01873 840208
Fax	01873 840208
Email	boyle@penpergwm.co.uk
Web	www.penplants.com

Entry 668   Map 7

Pembrokeshire

Penfro

This is fun – idiosyncratic and a tad theatrical, rather than conventional and uniformly stylish. The Lappins' home is a tall, impressive Grade II*-listed Georgian affair, formerly a ballet school. Judith's taste – she's also a WW1 expert – is eclectic verging on the wacky and she minds that guests are comfortable and well-fed. You eat communally, and very well, at the big scrubbed table in the flagged, Aga-fired kitchen at garden level… the garden's big and beautiful so enjoy its conversational terrace and hammocks. And discuss which of the three very characterful bedrooms will suit you best, plumbing and all!

Ethical Collection: Food. See page 400 for details.

Travel Club Offer: see page 392 for details.

Price	£65-£90. Singles from £45.
Rooms	3: 1 double; 1 double, 1 twin both with separate bathroom.
Meals	Packed lunch from £8. Pub 250 yds.
Closed	Rarely.
Directions	A4075 Pembroke; 2 miles to mini r'bout. Straight ahead, down hill, bear right. Right lane past castle; T-junc. bear right. Road widens by Chapel Pembroke Antique Centre. House on right.

	Judith Lappin
	Penfro,
	111 Main Street, Pembroke,
	Pembrokeshire SA71 4DB
Tel	01646 682753
Mobile	07763 856181
Email	info@penfro.co.uk
Web	www.penfro.co.uk

Entry 669 Map 6

Pembrokeshire

Bowett Farm

An ancient bluebell wood pulsates with colour in the spring and wild flowers of all kinds bloom in profusion; if you're lucky, you might see a badger. This is a friendly, relaxed house; take tea in the garden or bring wine and Ann will provide the glasses. Relax in the evening in a comfortable sitting room filled with gorgeous Welsh antiques – then to bed. One of the rooms has a fine, restored half-tester bed and a giant bathroom with Victorian washstand. Breakfast on local produce, homemade jams and marmalades, fresh fruit salad and yogurt… the Pembrokeshire coastal path runs nearby.

Price	£70-£75. Singles £45.
Rooms	3: 1 double with separate bath; 1 twin/double with separate shower; 1 single (same party only).
Meals	Packed lunch £6. Pub/restaurant 0.5 miles.
Closed	Mid-October to Easter.
Directions	B4320 from Pembroke for Hundleton. After woods, house 1st on right. Approx. 1 mile from Pembroke centre.

	Ann & Bill Morris
	Bowett Farm,
	Hundleton,
	Pembroke,
	Pembrokeshire SA71 5QS
Tel	01646 683473
Email	bowett@pembrokeshire.com
Web	www.bowettfarmhouse.co.uk

Entry 670 Map 6

Pembrokeshire

Furzehill Farm

Horse experts Val and Paul's new-build farmhouse is a friendly place for families and walkers. The Aga-driven kitchen is the hub and Paul will do you a grand breakfast, and something tasty and local for supper too. There are hunting prints, a modern leather sofa and a brick-surround open fire in the sitting room, and cosy carpeted bedrooms upstairs – one with a shower, two sharing a jazzy jacuzzi. Eco credentials include ground-sourced heating and the young garden promises an above-ground pool. This is a deeply rural spot with a good pub to walk to and the birds of the lovely Cleddau Estuary to admire.

Ethical Collection: Environment; Food.
See page 400 for details.

 Travel Club Offer: see page 392 for details.

Price	£60–£90. Singles from £30.
Rooms	3: 1 family for 4; 1 double, 1 room with bunkbeds, sharing separate bath.
Meals	Dinner, 3 courses, £25. Supper from £12. Packed lunch £5. Pub/restaurant 3 miles.
Closed	Christmas Day.
Directions	A40 to Canaston Bridge. A4075 for Pembroke. Right at Crosshands; after sharp bend, left (Cresswell Quay); left again at T-junc (Cresswell Quay). 2nd entrance on left.

	E V Rees Furzehill Farm, Martletwy, Narberth, Pembrokeshire SA67 8AN
Tel	01834 891480
Mobile	07887 592218
Email	val@furzehillfarm.com
Web	www.furzehillfarm.com

Entry 671   Map 6

Pembrokeshire

Knowles Farm

Two charming owners, great food, sparkling night skies and a quirky pub a short drive. The Cleddau estuary winds its way around this 1,000-acre organic farm – its lush grasses feed the cows that produce milk for the renowned Rachel's yoghurt. Your hosts love the area, are passionate about its conservation and let you come and go as you please; picnic in the garden, explore the woods. Gini rustles up scrumptious organic dinners and serves them at a candlelit table that seats 12. Bedrooms are simple and well-maintained, with comfy beds and fresh woodland flowers. Traditional, real-farmhouse B&B.

Travel Club Offer: see page 392 for details.

Price	From £64.
Rooms	3: 2 doubles; 1 twin with separate bath.
Meals	Supper from £12. Dinner, 4 courses, £22. Packed lunch £6. Pub 1.5 miles, restaurant 3 miles.
Closed	Rarely.
Directions	A4075 to Cresselly; turn right. Follow signs for Lawrenny to first x-roads; straight over; next x-roads right; 100 yds on left.

	Ms Virginia Lort Phillips Knowles Farm, Lawrenny, Pembrokeshire SA68 0PX
Tel	01834 891221
Fax	01834 891221
Email	ginilp@lawrenny.org.uk
Web	www.lawrenny.org.uk

Entry 672   Map 6

Pembrokeshire

Boulston Manor

A lush descent through ancient woodland, with tantalising glimpses of open water, takes you to the ivy-clad 1790s house and a great place to stay. A country-house drawing room with veranda and Cleddau views is yours to use; soft sofas, horsey pictures, fresh flowers and a grand piano set the tone. Perfectly refurbished bedrooms and bathrooms are roomy and glamorous: yards of thick fabrics, dazzling white linen, stone fireplaces, marble tiling, and, in one, a jucuzzi with the grandest parkland views. Generous Jules and Rod are lively and fun, you will eat good, local food and there's miles of walking in the National Park.

Pembrokeshire

Pentower

Curl up with a cat and watch the ferries coasting to Ireland; porpoises, too, may be spotted! French windows open onto the terrace and a glorious vista stretches out before you. Mary and Tony are easy-going and friendly and have done an excellent restoration on the turreted 1898 house, keeping its quarry tiled floors, decorative fireplaces and impressive staircase. Pretty bedrooms are light and airy, with ample wardrobes and huge showers; the Tower Room has the views. There's a tiled dining/sitting room for full English (or Welsh) breakfasts, a 'temple' in the garden for summer and Fishguard is a short stroll away.

📖 Travel Club Offer: see page 392 for details.

Price	£60–£100.
Rooms	3 doubles.
Meals	Supper £15. Dinner from £25.
Closed	Never.
Directions	From Salutation Square (County Hotel) Haverfordwest, take Uzmaston Road past Popes Garage. Through Uzmaston, past Goodwood (signed Boulston). Continue for 1.5 miles and follow Boulston signs.

Price	£65–£70. Singles £40.
Rooms	3: 2 doubles, 1 twin.
Meals	Packed lunch £5. Pubs/restaurants 500 yds.
Closed	Occasionally.
Directions	A40 to Fishguard town; at r'bout, 2nd exit onto Main Street. Before sharp left bend, right fork onto Tower Hill; 200 yds on, through house gates.

	Mr & Mrs Roderick Thomas
	Boulston Manor,
	Haverfordwest,
	Pembrokeshire SA62 4AQ
Tel	01437 764600
Email	info@boulstonmanor.co.uk
Web	www.boulstonmanor.co.uk

	Tony Jacobs & Mary Geraldine Case
	Pentower,
	Tower Hill,
	Fishguard,
	Pembrokeshire SA65 9LA
Tel	01348 874462
Email	sales@pentower.co.uk
Web	www.pentower.co.uk

Entry 673   Map 6

✗ 🐾

Entry 674   Map 6

Powys

Llangattock Court

Built in 1690 and mentioned in Pevsner as an 'outstanding example of a country house in this style', this is indeed grand and sits in the middle of the sleepy village, surrounded by a large garden. Both bedrooms are a good size (one has a big French bed and a small shower room) with lovely antiques and a fresh feel; views from one soar across to the Black Mountains. Breakfast in style in the enormous dining room overlooked by framed relatives, stroll through the rose garden, visit a castle or historic house, walk to the local pub for dinner. Morgan is a painter; some of his paintings are on display.

Powys

Tyr Chanter

Warmth, colour, children and activity: this house is fun. Tiggy welcomes you like family; help collect eggs, feed the lambs or the pony, drop your shoes by the fire. The farmhouse and barn are stylishly relaxed; deep sofas, tartan throws, heaps of books, views to the Brecon Beacons and Black Mountains. Bedrooms are soft, simple sanctuaries with Jo Malone bathroom treats. Children's rooms zing with murals; toys, kids' sitting room, sandpit – child heaven. Walk, fish, canoe, book-browse in Hay or stroll the estate. Homemade cakes, whisky to help yourself to: fine hospitality.

Travel Club Offer: see page 392 for details.

Price	£50-£80. Singles £45.
Rooms	2: 1 double, 1 suite with four-poster and twin.
Meals	Restaurants/pubs within 1 mile.
Closed	Christmas & New Year; 1-2 weeks October.
Directions	From A465 take B4777 into Gilwern, follow signs to Crickhowell. In Legar, left at Vine Tree Inn. Pass Horse Shoe Inn on right; after 60 yds turn right, then right again 50 yds beyond church signed to Dardy. 1st on left.

Polly Llewellyn
Llangattock Court,
Llangattock,
Crickhowell,
Powys NP8 1PH
Tel 01873 810116
Email morganllewellyn@btinternet.com
Web www.llangattockcourt.co.uk

Entry 675　Map 7

Price	£85. Singles £55.
Rooms	4: 1 double; 1 double with separate bath/shower; 2 children's rooms.
Meals	Packed lunch £6. Pub 1 mile.
Closed	Christmas.
Directions	From Crickhowell, A40 towards Brecon. 2 miles left at Gliffaes Hotel sign. 2 miles, past hotel, house is 600 yds on right.

Tiggy Pettifer
Tyr Chanter,
Gliffaes, Crickhowell,
Powys NP8 1RL
Tel 01874 731144
Mobile 07802 387004
Email tiggy@tyrchanter.com
Web www.tyrchanter.com

Entry 676　Map 7

Powys

Powys

The Old Post Office

Unpretentious, simple B&B in the most glorious surroundings. Bedrooms are large, colourful and delightfully quiet; beds are comfortable. Fresh flowers and good books abound, there's a guests' sitting room in which exhausted hikers – and their dogs – can collapse after a recce in the Black Mountains, and it's a one mile walk across fields for all the delights of Hay-on-Wye. Whatever you do, you'll be captivated by the region. Linda serves delicious, cooked vegetarian breakfasts at a long communal table; she and Ed tend to keep to their own part of the house and you come and go as you please.

Hafod Y Garreg

A unique opportunity to stay in the oldest house in Wales – a 1402 cruck-framed hall house, built for Henry IV as a hunting lodge. Annie and John have filled it with a fascinating mix of Venetian mirrors, Indian rugs, pewter plates, gorgeous fabrics and oak furniture. Dine by candlelight – maybe pheasant pie with chilli jam and hazelnut mash: delicious. Bedrooms are stylish and comfortable with Egyptian cotton bed linen. You reach the Grade II*-listed house by a bumpy track across gated fields crowded with chickens, cats, goats, birds... a very special, peaceful and secluded place.

Price	£70. Singles from £35.
Rooms	3: 1 double, 1 twin/double, 1 double (extra bed).
Meals	Pub 2 miles. Pubs/restaurants in Hay-on-Wye.
Closed	Rarely.
Directions	Hay-on-Wye to Brecon; 0.5 miles, left, for Llanigon; on for 1 mile, left before school. On right opp. church.

Price	£65. Singles from £60.
Rooms	2 doubles.
Meals	Dinner, 3 courses, £19.50. BYO. Pubs/restaurants 2.5 miles.
Closed	Christmas.
Directions	From Hay-on-Wye, A479 then A470 to B. Wells. Through Llyswen, past forest on left, down hill. Next left for Trericket Mill, then immed. right & up hill. Straight through gate across track to house.

	Linda Webb & Ed Moore
	The Old Post Office,
	Llanigon,
	Hay-on-Wye,
	Powys HR3 5QA
Tel	01497 820008
Web	www.oldpost-office.co.uk

	Annie & John McKay
	Hafod Y Garreg,
	Erwood, Builth Wells,
	Powys LD2 3TQ
Tel	01982 560400
Email	john-annie@hafod-y.wanadoo.co.uk
Web	www.hafodygarreg.co.uk

Entry 677   Map 7

Entry 678   Map 7

Powys

Trericket Mill Vegetarian Guesthouse

Part guest house, part bunk house, all very informal — all Grade II*-listed. The dining room has been created amid a jumble of corn-milling machinery: B&B guests, campers and bunkers pile in together to fill hungry bellies with Nicky and Alistair's delicious and plentiful veggie food from a chalkboard menu. Stoves throw out the heat in the flagstoned living rooms with their comfy chairs; the bedrooms are simple pine affairs. Set out to explore from here on foot, horseback, bicycle or canoe; lovers of the outdoors looking for good value and a planet-friendly bias will be in heaven.

Price	£58-£73. Singles £39-£49.
Rooms	3: 2 doubles, 1 twin.
Meals	Dinner, 3 courses, £18. BYO. Simple supper £8. Pub/restaurant 2 miles.
Closed	Christmas.
Directions	12 miles north of Brecon on A470. Mill set slightly back from road, on left, between Llyswen & Erwood. Train to Llandrindod Wells; bus to Brecon every 2 hrs will drop at mill on request.

Alistair & Nicky Legge
Trericket Mill Vegetarian Guesthouse,
Erwood, Builth Wells,
Powys LD2 3TQ
Tel   01982 560312
Email   mail@trericket.co.uk
Web   www.trericket.co.uk

✗ ☉ ⌇

Entry 679   Map 7

Powys

The Old Vicarage

For devotees of Victoriana, the house, designed by Sir George Gilbert Scott, is a delight. Your host, charming and fun, ushers you in to a rich confection of colours, dark wood and a lifetime's collecting: you could stay here a dozen times and still see something new. Splendid brass beds, cast-iron radiators, porcelain loos, sumptuous bedspreads and a garden with grotto, waterfall and rill. Dine by candlelight (the food is superb), ring the servants' bell for early morning tea. You are on the English side of Offa's Dyke: look north to the heavenly Radnorshire hills, south to all of Herefordshire.

▐▌ Travel Club Offer: see page 392 for details.

Price	From £92.
Rooms	3: 2 doubles, 1 twin.
Meals	Dinner, 4 courses, £34. Restaurant 10-minute drive.
Closed	Rarely.
Directions	B4355, between Presteigne & Knighton; in village of Norton, immed. north of church.

Paul Gerrard
The Old Vicarage,
Norton, Presteigne, Radnorshire,
Powys LD8 2EN
Tel   01544 260038
Email   paul@nortonoldvic.co.uk
Web   www.oldvicarage-nortonrads.co.uk

✗ ✉ ☉ ⌇ ♦

Entry 680   Map 7

Powys

Cwmllechwedd Fawr

Wild Wales at its best – drive across the moor where the ponies run free. This is a place for big walks and fresh air – where healthy appetites will be rewarded with wholesome and delicious food, much courtesy of the organic vegetable plot. It's an 1815 house on a working farm, so expect sheep dogs, chickens and cats in the yard. Inside, a breakfast table by a warm Aga, a dining table on worn slate flags, a sitting room cosy with piano and books. Bedrooms have plain wooden furniture and colourful rugs. For summer, a large sheltered terrace with long, lush views. Good people, great value.

Price	£60. Singles £35.
Rooms	2: 1 double, 1 twin/double.
Meals	Dinner, 3 courses, £18. BYO.
Closed	Rarely.
Directions	From A483 to Llanbister on B4356. Follow for 2 miles past chapel on right; across common. Immed. sharp left to Llanbadarn Fynydd; follow hedge on right for 0.3 miles to gate.

John Rath & John Underwood
Cwmllechwedd Fawr,
Llanbister, Llandrindod Wells, Powys
LD1 6UH
Tel   01597 840267
Fax   01597 840267
Email   postmaster@cwmllechwedd.u-net.com
Web   www.cwmllechwedd.u-net.com

Entry 681   Map 7

Powys

The Old Vicarage

Come for vast skies, forested hills and quilted fields that stretch for miles. This Victorian vicarage is a super base: smart, welcoming, full of comforts. You get a log fire in a cosy sitting room, a super-smart dining room with long country views and fancy bedrooms that spoil you all the way. Tim's food is just as good. Local suppliers are noted on menus, but much is grown in the garden, where chickens run free. Resist laziness and take to the hills – the Kerry Ridgeway is on your doorstep as is Powis Castle – for glorious walking, then home and afternoon tea. *Children over 12 welcome.*

Ethical Collection: Environment; Food. See page 400 for details.

Travel Club Offer: see page 392 for details.

Price	£95. Singles £65.
Rooms	3: 1 twin/double, 2 doubles.
Meals	Dinner, 3 courses, £25. Packed lunch available.
Closed	Rarely.
Directions	A483, 3.5 miles from Newtown towards Llandrindod Wells, left on sharp right bend, house first on left.

Tim & Helen Withers
The Old Vicarage,
Dolfor, Newtown,
Powys SY16 4BN
Tel   01686 629051
Mobile   07753 760054
Email   tim@theoldvicaragedolfor.co.uk
Web   www.theoldvicaragedolfor.co.uk

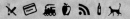

Entry 682   Map 7

Powys

Talbontdrain

Way off the beaten track, remote and wild, sits a white-painted stone farmhouse. The Cambrian mountains stretch to the south, the river Dovey lies in the vale below and kind Hilary knows all the walks and can sort special routes for you. She cooks a hearty breakfast too, or a farmhouse supper, and gives you colourful bedrooms – not swish, but with everything you need. There are photographs of garden plants, a pianola, and furniture in such a mix of styles that it all gives a feeling of great informality. The peace is deep – even the cockerel stays quiet until a respectable time – and walkers will adore it.

Wrexham

Worthenbury Manor

Homemade bread and Hepplewhite! This is a good, solid house of generous proportions and your hosts live in part of it. Wallow in an antique oak four-poster in a rose-carpeted, chandeliered bedroom full of comfort (books, games and flowers adding a cosy touch) and breakfast on local bacon, sausages and black pudding. Ian, history buff and ex-chef, is gentle, thoughtful and looks after you properly; dinner is quite an occasion. The listed house is close to Chester yet in a quiet, birdsung setting; the original building was enlarged in the 1890s in the William and Mary revival style.

 Travel Club Offer: see page 392 for details.

Price	£56-£66. Singles £28.
Rooms	4: 1 double, 1 family room for 3; 1 twin/double, 1 single sharing shower.
Meals	Dinner, 2 courses & coffee, £18. Packed lunch £6.
Closed	Christmas & Boxing Day.
Directions	Leaving Machynlleth on A489, 1st right signed Forge. In Forge bear right to Uwchygarreg up 'dead end'. 3 miles, pass phone box on left, up steep hill. House on left at top.

Price	£60-£80. Singles £38-£49.
Rooms	2: 1 four-poster; 1 four-poster with separate bath.
Meals	Dinner, 3 courses, £25. Lunch £15.
Closed	December-February.
Directions	Between A525 Whitchurch - Wrexham & A41 Whitchurch - Chester, on B5069 between Bangor-on-Dee (also called Bangor-is-y-coed) and Malpas. Manor on right before bridge.

	Hilary Matthews
	Talbontdrain,
	Uwchygarreg,
	Machynlleth,
	Powys SY20 8RR
Tel	01654 702192
Email	hilary@talbontdrain.co.uk
Web	www.talbontdrain.co.uk

	Elizabeth & Ian Taylor
	Worthenbury Manor,
	Worthenbury,
	Wrexham LL13 0AW
Tel	01948 770342
Email	enquiries@worthenburymanor.co.uk
Web	www.worthenburymanor.co.uk

Entry 683   Map 8

Entry 684   Map 7

Becoming a member of Sawday's Travel Club opens up hundreds of discounts, treats and other offers at many of our Special Places to Stay in Britain and Ireland, as well as promotions on Sawday's books and other goodies.

Where you see the 💼 symbol in this book it means the place has a special offer for Club members. It may be money off your room price, a bottle of champagne or a day's trout fishing. The offers for each place are listed on the following pages. These were correct at the time of going to print, but owners reserve the right to change the listed offer. Latest offers for all places can be found on our website, www.sawdays.co.uk.

Membership is only £25 per year. To see membership extras and to register visit www.sawdays.co.uk/members. You can also call 01275 395433 to set up a direct debit.

The small print

You must mention that you are a Travel Club member when booking, and confirm that the offer is available. Your Travel Club card must be shown on arrival to claim the offer. Sawday's Travel Club cards are not transferable. If two cardholders share a room they can only claim the offer once. Offers for Sawday's Travel Club members are subject to availability. Alastair Sawday Publishing cannot accept any responsibility if places fail to honour offers; neither can we accept responsibility if a place changes hands and drops out of the Travel Club.

England

Bath & N.E. Somerset

1   10% off stays Monday-Friday.
5   Half a decanter of sherry in your room.

Cambridgeshire

18   Chapel cocktail on arrival or Bucks Fizz with breakfast.

Cheshire

23   Local 'goodies' in the room.

Cornwall

31 Arrangement for St Enodoc golf (green fee not included). Talk about Cornish gardens or coastal and moor walks over a glass of wine.

36 Bottle of wine with dinner. Late checkout (12pm).

39 Drink on arrival.

40 Bottle of house wine in your room on arrival and pick-up from local train station.

41 Talk about St Ives artists with a glass of wine.

44 Truffles & glass of champagne on arrival.

46 Use of owner's studio.

48 Local food/produce in room.

51 Homemade cake on arrival. Bottle of wine with dinner. Discounts on Jane and John's books.

55 Reiki or reflexology therapy session per room on minimum 7 nights stay.

58 10% off minimum 5 nights, pick-up from Penryn station and a decanter of sherry in room.

66 Bottle of wine with dinner. Local chocolates in room.

67 Use of two fold-up bikes and helmets (must be pre-booked).

Cumbria

77 Bottle of Moet champagne for stays of 2+ nights.

82 Guided woodland/nature walks, including badger watching. Local maps available on loan and help planning days in the Lake District.

85 Late checkout (12pm). 20% off purchases of our sausage, bacon and eggs to take home.

86 Bottle of organic wine with 2-night stay.

87 Bottle of wine with 2-night stay.

Derbyshire

93 5% off stays of 3+ nights in a double ensuite room, Monday-Thursday.

Devon

98 Cream tea on arrival or following afternoon.

99 10% off stays Monday-Thursday.

105 Bottle of wine with evening meal.

106 Bottle of wine with first dinner.

111 Drink on arrival. 10% off stays Monday-Thursday. Transport to foot ferry.

113 10% off stays of 2+ nights, Monday-Thursday. Late checkout (12pm) and lift to local pubs.

119 10% off stays Monday-Thursday.

127 Sunday-Thursday nights – either upgrade when available or 10% discount.

131 10% off stays of 2+ nights. Welcome drinks tray.

133 Bottle of house wine with dinner. Pick-up from Exeter St Davids mainline train station.

134 10% off stays of 2+ nights, Monday-Thursday.

137 Devon cream tea on arrival, 4-6pm. After 6pm a glass of wine.

140 Glass of wine on arrival or homemade tea.

141 Glass of wine or gin and tonic for each night of your stay.

143 Waived charge for dogs or decanter of port.

144 Late checkout (12pm).

Dorset

147 Homemade organic Dorset cream tea or aperitif with nibbles for each night of stay. Served on sunny terrace or by log fire.

149 Half a bottle of bubbly on arrival. 10% off stays of 3+ nights Sunday-Thursday.

150 10% off stays Monday-Thursday. Or pick-up from Yeovil train station.

152 Locally made chocolate truffles and a bottle of truffle oil in your room.

154 Bottle of wine and box of 'Fudges' award-winning Dorset cheese biscuits.

158 Glass of wine on arrival.

162 10% off stays Monday-Thursday, pick-up from the local train station, welcome drink and guided tour of local area.

169 10% off stays Monday-Thursday.

171 Glass of champagne on arrival.

Essex

180 Welcome drink on arrival – tipple depending on season, weather and hour!

Gloucestershire

184 10% off stays of 3+ nights.

187 Discount available for stays of 3+ nights, November-April.

200 Bottle of wine.

201 Bottle of wine on arrival.

203 Coffee & tea on arrival. Glass of wine with dinner. 10% off stays Mon-Thurs.

Hampshire

209 10% off stays of 3 or more nights. Bottle of wine with dinner.

212 10% off stays Monday-Thursday.

219 Glass of champagne on arrival. 10% off stays of 2+ nights Monday-Thursday. Farm tour by John.

220 Tea on arrival.

Herefordshire

226 Pot of tea or coffee with cake and biscuits on arrival.
227 Bottle of wine for members celebrating a birthday, honeymoon or anniversary.
231 Tea and homemade cake or drinks on arrival with biscuits/cake in room
     for those needing an extra snack.
232 10% off stays Monday-Thursday. Pick-up from Ledbury station.
234 10% off stays Monday-Thursday. Cream tea on arrival.
235 Foodie treats in your room on arrival.

Kent

244 10% off second night (double occupancy) at weekends.
250 Bottle of wine for minimum 2-night stays.
254 Bottle of wine. Morning newspaper. Checkout at 11am with snack for journey.
261 Six greeting cards of your choice drawn by your host David Gurdon.
262 Bottle of house wine with dinner.
264 Sherry and homemade biscuits in your room. Pot of homemade jam or
     marmalade to take home.
265 Pick-up from local train station.

Lancashire

270 Pick-up from local train station. Fridge full of beverages. Late checkout.

Leicestershire

274 Bottle of wine with dinner. Late checkout.
275 Glass of wine on arrival.

Lincolnshire

279 Tea on arrival, house drink per person for each night of stay and pick-up from
     local train station.
281 10% off 4-night stays Monday-Thursday.
282 Home-grown produce on departure.
284 10% off Monday-Thursday, not July and August.
286 Locally produced Belvoir cordials in room.
288 10% discount on third night Monday-Thursday.

London

294 Evening drink or afternoon tea on arrival.

298 Half bottle of champagne for stays of 2+ nights.

302 Gin and tonic, glass of wine or other refreshment on arrival.

309 Jar of house preserve in room, pick-up from local station and bottle of house wine with dinner.

317 Pick-up from local tube. Refreshments on arrival. Late checkout.

Norfolk

327 10% off stays Sunday-Thursday. Bottle of wine on arrival.

328 Bottle of house wine per room.

333 10% off stays Monday-Thursday. Norfolk handmade soap.

337 Bottle of wine.

Northamptonshire

344 Late checkout (12pm).

345 Selection of local goodies and bottle of wine on arrival for stays of 2+ nights.

Northumberland

354 Pick-up from local station and late checkout (12pm).

Nottinghamshire

359 Occasionally fruit and vegetables from the garden for guests to take home.

Oxfordshire

370 10% off stays Monday-Thursday. Minimum 2-night stay.

374 25% discount on Pilates or Alexander Technique lesson.

Shropshire

381 Bottle of sparkling wine, minimum 2-night stay.

385 Bowl of fruit in room.

388 5% off stays Monday-Thursday.

389 10% off stays Monday-Thursday.

391 Afternoon tea on arrival. Guided tour of the heronry when appropriate.

392 Bottle of wine with dinner. Homemade muffins to take away.

393 Pick-up from local train station. Glass of wine on arrival. Fruit in bedroom.

394 Pick-up from local train station.

Somerset

400 10% off stays Monday-Thursday.

401 10% off stays Mon-Fri, selection of local food on arrival, late checkout (12pm),

pick-up from local station, lifts to walking start points with advice, map and guide, laundry service.

413 Bottle of wine per couple on arrival. Pick-up from airport and Yatton station.

415 10% off stays Monday-Thursday.

417 Escorted local walks.

422 Pick-up from Castle Cary station. House cocktail per person per night and 15% off room price for 2nd night of stay, Monday-Thursday.

424 10% off stays Monday-Thursday.

432 10% off stays Monday-Thursday, local food in your room on arrival, late checkout (12pm) and bottle of wine with dinner.

434 10% off stays Tuesday-Thursday.

Staffordshire

440 Late checkout (12pm). Tea and coffee and homemade shortbread.

Suffolk

446 10% off first night, minimum 2-night stay.

447 Pick-up from local station.

457 10% off stays Monday-Thursday except during August and Aldeburgh Festival.

459 For two night stays including Saturday, third night charged at single rate.

460 Half bottle of wine or Aspall apple juice in room on arrival.

Surrey

463 Drink of spirits, beer or wine each evening. Pick-up from local station.

Sussex

472 10% off stays Monday-Thursday.

483 10% off stays Monday-Thursday. Bottle of wine in room.

488 Glass of wine at dinner. Late checkout.

Warwickshire

499 10% off stays of 3+ nights.

500 Pick-up from Warwick Parkway station. 10% discount for Armed Forces.

502 10% off stays Monday-Thursday and bottle of house wine with dinner.

Wiltshire

510 £5 reduction per night after first night.

519 On arrival a cup of tea and Glebe Home Fruit Cake. On departure homemade jam or marmalade.

520 10% off stays Monday-Thursday and for 3-night stays over a weekend.
     Selection of fresh fruit in your room.
521 Postcards, bottle of house wine with dinner, late checkout (12pm)
     and pick-up from local train station.

Worcestershire
527 10% off stays of 3+ nights.

Yorkshire
532 Bottle of house wine for a minimum 2-night stay.
534 10% off stays of 2+ nights Monday-Wednesday.
536 10% off stays Monday-Thursday.
544 10% off stays Monday-Thursday.
548 Jar of local honey or 6 eggs from the farm.
554 Bottle of wine with dinner.
555 Choice of any bottle of wine from list with first dinner.
556 10% off stays Monday-Thursday. Does not apply to online bookings.
559 Bottle of wine for stays of 3+ nights.
560 Tour of the working farm.
564 Drink on arrival and late checkout.

Scotland
Aberdeenshire
565 Freshly made scones and afternoon tea on arrival 4-6pm.
569 Afternoon tea for early arrivals. Pre-dinner drink and house wine
     with dinner.

Angus
571 One free supper, minimum 3-night stays (1 November-1 June).

Argyll & Bute
580 3 nights for the price of 2.

Dumfries & Galloway
589 Tea & scones on arrival. Drink & wine with dinner. Plate of fruit in bedroom.

Edinburgh & the Lothians
596 Bottle of wine and chocolates in room on arrival.
597 Fresh flowers and bottle of wine in room on arrival.

Fife

606 Tea and cake on arrival, drinks before dinner and wine with dinner.

608 Decanter of whiskey, supplies of tea and coffee, homebaking available in guests sitting room. Bottle of house wine with dinner. No set checkout time.

Highland

613 50% off 4th night.

619 Glass of wine or whisky on arrival.

Scottish Borders

634 Toasted teacakes with homemade jams and tea or coffee on arrival.

Wales

Carmarthenshire

649 Bottle of wine with dinner, pick-up from local train station, maps drawn to order for walkers and late checkout (12pm).

650 Glass of wine on arrival and pick-up from local station.

Flintshire

657 10% off stays Monday-Thursday.

Gwynedd

659 Stay 4+ nights for a guided walk (half day) with a mountain guide.

663 Bottle of house wine with dinner.

Pembrokeshire

669 Penfro Jam or similar. Subsequent visits of 2+ nights £5 per night discount.

671 Bottle of wine with dinner.

672 Glass of wine with dinner, or evening of first night if dining out.

674 Homemade Welsh recipe cakes in room. Bottle of wine for stays of 2+ nights.

Powys

675 10% off mid-week stays. Pick-up from railway station.

680 Bottle of house wine with dinner or welcome drink if dinner not taken/available.

682 25% off stays of 2+ nights.

Wrexham

684 3 nights for the price of 2. For stays of 2+ nights half bottle of house wine per person with dinner.

Many of you may want to stay in environmentally-friendly places. You may be passionate about local, organic or home-grown food. Or perhaps you want to know that the place you are staying in contributes to the community? To help you we have launched our Ethical Collection, so you can find the right place to stay and also discover how each owner is addressing these issues.

The Collection is made up of places going the extra mile, and taking the steps that most people have not yet taken, in one or more of the following areas:

• **Environment** Those making great efforts to reduce the environmental impact of their Special Place. We expect more than energy-saving light bulbs and recycling – in this part of the Collection you will find owners who make their own natural cleaning products, properties with solar hot water and biomass boilers, the odd green roof and a good measure of green elbow grease.

• **Community** Given to owners who use their property to play a positive role in their local and wider community. For example, by making a contribution from every guest's bill to a local fund, or running pond-dipping courses for local school children on their farm.

• **Food** Awarded to owners who make a real effort to source local or organic food, or to grow their own. We look for those who have gone out of their way to strike up relationships with local producers or to seek out organic suppliers. It is easier for an owner on a farm in rural Wales to produce their own eggs than for someone in central London, so we take this into account.

How it works

To become part of our Ethical Collection owners choose whether to apply in one, two or all three categories, and fill in a detailed questionnaire asking demanding questions about their activities in the chosen areas. You can download a full list of the questions at www.sawdays.co.uk/ethical_collection

We then review each questionnaire carefully before deciding whether or not to give the award(s). The final decision is subjective; it is based not only on whether an owner ticks 'yes' to a question but also on the detailed explanation that accompanies each 'yes' or 'no' answer. For example, an owner who has tried as hard as possible to install solar water-heating panels, but has failed because of strict conservation planning laws, will be given some credit for their effort (as long as they are doing other things in this area).

We have tried to be as rigorous as possible and have made sure the questions are demanding. We have not checked out the claims of owners before making our decisions, but we do trust them to be honest. We are only human, as are they, so please let us know if you think we have made any mistakes.

The Ethical Collection is a new initiative for us, and we'd love to know what you think about it – email us at ethicalcollection@sawdays.co.uk or write to our Green Editor. And remember that because this is a new scheme some owners have not yet completed their questionnaires – we're sure other places in the guide are working just as hard in these areas, but we don't yet know the full details.

Ethical Collection in this book
On the entry page of all places in the Collection we show which awards have been given.

A list of the places in our Ethical Collection is shown below, by entry number.

Environment
18 • 31 • 39 • 44 • 55 • 67 • 165 • 195 • 229 • 239 • 325 • 374 • 396 • 401 • 431 • 445 • 604 • 649 • 659 • 663 • 667 • 671 • 682

Community
143 • 325 • 445 • 502 • 532 • 548 • 604 • 649 • 659

Food
18 • 31 • 39 • 44 • 52 • 55 • 67 • 74 • 85 • 93 • 102 • 136 • 143 • 145 • 195 •

209 • 229 • 244 • 312 • 325 • 341 • 350 • 360 • 396 • 414 • 431 • 445 • 472 • 495 • 502 • 532 • 548 • 555 • 564 • 649 • 659 • 663 • 667 • 669 • 671 • 682

Ethical Collection online
There will be stacks more information on our website, www.sawdays.co.uk. You will be able to read some of the answers each owner has given to our Ethical Collection questionnaire and get a more detailed idea of what they are doing in each area. You will also be able to search for properties that have particular awards.

Quick reference indices

Wheelchair-accessible
At least one bedroom and bathroom accessible for wheelchair users. Phone for details.

England

Scotland

Wales

On a budget?
These places have a double room for £70 or under.

England

Stay all day

You can stay all day at these places if you wish.

Quick reference indices

Quick reference indices

National Cycle Network
These Special Places are within two miles of the NCN.

Quick reference indices

If you have any comments on entries in this guide, please tell us. If you have a favourite place or a new discovery, please let us know about it. You can return this form or visit www.sawdays.co.uk.

Existing entry

Property name: _____

Entry number: _____ Date of visit: _____

New recommendation

Property name: _____

Address: _____

_____

Tel/Email/Web: _____

Your comments

What did you like (or dislike) about this place? Were the people friendly? What was the location like? What sort of food did they serve?

_____

_____

_____

_____

_____

Your details

Name: _____

Address: _____

_____

_____ Postcode: _____

Tel: _____ Email: _____

Please send completed form to:
BBB, Sawday's, The Old Farmyard, Yanley Lane, Long Ashton, Bristol BS41 9LR, UK

Have you enjoyed this book? Why not try one of the others in the Special Places to Stay series and get 35% discount on the RRP *

British Bed & Breakfast (Ed 13)	RRP £14.99	Offer price £9.75
British Bed & Breakfast for Garden Lovers (Ed 4)	RRP £14.99	Offer price £9.75
British Hotels & Inns (Ed 10)	RRP £14.99	Offer price £9.75
Devon & Cornwall (Ed 1)	RRP £11.99	Offer price £7.80
Scotland (Ed 1)	RRP £9.99	Offer price £6.50
Pubs & Inns of England & Wales (Ed 5)	RRP £14.99	Offer price £9.75
Ireland (Ed 6)	RRP £12.99	Offer price £8.45
French Bed & Breakfast (Ed 10)	RRP £15.99	Offer price £10.40
French Holiday Homes (Ed 4)	RRP £14.99	Offer price £9.75
French Hotels & Châteaux (Ed 5)	RRP £14.99	Offer price £9.75
Paris Hotels (Ed 6)	RRP £10.99	Offer price £7.15
Italy (Ed 5)	RRP £14.99	Offer price £9.75
Spain (Ed 7)	RRP £14.99	Offer price £9.75
Portugal (Ed 4)	RRP £11.99	Offer price £7.80
Croatia (Ed 1)	RRP £11.99	Offer price £7.80
Greece (Ed 1)	RRP £11.99	Offer price £7.80
Turkey (Ed 1)	RRP £11.99	Offer price £7.80
Morocco (Ed 2)	RRP £11.99	Offer price £7.80
India (Ed 2)	RRP £11.99	Offer price £7.80
Green Places to Stay (Ed 1)	RRP £13.99	Offer price £9.10
Go Slow England	RRP £19.99	Offer price £13.00

*postage and packing is added to each order

To order at the Reader's Discount price simply phone 01275 395431 and quote 'Reader Discount BBB'.

The Book of Rubbish Ideas
An interactive, room by room, guide to reducing household waste
£6.99

This guide to reducing household waste and stopping wasteful behaviour is essential reading for all those trying to lessen their environmental impact.

Ban the Plastic Bag
A Community Action Plan
£4.99

In May 2007 Modbury in South Devon became Britain's first plastic bag free town.
This book tells the Modbury story, but uses it as a call to action, entreating every village, town and city in the country to follow Modbury's example and... BAN THE PLASTIC BAG.

One Planet Living
£4.99

"Small but meaningful principles that will improve the quality of your life."
Country Living

Also available in the Fragile Earth series:

The Little Food Book   £6.99
"This is a really big little book. It will make your hair stand on end" *Jonathan Dimbleby*

The Little Money Book   £6.99
"Anecdotal, humorous and enlightening, this book will have you sharing its gems with all your friends" *Permaculture Magazine*

To order any of the books in the Fragile Earth series call 01275 395431 or visit www.fragile-earth.com

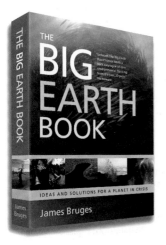

The Big Earth Book
Updated paperback edition
£12.99

We all know the Earth is in crisis. We should know that it is big enough to sustain us if we can only mobilise politicians and economists to change course now. Expanding on the ideas developed in *The Little Earth Book*, this book explores environmental, economic and social ideas to save our planet. It helps us understand what is happening to the planet today, exposes the actions of corporations and the lack of action of governments, weighs up new technologies, and champions innovative and viable solutions. Tackling a huge range of subjects – it has the potential to become the seminal reference book on the state of the planet – it's the one and only environmental book you really need.

What About China? £6.99
Answers to this and other awkward questions about climate change

"What is the point of doing anything when China opens a new power station every week?"

All of us are guilty of making excuses not to change our lifestyles especially when it comes to global warming and climate change. *What About China?* explains that all the excuses we give to avoid making changes that will reduce our carbon footprint and our personal impact on the environment, are exactly that, excuses! Through clear answers, examples, facts and figures the book illustrates how any changes we make now will have an effect, both directly and indirectly, on climate change.

"An excellent debunking of the myths that justify inaction" *The Ecologist*

① Cornwall

Cornwall

Calize Country House

② Beneath wheeling gulls and close to blond beaches, the big square 1870 house has amazing views of skies and sea. Virginia Woolf's lighthouse is in the bay and winter seals cavort at the colony nearby. A fresh, uncomplicated décor brings the tang of the sea to every room. Artworks recall a world of surf; deckchair stripes clothe the dining table and dress the window; traditional sofas call for quiet times with a book. Upstairs, patterned or pale walls, practical bath or shower rooms, perhaps a sea view. Jilly and Nigel are testament to the benefits of sea air and look after you beautifully.

③ Ethical Collection: Environment; Food. See page 400 for details.

④ 🧳 Travel Club Offer: see page 392 for details.

⑤ Price	£80–£90. Singles £55.
⑥ Rooms	4: 2 doubles, 1 twin, 1 single.
⑦ Meals	Packed lunch £5. Pub 350 yds.
⑧ Closed	Rarely.
⑨ Directions	Exit A30 at Camborne (west) A3047. Left, then right at r'bout. Right on entering Connor Downs, then on for 2 miles. House on right after sign for Gwithian.

Jilly Whitaker
Calize Country House,
Gwithian, Hayle,
Cornwall TR27 5BW

Tel	01736 753268
Fax	01736 753268
Email	jilly@calize.co.uk
Web	www.calize.co.uk

⑩   ✗ 🚂 🐴 ♿

⑪   Entry 39   Map 1

Treglisson

A short drive from St Ives, the glorious bay and some nifty surfing beaches. Inside the old farmhouse, all is calm and peaceful. Stephen and Heather are thoughtful, fun, easy-going and filled with enthusiasm for looking after you: large light bedrooms in soft colours, generous beds with lovely linen, modern white bathrooms, good art on the walls, a beautiful antique-marble hall floor. Cornish Aga-cooked breakfasts can be relished late if you prefer; in the evening, take a sundowner to the garden in summer or relax by the log fire in winter. There's a heated indoor pool too.

🧳 Travel Club Offer: see page 392 for details.

Price	£55–£75. Singles from £35.
Rooms	4: 1 double, 1 twin, 2 family rooms.
Meals	Pubs/restaurants 2-5 miles.
Closed	Christmas & New Year.
Directions	A30 to Hayle; 4th exit on r'bout into Hayle. Left at mini r'bout into Guildford Rd; up hill for 1 mile. Turn left at green sign into lane.

Stephen & Heather Reeves
Treglisson,
Wheal Alfred Road,
Hayle,
Cornwall TR27 5JT

Tel	01736 753141
Email	steve@treglisson.co.uk
Web	www.treglisson.co.uk

🛏 ✗ 📖 🚂 📶 🐴 🚜 🏊

Entry 40   Map 1